Pro Linux Embedded Systems

Gene Sally

Apress®

Pro Linux Embedded Systems

ISBN-13 (pbk): 978-1-4302-7227-4

ISBN-13 (electronic): 978-1-4302-7226-7

Printed and bound in the United States of America 9 8 7 6 5 4 3 2 1

Trademarked names may appear in this book. Rather than use a trademark symbol with every occurrence of a trademarked name, we use the names only in an editorial fashion and to the benefit of the trademark owner, with no intention of infringement of the trademark.

President and Publisher: Paul Manning
Lead Editor: Michelle Lowman
Technical Reviewer: William von Hagen
Editorial Board: Clay Andres, Steve Anglin, Mark Beckner, Ewan Buckingham, Gary Cornell, Jonathan Gennick, Jonathan Hassell, Michelle Lowman, Matthew Moodie, Duncan Parkes, Jeffrey Pepper, Frank Pohlmann, Douglas Pundick, Ben Renow-Clarke, Dominic Shakeshaft, Matt Wade, Tom Welsh
Coordinating Editor: Jim Markham
Copy Editor: Tiffany Taylor
Compositor: Bronkella Publishing LLC
Indexer: nSight Indexers
Artist: April Milne
Cover Designer: Anna Ishchenko

Distributed to the book trade worldwide by Springer-Verlag New York, Inc., 233 Spring Street, 6th Floor, New York, NY 10013. Phone 1-800-SPRINGER, fax 201-348-4505, e-mail orders-ny@springer-sbm.com, or visit http://www.springeronline.com.

For information on translations, please contact Apress directly at 2855 Telegraph Avenue, Suite 600, Berkeley, CA 94705. Phone 510-549-5930, fax 510-549-5939, e-mail info@apress.com, or visit http://www.apress.com.

Apress and friends of ED books may be purchased in bulk for academic, corporate, or promotional use. eBook versions and licenses are also available for most titles. For more information, reference our Special Bulk Sales–eBook Licensing web page at http://www.apress.com/info/bulksales.

The source code for this book is available to readers at http://www.apress.com.

For Tammi and our sons, Jonah, Benjamin, and Adam.

Contents at a Glance

Contents

About the Author

Gene Sally got mixed-up with computers at a young age, his fascination sparked by an Apple II, with the Lemon cooling system add-on, no less. As a software professional, Gene got his first job writing make files and then moved on to more exciting (for certain values of exciting) things like accounting, insurance processing, and social services systems. He first used Linux to set up a shared Internet connection and later used it when working on software that tested telecommunication management software; Gene was happy that a decent Unix-like environment could be had for free, and Linux became his axe of choice. Gene next found himself at a start-up that specialized in tools and distributions for embedded Linux, working in a variety of roles including engineer, trainer, technical support phone-answerer-guy, podcaster, and marketer. Presently, Gene is working at a company that creates safety products for retirement and assisted-living homes.

Gene resides outside of Pittsburgh, Pennsylvania in the rolling hills north of the city with his wife and three sons. When not working, writing, playing with kids, or tending to the never-ending repair list at home, Gene cycles, skis, and hikes throughout western Pennsylvania and eastern Ohio.

About the Technical Reviewer

 **William von Hagen (Bill)** has been a UNIX system administrator for over 20 years and a Linux fanatic since the early 1990s. He has worked as a systems programmer, system administrator, writer, application developer, drummer, and documentation manager. Bill has written or pco-written books on such topics as Ubuntu Linux, GCC, Linux Server Hacks, Linux Filesystems, SUSE Linux, Red Hat Linux, SGML, and Mac OS X.

Acknowledgments

First, I thank the good Lord for providing me with time, prosperity, curiosity, vigor, intellect, and health; I hope this work puts these gifts to proper use. During the time I spent writing this book, I received tremendous support from my family. I couldn't have done it without my wife and kids: you helped more than you know.

Writing a book is a team effort, and I am fortunate that the team working on this book was as excellent as any author could have ever expected. Thank you Bill von Hagen for being my technical reviewer, and Michelle Lowman and Frank Pohlmann for being my editors. All of the editors actually read what was written and provided feedback that made this book much better than it would have been without their efforts. I would also like to thank the production team at Apress, who created the cover, laid out the pages, and amazingly turned a collection of documents into the book you're holding now. Special thanks goes to James Markham, who somehow managed to tolerate my inability to meet a deadline with more patience than I deserved. Last, but not least, the open source community has provided me with an excellent education about Linux, both in mail and newsgroup traffic and in the source code itself.

Introduction

When I got started in embedded Linux nearly a decade ago, the question was, "Should I even use an operating system?" Going with Linux frequently meant porting the operating system to run on your target hardware and building to the tools to do so. Much has changed over the years, to the point that Linux is selected by default for many projects, and the decisions revolve around what features of the operating system can be used on the project. The question today is, "How should I configure my Linux distribution?" In technology terms, this is a seismic shift in developer attitudes in a very short time frame.

Linux is so pervasive in the embedded space that embedded processors and boards ship with Linux by default. Buyers simply expect that the board will boot Linux and they'll have the tools they need for embedded development provided along with the hardware. Unlike in the early days of Linux, as a developer, you won't be porting Linux to your board but rather configuring an already-running Linux kernel and root file system so that they suit your application.

With this background in mind, I wrote this book from the perspective of a user who is starting their project with a Linux distribution already running on the board. It may not the the distribution that eventually ships with the product, but it will likely serve as a starting point. Tasks like building the cross-compiler from scratch are documented in the book so you understand the process, but you will probably use a cross-compiler that has been provided with the board so you can concentrate on the application. However, learning how to build and configure the tools for a Linux system isn't a wasted effort, because when you need to squeeze every bit of memory out of your system, this is an essential skill.

Furthermore, with new System on a Chip (SOC) designs, the Linux distribution that comes on the board has all the drivers necessary for the devices on the chip. Only in the rarest events is driver development necessary. This means that most engineers spend time customizing the kernel rather than building new kernel components, and the total time spent doing any sort of kernel configuration or development is a fraction of what it was in years past.

As the processors in embedded devices become more powerful, developers are finding they can use languages other than C for development. It's common for C++ to be used for development as well as other higher-level language like Python, TCL, Java, and even Perl or PHP. To somebody who started doing embedded in assembly, using a language like Perl on an embedded target is nearly heresy, if not outright apostasy; however, these higher-level languages greatly increase the productivity of embedded development. In an industry where time-to-market is paramount, higher-level languages will become more mainstream.

Embedded projects have a development process unlike other software projects. First there is the design process, which usually involves creating a special enclosure and a user interface that's probably a small LCD display and some buttons; but more important are the deployment and update of the software. The code for the project isn't put on a CD or a web site but must be downloaded on the board along with the Linux distribution. After the initial installation of the software, you'll likely want to update the software with new versions that contain bug fixes and other goodies. Depending on how your system is configured, updating your system may be a project in itself.

If you're starting an embedded project for your work or have purchased one of the many, now very inexpensive board targeted to hobbyists, I wish you the best of luck in your endeavors. Using Linux in an embedded project is easier, and more fun, than ever.

CHAPTER 1

■ ■ ■

About Embedded Linux

Linux is an incredible piece of software. It's an operating system that's just as at home running on IBM's zSeries supercomputers as it is on a cell phone, manufacturing device, network switch, or even cow milking machine. What's more incredible is that this software is currently maintained by thousands of the best software engineers and it is available for *free*.

Linux didn't start as an embedded operating system. Linux was created by a Finnish university student (Linus Torvalds) who was smart enough to make his work available to all, take input from others and, most important, delegate to other talented engineers. As the project grew, it attracted other talented engineers who were able to contribute to Linux, increasing the burgeoning project's value and visibility and thus bootstrapping a virtuous cycle that continues to this day.

Linux was first written to run on the Intel IA-32 architecture and was first ported to a Motorola processor. The porting process was difficult enough that Linus Torvalds decided to rethink the architecture so that it could be easily ported, creating a clean interface between the processor-dependent parts of the software and those that are architecture independent. This design decision paved the way for Linux to be ported to other processors.

Linux is just a kernel, which by itself isn't that useful. An embedded Linux system, or any Linux system for that matter, uses software from many other projects in order to provide a complete operating system. The Linux kernel is written largely in C (with some assembler) and uses the GNU tool set, such as make; the GCC compiler; programs that provide an interface to the kernel; and a host of others that you'll encounter in this book. Much of this software already existed at Linux's genesis, and, fortunately, much of it was written with portability in mind. The fact that this software could be used on an embedded system or could be modified to make it suitable for embedded deployment contributed greatly to the acceptance of Linux for devices other than desktop machines.

■ **Note** Linux exists in no small part because of the GNU (Gnu's Not Unix) project, which was (and still is) developing an open source implementation of Unix. The GNU project provided a high-quality compiler and command-line make environment along with basic utilities expected on a Unix-like system.

This book takes you through using Linux for your embedded project. Because Linux and its associated projects are open source, you learn how to build everything you need for an embedded project from scratch. The entire Linux environment has advanced to the point that this undertaking is no longer a quixotic exercise; it falls squarely within the reach of any engineer willing to put in a reasonable amount of time and effort. Building a complete Linux system is the best training for creating a small Linux system; as a result, doing so is more than a morale-building exercise.

Why Use Embedded Linux?

Embedded Linux is just like the Linux distributions running on millions of desktops and servers worldwide, but it's adapted to a specific use case. On desktop and server machines, memory, processor cycles, power consumption, and storage space are limited resources—they just aren't as limiting as they are for embedded devices. A few extra MB or GB of storage can be nothing but rounding errors when you're configuring a desktop or server. In the embedded field, resources matter because they drive the unit cost of a device that may be produced in the millions; or the extra memory may require additional batteries, which add weight. A processor with a high clock speed produces heat; some environments have very tight heat budgets, so only so much cooling is available. As such, most of the efforts in embedded programming, if you're using Linux or some other operating system, focus on making the most with limited resources.

Compared to other embedded operating systems, such as VxWorks, Integrity, and Symbian, Linux isn't the most svelte option. Some embedded applications use frameworks such as ThreadX[1] for application support; the framework runs directly on the hardware, eschewing an operating system altogether. Other options involve skipping the framework and instead writing code that runs directly on the device's processor. The biggest difference between using a traditional embedded operating system and Linux is the separation between the kernel and the applications. Under Linux, applications run in a execution context completely separate from the kernel. There's no way for the application to access memory or resources other than what the kernel allocates. This level of process protection means that a defective program is isolated from kernel and other programs, resulting in a more secure and survivable system. All of this protection comes at a cost.

Despite its increased resource overhead compared to other options, the adoption of Linux continues to increase. That means engineers working on projects consider the increased overhead of Linux worth the additional cost. Granted, in recent years, the costs and power demands of system-on-chip (SOC) processors has decreased to the point that they cost no more than a low-power 8-bit microcontroller from the past, so using a more sophisticated processor is an option when it might not have been before. Many design solutions use off-the-shelf SOC processors and don't run the leads from chip for the Ethernet, video, or other unused components.

Linux has flourished because it provides capabilities and features that can't be made available with other embedded solutions. Those capabilities are essential to implementing the ever more sophisticated designs used to differentiate devices in today's market. The open source nature of Linux means embedded engineers can take advantage of the continual development happening in the open source environment, which happens at a pace that no single software vendor can match.

Technical Reasons to Use Embedded Linux

The technical qualities of Linux drives its adoption. Linux is more than the Linux kernel project. That software is also at the forefront of technical development, meaning that Linux is the right choice for solving today's technical problems as well as being the choice for the foreseeable future.

For example, an embedded Linux system includes software such as the following:

---

[1] I can't comment about the usefulness or features of ThreadX, but I can attest that the stuffed monkeys given away at every trade show for the last ten years are adorable. This company also sponsored a booth one year that had actors in *Star Trek* get-ups explaining what ThreadX did; I wasn't paying attention, but I got another stuffed monkey after the presentation.

- *SSL/SSH:* The OpenSSH project is the most commonly used encryption and security mechanism today. The open nature of the project means that thousands of security experts are constantly evaluating it; when problems are found, updates occur in a matter of hours, provided the update is not included with the exploit itself.

- *Apache and other web servers:* The Apache web server finds its way into embedded devices that need a full-featured web server. For devices with less demanding requirements, users can pick from smaller web servers like Boa, lighttp, and (a personal favorite) micro_httpd.

- *The C Library:* The Linux environment has a wealth of options in this area, from the fully featured GNU C Library to the minimalist dietlibc. If you're new to embedded Linux development, having a choice in this area reinforces the open nature of open source.

- *Berkeley sockets (IP):* Many projects move to Linux from another operating system because of the complete, high-performance network stack included in the operating system. A networked device is becoming the rule and not the exception.

The following sections explain why the Linux operating system is the best technological fit for embedded development.

Standards Based

The Linux operating system and accompanying open source projects adhere to industry standards; in most cases, the implementation available in open source is the canonical, or *reference*, implementation of a standard. A reference implementation embodies the interpretation of the specification and is the basis for conformance testing. In short, the reference implementation is the standard by which others are measured.

If you're new to the notion of a reference implementation, it may be a little confusing. Take for example the Portable Operating System Interface for Unix (POSIX) for handling threads and interprocess communication, commonly called *pthreads*. The POSIX group, part of the Institute of Electrical and Electronics Engineers (IEEE) is a committee that designs APIs for accomplishing the tasks of interacting with a thread but leaves the implementation of that standard to another group. In practice, when work begins on a standard, one or more of the participants on the committee volunteer to create the code to bring the standard to life, creating the reference implementation. The reference implementation includes a test suite; other implementations consider the passage of the test suite as evidence that the code works as per the specification.

Using standards-based software is not only about quality but also about independence. Basing a project on software that adheres to standards reduces the chances of lock-in due to vendor-specific features. A vendor may be well meaning, but the benefits of those extra features are frequently outweighed by the lack of interoperability and freedom that silently become part of the transaction and frequently don't receive the serious consideration they merit.

Standards are increasingly important in a world where many embedded devices are connected, many times to arbitrary systems rather than just to each other. The Ethernet is one such connection method, but others abound, like Zigbee, CANbus, and SCSI, to name a few.

Process Isolation and Control

The Linux kernel, at its most basic level, offers these services as a way of providing a common API for accessing system resources:

- Manage tasks, isolating them from the kernel and each other

- Provide a uniform interface for the system's hardware resources

- Serve as an arbiter to resources when contention exists

These are very important features that result in a more stable environment versus an environment where access to the hardware and resources isn't closely managed. For example, in the absence of an operating system, every program running has equal access to all available RAM. This means an overrun bug in one program can write into memory used by another program, which will then fail for what appear to be mysterious, unexplainable reasons until all the code on the system is examined. The notion of resource contention is more complex than just making sure two processes don't attempt to write data to the serial port simultaneously—the scarcest resource is time, and the operating system can decide what tasks run when in order to maximize the amount of work performed. The following sections look at each item in more detail.

Manage and Isolate Tasks

Linux is a multitasking operating system. In Linux, the word *process* describes a task that the kernel tracks for execution. The notion of multitasking means the kernel must keep some data about what is running, the current state of the task, and the resources it's using, such as open files and memory.

For each process, Linux creates an entry in a process table and assigns the process a separate memory space, file descriptors, register values, stack space, and other process specific information. After it's created, a process can't access the memory space of another process unless both have negotiated a shared memory pool; but even access to that memory pool doesn't give access to an arbitrary address in another process.

Processes in Linux can contain multiple execution threads. A thread shares the process space and resources of the process that started it, but it has its own instruction pointer. Threads, unlike processes, can access each other's memory space. For some applications, this sharing of resources is both desired and convenient; however, managing several threads' contention for resources is a study unto itself. The important thing is that with Linux, you have the design freedom to use these process-control constructs.

Processes are isolated not only from each other but from the kernel as well. A process also can't access arbitrary memory from the kernel. Access to kernel functionality happens under controlled circumstances, such as syscalls or file handles. A *syscall*, short for system call, is a generic concept in operating system design that allows a program to perform a call into the kernel to execute code. In the case of Linux, the function used to execute a system call is conveniently named `syscall()`.

When you're working with a syscall, as explained later in this chapter, the operation works much like a regular function call for an API. Using a file handles, you can open what appears to be a file to read and write data. The implementation of a file still reduces to a series of syscalls; but the file semantics make them easier to work with under certain circumstances.

The complete separation of processes and the kernel means you no longer have to debug problems related to processes stepping on each other's memory or race conditions related to trying to access shared resources, such as a serial port or network device. In addition, the operating system's internal data structures are off limits to user programs, so there's no chance of an errant program halting execution of the entire system. This degree of survivability alone is why some engineers choose Linux over other lighter-weight solutions.

Memory Management and Linux

Linux uses a virtual memory-management system. The concept of virtual memory has been around since the early 1960s and is simple: the process sees its memory as a vector of bytes; and when the program reads or writes to memory, the processor, in conjunction with the operating system, translates the address into a physical address.

The bit of the processor that performs this translation is the *memory management unit* (MMU). When a process requests memory, the CPU looks up the address in a table populated by the kernel to translate the requested address into a physical address. If the CPU can't translate the address, it raises an interrupt and passes control to the operating system to resolve the address.

The level of indirection supplied by the memory management means that if a process requests memory outside its bounds, the operating system gets a notification that it can handle or pass along to the offending process. In an environment without proper memory management, a process can read and write any physical address; this means memory-access errors may go unnoticed until some other part of the program fails because its memory has been corrupted by another process.

Programs running in Linux do so in a virtual memory space. That is, when a program runs, it has a certain address space that is a subset of the total system's memory. That subset appears to start at 0. In reality, the operating system allocates a portion of memory and configures the processor so that the running program thinks address 0 is the start of memory, but the address is actually some arbitrary point in RAM. For embedded systems that use paging, this fiction continues: the kernel swaps some of the available RAM out to disk when not in use, a feature commonly called *virtual memory*. Many embedded systems don't use virtual memory because no disk exists on the system; but for those that do, this feature sets Linux apart from other embedded operating systems.

Uniform Interface to Resources

This sounds ambiguous because there are so many different forms of resources. Consider the most common resource: the system's memory. In all Linux systems, from an application perspective, memory from the heap is allocated using the `malloc()` function. For example, this bit of code allocates 100 bytes, storing the address to the first byte in `from_the_heap`:

```
char* from_the_heap;
from_the_heap = (char*) malloc(100);
```

No matter what sort of underlying processor is running the code or how the processor accesses the memory, this code works (or fails in a predictable manner) on all Linux systems. If paged virtual memory is enabled (that is, some memory is stored on a physical device, like a hard drive) the operating system ensures that the requested addresses are in physical RAM when the process requests them.

Memory management requires interplay between the operating system and the processor to work properly. Linux has been designed so that you can access memory in the same way on all supported processors.

The same is true for accessing files: all you need to do is open a file descriptor and begin reading or writing. The kernel handles fetching or writing the bytes, and that operation is the same no matter what physical device is handling the bits:

```
FILE* file_handle;
file_handle = fopen("/proc/cpuinfo", "r");
```

Because Linux is based on the Unix operating system philosophy that "everything is a file," the most common interface to system resource is through a file handle. The interface to that file handle is identical no matter how the underlying hardware implements this functionality. Even TCP connections can be represented with file semantics.

The uniformity of access to resources lets you simulate a target environment on your development system, a process that once required special (and sometimes costly) software. For example, if the target device uses the USB subsystem, it has the same interface on the target as it does on the development machine. If you're working on a device that shuffles data across the USB bus, that code can be developed, debugged, and tested on the development host, a process that's much easier and faster than debugging code on a remote target.

System Calls

In addition to file semantics, the kernel also uses the idea of syscalls to expose functionality. Syscalls are a simple concept: when you're working on the kernel and want to expose some functionality, you create an entry in a vector that points to an entry point of for the routine. The data from the application's memory space is copied into the kernel's memory space. All system calls for all processes are funneled through the same interface.

When the kernel is finished with the syscall, it transfers the results back into the caller, returning the result into the application's memory space. Using this interface, there's no way for a program in user space to have access to data structures in the kernel. The kernel can also keep strict control over its data, eliminating any chance of data corruption caused by an errant caller.

Peripheral Support

``At last count, Linux supported more than 200 network adapters, 5 vendors of flash memory, and 10 USB mass storage devices. Because SOC vendors use Linux as their testing system for the chip, support for the chip itself implies support for the components on the device.

Wide device support is an artifact of the fact that Linux runs on millions of desktops and servers, representing a customer base that device manufacturers can't ignore. Plus, the open nature of Linux allows device vendors to create drivers without getting a development license from an operating system vendor.

What really differentiates peripheral support on Linux is that the drivers are (primarily) written in C and use the kernel's API to implement their functionality. This means that once a driver has been written for the x86 Linux kernel, it frequently requires zero or a small amount of work for a different processor.

Security

Security means access to data and resources on the machine as well as maintaining confidentiality for data handled by the computer. The openness of Linux is the key to its security. The source code is available for anyone and everyone to review; therefore, security loopholes are there for all to see, understand, and fix.

Security has a few different dimensions, all of which may be necessary for an embedded, or any other, system. One is ensuring that users and programs have the minimal level of rights to resources in order to be able to execute; another is keeping information hidden until a user with the correct credentials requests to see or change it. The advantage of Linux is that all of these tools are freely available to you, so you can select the right ones to meet your project requirements.

SELinux

A few years ago, a governmental agency with an interest in security—the National Security Agency (NSA)—and with several other private companies with similar interests took it upon themselves to examine the Linux kernel and introduce concepts such as data protection, program isolation, and security policies, following a Mandatory Access Control (MAC) model. This project is called SELinux (where *SE* stands for *Security Enhanced*), and the changes and concepts of the project were made part of the 2.6.0 release of the Linux kernel.

The MAC concepts in SELinux specify controls whereby programs must be assigned the rights to perform certain activities, like opening a socket or file, as part of their security policy. The assignment must come from an administrator; a regular user of the system can't make changes. SELinux systems operate under the principle of least privilege, meaning that a process has only the rights granted and no more. The least-privilege concept makes errant or compromised programs less dangerous in a properly configured environment, because the administrator has already granted a program the minimal set of rights in order to function. As you may guess, creating security policies can be a project itself. I'll spend some time talking about how to go about doing this on an embedded system.

PAM

Pluggable Authentication Modules (PAM) are a way to create a uniform interface to the process of authenticating users. Traditionally, user authentication on a Linux system occurs by looking up the user name in the /etc/passwd file and checking the password encrypted therein (or using the shadow password file). The PAM framework also provides session management: performing certain actions after a user is authenticated and before they log out of the system.

The open design of the PAM system is important for embedded projects that are attached to a network in a corporate environment. For example, if the device serves as a shared drive, some of your target market may use LDAP to decide who has access to the device, whereas others may put use accounts in an NT domain. PAM works equally well with both of these technologies, and you can switch between the two with simple configuration changes.

IPsec

IPsec is a system for authenticating and transmitting data between two trusted hosts over an IP network. IPsec at level 3, the Network Layer of the OSI stack, isn't a single piece of software but rather a collection of tools working together to provide secure communication. By operating at this layer, IPsec can provide secure communication between hosts with no participation by the protocols running further up the stack.

A classic use for IPSec is encrypting virtual private network traffic. It can also be used in cases where you want to use a simple protocol for sending data, like HTTP or even plain text, but you want this data to be kept secure.

One of the nice things about embedded Linux is that you can perform all the configuration work to use IPsec on a pair of desktop machines and transport those configuration files to the embedded target. This is possible because when you create an embedded Linux system, you can use the same software that is running on the target on the desktop used for development, making it an ideal platform for emulating your target hardware.

Commercial Reasons to Use Embedded Linux

In addition to the outstanding technical aspects of Linux that make it advantageous to use for an embedded device, there are also compelling commercial reasons to choose Linux over other commercial offerings. Some of these reasons, such as lower costs, will appeal to the bean-counters in your organization; but the key difference is that you'll have greater control over a critical aspect of your development project.

Complete Software Ecosystem

The universe of software around Linux is vast and varied. If you're new to Linux, you'll soon find that Linux is a more than its namesake kernel: it's a collection of software that works together. The nice thing about Linux is that what's available on your desktop can be used on an embedded system. Even better, the ability to run and test software on a regular desktop gives you the chance to see if the software offers the right feature set for the application.

The nature of open source gives you plenty of choices for nearly every piece of your configuration, and that can cause consternation if you're trying to pick the right package. Oddly, the large amount of choice is posited by commercial vendors as a reason to use their closed source or highly structured Linux distribution. Don't fall for this line of reasoning! You're reading this book so you can take advantage of what open source has to offer.

Open source software is always available as source code. Most of the time, the authors have written both the package itself and the build instructions so that the project isn't architecture dependent and can be built for the target system. Software that is part of the root file system is nearly always completely portable, because it's written in a high-level language like C. Because of the nice job done in the Linux kernel to isolate architecture-dependent code, even a vast amount of kernel code is portable.

■ **Note** Cross compiling and a root file system are two key concepts for embedded developers. During *cross compilation*, the compiler produces code that doesn't run on the processor or operating system of the machine that performed the compilation. Compiling Java into bytecode that runs on a Java Virtual Machine (JVM) is an example. If you've written a Netware Loadable Module, you've also done cross-compilation. The root file system is the population of files and folders under the / folder of a computer. Developers creating enterprise systems rarely give this part of the system a second thought; but embedded developers put care and effort not only into selecting the right sort of root file system, but also into populating it efficiently in order to conserve space and reduce hardware costs and power requirements. I'll cover both of these topics in detail.

The key to using what's available in open source is two-fold: having a cross-compiler and having the build scripts work when you're cross-compiling. The vast majority of packages use the automake/autoconf project for creating build scripts. Automake and autoconf by default produce scripts suitable for cross-compilation. Later in this book, I explain how to use them properly. I talk about the cross-compiler that later in this chapter and tell you how to build your own from source.

Although constraints like memory and storage space may make some choices impractical, if you really need certain functionality, the source is there for you to reduce the size of the package. Throughout the book, you'll find references to software projects typically used by embedded engineers.

No Royalties

Royalties, in the software sense, are the per-unit software costs paid for every unit shipped, which compensate an owner of intellectual property for a license granted for limited use of that property. Royalties increase the Bill of Materials (BOM) cost of every unit shipped that contains the licensed intellectual property. A licensee must make regular reports and prompt payment and must avail itself for audit so that the holder of the licensed property can ensure the monies paid accurately reflect what was shipped.

In this model, forms must be filled out, checked, and signed. Paper must be shuffled, and competitive wages and benefits need to be paid to those doing the shuffling. With a contract to sign, expect a bill from your attorney as well. The entire cost of the royalty is greater than what appears on the BOM.

Royalties impose another cost: lack of flexibility. Want to experiment with a newer processor? Want to create a new revision of the product or add features? All these activities likely require permission from the vendor and, when you ship a new product, a new royalty payment to not only make but properly administer.

When presenting an embedded operating system that has royalties, the salescritter[2] will explain that the payments represent a small concession compared to what the software they're selling brings to the table. What they leave out is the loss of liberty with respect to how your company structures its development operations and the additional administrative and legal costs that never make it into the calculations showing your "savings." *Caveat emptor.*

Control

This is an often-missed reason to use Linux: you have the sources to the project and have complete control over every bit of software included in the device. No software is perfect, but with Linux you aren't at the mercy of a company that may not be interested in helping you when a defect becomes apparent. When you have trouble understanding how the software works, the source code can serve as the definitive reference.

Unfortunately, this amount of control is frequently used to scare people away from Linux. "You may have the source code, but you'll never figure anything out … it's so complex," the fear mongers say. The Linux code base is well written and documented. If you're capable of writing a commercial embedded Linux application, you no doubt have the ability to understand the Linux project—or any other open source project, for that matter.

10,000-Foot Embedded Linux Development Flyover

This section contains a quick and dirty explanation of the embedded Linux development process. Embedded Linux is a topic with many interdependencies; this section lays out the big points and purposely lacks detail so you can see the big picture without getting distracted by the fine details. The heft of this book should indicate that more details are forthcoming.

Target Hardware

Nearly every project involves selecting the processor to be used. A processor is just a chip and not much more until it's soldered on a board with some peripherals and connectors. Processor vendors frequently create *development boards* containing their chip and a collection of peripherals and connectors. Some companies have optimized this process to the point that a board with connectors and peripherals is connected to a small daughter board containing the processor itself, allowing the base board to be shared across several different processor daughter boards.

Development boards are large, bulky, and designed to be easily handled. Every connector is supported by the processor because the vendor wants to create only one board to ship, inventory, and support. The development kit for a cell phone occupies as much space as a large laptop computer.

---

[2] You're paying for them, too.

In a majority of products, the development board isn't used in the final product. An electrical engineer lays out a new board that fits in the product's case and contains only the leads for the peripherals used in the final application, and he probably sneaks in a place to connect a serial or JTAG port for debugging.

Obtaining Linux

Linux is nearly always included with a development board and has support for the peripherals supported by the chip or the development board. Chances are, the board was tested with Linux to ensure that the processor and connectors work as expected. Early in the history of embedded Linux, there were porting efforts to get Linux running on a board; today, this would be an anomaly.

If the board is an Intel IA-32 (frequently called x86) architecture, you can boot it (under most circumstances) with any desktop distribution of Linux. In order to differentiate their IA-32 boards, vendors frequently include a Linux distribution suitable for an embedded project.

Just as the development board has every known connector, the Linux included with the board is suited for development and not for final deployment. Part of using Linux is customizing the kernel and the distribution so they're correct for the application.

Booting Linux

Because most board vendors supply a Linux distribution with a board, getting Linux booted is about configuring the software services Linux needs to boot and ensuring the cabling is proper and attached. At this point, you probably need a null modem serial cable, a null modem Ethernet cable (or a few cables and an Ethernet concentrator or switch), and maybe a USB cable. Unlike a desktop system with a monitor, the user interface for an embedded target may be just a few lights or a one-line LCD display. In order for these boards to be useful in development, you connect to the board and start a session in a terminal emulator to get access to a command prompt similar to a console window on a desktop Linux system.

Some (enlightened) vendors put Linux on a Flash partition so the board runs Linux at power up. In other cases, the board requires you to attach it to a Linux host that has a terminal emulator, file-transfer software, and a way to make a portion of your Linux system's hard drive remotely accessible.

In the rare cases where the board doesn't include Linux (or the board in question hails from before you welcomed the embedded Linux overlords), the process requires you to locate a kernel and create a minimal root file system.

Development Environment

Much of the activity around embedded development occurs on a desktop. Although embedded processors have become vastly more powerful, they still pale in comparison to the dual core multi-gigabyte machine found on your desk. You run the editor, tools, and compiler on a desktop system and produce binaries for execution on the target. When the binary is ready, you place it on the target board and run it. This activity is called *cross-compilation* because the output produced by the compiler isn't suitable for execution on your machine.

You use the same set of software tools and configuration to boot the board and to put the newly compiled programs on the board. When the development environment is complete, work on the application proper can begin.

System Design

The Linux distribution used to boot the board isn't the one shipped in the final product. The requirements for the device and application largely dictate what happens in this area. Your application may need a web server or drivers for a USB device. If the project doesn't have a serial port, network connection, or screen, those drivers are removed. On the other hand, if marketing says a touch-screen UI is a must-have, then a suitable UI library must be located. In order for the distribution to fit in the amount of memory specified, other changes are also necessary.

Even though this is the last step, most engineers dig in here first after getting Linux to boot. When you're working with limited resources, this can seem like a reasonable approach; but it suffers from the fact that you don't have complete information about requirements and the person doing the experimentation isn't aware of what can be done to meet the requirements.

Anatomy of an Embedded Linux System

Campus Network
The connection to the network at the office and the Internet.

Development Host
This is a desktop machine where the kernel and application are built.

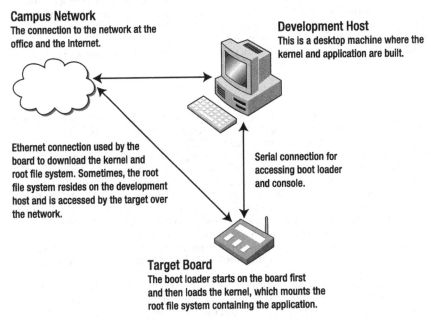

Ethernet connection used by the board to download the kernel and root file system. Sometimes, the root file system resides on the development host and is accessed by the target over the network.

Serial connection for accessing boot loader and console.

Target Board
The boot loader starts on the board first and then loads the kernel, which mounts the root file system containing the application.

Figure 1-1. Embedded Linux Development Infrastructure.

At runtime, an embedded Linux system contains the following software components:

- *Boot loader:* What gets the operating system loaded and running on the board.

- *Kernel:* The software that manages the hardware and the processes.

- *Root file system:* Everything under the / directory, containing the programs run by the kernel. Every Linux system has a root file system. Embedded systems have a great amount of flexibility in this respect: the root file system can reside in flash, can be bundled with the kernel, or can reside on another computer on the network.

- *Application:* The program that runs on the board. The application can be a single file or a collection of hundreds of executables.

All these components are interrelated and thus depend on each other to create a running system. Working on an embedded Linux system requires interaction with all of these, even if your focus is only on the application.

If you're new to Linux but have used other commercial embedded solutions, the notion of a distinct kernel and root file system can be disorienting. With a traditional embedded solution, the application code is linked into a binary image with the rest of the embedded OS. After initialization, the operating system calls a function that is the entry point into your code and starts running.

Next, I define these components so you understand what they do and how they work together.

Boot Loader

Boot loaders can be laden with features, but their primary responsibility is to get the processor initialized and ready to run the operating system. Later in the book, I go through the boot-up process from beginning to end; but for practical purposes, this is the software that's first run on the system.

In most modern embedded Linux systems, the kernel is stored in a partition in flash memory. The boot loader copies that flash partition into a certain location in RAM, sets the instruction pointer to that memory location, and tells the processor to start executing at the instruction pointer's current location. After that, the program that's running unceremoniously writes over the boot loader. The important thing to note is that the boot loader is agnostic with respect to what is being loaded and run. It can be a Linux kernel or another operating system or a program written to run without an operating system. The boot loader doesn't care; it performs the same basic actions in all these use scenarios.

As boot loaders have matured, they've become more like operating systems with network, video, and increasing support for flash storage devices. Later in this book, I look at the popular boot loaders you may encounter when working with Linux.

One more important note: boot loaders are now ubiquitous. Rarely as an embedded Linux developer do you need to port a boot loader for your board. You may want to recompile the boot loader (I'll cover that, too) to remove functionality to conserve space and increase boot time, but the low-level engineering is done by the board vendor. Users of Intel-based systems that use the Phoenix BIOS boot loader have no opportunity to change this code, because it's baked into the board design.

WHAT ABOUT GRUB AND LILO?

If you're familiar with Linux systems running on PC-type hardware, you're no doubt familiar with Grub and LILO. If you're not, hit the reset button and wait. You see one or the other as the computer starts. Technically, these aren't boot loaders, but loaders for Linux. Old-school Linux users remember running a similar program, loadlin, from the DOS prompt in order to begin running Linux after the PC first booted DOS or Windows; in this case, MS-DOS acted as the boot loader for Linux. The boot loader contained in the BIOS of the machine read these programs from a certain sector of a disk and begins running them.

Kernel

As discussed earlier, the Linux kernel was created by a Finnish computer science student as a hobby project and was first released in August 1991. The operating system originally ran only on x86 hosts and was modeled on a teaching aid operating system, MINIX. The Linux kernel was first ported to the Motorola 68KB processor, a painful process resulting in Linus Torvalds designing the kernel for portability. By doing the right thing, he laid the groundwork for Linux being ported to nearly every major processor over the following decade.

Due to the maturity and wide device support of Linux, engineers spend less time doing kernel development work such as creating device drivers (for example, to drive an LCD) and more time and effort creating applications the user values (like displaying the current weather conditions). Some effort may go into customizing the kernel by removing unneeded components or making other tweaks to increase booting time, but generally you don't need to do the low-level programming necessary to get the Linux kernel running in the first place.

Although it's an essential and vital component, the kernel has a symbiotic[3] relationship with the software it runs. The point isn't to give the Linux kernel short shrift or minimize its importance! The point is to make clear how the kernel fits into the overall functioning of a Linux system. Without something to run, the kernel stops executing and panics. That's where the root file system and your application come into play.

Root File System

A *file system* is a way of representing a hierarchical collection of directories, where each directory can contain either more directories or files. For computer science types, this hierarchy is a tree structure in which the files are always leaf nodes and directories are internal nodes when they contain something and leaf nodes otherwise. The point of making this trip down data-structure memory lane is that the top node in a tree structure is the *root node* and that, in Linux, the file system mounted at the top node is aptly called the *root file system*.

On your desktop Linux system, you can see what's mounted as the root file system by doing the following:

```
gene@imac-2:~$ mount | head -1
/dev/hda3 on / type ext3 (rw,errors=remount-ro)
```

---

[3] The biologically minded may think about the type of symbiotic relationship. I classify it as obligate mutualism, because neither can survive without the other. If you can discuss this topic with your significant other, they're a keeper.

Just typing mount shows all the file systems mounted. Most Linux systems have several file systems mounted, but all the file systems are mounted relative to the root file system.

When the Linux kernel boots, it must be able to mount a root file system. During the boot process, the root file system can be replaced with another, but only one root file system can be mounted at a time. Failure to mount a root file system means that the system can't find something to run, because a file system is a container for your program and the kernel panics and halts.

Depending on the board's hardware and application requirements, you're free to select any number of root file system types. A completed device contains a single file system mounted at root but likely uses several different file systems mounted at other directories within the root file system. Only one file system can be mounted at the root (/ directory), but Linux allows for an arbitrary number of file systems to be mounted at other locations in the root file system. For example, a system that uses flash memory for storage mounts a RAM-based file system for temporary storage because it's faster, and flash memory has a much smaller duty cycle than RAM. In the chapters that follow, this book covers how to select a root file system type and how to build one from the ground up.

Your Application

After the boot loader loads the kernel and the kernel mounts the root file system, it's time for something to start running that you and your boss view as useful. When Linux starts, it looks for a program to execute by default, or you can supply it with the name of something to run. This program runs as the first process and must continue to run. When this process stops, the kernel, and thus the entire system, stops running.

On your desktop Linux system, this program is likely init. You can find out by doing the following:

```
gene@imac-2:~$ ps aux | head -2
USER       PID %CPU %MEM    VSZ   RSS TTY      STAT START   TIME COMMAND
root         1  0.0  0.2   1692   516 ?        S     Dec07   0:01 init [2]
```

Later in the book, I cover what init does and how it's used in an embedded system, if at all.

It's important to note that your application can be anything that can be executed by Linux: a shell script, a C program, a Perl script, or even an assembly written in C# (the Mono project is a robust, open source C# platform)—you name it. As long as it can be executed by Linux, it's fair game to be the application. This is obvious to those who have already worked with Linux; and it's liberating almost to the point of disbelief for embedded engineers new to Linux. In addition, you can implement a solution using a few different languages if necessary.

All the shared libraries and other supporting files for the application must be present in the root file system deployed on the board. The mechanics for gathering what's necessary for your application are covered in a later chapter.

Cross-Compiler

So far, I've discussed the software components that are on the board. A cross-compiler is part of the development environment and, in the most basic terms, produces code that runs on a different processor or operating system than where the compiler ran. For example, a compiler that runs on a Linux x86 host that produces code to execute on an ARM9 target is a cross-compiler. Another example is a compiler running on Windows that produces code that runs on a x86 Linux host. In both cases, the compiler doesn't produce binaries that can be executed on the machine where the compiler ran.

In Linux, the cross-compiler is frequently referred to as a *tool chain* because it's a confederation of tools that work together to produce an executable: the compiler, assembler, and linker. The debugger is a separate software component. The book later describes how to obtain or create a tool chain for your target processor based on the GNU Compiler Collection (GCC) project.

Linux is GNU licensed software, and subsequently users who receive a Linux kernel must have the ability to get the source code for the binaries they receive. Having the source code is just one part of what's necessary to rebuild the software for the board. Without the cross-compiler, you can't transform that source into something that can run on the remote target.

The de facto compiler for Linux is GCC, but this need not always be the case. Several chip vendors market compilers that produce highly optimized code for their processors. The Linux operating system, although written in C and assembler, requires GCC for compilation. However, you can compile programs to be run on the system with a different compiler.

For a certain segment of embedded boards, a cross-compiler isn't necessary. Many PowerPC boards are as powerful as your desktop system; and some embedded systems are, for all intents and purposes, PCs in a different case. In these cases, development can happen right on the board. The compiler runs on the board, which produces code that runs in the same environment; the development cycle is much like that of a regular software project.

Tools of the Trade

Embedded development can be done with a simple collection of tools. This section covers the most frequently used tools so you can understand what they do and how they fit into an embedded system. This book covers each of these in great detail, to provide *terra firma* on which to stand if you're new to the world of embedded development. One of the most confusing aspects of embedded Linux is that there are many interrelated tools, it's difficult to talk about any one in isolation.

This is just a subset of the tools used during any development project, but it represents the bare minimum subset. Most projects of any consequence use a variety of tools in addition to the ones mentioned.

The GNU Compiler Collection

The GCC compiler, like the kernel, is designed for portability. Like all open source programs, GCC is available in source form, and you can compile the code to create your own compiler. Part of the compilation process of GCC involves configuring the project; during that step, you can configure GCC to produce code for a different target processor and thus become a cross-compiler.

However, the compiler is only one part of the tool chain necessary to produce running code. You must also get a linker, a C standard library, and a debugger. These are separate, albeit related, projects in Linux. This separation is vexing for engineers used to tools from a certain company in Redmond, Washington, where the tools are monolithic in nature. But not to worry; when you're working on an embedded project, this separation is an advantage, because the additional choice lets you select the right tool for your application.

The GCC compiler installed on your host machine is preconfigured to use the GNU C Standard Library, frequently called glibc. Most embedded projects use an alternate, smaller library called uClibc for embedded development; it's discussed later in this chapter.

GDB

The GNU Debugger (GDB) project deserves a special mention. It's the most commonly used debugger on Linux systems. Although it's frequently included in the tool chain, GDB is a separate, independent project.

For embedded development, GDB is compiled so that it can debug code running on a different processor than the debugger, much like GCC can cross-compile code. This sort of debugging adds another complication: the machine running the debugger is rarely the machine running the code to be debugged. Debugging code in this fashion is called *remote debugging* and is accomplished by running the program to be debugged with a stub program that communicates with another host where the debugger is running.

The stub program in this case is gdbserver, and it can communicate by serial or TCP connection with a host running GDB. Using gdbserver also has practical considerations because at only 100KB, give or take, it's small enough in terms of size and resources required when running on even the most resource constrained targets.

BusyBox

BusyBox is a multicall (more later on what this means) binary that provides many of the programs normally found on a Linux host. The implementations of the programs are designed so that they're small both in size but also with respect to how much memory they consume while running. In order to be as small as possible, the programs supply a subset of the functionality offered by the programs running on desktop system. BusyBox is highly configurable, with lots of knobs to turn to reduce the amount of space it requires; for example, you can leave out all the command-line help to reduce the size of the program.

As for the multicall binary concept, BusyBox is compiled as a single program. The root file system is populated with symlinks to the BusyBox executable; the name of the symlink controls what bit of functionality BusyBox runs. For example, you can do the following on an embedded system:

```
$ls -l /bin/ls
/bin/ls -> /bin/busybox
```

When you executes /bin/ls, the value of argv[0] is "/bin/ls". BusyBox runs this argument through a switch statement, which then calls the function ls_main(), passing in all the parameters on the command line. BusyBox calls the programs it provides *applets*.

■ **Note** If you're new to Linux (or Unix-like operating systems), a *symlink* (symbolic link) is a new concept. A symlink is a pointer to another file in the file system, called the *target*. The symlink functions just like its target file; opening and reading from a symlink produces the same results as opening and reading from the target file. Deleting a symlink, however, results in the link being deleted, not the target file.

BusyBox is a key component of most embedded systems. It's frequently used in conjunction with the uClibc project to create very small systems. I dedicate a chapter to the nuances of BusyBox and uClibc so you can understand when and how to take advantage of these great projects.

uClibc

As you'll find out reading this book, nearly everything in an embedded Linux system is fair game for some sort of substitution—even things you take for granted. One such item that most engineers use frequently but never give much consideration to is the implementation of the standard C library. The C language contains about 30 keywords (depending on the implementation of C), and the balance of the language's functionality is supplied by the standard library.[4] This bit of design genius means that C can be easily implemented on a new platform by creating a minimal compiler and using that to compile the standard library to produce something sufficient for application development.

The separation between the core language and the library also means there can be several implementations. That fact inhibited the adoption of C for a while, because each compiler maker shipped a C standard library that differed from their competitors', meaning a complex project needed tweaking (or major rework) in order to be used with a different compiler.

In the case of Linux, several small library implementations exist, with uClibc being the most common. uClibc is smaller because it was written with size in mind and doesn't have the platform support of glibc; it's also missing some other features. Most of what's been removed has no effect on an embedded system. Later in the book, I cover the finer points of uClibc as well as some of the other small libc implementations.

Automake/Autoconf

Open source software is designed to be distributed in source code form so that it can be compiled for the target platform. When target platforms were diverse, this made perfect sense, because there was no way for a binary to work on a wide range of targets. For example, one key part of the target system was the C library. Most open source software is written in C; when compiled, the binary attempts to use the C library on the target system. If the C library used for compilation wasn't compatible with the library on the target system, the software wouldn't run.

To make sure the software could be compiled on a wide range of systems, open source software developers found themselves doing the same sort of work, such as detecting the existence of a function or the length of a buffer in order to compile properly. For a project to be widely adopted, not only did it need to work, but users also needed to be able to compile it easily.

The Automake and Autoconf projects solve the problem of discovering the state of the target environment and creating make files that can build the project. Projects using Automake and Autoconf can be compiled on a wide range of targets with much less effort on the part of the software developer, meaning more time can be dedicated to improving the state of the software itself rather than working through build-related problems.

Packaging Systems

As Linux became more mainstream, *distributions* were developed. A distribution is a kernel and a group of programs for a root file system, and one of the things on the root file system is the C library. The increasing use of distributions means a user can compile open source software with the expectation that it will run on a computer with a certain target distribution.

Distributions added another layer with the concept of *packages*. A package is a layer of indirection on top of an open source project; it has the information about how to compile the software it contains, thereby producing a binary package. In addition to the binaries, the package contains dependency information such as the version of the C library that's required and, sometimes, the ability to run arbitrary scripts to properly install the package. Distributions typically built a group of packages as a set; you install a subset of those packages on your system. If you install additional packages, then as long as

---

[4] When it was popular to quiz engineers during an interview, a common tactic was to let the interviewee identify the keywords in a sampling of C code. Many candidates thought printf and putc were keywords. I'm glad those days are over, because I think this sort of quiz didn't do much to sort out good programmers from poor ones.

they come from the same set used to create the distribution, the dependencies are satisfied or can be satisfied by using other packages in the set.

Several packaging systems are available. RPM (neé Red Hat Package Manager, now RPM Package Manager) and deb (the packaging system used by the Debian project first and then Ubuntu) are two of the more popular packages for desktop systems. Some embedded distributions use these packing systems to create a distribution for embedded targets. In some cases, it makes sense to use a packaging system; in this book, I cover what's available for embedded developers and when using a packing system makes sense.

Patch

You hear a lot about patches when working with Linux. You may even make one or two yourself. A patch is nothing other than a file containing a *unified diff*, which is enough information that it can be used to non-interactively edit a file. This information is frequently referred to as a *change set*. The file to which the changes are applied is called the *target file*. Change sets can specify that lines can be changed, removed from, or added to the target. Although patches are typically created for text files, a patch can be created for a binary program as well.

A patch is just a data file. To update the target files, another program must be used, and that program is patch. Created by the Perl guy Larry Wall, patch does the work of reading the patch file, locating the file to be edited, and applying the changes. Patch is clever in that it can apply changes even if the file to be patched is a little different than the one used to create the patch.

You can create patches using the diff program, like so:

```
diff -Naur old-something new-something > patch-file
```

However, many source code control systems generate a patch based on the current contents of your directory versus what's stored in the source code control repository. No matter how you create your patch, applying it works the same:

```
patch < patch-file
```

If the patch program can't make the changes requested, it produces error messages and creates *reject files* so you can see where things went wrong.

Make

Make is a core underpinning of open source software. It works by scanning a list of rules and building a dependency graph. Each rule contains a target, which is usually a file and a list of dependencies. A dependency can be either another target or the name of a file. Make then scans the file system to determine what files aren't present and figures out what targets to run in what order to create the missing files.

Make has been around since 1977 and has been rewritten several times. The version used on Linux systems is GNU Make.

Make uses a combination of a terse syntax in conjunction with many preset defaults, such that the way a make file works is nearly magic. Consider this:

```
mybinary: file1.c file2.c
```

This is sufficient to give make the proper instructions to compile the file `mybinary.c` into the executable `mybinary`. The defaults tell make how to compile and link a C file from the files in the make rule.

Using make for embedded development isn't much different from using make for desktop development. One big difference is that when you're doing embedded development, you need to tell make to invoke a cross-compiler or compile under emulation. In the previous example, it's as simple as this:

```
LD=arm-linux-ld
CC=arm-linux-gcc

mybinary: file1.c file2.c
```

Although this is the simplest approach, it can probably be done more elegantly so that changing the compiler requires fewer changes to the make file. I dedicate time to creating make files so you can use a different compiler with minimal impact.

Using make along with your favorite editor is all you need to do embedded development. IDE tools like KDevelop and Eclipse scan the project to create a make file that is then executed to perform a build. You may decide to use an IDE, but having a firm understanding of what's happening under the covers is important when you're working with other open source projects or creating automated builds.

Where to Get Help

All software developers depend on little helpers, whether visible or invisible. Open Source developers tend to call upon a large number of resources to get help, very few of which require a contract or a well-stocked bank account. I introduce a selection of them here to make your life a little easier, but please be aware of the fact that new resources are being created all the time. This is just meant to get you started.

University of Google

As far as I know, Google doesn't have a university—yet. But searching via Google seems to be the best first approach. When you search, make sure you take advantage both the web search (`www.google.com`) and the newsgroup search (`groups.google.com`). Google has an archive of newsgroup messages since before the advent of Linux. Many talented engineers share what they know through personal pages, project pages, and blog postings; and Google, as you know, is the perfect way to find this sort of information on the Web.

Some crafty web sites grab the contents of mailing lists and/or newsgroups and wrap them in a web page as a way of attracting visitors to their ad-laden slices of hell; they don't have any better content than you find on a newsgroup, so feel free to look elsewhere.

Mailing Lists and Newsgroups

Mailing lists constitute the primary means of communication and serve as the mechanism of record for open source projects. A mailing list is nothing more than a system whereby communications are posted via e-mail and the postings are then forwarded to the list's subscribers. The software managing the mailing list keeps an archive of the messages, usually grouped by month and then organized by topic. Reading the archives is a great way to understand how people use the software you're interested in and what sorts of problems are common.

You should also feel free to subscribe to the mailing lists of projects in which you have greater interest. To do this, you need to supply your e-mail address. Don't worry about being spammed—these sites are run by people like you and aren't interested in enhancing anything other than your technical knowledge. As a subscriber to the list, you can choose to receive messages as they're posted or once a day, in *digest* mode. Digest mode is fine for occasional readers; but if you find yourself more involved in the project, once-a-day updates introduce too much latency.

For the newbie, the mailing list archives offer a wealth of knowledge. The open source community is large enough that somebody has worked through a problem like yours before. Google searches the mailing lists, but reading them directly gives you more context and understanding than reading a few messages in isolation. If you ask a question on the mailing list, you may get a reply that this has already been resolved or answered and a pointer to a URL of a message in the archives.

Throughout the book are recommendations for mailing lists devoted to various topics.

Etiquette

When groups of people regularly get together, rules form to make interaction pleasant for all those involved; this is the notion of *etiquette*. Etiquette involves thinking about others before yourself and making life easier for them. Now, stop slouching and start using the proper fork for your salad.

If you're new to using mailing lists or newsgroups, here are some basic rules:

- *No spam:* If it's not related to the mailing list, don't post it. If you're asking about C++ syntax corner cases on a C mailing list, somebody will likely tell you nicely that your question is off topic. Posting about your latest medical procedure or trying to sell something is verboten.

- *Keep it short and to the point, and use simple English.* This makes your message easy to download and easy to read for non–English speakers who may be participating. Don't include large attachments with your message (where *large* is more than a few kilobytes).

- *Post in plain text.* Many people reading the mailing list don't have a mail client that renders the message with fancy formatting.

- *Don't post in ALL CAPS.* It's the computer equivalent of shouting.

- *When replying, don't include all the text from the prior poster.* Clip out what you need to reference, and include that in the message.

- *Don't post "questions" that are thinly veiled invitations for somebody else to do your work.* Likewise, don't set deadlines or make demands of your fellow readers.

Open source somehow has attracted some of the smartest people and also some of the nicest. Fear not when posting a message; be reasonable and respectful, and your treatment will be the same.

Vendor-Sponsored Resources

Because having Linux running on a board is an important part of a vendor's release strategy, many vendors also offer support in varying degrees for the Linux distributed with the board. For some vendors, the only way to get Linux is to download it from their site.

The advantage of using one of these sites is that you have access to the Linux kernel and root file system that have been tested with the board and at the same time have access to a group of engineers who are working with the same hardware and software platform, because most vendor sites include a mailing list or web-based forum for support. Depending on the enlightenment of the hardware vendor and the dedication of its Linux-using customer base, the site may also contain technical articles or technical support offered directly by the company.

The trend among hardware vendors is to ensure that the changes to the Linux kernel that are required for it to run on a board make it into the mainline Linux kernel project. Due to the coordination efforts involved in the main kernel release process, processor and board vendors are always a little unsynchronized with the main kernel release, but not to the extent they were a few years back.

Trade Group and Community Interest Sites

Creating embedded Linux distributions is a much more pedestrian activity than it was a few years back, when creating a Linux distribution from scratch was a mysterious process. Several projects grew out of the need to create an embedded distribution; they built an infrastructure to help users configure and build an embedded Linux distribution. Frequently, the distributions created by these sites target a family of processors for a particular type of distribution, like a mobile phone.

These sites have great starting points for application development, if you're working on a project similar to that of the distribution. If you're doing something different, you need to learn the underlying build system for the project in order to build a distribution for your project. The build systems are great pieces of software that commendably do a difficult job and can be helpful for your project. You must evaluate the project and see if it can be helpful for your efforts.

Following are several embedded Linux distributions. This is by no means an exhaustive list:

- *Openmoko and OpenEmbedded* (http://openmoko.org and http://openembedded.org): The Openmoko distribution runs on Neo FreeRunner phones. It's targeted for an ARM9 processor and includes software for a touch device, a small Linux desktop environment, and, of course, the software necessary to run a cell phone. Openmoko grew-up around the BitBake build system, which has a bit of a learning curve. OpenEmbedded is the generic embedded distribution used in the creation of Openmoko.

- *OpenWRT* (http://openwrt.org): This distribution appeared to support Linksys routers that were running Linux and had branched out to support additional boards. It's geared toward networking devices. The build for this project is built up make and downloads and installs all the software and patches necessary to build a distribution. If you're comfortable with make, using this project should be fairly easy.

- *Android* (http://source.android.com): This is the open source project for the platform that runs the Google phone, which runs an ARM9 processor. It contains components for a UI and, most interesting, a smallish Java runtime environment. The documentation for the project explains how to use the IDE Eclipse environment to create and debug applications.

- *Linux from Scratch* (http://linuxfromscratch.org): This distribution is primarily targeted at Intel IA-32 processors. It's very configurable and gives you considerable control over the Linux that's being built. A variant of this project, CLFS, is designed to cross-build the distribution. The build system uses an XML file containing the build instructions.

The following is a list of sites focused on hardware vendors. Some of these sites are run by enthusiasts, and others are sponsored by the companies that make the hardware:

- *Linux4SAM* (`http://linux4sam.org`): This site contains information supporting the Atmel SAM9xxx processors. It provides a Linux distribution for each of Atmel's ARM boards and also has ancillary tools such as the flash programmer (SAM-BA) used to program the boot loader on the board.

- *Penguin PPC* (`http://penguinppc.org`): A wealth of information resides on this site regarding Linux running on PowerPC boards. The site has a link to a group of pages that address using PowerPC chips in embedded systems.

- *ARM, Ltd* (`www.arm.com/products/os/linux_download.html`): This is part of the official ARM, Ltd site and contains Linux distributions for most of the development boards offered by the company. The distributions contained on this page are good enough to quickly boot an ARM board. No mailing list or community support is offered on the site. If you have an ARM board and want to get Linux running quickly, this is the page to visit.

- *Linux/MIPS* (`www.linux-mips.org`): This site contains distributions, hardware information, porting guides, and patches for getting Linux running on a variety of MIPS-based systems. A group of pages explain the level of Linux support for all the MIPS architectures and even spell out things like how the 4Kc design is different than 4Kp. This site also has information about MIPs hardware manufacturers and includes a well-frequented mailing list.

Finally, these are general-purpose embedded Linux sites. They don't have much depth about any one processor or type of project. What they lack in depth, however, is made up for in breadth:

- *Linux Devices* (`www.linuxdevices.com`): This news site has more "Look! Linux runs on this hardware" articles than it has about Linux itself. Recently, the site has been focusing more on Linux software, with articles about deploying Linux on a variety of boards. Unlike many news sites, Linux Devices doesn't have community features; it's one of the few read-only news sites.

- *Free Electrons* (`www.free-electrons.com`): This started as a site with great training content and has built on that with a blog, technical videos, and other training information. It's a great resource for those new to embedded Linux. Many courses of the practical labs contain high-quality, step-by-step exercises to reinforce the concepts laid out in the training materials.

- *LWN* (`http://lwn.net/`): This is a general Linux news site that also covers embedded Linux. The site operates by subscription, with newer articles for subscribers only. LWN does a great job of summarizing the features of each new Linux distribution, explaining critical new features and bug fixes in detail. Although the site covers Linux in general, it provides a decent amount of news coverage about embedded topics and is worth a regular visit.

- *IBM developerWorks* (`www.ibm.com/developerworks/linux/library/l-embl.html`): You may not expect IBM to have so much high-quality information about embedded Linux. The mix of content is incredible, from articles demystifying open source licensing to in-depth articles explaining how Linux's virtual memory subsystem works. The site contains very few how-to step-by-step articles, instead favoring articles that explain Linux's technology in depth.

IRC

Internet Relay Chat (IRC) is a communication protocol that lets you communicate quickly by sending short messages either through a public channel or privately. IRC messages hosted by a server and channels can be thought of as existing on that server. Some projects or companies maintain their own IRC services. Client software required to use IRC is part of a standard Linux distribution. Windows users can download one of several IRC clients for that platform.

This communication medium has some rules to make it useful and easy for those who participate. Like using a mailing list, you should be courteous and respectful to the people participating:

- *Keep it short:* The purpose of IRC is to exchange short messages, maybe a line or so. The act of being verbose is called *flooding* and is frowned on.

- *Don't send status messages:* Some IRC clients let you change your user name or send out messages after a span of inactivity. In a channel frequented by many people, this is nothing but noise and makes it hard for others participating to see the real discussion of the channel.

- *Don't use Caps Lock:* As in e-mail, it's the same as shouting.

- *Don't ask somebody to solve your problem:* Also as on a mailing list, you can ask questions to get help, but the people in the channel have no obligation to help you or solve your problem. Just like any other online community, lots of people are willing to help you if you're willing to help yourself.

Next Up

Chapter 2 digs in and explains how to configure a host for embedded Linux development. The nature of embedded development requires some specialized software tools to communicate with the target board. The book also covers how to configure a Windows workstation so that it can be used for development. Of course, the tools necessary for development are free and open source (even on Windows); it's just a matter of getting them.

CHAPTER 2

■ ■ ■

Configuring the Software Environment

Getting ready for an embedded Linux project is a straightforward process. You need to collect the tools and install the necessary software components, which aren't usually found on a run-of-the-mill Linux or Windows distribution. Some of the preparation involves getting the right sort of cabling and understanding how to get everything wired up and ready to go.

Time spent configuring this aspect of the development environment correctly is an excellent investment. Even if your team consists of a single person, taking the time to document how the system is configured is important. If the team grows or the machine used for development dives into the bit-bucket, re-creating the environment using the documentation is much easier than trying to do so from memory alone.

The development environment is used for the following tasks:

- *Booting the board:* An embedded development board needs some special services in order to get started. When it's up and running, if the board contains an Ethernet port (most do), you can telnet or ssh to the board. During the development cycle, it's recommended that the serial console be active as a backup communication method in case the board can't be reached over the network.

- *Configuring and building the Linux kernel:* Most boards, although powerful, can't be used to compile the kernel. The memory and/or processing power isn't adequate. The development host is used to configure and compile the kernel and get it ready for use by the board.

- *Configuring and building the root file system:* The root file system contains the user programs that the kernel needs to work as well the application for the device. Without a root file system, the kernel would panic and stop running. In some cases, the root file system resides on the development host and is accessed over the network by the target board, which means the development host must be properly configured this to work.

- *Compiling and debugging your application:* Because most boards can't be used to compile the kernel and applications, the development host is used to compile the programs. That requires additional configuration steps.

Because the code is cross-compiled, the object code is executable only on the target device. This gives you more degrees of freedom when you're selecting a host environment. Many embedded Linux engineers use a Linux host for development, but this isn't a requirement. You can use an Apple machine (running OSX or Linux) or even a host running Windows.

Host Environment

Although you can use several operating systems to base your development environment on, all operating systems share quite a few services and of course, software development tools.

Linux

Linux is the simplest environment to get ready. Very little configuration is required; it's more a matter of getting the correct software on the system. Most systems require a few packages to be installed for development tools that aren't normally found on a desktop distribution, such as Automake, Autoconf, and, of course, GCC.

Development on Linux doesn't require superuser privileges. A root account on the system isn't necessary; however, if possible, configuring the system to get root access via sudo is a good idea, because in some cases commands must be executed as root. These include creating device nodes for root file systems, installing software, and performing other system-administration tasks. Having root access is less necessary than in years past because the software around building embedded Linux has matured.

Table 2-1 lists the software packages and what they do.

Table 2-1. *Tools Typically Used in Embedded Development*

Package	Purpose
Automake	A tool for creating make files that can be run on a variety of systems.
Autoconf	A tool for building the configure scripts that scan the system to figure out the system's state.
M4	A macro processing tool much like the pre-processor in C.
GCC	The GNU Compiler Collection. Many installations don't include GCC because of its size. When you install GCC, the system also installs some of the tools that GCC uses, such as the assembler (as) and linker (ld). If you type gcc on the command line, the C compiler provided by the GNU Compiler Collection will be invoked.
G++	The GNU C++ compiler command. Whenever you type g++ on the command line, the GNU C++ compiler will be invoked. This is required when you're using tools that use C++. Like GCC, G++ requires a lot of disk space; consequently, it doesn't make the cut for many CD-ROM based installations.
GDB	The GNU Debugger.
dhcp3-server	Dynamic Host Configuration Protocol—the software that's used to automatically assign IP addresses on a network.
nfs-user-server	Network File System—a tool from Sun that allows a remote computer to access storage on a remote computer.

tftpd	Trivial File Transfer Protocol—A simple protocol for transferring files over an IP network. This protocol is easy to implement and makes few demands on the boot loader.
minicom	An old school, text-based terminal emulation program. When you're talking to a board over a serial cable, minicom is the perfect tool.

Debian (Ubuntu) Systems

Debian systems use the dpkg system to manage the software installed on the host. Wrapped around dpkg is another suite of tools called the Advanced Packing Tool (APT) that you can use to download packages from a central repository. The examples in this chapter use the command-line method of working with packages; graphical tools like aptitude are also available. These tools make it easy to install the packages you need for embedded development.

You can install packages with one command and test to see (using the -s switch) what happens by doing the following:

```
$ sudo apt-get -s install automake autoconf m4 gcc gdb dhcp3-server nfs-user-
server↵
 tftpd minicom
```

This produces output like the following:

```
Reading package lists... Done
Building dependency tree
Reading state information... Done
autoconf is already the newest version.
m4 is already the newest version.
gcc is already the newest version.
gdb is already the newest version.
The following extra packages will be installed:
  autotools-dev openbsd-inetd portmap
Recommended packages:
  lrzsz
The following NEW packages will be installed:
  automake autotools-dev dhcp3-server minicom nfs-user-server openbsd-inetd
portmap↵
 tftpd
0 upgraded, 8 newly installed, 0 to remove and 233 not upgraded.
Inst autotools-dev (20070725.1 Ubuntu:8.04/hardy)
Inst automake (1:1.10.1-2 Ubuntu:8.04/hardy)
Inst dhcp3-server (3.0.6.dfsg-1ubuntu9 Ubuntu:8.04/hardy)
Inst minicom (2.3~rc1-2 Ubuntu:8.04/hardy)
Inst portmap (6.0-4 Ubuntu:8.04/hardy)
Inst openbsd-inetd (0.20050402-6 Ubuntu:8.04/hardy)
Inst tftpd (0.17-15ubuntu1 Ubuntu:8.04/hardy)
Inst nfs-user-server (2.2beta47-23 Ubuntu:8.04/hardy)
Conf autotools-dev (20070725.1 Ubuntu:8.04/hardy)
```

```
Conf automake (1:1.10.1-2 Ubuntu:8.04/hardy)
Conf dhcp3-server (3.0.6.dfsg-1ubuntu9 Ubuntu:8.04/hardy)
Conf minicom (2.3~rc1-2 Ubuntu:8.04/hardy)
Conf portmap (6.0-4 Ubuntu:8.04/hardy)
Conf openbsd-inetd (0.20050402-6 Ubuntu:8.04/hardy)
Conf tftpd (0.17-15ubuntu1 Ubuntu:8.04/hardy)
Conf nfs-user-server (2.2beta47-23 Ubuntu:8.04/hardy)
```

Some of these packages may already be installed on your system, and others may be out of date. In some cases, the requested packages require other packages in order to work correctly. No worries—apt-get sorts all that out, figuring out what packages must be installed in what order. After installing the packages, the system also runs any configuration scripts so the newly installed software is ready to run.

Running the command without -s produces output like the following:

```
$ sudo apt-get  install automake autoconf m4 gcc gdb dhcp3-server nfs-user-server⏎
 tftpd minicom

autoconf is already the newest version.
m4 is already the newest version.
gcc is already the newest version.
gdb is already the newest version.
The following extra packages will be installed:
  autotools-dev openbsd-inetd portmap
Recommended packages:
  lrzsz
The following NEW packages will be installed:
  automake autotools-dev dhcp3-server minicom nfs-user-server openbsd-inetd portmap
⏎
tftpd
0 upgraded, 8 newly installed, 0 to remove and 233 not upgraded.
Need to get 1261kB of archives.
After this operation, 4432kB of additional disk space will be used.
Do you want to continue [Y/n]?
```

Respond with Y, and press Enter. The packages are downloaded and installed on the system.

RPM

Systems based on RPM, like Red Hat and CentOS, use a program called yum[1] that provides the same functionality as apt-get. Yum interacts with a central repository, and when a user asks to install a package, it attempts to download it from that repository along with any dependent packages.

To start the installation process, enter the following command:

```
$ sudo yum install automake autoconf m4 gcc gdb dhcp3-server nfs-user-server tftpd
minicom
```

---

[1] Yum unpacks to Yellowdog Updater, Modified. Yellowdog is a distribution of Linux for PowerPC computers built with RPM packages. I use this excellent distribution for one of my kid's pre-x86 iMacs.

The software calculates the dependencies and shows a list of what will be upgraded and installed. The output looks similar to this, depending on the configuration of the host system:

```
================================================================================
Package        Arch      Version        Repository     Size
================================================================================
Installing:
autoconf       noarch       2.59-12         base        647 k
automake       noarch      1.9.6-2.1        base        484 k
gcc      i386      4.1.2-42.el5         base      5.2 M
gdb      i386      6.5-37.el5_2.2      updates       3.1 M
m4       i386      1.4.5-3.el5.1       base      133 k
Installing for dependencies:
binutils       i386       2.17.50.0.6-6.el5 base       2.9 M
glibc-devel      i386       2.5-24.el5_2.2      updates       2.0 M
glibc-headers      i386       2.5-24.el5_2.2      updates      611 k
imake      i386       1.0.2-3       base       319 k
kernel-headers      i386       2.6.18-92.1.22.el updates       854 k
libgomp      i386       4.1.2-42.el5        base       82 k
Updating for dependencies:
cpp      i386       4.1.2-42.el5        base       2.7 M
glibc      i686       2.5-24.el5_2.2      updates       5.2 M
glibc-common      i386       2.5-24.el5_2.2      updates      16 M
libgcc      i386       4.1.2-42.el5        base       93 k

Transaction Summary
================================================================================
Install 11 Package(s)
Update 4 Package(s)
Remove 0 Package(s)

Total download size: 40 M
Is this ok [y/N]:
```

Enter Y, and the system begins downloading and installing the packages. When the process completes, the environment has the necessary packages installed.

Windows

Using a Windows host for embedded Linux development is a reasonable choice if that's what is already on your desktop. Due to corporate standards, some users have no choice but to run Windows while on the corporate network. To use an MS Windows host for embedded development, you need software that emulates a Linux host to the point that it can be used to compile a kernel and the supporting tools. This means the software must implement the POSIX standard and supply the command-line tools commonly found on a Linux distribution. Cygwin is the preferred solution to accomplish this goal.

Cygwin

Cygwin is an open source project providing a complete Linux-like environment. It doesn't emulate a Linux host; rather, it implements a complete POSIX environment on Windows and provides the additional headers so you can compile code open source software and run it on Windows. Cygwin doesn't let you run binaries compiled for Linux, but it provides the infrastructure and runtime so those programs can be compiled and run. The core of Cygwin is a Dynamic Link Library (DLL) containing the implementation of the POSIX functions missing from Windows.

As a user, the primary way of interacting Cygwin is through a shell. When you install Cygwin, it includes a bash shell. The desktop icon launches this shell, giving you the familiar $ prompt and greatly advancing the functionality of your Windows machine. Because the programs compiled for Cygwin are native Windows programs, you can still execute them from the standard Windows command shell, if for some reason you prefer that option.

Installation

The basic process for installing Cygwin involves downloading a binary setup program and then downloading and installing a series of binary packages from the Cygwin site. After the packages have been downloaded, they're installed on the system. The Cygwin setup allows you to skip the download set and install the packages directly; however, downloading the packages lets the Cygwin configuration be easily re-created. In addition, the download process frequently fails, so by separating the download from installation, the system doesn't have a partially installed Cygwin.

Cygwin includes an installer that makes installation easy. To start the installation process, do the following:

1.   Visit www.cygwin.com. On the home page, click the Install Cygwin Now link.

2.   Save the setup.exe file. Some browsers let you run a program from a web site. Instead, save the file to a folder, such as c:\temp\cygwin-install\setup.exe.

3.   Run setup.exe. Use Explorer to go to the folder c:\temp\cygwin-install\setup.exe. Depending on the paranoia setting of Windows, a message may appear indicating that it isn't a signed program (see Figure 2-1). You can ignore this warning.

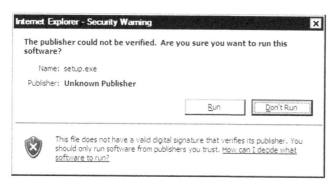

Figure 2-1. *Cygwin security warning dialog*

4.   The installation program shows you the installation splash screen. Click Next.

5.   Choose an installation type (see Figure 2-2). The recommended method is Download Without Installing, which fetches all the components that Cygwin needs to install and stores them on your system.

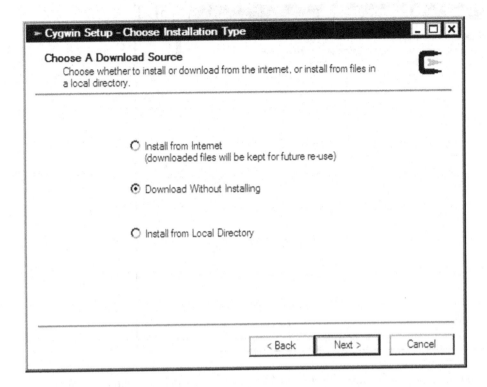

Figure 2-2. Cygwin installation: selecting the download source

6.   Select a local package directory (see Figure 2-3). This is where the packages are stored on your system after download. The default path is complex; change it to something easier to remember.

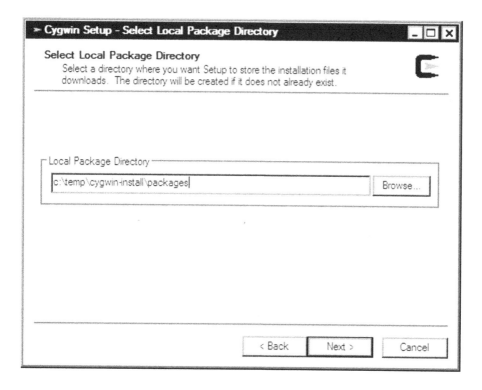

Figure 2-3. *Cygwin installation: selecting a directory in which to store the packages after download*

7. Select a connection type (see Figure 2-4). Generally, you can choose Direct Connection. However, if you have an Internet connection that requires making a connection, the IE5 settings make that connection for you before starting the download process. If your environment uses a proxy to connect to the Internet, select the third item, and enter the hostname and port for the proxy.

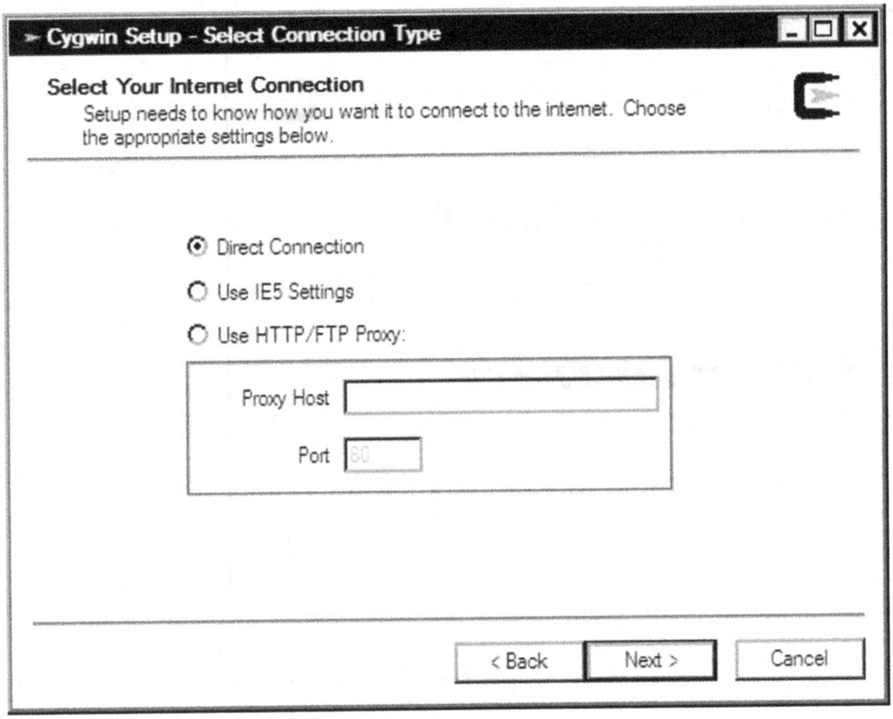

Figure 2-4. Cygwin installation, selecting Internet connection type.

8. Choose a download site (see Figure 2-5). The Cygwin project uses a collection of mirrors to host the binaries for installation, to conserve on bandwidth and give users around the world better download times. Pick a mirror close to you. I'm partial to .edu sites, because they typically have great bandwidth in the U.S.

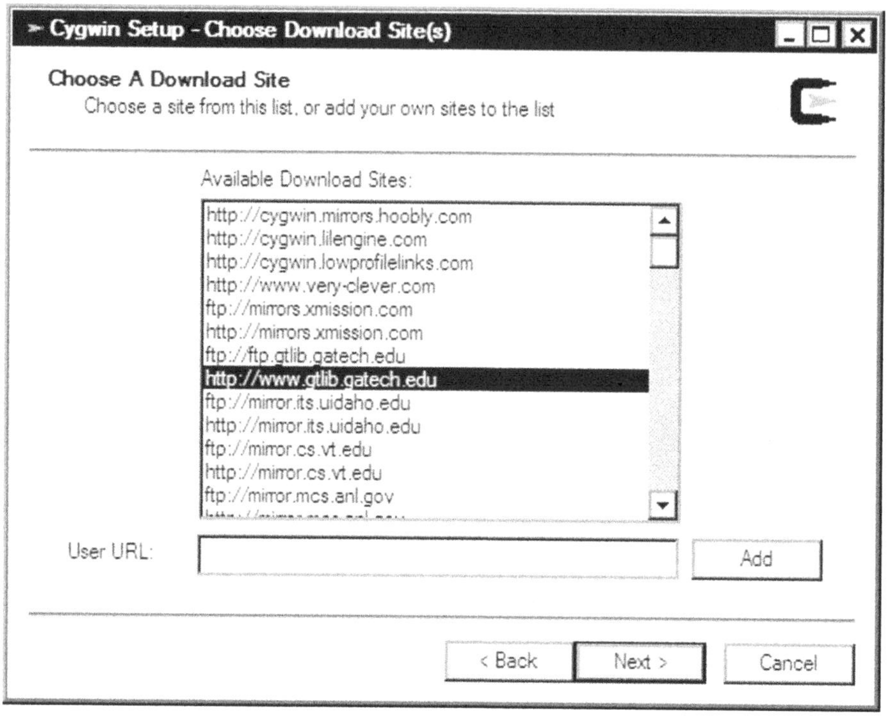

Figure 2-5. *Cygwin installation: selecting a download site*

9. Select the Packages you want (see Figure 2-6). The default set of packages is barely enough to get Cygwin running on your computer. For embedded development, you need to install more than the default. The selection process is a bit confusing. Figure 2-6 shows the packages organized by group; next to each group is text describing what will be installed, with all the groups set to Default. Clicking the Default text switches it to Install. Clicking the Default label next to the All tag installs all the packages, which is several hundred megabytes.

   The best way to install Cygwin is to select all packages for installation and then unselect the following categories: Audio, Database, KDE, Games, Gnome, Graphics, X11, and Publishing.

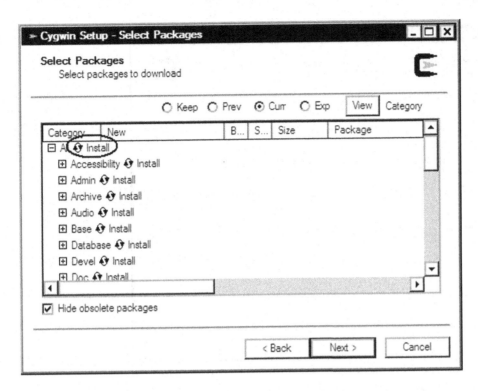

Figure 2-6. *Cygwin installation: selecting what packages to install*

10. The download process now begins. How fast the packages download depends on the speed of your Internet service and the mirror's Internet connection. Expect it to take a few hours for the files to download to your computer.

11. After the files have downloaded, run the installation program again, but install the files from the local cache. Run the setup program again, and this time, select Install from Local Directory and click Next (see Figure 2-7).

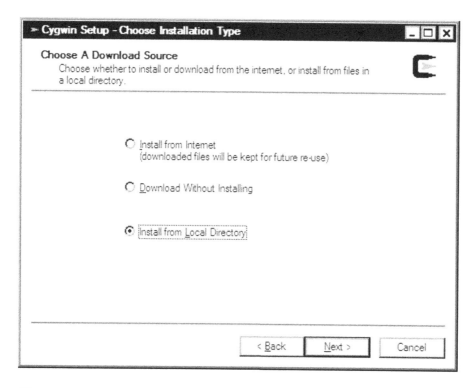

Figure 2-7. *Cygwin installation: installing using the downloaded packages*

12. You're asked where to install Cygwin (see Figure 2-8). This is the root of the
Cygwin installation: all the files are installed under this directory, and when
Cygwin is run, this directory maps to the root file system. I talk more about
what that means in the section "Cygwin's View of the File System." The
default, under most circumstances, is correct.

The Default Text File Type option determines how Cygwin handles text files.
You should select the recommended "Unix / binary," because in this mode, no
line-ending translation occurs. That means if you open a text file created by a
Cygwin program (say, you use vi to create a two-line file) with a program
expecting Windows line endings (such as Notepad), the Windows program
won't show a file with two lines. Again, more about this in "Cygwin's View of
the File System."

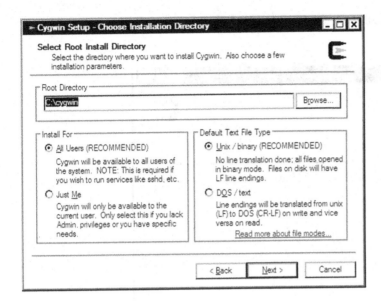

Figure 2-8. *Cygwin installation: selecting an installation directory*

13. The setup program shows the directory where the files were downloaded (see Figure 2-9).

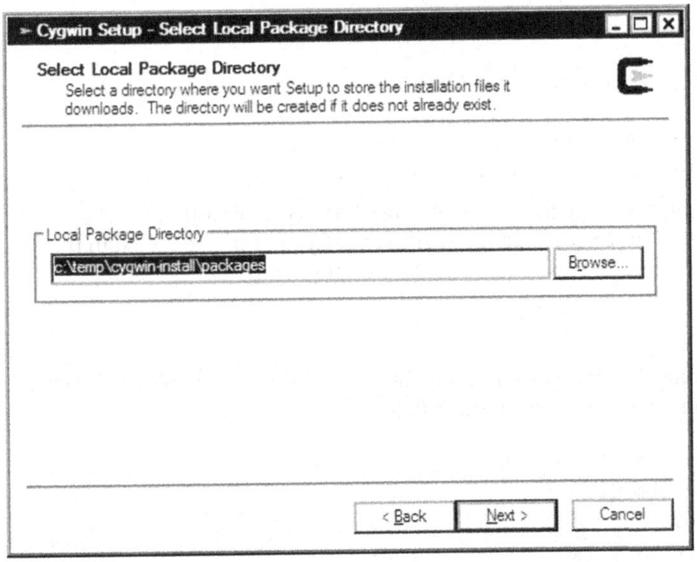

Figure 2-9. *Cygwin installation: selecting a local package directory*

14. On the next page, click the Default label next to All to install all the packages (see Figure 2-10).

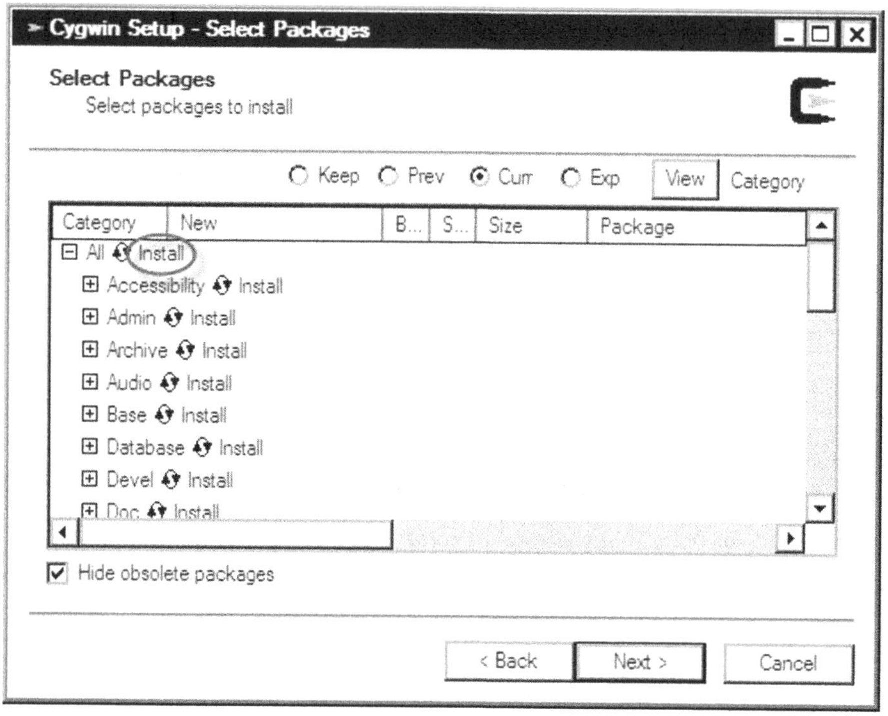

Figure 2-10. Cygwin installation: picking what packages to install

15. The installation process begins. The installer tallies the checksums of the downloaded files to make sure they aren't corrupt, and begins copying files.

When the install completes, you can have the installer put an icon in the Start menu or on the desktop to run the bash shell. This file is called `c:\cygwin\cygwin.bat` if Cygwin was installed in the default location. Running this program results in a command shell with a $ prompt.

Cygwin's View of the File System

In the bash shell on a Windows host, typing `ls /` shows you something that looks a lot like a file system on a regular Linux (or Unix) host. Issuing the `mount` command reveals

```
c:\Cygwin\bin on /usr/bin type system (binmode)
c:\Cygwin\lib on /usr/lib type system (binmode)
c:\Cygwin on / type system (binmode)
c:\temp on /tmp type system (binmode)
c: on /cygdrive/c type system (binmode,noumount)
d: on /cygdrive/d type system (binmode,noumount)
```

This shows that several directories in the file system have been associated with mount points from Cygwin's perspective. You can use `mount` to include arbitrary directories in the root file system, just as you do on a regular Linux system, except that the mounted device can only be a directory on the computer. Any time a Cygwin program is executed, it uses this mount table to locate a file. (The mount table for Cygwin is stored in the registry at `HKEY_LOCAL_MACHINE\SOFTWARE\Cygnus Solutions\Cygwin\mounts v2` if you want to take a peek.)

To easily access all the drives in a Windows system, Cygwin maintains a directory `/cygdrive` with a subdirectory for each drive letter present on the system; for example, to see the contents of the root of the `C:` drive, use the directory `/cygdrive/c`. This directory is kept in sync with the rest of the system so that when a USB drive is plugged in and Windows maps it to a drive, it appears in this directory as well.

Windows (DOS, really) and Linux have a different convention for indicating the end of a line in a text file. Windows uses two characters: a Carriage Return (CR) and a Line Feed (LF). Linux uses just one: LF.[2] When you install Cygwin, the setup program asks how to handle text files. The choices are as follows:

- *Unix/Binary:* If you select this choice, Cygwin doesn't attempt to translate the end-of-line character in text files. This is the default option, and it makes sense for the vast majority of users. Choosing this option means that files created with standard Windows tools like Notepad appear to have extra end-of-line characters when viewed from a program compiled in the Cygwin environment, like `cat`.

- *DOS/Text:* In this mode, Cygwin attempts to translate the end-of-line markers for files, so that files created with standard Windows editors and programs appear to programs running under Cygwin as having just a LF for an end-of-line marker. Cygwin doesn't perform this translation for files opened as binary (recall that you pass in a flag when opening a file, indicating if it's text or binary). Unless the environment uses some stubborn programs on the development host, you shouldn't select this option.

When you're working on code on a Windows host, it should use the Unix line-ending convention. Many free editors support this feature: joe, Emacs, and vi for the Linux user forced to use Windows; Notepad++, XEmacs, and Crimson Editor for Windows users forced to use Linux. Most tools for working with source files do the right thing—for example, code librarians like CVS and Subversion properly translate line endings by default. However, any failure to properly configure the tools becomes very difficult to diagnose. Little overhead is required for making sure the line endings are consistent, and doing so takes one possible source of problems off your list of things that could go wrong.

Virtual Linux Machines on Windows

Another approach you can take when working on a Windows host is to use virtualization software. Using this approach means that a virtual machine runs Linux on the Windows host. With today's commonplace multicore processor, multi-gigabyte machines, this is a reasonable approach. One of the advantages of running a virtual machine is that you don't need to compensate for Cygwin idiosyncrasies, because the virtual machine is running Linux.

When you run a virtual machine, a window opens on the desktop that looks like the monitor of the running machine. You can adjust this virtual monitor so that it occupies the entire screen area, which gives the applications running on the virtual machine more screen real estate. The virtual machine can also be minimized, and you can then use a terminal emulation program to connect via ssh (this is my preference.)

---

[2] This is a leftover from the days of teletypes. Some teletypes needed the Carriage Return to move the print head back to the start of the line and a Line Feed to advance the paper one line.

Several virtualization software packages exist:

- *Sun VirtualBox* (http://virtualbox.org): This is the recommended solution. VirtualBox is easy to install and lets you easily create new machines.

- *VMware* (http://vmware.com): VMware has been in the virtualization market for years and offers a very mature product. It's harder to configure than VirtualBox and requires registration.

- *QEMU* (http://bellard.org/qemu/): This is an open source tool for system emulation that runs best on Linux. There are distributions for Windows that are precompiled.

Using VirtualBox

VirtualBox is by far the easiest software to install and get running and is the recommended solution. It does a great job with the basics and also offers features like emulation of the serial and USB ports. This is important because the primary way to communicate with a board during startup is through the serial ports. To create a development environment, you need the following:

- *VirtualBox software from Sun:* Obtain this from the VirtualBox site, and run the installer. The http://www.virtualbox.org/wiki/Downloads page contains pointers to the URLs for the latest distributions. VirtualBox is a dual-licensed product, meaning that Sun can offer it as open source software and license its use under other circumstances. Commercial VirtualBox users can download and evaluate VirtualBox at no cost. If you're a commercial user, the VirtualBox terms of use require you to obtain a license.

- *An Ubuntu bootable CD image:* The Ubuntu project publishes CDs that are ready to boot a running Linux system (what's called a LiveCD) and can be used for installation as well. To download an Ubuntu LiveCD, visit http://www.ubuntu.com/getubuntu/download. The page asks for your location to find a close mirror. The download is a file that is a bit-image of a CD. Of course, any LiveCD distribution will do; there are plenty to choose from, and new ones appear on a regular basis. If you're partial to Red Hat/Fedora, you can use the distribution at http://fedoraproject.org/get-fedora; it boots from the CD and has an installer. Ubuntu is used as an example because of its trouble-free installation and wide hardware support.

When you've gathered the components, open VirtualBox and run the New Machine Wizard by clicking the New icon (see Figure 2-11).

Figure 2-11. *Start the New Machine Wizard by clicking New..*

The wizard asks for a machine name and the operating system type and version. Any text supplied can be the name, but the best thing to do is to select a name that relates to the type of machine, like "ubuntu-version". The next panel asks for the base memory size. The default is an acceptable value; click Next.

In the Virtual Hard Disk Panel, click New under Boot Hard Disk (see Figure 2-12). This lets you create a new "disk" for the virtual machine.

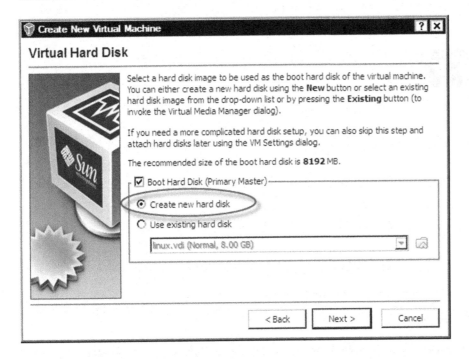

Figure 2-12. *Click New to create a "disk" for the virtual machine.*

Create a disk with dynamically expanding storage. This type of disk grows until it reaches its size limit, taking up only the space it needs as it grows. When you create this type of disk, feel free to create a large disk in case you need the space later in the project. The next panel suggests a disk size, usually 8GB; increase this value to at least twice the suggested size. In this panel, you also give the drive's file a name; use the name of the virtual machine, to make associating one with the other easier. Then, finish the Virtual Hard Disk Wizard. This is the last step in creating the virtual machine.

Before you boot the virtual machine, you must make two important changes:

- *Boot the machine from the virtual CD ROM drive:* The virtual machine that's been created has nothing on its hard drive. So, boot the machine with the Ubuntu CD-ROM image you downloaded earlier.

- *Change the network settings:* The default networking uses the machine where the virtual machine is running like a router. To make accessing the network easier, change the network configuration so that the virtual machine shares the network adapter.

You can make these changes through the machine's Settings panel (see Figure 2-13). Follow these steps:

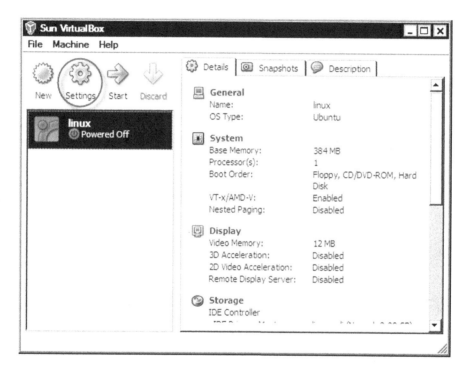

Figure 2-13. *The Settings panel*

1. In the CD/DVD-ROM section, click Mount CD/DVD ROM Drive, and then select ISO Image file. Using the control next to the drop-down, use the Virtual Media Manager dialog to add the Ubuntu ISO file you downloaded earlier. Doing so makes the virtual machine think that ISO image is in the virtual CD/DVD ROM drive.

2. Change the networking so that the virtual machine shares the network adapters on the host machine. To do so, select Network at the left in the Settings panel, and change Attached To to Host Interface (see Figure 2-14). The bottom part of the dialog shows a list that lets you select which host interface should be used by the virtual machine. If the computer where VirtualBox is located has only one adapter, no action is necessary. Click OK to save the settings.

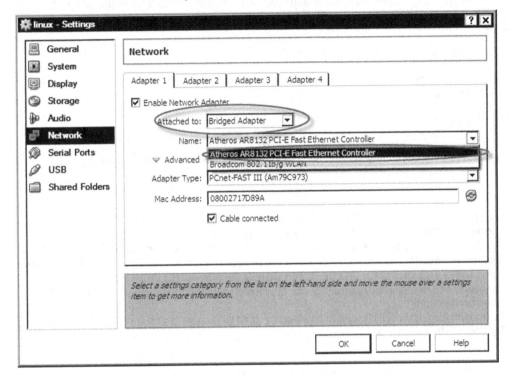

Figure 2-14. Change the network settings.

3. To start the machine, double-click it in the list of virtual machines. A booting message appears. The CD-ROM ISO image is mounted, and the Ubuntu boot-up message appears, asking if the distribution should be run from the CD ROM or installed on the machine. Click Install, and follow the instructions.

4. The biggest leap of faith occurs when Ubuntu asks if you want to reformat the current hard drive and use all of it for the Ubuntu installation. Click Yes. The drive being reformatted is the virtual drive, not the physical one on your system. In about 10 minutes, your Ubuntu machine is ready for use.

Host Services

After the software is installed, some additional configuration steps are necessary to get the packages in running order. This section goes through configuring each of the services and how to perform some testing and trouble shooting. The time you devote to making sure the services work as expected is well spent, because the boot loader provides little feedback in the event of failure. Knowing that software is in a working state removes one thing from the list when you're troubleshooting.

Turn Off Your Firewall

Some systems run a firewall by default; this should be turned off. The system used for booting an embedded board shouldn't be on the public side of the firewall, subject to attack from the general Internet.

Turning off the firewall is as easy as

```
$ sudo /etc/init.d/iptables off
```

That command turns off the firewall until the next reboot. To turn it off forever, delete the symlink used to run the service during system startup:

```
$ sudo chkconfig iptables off
```

Firewalls work silently, so if the board attempts a TFTP connection that the firewall blocks, the board reports that it can't make a connection. This is accurate but not a complete description.

TFTP

TFTP, a lightweight file transfer protocol, uses other software to get running: xinetd. The xinetd program performs a neat job: it waits for network connections on ports (as specified in the /etc/services file) and, when a connection occurs, remaps the standard in and out to the read and write of the network connection. This trick means that the program run by xinetd has code that uses file semantics (like scanf() and printf()) and reads and writes over a network connection. Not all distributions have xinetd installed by default, so you may need to install it using your distribution's package-management system.

The configuration file for the TFTP service handled by xinetd resides at /etc/xinetd.d/tftp. Listing the files reveals the following:

```
# default: off
# description: The tftp server serves files using the trivial file transfer
#       protocol. The tftp protocol is often used to boot diskless
#       workstations, download configuration files to network-aware printers,
#       and to start the installation process for some operating systems.
service tftp
{
        socket_type             = dgram
        protocol                = udp
        wait                    = yes
        user                    = root
        server                  = /usr/sbin/in.tftpd
        server_args             = -s /tftpboot
        disable                 = yes
        per_source              = 11s
        cps                     = 100 2
}
```

The lines of interest in this file are `server_args`, which indicates the directory where TFTP stores and looks for files. The kernel that is downloaded to the board needs to be placed in this directory. Change the default value `/tftpboot` to something more convenient for you.

The second line of interest is

```
disable                 = yes
```

At first glance, you may think that `yes` means it's enabled, but it means the opposite. Sneaky! Change this line to read

```
disable                 = no
```

After you've made the changes, restart the `xinet.d` service:

```
$ sudo /etc/init.d/xinet.d restart
```

If the `/etc/xinetd.d/tftp` file contains errors, a message appears. Testing the TFTP server is as easy as creating a file and trying a `put` and a `get`:

```
$ date > /tmp/tftptest
$ tftp
tftp> connect localhost
tftp> put /tmp/tftptest
tftp> get tftptest /tmp/get.tftptest
```

You can try the same test on another computer on the network, to ensure that you can connect to the host from another machine (*across the wire*, as a network-person would say). If TFTP works from localhost but not from another computer, chances are the firewall is still running. Stop this service, and try again.

DHCP

Some boards request an IP address during initialization. If the board is using an NFS-mounted file system, it certainly needs the network stack up and running. The DCHP protocol works by having a host send a broadcast packet requesting an address from a DHCP server and waiting for a reply. If an answer comes back before the timeout ends, the board uses the information in the reply to configure the network adapter. Take care when starting a DHCP server, because a typo in the configuration can result in the server merrily assigning addresses to computers other than the target board.

The following configuration only assigns addresses based on Media Access Control (MAC) addresses. The MAC address is a unique number assigned to the board by the manufacturer, so the chance of two machines on the network having the same MAC address is close to zero. It's not exactly zero, because sometimes MAC address are duplicated across vendors (that is, Vendor B issues MAC addresses that only Vendor A should issue); more commonly, the board is given a MAC address during configuration that matches an existing address on the network. Duplicate IP addresses result in general network mayhem, result in at least three all-hands IT meetings; it's not the type of attention you want.

The software providing the reply is called the DHCP server and gets its settings from a file stored in `/etc/dhcpd.conf`. This file is read when the DHCP service starts, so this server must be restarted in order for changes to take effect.

A typical `/etc/dhcpd.conf` file looks like this:

```
ddns-update-style ad-hoc;
authoratative;
subnet 10.0.0.0 netmask 255.0.0.0 {
```

You structure the DHCP file to supply information on a per-host basis. A DCHP configuration file can have many of these host sections:

```
host myboard {
 hardware ethernet 02:03:04:f5:d6:07;
 fixed-address 10.0.0.2;
 server-name "10.0.0.1";
 option router "10.0.0.1";
 option root-path "/var/board/rfs";
```

The root path is used by boards that mount an NFS file system.

The host name can be different from the host part of this definition. This is the value that Linux writes into /etc/hostname:

```
 option host-name "board";
```

Configuring a DHCP service for an enterprise is a complex business; however, for the case of booting a board, the configuration is as minimal as possible. In this example, the file has been configured so that it replies only to hosts with a MAC address of 02:03:04:f5:d6:07. You need to change this value for the board being booted. There are several ways to get the IP address for the board:

- *Look at the board:* The MAC address is occasionally printed on a sticker. This is the low-tech solution.

- *When the board boots, the boot loader may show you the MAC address:* Or, at the boot loader prompt, you can ask for the state of the environment. The exact method varies per boot loader; however, many boards use U-Boot, and the bdi command shows the following output along with some other information:
  ```
  ethaddr    = :02:03:04:f5:d6:07;
  ```
  If you're new to embedded systems, U-Boot is boot-loader software that runs after the board boots but before the operating system as started. Chapter 7 talks about the role of boot loaders in detail.

- If all else fails, you can attach the board to the network, start the board, and have it attempt to find an address while running a packet sniffer on your desktop. This is the most hackerish way of getting the address; for some boards with primitive boot loaders, it's sometimes the fastest way.

- To sniff the network, use a tool called tcpdump to print out all broadcast packets on the network, and wait for the output. The tcpdump utility reports the MAC address of the machines broadcasting for a DHCP reply. For example:

```
# tcpdump ip broadcast
tcpdump: verbose output suppressed, use -v or -vv for full protocol decode
listening on eth0, link-type EN10MB (Ethernet), capture size 96 bytes
22:30:39.791184 IP localhost.bootpc > 255.255.255.255.bootps: BOOTP/DHCP, Request
↵
```

```
from :02:03:04:f5:d6:07 (oui Unknown), length 300
```

After obtaining the MAC address, the next interesting line is

```
fixed-address 10.0.0.2;
```

This is the address that is assigned to the host. The address should be one that is acceptable on your network and shouldn't clash with other addresses. Specifying fixed-address means that when the DHCP server sees a request for an address from the MAC address in this section, it always returns the same IP address. Experimentation shows that a DHCP server frequently assigns the same IP address to a computer; this isn't guaranteed by the specification but is an implementation artifact. By associating a MAC address with a fixed IP address, the board always gets the same IP address assignment.

NFS

The Network File System (NFS) protocol is a way for a machine to make a storage location (the so-called *export* in NFS parlance) available to other hosts on the network. NFS isn't a requirement for embedded development, although it does make development easier because the root file system used by the target board can be easily updated when it's stored as a directory somewhere on the development host. Embedded boards that use flash memory (the same technology as USB drives) must have their file systems built and then placed on the board, and that process can be time consuming early in the development process when changes are frequent.

NFS exports are mounted like any other device in Linux, via mount:

```
# mount -t nfs nfsserver.yourdoman.com:/some/path a-directory/that-exists
```

After mounting, you can read or write to /mnt/nfs according to the permissions granted to you. Informing the NFS server of a mount is done through the /etc/exports file. The format of this file is very simple; for example, to export a directory containing a root file system to be mounted by a board, the file contains the following line:

```
/var/rfs                *(rw,no_root_squash)
```

This line says, "export /var/rfs, allow anyone to connect, allow reads and writes, and if a user with UID=0 connects, don't attempt to remap the UID to something less dangerous." The * means to allow connections from any host. Reading the man page for this file reveals that the user has great control over what hosts can mount an export: the user can enter host names, IP addresses, and IP address masks. All this is necessary for NSF servers deployed in an enterprise or public network, but is overkill for the purposes of booting a board, and is a generator of problems.

Restart the NFS server by doing the following:

```
# /etc/init.d/nfs-user-server restart
```

You should test the NFS server from another Linux host, to duplicate how the board mounts the share. Here's the command:

```
# mkdir -p /mnt/nfs
# mount -t nfs <nfs-server-host-name>:/var/nfs /mnt/nfs
```

Of course, replace *nfs-server-host-name* with the host name or IP address of the NFS server. After you've connected, test the connection by writing a file and printing the contents:

```
# echo 1 > /mnt/nfs/file
# cat /mnt/nfs/file
```

The most common problem with NFS is not having permissions to write files on the NFS server or misspelling name of the export in the /etc/exports file or the mount command. When you make changes, remember to restart the NFS server after changing the /etc/exports file.

NFS with Cygwin

Configuring the NFS server included with Cygwin requires some extra finessing. The NFS server must run as a Windows service, and you must do some mapping between the Windows and Unix security models. Fortunately, a script has been written that does this configuration work: nfs-config-server. You must run this script in order for NFS to function under Cygwin. For this script to work, the account logged in to the Windows computer must have local administrator rights. You probably have local administrator rights, unless your IT department is more draconian than most.

Open a Cygwin bash shell, and do the following:

```
bash-3.2$ ./nfs-server-config
This script sets up a default configuration for running an NFS server under
Cygwin. As part of this setup, the script will do the following:

  1) Create a user account to run the services under. [OPTIONAL]
  2) Install portmap, mountd, and nfsd as Windows services.
  3) Create a sample exports file.
  4) Create a sample uid/gid mapping file.

After installing, please read the nfs-server README for Cygwin:

  /usr/share/doc/Cygwin/nfs-server-2.3-*.README

This document contains notes on installation and documents known problems
and workarounds with the NFS server; ex:

  - ISSUE : Recommend using ntsec
  - ISSUE : Daemons are single-threaded
  - ISSUE : Daemons require 'impersonate logged on user' right.
  - ISSUE : Daemons cannot re-export mapped network drives
  - ISSUE : Daemons expect 'nobody' or 'Guest' as anonymous user
  - ISSUE : Portmap service fails to start
  - ISSUE : Cannot export Windows directories not under Cygwin root
  - ISSUE : Considerations when mapping UIDs/GIDs
Do you want to continue? (yes/no)
```

Reassuring, huh? Answer Yes. The script fishes around to make sure there isn't another Cygwin-like program that could cause problems. If all goes well, the following appears:

```
Checking for other Unix environments on this system ...
Good! There doesn't seem to be any other Unix environments installed.
```

You can choose to install the services so that they run under the local system
account, or under a separate user account. Which option you should choose
depends on which version of Windows you are running:

```
Windows 2000 : You may run nfsd under either a local system account or
                a separate user account. You _probably_ want to run under
                the local system account.
Windows XP   : You _must_ run nfsd under a separate user account.
```

If you choose to run nfsd under a separate user account, you will be prompted
for a user name and password. If the user name you supply does not exist,
it will be created.

Do you want to run nfsd under a separate user account? (yes/no)

Respond with Yes, and you're asked for a username and password to create a new account:

```
User name : nfs-server
Password  :

Creating user nfs-server ...
The command completed successfully.

Adding nfs-server to Administrators group ...
The command completed successfully.

Assigning required privileges to user nfs-server ...
Adding user nfs-server to /etc/passwd ...
Ensuring user nfs-server has write persmissions in /var/log ...

Installing portmap service ...
Installing mountd service ...
Installing nfsd service ...
```

The services are installed and ready for use. The /etc/exports file also contains a parameter so
that the NFS server can map the User and Group ID (UID/GID) of the mounting NFS server into a user
and group that have read/write permissions in the Cygwin directory. This is an example file:

```
/temp   192.168.2.86(rw,no_root_squash,map_static=/etc/nfs/new.map)
```

The fie /etc/nfs/new.map contains this data:

```
uid    0-1000   500      # user id for Administrator
gid    0-1000   513      # group id for Administrator
```

This file means that incoming UIDs and GIDs between 0 and 1000 should be mapped to the User ID and Group ID of the Administrator on the local machine. To figure out the User and Group ID of the Administrator, do the following:

```
$ mkpasswd.exe -l -u Administrator
Administrator:unused_by_nt/2000/xp:500:513:HOSTID\Administrator,S-1-5-21-
9999999999-↵
2222222222-5555555555-500:/home/Administrator:/bin/bash
```

These two numbers are the UID and GID.
You can now start the NFS service by doing the following:

```
$ cygrunsrv --start nfsd
```

PXE

Preboot Execution Environment (PXE) is a specification for booting a system over a network. This technology was spearheaded by Intel as part of its management framework for networked computers. I'll spare you the gory details behind the protocol; PXE works by adding additional information to the DCHP broadcast packet and behaving differently if it gets back a DHCP packet from a server supporting the PXE protocol.

Because few boards use PXE, this package isn't a part of most distributions.. To install PXE on Ubuntu, do the following:

```
# apt-get install pxe syslinux
```

On Red Hat systems, use yum:

```
# yum install pxe syslinux
```

Configuring PXE requires an update to the DHCP record for the board. This uses the previous example:

```
host myboard {
 hardware ethernet 02:03:04:f5:d6:07;
 fixed-address 10.0.0.2;
 server-name "10.0.0.1";
 filename "pxelinux.0";
 next-server <ip-address-of-tftp-server>;
}
```

The last two parameters are used by the PXE software on the host to download the file pxelinux.0 from the host *ip-address-of-tftp-server*. The PXE specification requires the use of an IP address for the TFTP server, because this eliminates the code and execution time for resolving the host name into an address. The pxelinux.0 file is installed as part of the syslinux package and needs to be put in the tftpboot directory so the board can locate it during the boot-up process:

```
cp /usr/lib/syslinux/pxelinux.0 /tftpboot
```

pxelinux.0 is a program that goes fishing for a configuration file on the TFTP server to continue the booting process. Creating a default configuration file is the best approach; use the following steps:

```
$ Mkdir -p /tftpboot/pxelinux.cfg
$ touch /tftpboot/pxelinux.cfg/default
```

The /tftpboot/pxelinux.cfg/default file contains instructions on what kernel and initial RAM disk to use to boot the system, similar to the information stored grub's configuration file. A minimal configuration file looks like the following:

```
label board
kernel board/kernel
append initrd=board/initrd
```

This results in the PXE software attempting to download board/kernel from the /tftpboot directory. When the kernel and initial RAM disk are ready for the embedded board, they're copied to this location.

Cabling

Booting an embedded target requires some cabling that may not be handy. A typical commercial embedded development kit includes cables; however, they tend to get lost over time. If the board in question doesn't have an integrated display (or display adapter) and keyboard connector, at least a null modem serial cable is required. It's best to locate these components now, because you'll need them.

Serial (for Console)

Nearly every embedded development board has a serial console connector in the form of a DB-9 connector. Most boards require a null modem cable that swaps the send and receive pins and connects the clear to send and request to send pins. You can buy a null modem cable at any self-respecting electronics store and most big-box office supply stores. When confronted with the task of finding a null modem cable in a jumble of cables at work, look for one with female connectors on both ends; this doesn't guarantee that the cable in question is properly wired, but chances are that it is. You can also purchase a null modem converter that makes a regular straight-through cable a null modem.

Some boards use a USB connection for the serial console. Linux and Windows include device drivers to make communicating over USB essentially the same as using serial. From a cabling perspective, all you need to do is find a USB cable with the right connectors. The USB specification ensures that the device and computer are wired properly; there's no need for special cabling.

Network

A network connection is also a common way for a board to communicate with the outside world. The Linux kernel is large enough that downloading via a serial cable (even if the connection is fast) is slow. When the boot loader uses the network adapter, downloading the kernel takes just a few seconds.

You can attach an embedded board with an Ethernet port to the network using a standard network cable. However, if the board is connected directly to another network adapter (see the next section), the Ethernet equivalent of a null modem cable is necessary; it's called a cross-over cable. This Ethernet cable is wired to the serial null modem: the data wires are swapped from input to output, and the flow control pins are crossed. These cables are readily available at electronics stores but are difficult to find elsewhere. Unlike serial cables, a null modem converter for Ethernet cables isn't readily available. In a pinch, using a Ethernet hub is a workaround, because when it moves data from one port to the next, it does roughly the same as a null modem converter.

Avoiding an Angry Visit from IT

Embedded development requires the configuration and setup of software that may interfere with the corporate network. Making a mistake in the DHCP file may result in two hosts on the network getting the same IP address, resulting in a flurry of network messages, system-management warnings, and other events that will probably require somebody, somewhere to file a report. The best way to avoid this sort of attention is taking preventative measures.

Dual-Homed Host

Dual homing means putting two network adapters in your host. One of these adapters can be attached to the corporate network, get its address via DCHP, and otherwise function like a network adapter always does. You can configure the other adapter with a fixed IP address; it frequently uses a different address class and is used to work with the embedded target.

The IP address range blocks out three ranges of addresses (A, B, and C) that are only for use in private networks, such as your home or business. See Table 2-2.

Table 2-2. *Private (or Nonroutable) IP Address Ranges*

Class	Range (Mask)
A	10.0.0.0–10.255.255.255
B	172.16.0.0–172.31.255.255
C	192.168.0.0–192.168.255.255

Inspect the network address of the corporate network assigned to the host, and use the table to choose another address class for the second adapter. Most companies use either A or C, and nearly all home routers default to C. It doesn't matter which address range you pick, as long as the address range isn't what the company or the rest of your home is using.

When you assign an IP address to the board, choose one in the same range as that used for the second adapter. Figure 2-15 illustrates this configuration.

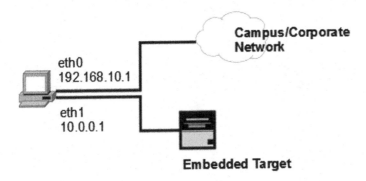

Figure 2-15. *Dual-homed network*

Note that the embedded target is attached directly to the host machine. This is a case where a cross-over network cable would be necessary; however, two patch cables and a switch/concentrator can also do the trick.

Of the services in this section, DHCP is the most dangerous, so it should be running on its own adapter. The DHCP server has a configuration file (`/etc/default/dhcp3-server`) where you can specify what adapter the server should use to run the server, instead of listening on all adapters.

For example, if adapter eth0 is on the company network and eth1 is used for the embedded board, the `/etc/default/dhcp3-server` file needs to contain the following line:

```
INTERFACES="eth1"
```

You must restart the server for the changes to take effect, by doing the following:

```
/etc/init.d/dhcp3-server restart
```

This command stops the existing DHCP server if it's running and then starts it again. When the server restarts, it uses the arguments in the configuration file to answer address requests on the appropriate adapter.

CHAPTER 3

■■■

Target Emulation
and Virtual Machines

Virtualization is a mature technology that lets several operating systems share the physical resources of a machine, such that that each thinks it has exclusive use of the resources. *Emulation* means that a program impersonates another—or, in this case, that a processor impersonates another.

In Chapter 2, I proposed virtualization as a way to run an instance of a Linux host on a Windows machine; Cygwin is software that emulates a POSIX system on a Windows machine. In this chapter, I look at software for emulating a target board. If the target processor happens to be an x86, the virtualization software discussed in Chapter 2 is perfect for the task.

However, when you're emulating a processor different than the host, you have fewer options. Emulating a different processor requires software that, in effect, translates the op-codes of the emulated processor into the op-codes for the host processor. There are some additional complications, such as sharing devices like video and network, but this book's focus is on how to use these tools and not the details of their construction.

Why Target Emulation?

In a word: convenience, but in two respects. The first convenience is that the target board is likely being developed at the same time as the software that's supposed to run on the board. Second, running in an emulator greatly reduces the complications of communicating with a remote target.

A common practice in embedded engineering is to write code that is compiled and tested on the development host. This makes sense, because the C language is portable enough to make this possible. Although large amounts of code can be written, compiled using the native tools, and tested without the benefit of an emulator, some things, such as the following, require testing using the target processor or emulator:

- *Inline assembly:* This is the most obvious. Code that has inline assembly for an ARM target won't compile on that nice new quad core Intel 64 bit host, no matter how much you want it to.

- *Endiannesss:* This describes the byte order used to store data. In a big-endian system, the high-order bytes precede the low-order bytes; little-endian is the reverse. The date 2009-01-31 is big endian, whereas 31-01-2009 is little-endian.[1] If endianness isn't agreed on, imagine the confusion with a date like 02-05-2009, where the month and day aren't obvious. This is an example to make plain the notion that endianness, as the internal storage format for a date in a computer, is usually an integer.

- *Floating point:* The floating-point capacities aren't the same for all processors and the emulator. One processor's very large number is another processor's overflow. Not many embedded systems need high precision, but the ones that do should take these limitations into consideration.

- *Optimization:* The GCC compiler is smart enough to optimize not only by refactoring and re-ordering the code but also by selecting machine instructions that execute more quickly. This means the classic speed for time optimization may be very different on the host than the target. Optimization is also likely to find bugs in the code generated by GCC

Emulation via QEMU

QEMU is a growing emulation project started by Fabrice Bellard. It's available for Linux and Windows hosts and emulated PowerPC, ARM, MIPS, and SPARC targets. QEMU takes the approach of providing a minimal translation layer between the host and target processor. The host processor is the one running the emulator, and the target processor is what's being emulated.

QEMU also provides support for USB, serial, graphics, and network devices by mapping them to a real device on the host machine. For an embedded board, this support makes it possible for QEMU to be a reasonable stand-in for kernel and application development. In addition to being a useful tool to emulate an entire system, QEMU can also execute programs compiled from the target machine on the host machine. This means you can test or debug a program without starting an entire emulated system, thus making it even easier to quickly debug and test programs.

QEMU provides both virtualization software and emulation. This chapter looks at using QEMU as an emulator. If the target machine happens to be the same as the host machine, the software performs virtualization, but that's an implementation detail. QEMU has a kernel module for accelerating virtualization; unless your target machine is also a x86, this feature isn't that helpful.

Compiling QEMU

QEMU is available in source form; the site has precompiled binaries as well. In spite of the binary distribution, this is open source software, so knowing how to compile it is important in case a patch becomes available—or just because it's open source, and compiling from source is the right thing to do.

QEMU requires GCC 3.0 in order to build. To check what version of GCC is currently installed, do the following:

```
$ gcc -dump-version
4.2.3
```

---

[1] In the U.S., dates are typically middle-endian, following the format *Month-Day-Year.*

If it does present you with a 4.0 or higher version number, install the GCC 3.4 package. Don't worry about multiple GCC installations on the system. GCC installs as gcc-‹version› and creates a symlink gcc that points at the newest version. If you set the environment variable CC to gcc-3.4, that executable is used instead of the most recent gcc:

```
$ apt-get install gcc-3.4
$ export CC=gcc-3.4
```

QEMU's build also requires some additional development libraries in order to build. Fetch these by doing the following on an Ubuntu or a Debian system:

```
$ sudo apt-get install libsdl-gfx1.2-dev zlib1g-dev
```

Start compiling QEMU by getting the source code at http://bellard.org/qemu/download.html. The current version is 0.9.1; you can download it using wget, like so:

```
$ cd ~
$ wget http://bellard.org/qemu/qemu-0.9.1.tar.gz
```

Then, untar:

```
$ tar zxf qemu-0.9.1.tar.gz
```

Start the build process by doing a configure:

```
$ cd qemu-0.9.1
$ ./configure
```

Does this message appear?

```
WARNING: "gcc" looks like gcc 4.x
Looking for gcc 3.x
gcc 3.x not found!
QEMU is known to have problems when compiled with gcc 4.x
It is recommended that you use gcc 3.x to build QEMU
To use this compiler anyway, configure with --disable-gcc-check
```

This message means the GCC installed on the system isn't a 3.x version. Check that GCC 3.4 has been installed, and make sure the environment has the CC variable set to gcc-3.4. Running configure with the -disable-gcc-check flag results in the configure step working correctly, but the compilation fails.

After the configure step, typing

```
$ make
$ sudo make install
```

builds and installs QEMU.

For Windows users, a precompiled package is available at http://www.h7.dion.ne.jp/~qemu-win/. It's recommended that QEMU users on Windows start with this precompiled package.

Using QEMU to Emulate a Target

The QEMU maintainer has thoughtfully included ready-to-boot packages for the following processors:

- MIPS
- ARM
- X86
- ColdFire

Visit http://bellard.org/qemu/download.html and scroll to the bottom to see the current distributions available. Using the ARM distribution as an example, here is how to use one of these boot packages to quickly get a system up and running and prove that the QEMU that you built works as expected.

The packages include a kernel and an initrd root file system. These systems are self-contained and immutable since the initrd file system is loaded into RAM memory at boot time and there's no way to save the changes between boots. This has both benefits and drawbacks. The greatest benefit is that no matter what you change or delete, completely resetting the environment is just a few keystrokes away. This is also a drawback, because changes to the file system can't be easily stored for the next power cycle without re-creating the initial RAM disk. Because you're using these file systems to test the board, the benefits outweigh the drawbacks.

Follow these steps to download and unpack the file:

```
$ cd ~
$ wget http://bellard.org/qemu/arm-test-0.2.tar.gz
$ tar xzf arm-test-0.2.tar.gz
```

Use these commands to start the machine without a graphical terminal:

```
$ cd arm-test
$ ../qemu-0.9.1/arm-softmmu/qemu-system-arm  -kernel zImage.integrator
-initrd arm_root.img -nographic -append "console=ttyAMA0"
```

A lot of parameters are passed into QEMU to make things work. Table 3-1 describes what they mean. QEMU is performing the job of a boot loader, so at the least, it needs to know what kernel to boot.

Table 3-1. *QEMU kernel boot parameters e*

Parameter	Purpose
-kernel <kernel image>	Indicates what kernel to use. This file is a kernel image that's been compressed. It looks for the kernel file in the current directory if one isn't specified.
-initrd <initial ram disk image>	The initial RAM disk to load for the kernel. This is the only file system used by the emulated target.
-nographic	QEMU configures a VGA device for the board if this isn't specified. The board being booted doesn't have graphics support, so there's no need for QEMU to emulate graphics.

-append <*parameters*> This is what appears when you add append to the end of the kernel's command line. The kernel's command line is similar to the parameters passed into a program. In this case, setting console=ttyAMA0 means the kernel should use the /dev/ttyAMA0 device for the console. This device is created by QEMU so the board has a pseudo-serial device to use for a terminal.

In a few seconds, the kernel boot-up message appears. Log in as root (no password is necessary), and verify that the machine is an ARM target:

```
# cat /proc/cpuinfo
Processor        : ARM926EJ-Sid(wb) rev 5 (v5l)
BogoMIPS         : 137.21
Features         : swp half thumb fastmult edsp java
CPU implementer  : 0x41
CPU architecture : 5TEJ
CPU variant      : 0x0
CPU part         : 0x926
CPU revision     : 5
Cache type       : write-through
Cache clean      : not required
Cache lockdown   : not supported
Cache format     : Harvard
I size           : 4096
I assoc          : 4
I line length    : 32
I sets           : 32
D size           : 65536
D assoc          : 4
D line length    : 32
D sets           : 512

Hardware         : ARM-IntegratorCP
Revision         : 0000
Serial           : 0000000000000000
```

Pretty neat! A little investigation reveals that this is a fairly basic root file system, but it does the job of starting the board and providing a prompt. At this point, you may be tempted to use the root file system here as the starting point for your project; and that isn't an outlandish notion if the project in question only has a few additional executable files. More complex projects require enough changes to the kernel and root file system to merit a rebuild, because the amount of effort to modify or build is similar.

To quit the emulator, press Ctrl+A followed by X. The machine is terminated, and control returns to the terminal prompt. There's no confirmation to quit, so be careful not to unintentionally shut down the machine.

By creating this machine, you can test development work on the emulated host before the hardware for the project arrives, allowing activities that were once serialized to have some degree of overlap. This is very helpful in situations where the board hardware is in short supply or the project is distributed geographically and getting hardware to engineers is difficult. In addition, having QEMU run the board also shortens the iteration time for testing new root file systems and boot-up scripts.

Using QEMU to Compile under Emulation

QEMU also supports a user-space mode in which instead of running an entire virtual machine to run a program, QEMU runs a user program. To run that user-space program, you need a binary and all the libraries used by that binary. The simplest way to get this for an ARM processor is to download it from ARM directly:

```
$ cd ~
$ wget http://www.arm.com/linux/armbase_2.5.cramfs
```

If this link is no longer available, visit ARM's distribution page at http://www.arm.com/products/os/linux.html. After it's downloaded, you can loop-back mount the image using this command:

```
$ sudo mkdir -p /mnt/arm-rfs
$ sudo mount -o loop -t cramfs ./armbase_2.5.cramfs /mnt/arm-rfs/
```

Loop-back mounting is a way to connect a file with a block device and then mount the device as if it were a physical block device. When it's mounted, the /mnt/arm-rfs directory contains a file system that has the necessary libraries to run the programs in the /mnt/arm-rfs/bin directory. When QEMU attempts to run a program that has shared libraries, it needs to know the location of the shared library loader and be able to load the libraries.

On a Linux system, programs that use shared libraries depend on an executable to do the final link step so the executable can run. On a Linux desktop system, that file is usually /lib/ld-linux.so.2, but it can have any file name.

When QEMU is built, it looks for these library-handling files in the /usr/gnemul/qemu-arm directory by default. In order for QEMU to find those files, copy the contents of the lib directory of /mnt/arm-rfs to that location. A copy is better than creating a symlink, because that symlink is invalid when the file system is unmounted from /mnt/arm-rfs:

```
$ sudo mkdir -p /usr/gnemul/qemu-arm
$ sudo cp -a /mnt/arm-rfs/lib /usr/gnemul/qemu-arm
```

Now that everything is in place, run a command by doing the following:

```
$ cd /mnt/arm-rfs
$ qemu-arm  /mnt/arm-rfs/bin/ls
```

The first reaction to this is, "That's nice, but why?" One important group of programs that you can run includes the configuration scripts and the compiler. By taking this approach, no cross-compilation is necessary, because the code thinks it's running on an ARM (or whatever) host. Later in the book, I cover using a native compiler running under an emulator as opposed to a cross-compiler for building a system.

The examples in this section have covered ARM processors, but remember that QEMU supports more than just the ARM processor.

Virtualization Software for x86 Hosts

If you're developing code for an x86 host, why bother using virtualization? The host and target are identical, so using virtualization software introduces overhead. Some of the problems introduced by a homogeneous host and target can be latent in nature, resulting in unexpected problems if the software happens to work by chance on the host environment.

Virtualization still makes sense as part of the development process for the following reasons:

- *Isolates development target dependencies:* It's easy to become careless when you're compiling programs and depend on a library or configuration file that is present on the host computer but won't be available when the software is deployed. Testing and validating the boot-up sequence is best done using a clean computer, because the host environment can interfere in unexpected ways.

- *Constrains resources:* If the target machine has 8MB RAM, a virtual machine can handle that without any problems. If the target device doesn't have certain hardware like network adapters or serial ports, you can also do that in the virtual machine. For example, many embedded x86 targets have little or no video memory.

- *Is highly repeatable:* Nearly all virtual machines support the notion of fixed storage, which lets you make writes during the run of the application that are disposed of when the machine reboots. Using virtualization software, the computer can always be returned to a known state.

Approaches to Virtualization

You can use several approaches for x86 virtualization: Sun's VirtualBox, VMware, and QEMU. VirtualBox and VMware are much easier to use than QEMU; however, QEMU is very Linux oriented and lets you start a virtual machine from a kernel image and an initial RAM disk file, features that VirtualBox and VMware lack. VMware and VirtualBox are commercial software packages that have licensing terms restricting their use in certain commercial situations. Please consult the terms included with the product to determine if you need to purchase a license.

You may be curious about Xen, which is a hypervisor for x86-based systems. Xen is more like an operating system that runs operating systems efficiently. It[2] differs from QEMU or VMware in that operating systems run on a Xen pseudo-hardware layer which then partitions the hardware resources to the virtual machines. Installing Xen means overwriting your current operating system and installing Xen on top, which is probably not what you have in mind.

When you use either VirtualBox or VMware, you can boot the target machine over the network using PXE (described in Chapter 2) as the boot loader. In the VirtualBox user interface, you configure a machine to boot from a network device by opening the virtual machine's definition, selecting General at left, and then clicking the Advanced tab.

In the Boot Order list, unselect every item except Network (see Figure 3-1). When the machine boots, it uses DHCP to request an address and boot information and proceeds to download a kernel and root file system; then, the machine starts running. If you're planning to use PXE for booting during development or deployment, using virtualization software makes testing the PXE configuration much easier than power-cycling a board, even if the Power On Self Tests (POSTs) are disabled.

---

[2] Xen is a technology right out of the late 1960s. IBM's mainframes ran VM/370 on their multiprocessor computers as the base operating system, which then ran the guest operating system (at the time, CMS). This technology is still around, but the guest operating system is Linux.

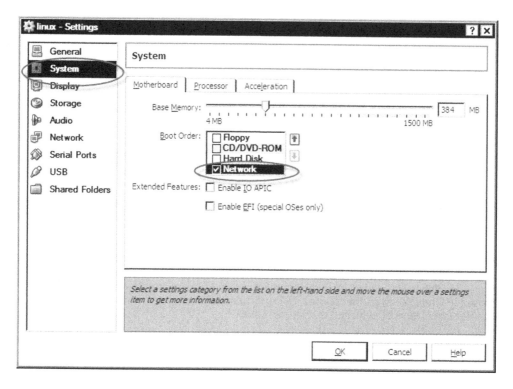

Figure 3-1. *Configuring Network Booting in VirtualBox*

Summary

This chapter covered some commonly used tools for virtualization. This technology is very useful when you don't yet have your hardware but you still want to experiment. QEMU is the best tool for emulating machines other than x86 and is becoming a popular item in the embedded developer's toolbox. In the next chapter, you look at what happens when the hardware arrives and you need to make an assessment of what you've received. Most embedded boards come with some type of Linux; Chapter 4 helps you understand how to do a gap analysis and figure out what else you need for your project.

CHAPTER 4

■ ■ ■

Starting Your Project

Embedded projects start with selecting hardware. Based on the requirements of the project, such as cost, battery life, communications, and user interface, a few processors and technologies become obvious choices. For example, low-power consumer devices frequently use ARM processors, and industrial control applications frequently use Intel x86 parts. The hardware selection doesn't occur in isolation; the team selecting the hardware must at the same time consider the peripheral devices and driver availability. Chapter 17 goes into detail regarding the development process unique to embedded projects.

The trend is toward purchasing off-the-shelf hardware and peripherals and putting them together with standard interconnects, like a PCMCIA or USB bus. Because most chips are SOC designs, that means the system on the chip is most of the hardware found on a typical computer; the peripherals that aren't on the chip are a bit esoteric, proprietary, or costly, and drivers may not be available in all cases. For instance, wireless network interfaces aren't part of an SOC and are sold as a separate module that attach to the PCI, USB, or PCMCIA bus on the board.[1] Many SOC designs don't contain storage or RAM, because those are higher cost and power consumption items. In addition, RAM and storage requirements vary greatly between designs.

Embedded projects fall into one of two categories:

- *Those that ship with standard-sized hardware boards (COTS):* A perfect example of this sort of project is a kiosk containing a consumer application. The case around the device is sufficiently large that the size of the board is of little concern. In fact, for a kiosk, you want to create a casing large and heavy enough to prevent tipping or theft. Although the marketing group at your company may try to give the device a fancy appearance, a PC-AT device can fit into the case with room left over for some eight-track tapes, a turn table, and a boom box. The size and form factor of the board aren't important because there's plenty of room due to the design of the case itself. Industrial devices also fit into this classification; most factory floors aren't space constrained, and the appearance of the end product isn't as important as it is for a device used by a consumer.

---

[1] An example of this trend is the Toshiba S3C24xx line of SOC designs, which contain a processor, some flash memory, a camera, an LCD interface, an analog to digital converter, and a small audio-processing module.

- *Those that require custom hardware design (custom):* Cell phones are great examples of these devices. For these projects, an industrial designer has authored a case that the hardware must fit into without altering the design too much. For a cell phone, the appearance as much as the capabilities matter to the end user. Products that fall into this class usually have strict power budgets for two reasons: battery life is a selling point, and the battery is the largest and heaviest (and sometimes costliest) component in the design. Making the most out of the battery means more freedom for the designers and a greater profit margin for the manufacturers. Frequently, these projects are built in high volume, so the work put into reducing the per-unit cost can be amortized over tens of thousands of units, making the effort worthwhile.

A half step is emerging between these categories: the *stamp* form factor, where a small board contains the processor and a few peripherals, like memory or flash, and has leads so it can be plugged into a daughter board. The task of the hardware designer is much less complex than when designing a complete board but much more involved than using a COTS board. The hybrid approach means lower hardware-design costs, a smaller form factor, and more control over the power consumption of the board, because the hardware designer can pick and choose the exact set of peripherals included on the board.

Understanding which category your project falls into helps you understand the development approach and how Linux can be used. In both cases, development begins on a (aptly named) development board that has nearly all the peripherals supported by the chip. Chip vendors like to target their chips to certain market segments (such as cell phone, automotive, or industrial control); they sell development kits containing a board with the processor bundled with the peripherals used by those developers so the engineers can quickly prototype a system. For example, a cell phone development kit includes a small screen, a numeric keypad, and GPRS hardware so software and hardware engineering can begin quickly. The final hardware design includes the same, or a similar, CPU chip on a custom-designed board with the necessary peripherals for the design that are similar to those included with the development kit.

However, teams of the COTS variety select a development board that best meets their requirements and use it as is for the product. Such users pick a standard form factor (like mini-itx) so the company making the case can put the mounting hardware in the right place inside the kiosk or the right case can be sourced for the project. When you're working on a COTS project, the board used for development is identical to the board deployed in the product. Although a COTS board is more expensive on a per-unit basis, there is little hardware engineering fixed cost to amortize over the production run. Designing a custom board costs at least $50,000, and tooling costs for fabrication are at least that much again, so a product with a production run of a few hundred units has an average cost much higher than the average cost of purchasing an off-the-shelf board.

Most Boards Include a Linux Distribution

Unless the selected processor doesn't have the capability to run Linux, it ships with a Linux distribution in the box or one is available. (Early on in the embedded Linux lifeline, this wasn't true, and getting Linux for a board involved a Quixotic search or custom engineering.) This principle holds true for COTS boards and prototyping boards for custom hardware. Linux vendors typically vie for information about their product to be included in the packing material for the board, in hopes it will boost sales or interest in their product.

The key is understanding what is packaged for the board. Some board vendors treat their Linux distribution as a check-off requirement, which is marketing speak for something that's good enough to claim support but not adequate for project development. Other board vendors put a great deal of effort into delivering a Linux distribution that's ready for development.

The worksheet in Table 4-1 serves as an aid for evaluating the Linux received with the board. The remainder of the chapter goes over the details.

Table 4-1. Linux Distribution Inventory

Item	Version	Sources? (Yes/No)	Notes
Kernel			Sources must be supplied. Sometimes patches are included as well. Make sure you locate all of them and that the patches work.
GCC cross-compiler			Some kernels and root file system components require a certain version of GCC. Understand the requirements necessary to build the kernel and root file system.
C library			The kernel doesn't require a C library, but the supporting programs, like the configuration system, do. Kernel building has few constraints; for packages in the root file system, anything is possible; but usually there are no special requirements.
Supported devices			Check out what's on the board.
Supported file systems			Are any of these useful for the project? A file system not supported in the kernel doesn't mean it's unavailable, just that it isn't in this build of the kernel.
Root file system format			How has the root file system been formatted?
Root file system contents			Are sources available? What packages have been supplied?

What to Do After Unpacking the Board

The best way to assess what is supplied with the board is to plug in the board and get Linux up and running. If you have problems locating what's necessary to boot the board, that fact is a good indication of the work that lies ahead.

The board contains a guide with important information regarding the physical configuration of the hardware: what the DIP switches do and the location of the serial, video, USB, and other ports. In the trade, this is called a *data sheet*, leaving you with the impression that it's one page; but it's usually 50 to over 100 pages long. Depending on the board, these ports may not have connectors. The guide also contains information about how the board's serial port is configured: this is important information, because figuring out the communication parameters is a trial and error process otherwise. These guides are usually very well organized; you can scan the index for the chapter on booting the board.

Have Linux? Boot It!

The easiest way to see what the kernel supports is to boot the board and have it tell you what it supports. To boot Linux, you need to check whether the distribution contains the following in binary form:

- Compiled Linux kernel with an initrd

- Root file system

There isn't a dependable way to determine by inspection what these files are, so the documentation is key at this point. Here are some conventions:

- Kernels are frequently in zImage format, so file names have these patterns:

  - `zFileName`

  - `FileName.zimage`

- If the kernel is for an x86 board, it's usually in bzImage format. A *bzImage* is a compressed image that looks like a x86 boot sector, only it's larger than the boot sector size. It's compressed with gzip, not bzip2, as the *bz* leads some to believe. Here are the file name patterns:

  - `bzFileName`

  - `FileName.bzImage`

- If the board uses the U-Boot boot loader (the board's manual explains if it does), the kernel is named like the following. A *uImage* is a zImage with some additional information for the U-Boot boot loader:

  - `uFileName`

Copy the kernel file into the `/tftpboot` directory. This is the default location where the TFTP server looks for files. If this is an x86 using PXE boot, copy the file to the `/tftpboot/default` directory.

The root file system is easier to find. It's usually a compressed tar file. *Tar* means *tape archive* and is a holdover from the early days of Unix when it was a tool for creating backups on reel-to-reel media. There are two ways to compress a tar file but several ways to name the file for each compression type, as shown in Table 4-2.

Table 4-2. Tar Naming Conventions

Extensions	Unarchive Command	View Contents Command
tar.gz, tgz	tar xzf <*file*>	tar tzf <*file*>
tar.bz2, tbz2	tar xjf <*file*>	tar tjf <*file*>

Unlike with the kernel, you can determine if a tar file contains a root file system by inspection. Use the view-contents command from Table 4-2 to output the list of files in the archive to the console, and use the less pager to look at the contents:

```
# tar tzf <file> | less
```

It should contain what looks like the file system on your desktop. It should have the /dev, /etc, /bin, and /sbin directories. If this appears to be the root file system, extract it into the directory exported in the /etc/exports directory.

The board now needs to be cabled-up, usually via the serial connector. Start minicom:

```
# minincom -o
```

Minicom usually does the right thing by default. Press the spacebar a few times, and the boot loader should appear. Nothing on the display? Make sure the following are correct:

1. Check the cables. Are they securely attached? Is the cable a null modem? A null modem is a cable in which the send and receive lines have been crossed along with the clear-to-send and ready-to-send lines. Two serial ports can be connected with this cable; when data is transmitted by one, it appears as input on the other. The clear-to-send and ready-to-send pins handle flow control, so the machine at the receiving end can ask the sender to wait as it processes data.

2. Working with the right port and settings? Press Ctrl+A, O to open the configuration menu, and select Serial Port Setup. Make sure the serial device is the one that the board is attached to and that flow control is off (although your null modem cable may be configured to handle flow control, it isn't frequently implemented in a boot loader). After updating, select Save as dflt so the changes are stored as the default options.

3. Check the communication speed. Adjust it by pressing Ctrl+A, P. You can choose a few other options: start at the slowest speed and work upward. After you select a speed, press the spacebar a few times to see if that made a difference.

4. Still having problems? Check the cables again, and consult the data sheet. Chances are, you skipped checking everything thoroughly the first time. The communication configuration for the board may also be nonstandard: you may have attached the cable to the wrong port if the board has several serial connectors.

The board should include instructions for using the boot loader and what commands to use to load the kernel into memory and start execution. This is different for every board. You need to know the following, though, no matter what boot loader is being used:

- The IP address of the machine running the TFTP server

- The IP address of the machine running the NFS server, if the board includes a file system suitable for mounting via NFS

- The name of the kernel

- The location of the root file system if it isn't packaged as part of the kernel binary

When Linux boots, a few pages of information scroll past. Those diagnostic messages tell you what hardware is discovered, what drivers are loaded, and much more. Chances are, the scroll-back buffer doesn't have enough room for all these messages. Use the following command to retrieve this information for review:

```
# dmesg | less
```

The less command results in a nice pager that lets you move forward and backward through the output. I explain critical parts of this output next; other noise output has been clipped. The dmesg command prints the contents of the kernel's ring buffer, which is the accumulated output from printk (the kernel analog to printf) function calls. You can configure the size of this buffer to just a few kilobytes to conserve space. A ring, or circular, buffer is one where capacity is fixed; when it's reached, the data at the start of the buffer is overwritten. This sort of buffer is failsafe in that it can't overflow in exchange for data fidelity.

The following tells you when the kernel was built and with what compiler. What appears here is completely under the control of the person building the kernel:

```
Linux version 2.6.17-rc3 (paul@wren) (gcc version 4.1.0 (CodeSourcery ARM))
#53 Thu May 4 15:05:18 BST 2006
```

■ **Note** The /proc and /sys directories contain a wealth of information about a Linux system. The /proc file system contains process system capability information, and /sys contains an inventory of devices and device driver information.

This is the CPU information:

```
CPU: ARM926EJ-Sid(wb) [41069265] revision 5 (ARMv5TEJ)
Machine: ARM-IntegratorCP
Memory policy: E
CC disabled, Data cache writeback
On node 0 totalpages: 32768
  DMA zone: 32768 pages, LIFO batch:7
CPU0: D VIVT write-through cache
CPU0: I cache: 4096 bytes, associativity 4, 32 byte lines, 32 sets
CPU0: D cache: 65536 bytes, associativity 4, 32 byte lines, 512 sets
Built 1 zonelists
```

It's the same data, more or less, that's contained in the /proc/cpuinfo file. After the kernel starts, print out the contents of /proc/cpuinfo to check. The data here isn't read from the chip: the programmer working on the chip-specific parts of the kernel populates a data structure containing this information. As you'll see later, the /proc file system contains information about the system hardware, kernel configuration, and networking information as well as information for all the processes running on the system. The /proc file system isn't really a file system—it's a view into the kernel's data structures structured as a file system.

The kernel can be passed parameters by the boot loader. This is done by having the boot loader and kernel agree on an area of memory where the parameters are placed by the boot loader before running the kernel. You can configure the kernel not to accept kernel parameters as well; however, this isn't usually the case, because the parameters let you control some parameters of the boot process that change frequently, like the location of the root file system or console device without a rebuild. You can also compile the kernel with default parameters. The parameters passed in during boot are appended to the ones compiled into the kernel. Being able to see this line make it obvious what the command-line parameters were when the kernel booted:

```
Kernel command line: console=ttyAMA0
```

This means the kernel found a valid initramfs image:

```
CPU: Testing write buffer coherency: ok
checking if image is initramfs... it is
```

The initramfs is a file system attached to the kernel that lets the kernel load additional device drivers if necessary. Some embedded systems use the initramfs as the only file system, which is something I investigate later in this book. The kernel always checks to see whether this file system exists and uses it if it does.

These are the serial ports on the board:

```
Console: switching to colour frame buffer device 80x30
Serial: AMBA PL011 UART driver
mb:16: ttyAMA0 at MMIO 0x16000000 (irq = 1) is a AMBA/PL011
mb:17: ttyAMA1 at MMIO 0x17000000 (irq = 2) is a AMBA/PL011
```

The kernel, as it's booting, is nice enough to tell you the device names for these ports. The kernel continues being nice by creating these device nodes for you in a little, temporary /dev file system that allows the kernel command line to refer to a console or fixed-storage device node before a /dev file system is properly mounted. This can be a source of confusion if you're learning about embedded Linux, because there are references to device nodes (/dev/something); however, because / hasn't been mounted, how does the kernel interact with a device in an unmounted file system?

This kernel has been configured for RAM disks:

```
RAMDISK driver initialized: 16 RAM disks of 8192K size 1024 blocksize
```

RAM disks are convenient when you have a flash-based file system because the /tmp directory can be mounted to a RAM disk. This reduces wear on the flash memory while increasing performance, because frequent create/delete cycles are slow in flash and many programs store small cache files in /tmp for the purpose of increasing performance. RAM disks waste space if they aren't used in the system. Make a note of this when you're optimizing the kernel for size.

This is the Ethernet driver starting up and showing the devices it has allocated. If the board has several Ethernet adapters, each appears in this list with its device name:

```
smc91x.c: v1.1, sep 22 2004 by Nicolas Pitre <nico@cam.org>
eth0: SMC91C11xFD (rev 1) at c8814000 IRQ 27 [nowait]
eth0: Ethernet addr: 52:54:00:12:34:56
```

These entries explain what input devices like keyboards and mice have been registered:

```
mice: PS/2 mouse device common for all mice
mmc0: MMCI rev 0 cfg 00 at 0x1c000000 irq 23,24
input: AT Raw Set 2 keyboard as /class/input/input0
input: ImExPS/2 Generic Explorer Mouse as /class/input/input1
```

If the board is attached to a touch screen driver, it appears in this section as well. The line starting with mmc0 isn't related to the mouse or keyboard; it's an entry for the flash driver used to read data from and write data to an SD card (this board has an interface for the sort of memory module used in a camera). It happened to load after the mouse but before the keyboard. The remainder of the output contains information about the TCP subsystem and configuration.

After booting, you need to inspect several other things. Most embedded engineers (rightly) concern themselves with the file system to be used by the board. A quick way to see what file systems the kernel supports is to inspect /proc/filesystems:

```
# cat /proc/filesystems
nodev    sysfs
nodev    rootfs
nodev    bdev
nodev    proc
nodev    binfmt_misc
nodev    sockfs
nodev    pipefs
nodev    futexfs
nodev    tmpfs
nodev    inotifyfs
nodev    eventpollfs
nodev    devpts
         ext2
         cramfs
nodev    ramfs
nodev    nfs
nodev    nfsd
nodev    smbfs
nodev    rpc_pipefs
```

Because Linux uses file systems as a communications mechanism between the kernel and the user or different processes, as well as a way to store data, there's always an abundance of registered file systems. File system drivers can be either directly built into the kernel or loaded in kernel modules, so this list isn't the complete population for this board. The file systems typically built into the kernel map to the type of storage mediums available on the board. For instance, boards containing flash memory should have at least one working flash file system like jffs2 or yaffs2. Make a note of what's here, because file systems not used in the production kernel are dead weight and need to be removed. The file systems here are those necessary to mount the root file system and get the system running.

Check what's mounted by doing the following:

```
# mount
/dev/sda1 on / type ext3 (rw,errors=remount-ro)
proc on /proc type proc (rw,noexec,nosuid,nodev)
/sys on /sys type sysfs (rw,noexec,nosuid,nodev)
varrun on /var/run type tmpfs (rw,noexec,nosuid,nodev,mode=0755)
varlock on /var/lock type tmpfs (rw,noexec,nosuid,nodev,mode1777)
udev on /dev type tmpfs (rw,mode=0755)
```

The format of these lines is as follows:

```
<device> on <mount point> type <type> <parameters>
```

Consider the first line:

```
/dev/sda1 on / type ext3 (rw,errors=remount-ro)
```

This line says that the ext3 type file system in the /dev/sda1 device has been associated with the / directory. The / is the root directory of the system, so it can be said that /dev/sda1 contains the root file system. ext3 must be a file system type that appears in /proc/filesystems, or the kernel won't know how to handle the data contained in the device. At this point, the parameters aren't that important; when the file system was mounted, these parameters were passed to the driver. Parameters are generally file-system specific. Although other file systems can be mounted and dismounted at will, because of the nature of the root file system being core to the operating system, you use special commands to change to a different root file system. Pay attention to the nodev file systems; they aren't associated with a physical device but rather act as a way for the kernel and user programs to communicate.

Next, look at the device drivers:

```
# cat /proc/devices
Character devices:
  1 mem
  2 pty
  3 ttyp
  4 /dev/vc/0
  4 tty
  5 /dev/tty
  5 /dev/console
  5 /dev/ptmx
  7 vcs
 10 misc
 13 input
 29 fb
128 ptm
136 pts
204 ttyAMA
```

```
254 rtc


Block devices:
  1 ramdisk
  7 loop
 43 nbd
254 mmc
```

Devices in Linux are of two types: *block* and *character*. Block devices are random access devices like disk drives, and character devices are serial like mice and keyboards. The first column contains the device's *major* number, and the second is the *symbolic name* for the device. A registry of major device numbers is kept in the devices.txt file in the Documentation directory in the Linux source tree, if you're curious. The contents of the file appear in numerical order as a convenience; they serve as identifiers only and aren't scalar. Like file systems, the entries in /proc/devices are for the device drivers currently loaded. Additional device drivers may also be available.

The next command outputs the configuration that was used to build the kernel. If you're new to Linux kernel building, the configuration consists of the options used to control how the kernel is compiled. The kernel, being a large project, has a configuration system for setting compilation options; I explain how this works in detail in Chapter 11. The output of the configuration process is a file that is used to control how the kernel is built. Some kernel developers thoughtfully include the contents of this file in the kernel, because including this information is one of the possible configuration options for the kernel. This file, in conjunction with the source code used to build the kernel, is sufficient to rebuild the currently running kernel. The kernel has the concept of building some code and incorporating it directly into the kernel and linking some code at runtime, similar to a program that has statically linked code and uses libraries loaded at runtime.

At this point, the best thing to do with this file is to save it to your development host system for future reference. If you're curious, use this command to output the contents to the console:

```
# gunzip -c /proc/config.gz | more
```

You see output that looks similar to the following. Of course, the kernel version, compilation date, and other information are different:

```
#
# Automatically generated make config: don't edit
# Linux kernel version: 2.6.17-rc3
# Thu May  4 15:05:06 2006
#
CONFIG_ARM=y
CONFIG_MMU=y
CONFIG_RWSEM_GENERIC_SPINLOCK=y
CONFIG_GENERIC_HWEIGHT=y
CONFIG_GENERIC_CALIBRATE_DELAY=y
CONFIG_VECTORS_BASE=0xffff0000

#
# Code maturity level options
#
CONFIG_EXPERIMENTAL=y
```

```
CONFIG_BROKEN_ON_SMP=y
CONFIG_INIT_ENV_ARG_LIMIT=32


#
# General setup
#
CONFIG_LOCALVERSION=""
```

Assess the Kernel

With kernel configuration, the next step is to get the kernel and prove that it can be rebuilt as it is on the board. Linux is GNU Public License (GPL) licensed, which means, briefly, that when somebody supplies a Linux kernel, they're also obligated to supply the source code used to build the kernel. Some board vendors include just the patches and the version of the kernel to which they can be applied; others include the kernel source tree with all the changes made for the board in question. Along with the source code, the supplier of the binaries must also supply a way to build the code.

The hardware vendors do their best to comply with the letter and spirit of the GPL. Board vendors aren't software companies, however, and frequently they lack the expertise to package software the way a software vendor should. Occasionally, board vendors deliver binary-only proprietary drivers, but this is more the exception than the rule. Because building the kernel is part of an embedded Linux project, gathering what's necessary at the start helps the rest of the process succeed.

Locate Sources and Patches

Patches are an interesting bit of technology. A *patch* is a file that contains roughly this information: the name of a file, and a set of changes that should be applied to the file on a line-wise basis. The file used to create a patch is called `diff`, and the program that updates a file with the contents of the patch is itself called `patch`. I spend more time later in the book discussing what is in a patch and how to make one; at this point, the goal is to understand what they do and how to apply them (if present) to the kernel sources so it can be built. If the patches don't apply to the kernel, it's helpful to know that so you can assess the quality of what was delivered.

The Linux kernel is intended to be distributed as source code. The hardware manufacturer or distributor built the kernel as a convenience to users so that a board could be booted quickly. The kernel source code is nearly always shipped at a compressed tar file, made with either bz2 or gzip, with the general format being

`Linux.X.Y.Z.B`

X, *Y*, *Z*, and *B* are the version, major revision, minor revision, and bug fix version, respectively. Along with the kernel sources, you may have some patches to apply to get a kernel built for your board. There are two strategies for handling patches:

- *Patches have been applied and included in the sources files delivered:* Although this is the easiest way to get started, it's more harmful in that this method obscures the changes made by the board vendor. If additional patches need to be made to the kernel, say to address a bug, those patches may conflict with changes made by the vendor.

- *Patches are in a separate file or files:* This is the preferred method, because it lets you see exactly what changes the vendor made (if any) before delivering the kernel. When you're applying other patches or upgrading kernel versions, having separate patches makes it easy to see what has changed and to possibly use those changes in the new version. When patches are included as separate files, most include a script that applies them in the right order. In the absence of this script or information, you need to discover and record the order.

If you have patches in separate files, applying them is easy using the `patch` command. The exact command used to unpack the kernel depends on the type of archive; this example starts from the point of the kernel sources being extracted. A patch file may contain changes to several files, and it's important to make sure the patch is *atomic* (highfalutin database-speak that means the entire patch file needs to be applied or none of it is applied)—a half-applied patch is worse than one not applied at all. To see if a patch will work, use this command:

```
$ cd <kernel source>
$ patch -p 1 --dry-run < /path/to/patch/file
```

The `-p` option means to ignore the first directory level in the patch file. This option is necessary because you're in the first level directory. The `--dry-run` option lets the patch check to see if the patches can be applied, without applying them. This means that if a few patches fail to apply, the other files aren't changed.

If there are no errors, apply the patch:

```
patch -p 1 < /path/to/patch/file
```

What if the patches don't work? Test the vendor's commitment to customer service and the GPL by letting them know and asking for patches that do apply or assistance with getting the right version of the kernel or patches that apply.

Locate the Configuration

The kernel uses a file called the *configuration* to control the software build. If the kernel included with the board contained a `/proc/config.gz` file, as described in the previous section, that is the configuration used to build that kernel. In other cases, the supplier includes a file with the configuration settings.

Many board vendors store a configuration file in the kernel sources. This is the friendliest method, because the kernel build system is designed to work nicely with these defconfig files. To see the configurations stored in the kernel source tree, do the following:

```
# make help ARCH=<your architecture>
```

<your architecture> is the architecture of the processor on the board. For example, in the 2.6.28.5 release of the kernel, this command yields the following for the ARM architecture:

```
afeb9260_defconfig        - Build for afeb9260
am200epdkit_defconfig     - Build for am200epdkit
ams_delta_defconfig       - Build for ams_delta
assabet_defconfig         - Build for assabet
at91cap9adk_defconfig     - Build for at91cap9adk
at91rm9200dk_defconfig    - Build for at91rm9200dk
```

```
at91rm9200ek_defconfig    - Build for at91rm9200ek
at91sam9260ek_defconfig   - Build for at91sam9260ek
at91sam9261ek_defconfig   - Build for at91sam9261ek
at91sam9263ek_defconfig   - Build for at91sam9263ek
at91sam9g20ek_defconfig   - Build for at91sam9g20ek
at91sam9rlek_defconfig    - Build for at91sam9rlek
ateb9200_defconfig        - Build for ateb9200
badge4_defconfig          - Build for badge4
cam60_defconfig           - Build for cam60
carmeva_defconfig         - Build for carmeva
cerfcube_defconfig        - Build for cerfcube
clps7500_defconfig        - Build for clps7500
cm_x300_defconfig         - Build for cm_x300
colibri_defconfig         - Build for colibri
collie_defconfig          - Build for collie
corgi_defconfig           - Build for corgi
csb337_defconfig          - Build for csb337
```

(Many lines have been clipped for brevity!)

```
realview-smp_defconfig    - Build for realview-smp
realview_defconfig        - Build for realview
rpc_defconfig             - Build for rpc
s3c2410_defconfig         - Build for s3c2410
sam9_l9260_defconfig      - Build for sam9_l9260
shannon_defconfig         - Build for shannon
shark_defconfig           - Build for shark
simpad_defconfig          - Build for simpad
spitz_defconfig           - Build for spitz
sx1_defconfig             - Build for sx1
tct_hammer_defconfig      - Build for tct_hammer
trizeps4_defconfig        - Build for trizeps4
usb-a9260_defconfig       - Build for usb-a9260
usb-a9263_defconfig       - Build for usb-a9263
versatile_defconfig       - Build for versatile
viper_defconfig           - Build for viper
xm_x2xx_defconfig         - Build for xm_x2xx
yl9200_defconfig          - Build for yl9200
zylonite_defconfig        - Build for zylonite
```

These files are stored under the arch/<*your architecture*> /configs directory in the kernel sources. You may find it easier to navigate to the directory and inspect the files one by one. Use the following command to get a briefer output of the defconfig files stored in the kernel:

```
# find ./arch -name "*_defconfig" -type f
```

If the board uses one of these files, the documentation indicates what file to use. If there's no documentation, inspect the list for something matching or similar to the board.

Understand the RFS

The kernel is only one part of a Linux system. The root file system is a necessary component for a running system and is frequently overlooked when assessing a Linux distribution supplied with a board. Because you have many more degrees of freedom when creating a root file system, making an inventory of what's present is important along with making sure the source code is available.

As in Chapter 2, the most common accounting unit for a root file system is a package. The package contains a set of files that provide certain functionality. Although there are package managers that aid in building desktop distributions, such as dpkg and RPM, a package need not be more than a tar file. The goal of the packaging system is to make it easy to build a root file system from packages so that the root file system can contain the necessary functionality while being as small as possible. Technologies like dpkg and RPM rely on technologies like tar[2] to gather files into a single binary and keep track of metadata like how to build the package, what types of files it contains, and scripts to run at installation to ensure the package is ready to use. RPM and dpkg contain package dependency information, meaning that each package can state what other packages must be installed for it to work correctly. This dependency information is perhaps the driving reason to use these systems over tar.

You must know three critical things about an RFS, each of which is summarized here and then discussed in its own a section:

- *The format of the file system:* How is the root file system packaged and made available to the kernel?

- *Sources, patches, and build instructions:* Where are the sources so the software can be rebuilt? If there are patches, how should they be applied?

- *Suitability for your project:* Can what's supplied serve as the core of the project, or what else is necessary?

File System Format

The root file system for an embedded board can be delivered in the following forms. The second and third options are about the same but are different enough to merit some separate discussion. The first case, where the root file system is delivered as a large file with the expectation that it will be copied onto a flash device, is a little more difficult to look at without booting the board:

- *As a file system image:* This is a file that is designed to be burned into flash on the board. File systems in this format are usually cramfs, jffs2, or yaffs2 file systems but can be any file system type.

- *As a tar file, probably compressed:* If delivered like this, the engineers who created the file system used the `tar create` command to put everything together.

- *As a directory containing the files for the root file system:* If the root file system is small enough and the distribution is on some type of CD media, the step of compressing the RFS was skipped.

- *Integrated with the kernel:* Initial RAM disks are becoming popular ways to include a root file system with a kernel, and for good reason, because they do the booting process. An initial RAM disk is a file system stored with the kernel and uncompressed into memory at boot time.

---

[2] RPM uses cpio to store data, which is, I think, superior to tar; although it's harder to use. For one, cpio archives special files like fifos and other things created by mknod. Second, you must pass in the files to be archived, making cpio much more deterministic.

In all cases, booting the board and using the on-board tools to view the contents is the fastest way to seeing what's in the root file system. However, the first three methods easily allow inspection of the file system without booting the board, which may be preferable if the vendor didn't include a working kernel. Extracting the root file system that is an initial RAM disk involves dissecting the kernel and extracting the root file system. You can do so as follows:

```
$ mkdir ~/board-rfs
$ cd ~/board-rfs
$ s<cross-tools>-objdump -j .init.ramfs -O binary <kernel image> \
             /dev/stdout | gunzip -cd | cpio -i
```

The last command uses the objdump tool to extract the section of the binary .init.ramfs where this data resides and write the output to /dev/stdout, which is the console. That output is piped to gunzup, which uncompresses it and then sends the results to cpio; cpio extracts the contents and writes them on the disk.

Extracting the data from the tar file is also easy. Do the following to put the RFS into the ~/board-rfs directory:

```
$ mkdir ~/board-rfs
$ cd ~/board-rfs
$ tar zxf ~/<file-with-rfs>.tar.gz
```

If the root file system is a file that's ready for burning onto flash, the process of viewing the content is a little more complex. The root file system is mounted via a *loopback* device instead of being unpacked into a directory. The notion of a loopback is simple: it makes the contents of a file appear to be a block device. You mount a cramfs file system via a loopback device like so:

```
# mount -o loop -t cramfs ~/board-rfs-file ~/board-rfs
```

However, mounting a jffs2 or yaffs2 file system the same way doesn't work. The jffs2 and yaffs2 file systems expect to mount a memory technology device (MTD), which isn't the block device that using -o loop creates. As explained in the chapter about file systems, MTDs are different from block devices and can't be treated as such. MTDs are flash memory, similar to what is used on a USB drive, but an MTD doesn't have the additional software to provide wear-leveling that's present on a USB drive. In order not to wear out flash memory, you must take care not to write to one area of the flash device much more frequently than another. The action of spreading writes over the flash media is called *wear leveling*; this is done by specialized file systems geared for using flash media. Note that USB flash drives contain wear-leveling software in the drive hardware.

To mount this sort of file system, the host system needs a mechanism for making a file look like it's a MTD device; the thing that does that is the mtdram module. This software emulates how an MTD device works in software and is available as a kernel module that is installed when you add the mtd-tools package:

```
# modprobe mtdram total_size=65536 erase_size=128
```

Check to make sure this works. The following also shows the name associated with the device:

```
# cat /proc/mtd
dev:    size    erasesize   name
mtd0: 04000000 00020000 "mtdram test device"
```

This is an in-memory file system that emulates a MTD device. Now, use the dd command to make a copy of the file system to the newly created device:

```
# dd if=rootfs.jffs2 of=/dev/mtdblock0
```

The /dev/mtdblockX (where X disambiguates multiple partitions) device is a simple block-oriented interface into an MTD device.

Now that the /dev/mtdX device contains a copy of the root file system, you can mount it as follows:

```
# mount -t jffs2 /dev/mtd0 ~/board-rfs
```

Next, look at the /bin directory to see if this is a file system containing BusyBox:

```
# ls -la ~/board-rfs/bin
```

If the directory contains mostly links to /bin/busybox, this is a BusyBox-based root file system. Chapter 14 is dedicated to BusyBox, but at this point know that it supplies smaller, limited-functionality implementations of hundreds of programs.

Next, look at the /lib directory to see what sort of libraries the system is using, if any:

```
# ls -l /lib
```

Some BusyBox-based root file systems don't have shared libraries because the file has been linked statically—that is, all the external symbols required for the program are linked into the executable. Look for the file

```
/lib/libc.so.6
```

This file can be run on the target machine or on the host machine if it's the same architecture as the target. Run it, and you get output that looks like following: (yes, you can run some libraries!):

```
GNU C Library stable release version 2.3.6, by Roland McGrath et al.
Copyright (C) 2005 Free Software Foundation, Inc.
This is free software; see the source for copying conditions.
There is NO warranty; not even for MERCHANTABILITY or FITNESS FOR A
PARTICULAR PURPOSE.
Compiled by GNU CC version 4.1.0 (Sourcery G++).
Compiled on a Linux 2.6.16-rc5 system on 2006-05-04.
Available extensions:
        GNU libio by Per Bothner
        crypt add-on version 2.1 by Michael Glad and others
        GNU Libidn by Simon Josefsson
        Native POSIX Threads Library by Ulrich Drepper et al
        BIND-8.2.3-T5B
        NIS(YP)/NIS+ NSS modules 0.19 by Thorsten Kukuk
Thread-local storage support included.
For bug reporting instructions, please see:
<http://www.gnu.org/software/libc/bugs.html>.
```

The first line tells you that this system is using the GNU C Library, or glibc. This printout also explains how this library was built. It has the following extensions:

- *libio:* This is the implementation of stdio functions like printf and its friends. Although this is considered an extension to glibc, you rarely find a build without this extension.

- *Libidn:* The purpose of Libidn is to encode UTF-8 domain names.

- *NPTL:* The Native POSIX Thread Library is the front end for the POSIX thread library primitives built into the Linux kernel. POSIX is a standard for handling threads, and this standard was, at one time, implemented in a separate library.

- *NIS(YP):* This extension handles Network Information Services, which is a way of publishing information for use by a network, like authentication data. This service was originally called the Yellow Pages (YP) until the developers received a cease and desist letter because that is a trademarked name.

If the libc.so.6 file isn't an executable and links to a file with the general format libuClibc-0.X.Y.so, the libc is based on the uClibc project. uClibc is an implementation of the C standard library that's designed to be small. uClibc doesn't have the same reporting as glibc (because that reporting takes space!), so there's no way to query how it's built. Having uClibc for the board is handy because it's smaller; and for some devices where space is a premium, uClibc offers a great solution. There's more on uClibc later in the book.

Locate Sources for the Root File System

With GPL, the supplier of a binary must also make available the source code used to create the binary as well as scripts for building the source code.[3] Many times, companies that create the Linux distributions for their boards omit the sources for the root file system.

When delivered, sources come in one of two forms: tar files (usually compressed) or files from a packaging system, like Debian or RPM. Files from a packaging system have the advantage of additional metadata that makes them easier to build. RPM source packages end in .src.rpm; sources distributed for the Debian build system end with .orig.tar.gz and have accompanying .dsc and diff.gz files.

If the packages were delivered as tar files, they should be in a folder on the CD media. Compressed tar files are the lowest common denominator for distributing source code. This isn't intended to cast aspersions on tar files; the point is that this format can be used on nearly any system. The source RPM and Debian packages rely on tar as their internal storage format for source files.

Devices and In-Memory File Systems

At this point, it's useful to see the contents of the /dev file system because it contains the device files that serve as the interface to device drivers in the kernel:

```
# ls -la ~/board-rfs/dev
```

---

[3] This doesn't mean you can demand the source code from any company that has GPL-based products. If the company hasn't supplied you with a binary (for which they can insist that you pay them), they're under no obligation to supply you with the source code.

Sometimes this directory contains just a few entries. In this case, the board is using udev to create device nodes when the board boots based on the hardware configuration. Udev is software that scans the /sys file system and creates device nodes based on the content. The /sys directory is a mounted sysfs file system containing directories and files representing the devices on the system with their properties. Using udev is fine for a demonstration or development board; however, most deployment board avoid udev in favor of creating device node files when building the production root file system. It's a good idea to record the contents of the dev directory by outputting the results to a file; for example, the following command, when run on the target, makes a record of the contents of the /dev file system:

```
# ls -la /dev > ~/board-rfs-dev
```

The next thing to check is whether there are other file systems mounted by the board. To get this data, look at the board's /etc/fstab:

```
$ cat ~/board-rfs/fstab
# <file system> <mount point>    <type>  <options>      <dump>  <pass>

proc            /proc            proc    defaults       0       0

sys             /sys             sysfs   defaults       0       0
```

This file contains the name of the file system's mount point, the type, and any parameters. When running, a system with this mount tab displays the following when you use the mount command on the target:

```
# mount
proc on /proc type proc (rw)
sysfs on /sys type sysfs (rw)
```

This board has sysfs and the proc file system mounted at /sys and /proc, respectively. These file systems aren't associated with a physical device but are instead views into the kernel's various data structures. The proc file system gives a view into the processes that are running and other machine-related data. There's a directory for each process, and under each process-directory are files that let you inspect memory, handles, and other information.

The sysfs file system exposes the internal set of kobjects in of the kernel. The purpose of a kobject (along with its posse of ksets and ktypes) is to drive the sysfs file system to let user programs inspect what devices have been registered. The sysfs is the data source for udev that's used to dynamically create device nodes when the system boots.

I cover both sysfs and procfs in detail later. The important thing is to inventory what's present. Although procfs and sysfs are the minimal set, a system with flash storage has a tmpfs file system mounted at /tmp, because that's much faster than using flash. Systems with write-only root file systems also have the /home directory mounted using a tmpfs file system. The tmpfs file system is a RAM-based file system that lets you limit the amount of memory it can consume.

Suitability for Your Project

It's time to decide whether the supplied root file system is adequate for your project. Although the supplied root file system won't be a perfect match, the question boils down to this: is the root file system close enough to be suitable for a starting point.? If the sources for the root file system aren't present, or what's necessary for the project is wildly different than what the root file system contains, starting from scratch is likely the best route.

For example, if the root file system includes all the binaries for handling graphics, and the device doesn't include a UI, these components are wasting space and should be removed. Conversely, if the device's root file system needs to fit a very small flash partition (where *small* for Linux means less than 1MB), nearly any root file system that hasn't been optimized for space is too large.

However, if the supplied root file system is about the right size and has the software ready for the way the device will be used, there's no reason, other than building character, to build the RFS from whole cloth; the best approach is to create the application, copy it into the file system, and rebuild the root file system binary image. Purists may treat this approach with disdain, but it's an acceptable route for many projects.

Root file systems that use uClibc have another constraint: uClibc makes no effort to be binary compatible with other versions of uClibc. That's not a defect, but rather a space-saving choice made by the developers of the project—binary compatibility requires additional code and therefore increases the size of a project whose stated goal is minimal size.

No matter what route you take with the root file system, you must change the startup scripts to make them run faster and require fewer resources. At a minimum, the startup scripts need to be modified to run applications created for the device.

The kernel must also be rebuilt for the project, because the one included with the board is likely missing the correct device drivers or has drivers that aren't necessary. In addition, the kernel must be rebuilt with common options to reduce its size and minimize boot time. Because the kernel needs to be rebuilt, you don't need to decide whether it can be used in its present condition.

Cross-Compiler

When you're assessing the support package for the board, don't forget to see whether the vendor included a cross-compiler. A cross-compiler isn't a required component for booting and frequently isn't included with the Linux software that's shipped with the board. Building a cross-compiler or using a native compiler running in an emulator is a much easier prospect than in previous years, but it still represents some effort that must be expended on the project.

If the board does ship with a cross-compiler, it's difficult to identify whether it was the compiler used to build the kernel and/or the root file system; but you can check the versions of the C library in the cross-compiler's directory to see if they match.

In the cross-compiler's directory, look in the `<arch>-linux/lib` directory for `libc.so.6`. The cross-compiler is located in a directory that's formatted like this

```
<arch>-linux
```

`<arch>` is something like `armv5l`, or `mipsel`, or even `i686`. To be sure you've located the correct directory, be sure it contains a `/bin` directory that contains, at least, a compiler, a preprocessor, and a linker:

```
<arch>-linux/bin/<arch>-linux-gcc
<arch>-linux/bin/<arch>-linux-cpp
<arch>-linux/bin/<arch>-linux-ld
```

There may be slight differences in the names of the files, because these are specified at build time and the values are only convention; the builder of the toolchain has a great degree of freedom over what these executables are named and sometimes picks nonstandard labels.

When you find something that appears to be a cross-compiler, double-check by requesting the version number:

```
# ./<arch>-linux/bin/<arch>-linux-gcc –dumpversion
4.1.0
```

After you locate the cross-compiler, look for the architecture's `lib` directory:

```
# ls -l ./<arch>-linux/<arch>-linux/lib/libc.so*
-rw-r--r-- 1 root root 386 Oct 20  2006 armv5l-linux/lib/libc.so
lrwxrwxrwx 1 root root 14 May  7  2007 armv5l-linux/lib/libc.so.6 -> libc-2.4.90.so
```

Look at what `libc.so.6` links to, and verify whether it's the same in the board's `lib` directory, If they're the same, chances are this compiler was used to build the root file system, although you can't prove it definitively.

Because the Linux kernel doesn't have any library dependencies, it indicates the version of GCC used. If that version matches what `–dumpversion` reports, it's a safe bet that the compiler was used to build the kernel, but this assertion can't be proved beyond any doubt.

No cross-compiler? Shouldn't the software include one to build the sources? With GPL software, the supplier of a binary must also supply the source but not necessarily a cross-compiler.

Moving Forward

At this point, you should be familiar with the contents of the Linux supplied with the board—both what it supplies and what's missing. Some Linux distributions offer nearly everything necessary for development and even supply a kernel and a root file system that closely approximate what is necessary in the production device; in other cases, the best approach is to start from the beginning. The important part is that you choose the route for your project after understanding what's included with the board.

The following chapter discusses getting Linux from an existing open source project, because a number of Linux system builder–type projects have come into existence over the past few years. In addition, I also dedicate a chapter to building a Linux distribution from scratch.

CHAPTER 5

■■■

Getting Linux for Your Board

After looking at the Linux distribution included with a board or sold by the board vendor, it may make sense to start your project with a Linux distribution created by an open source project or from a commercial vendor. Commercial vendors offer deep support for certain use cases (like graphics on consumer electronics devices or Linux certified for use in telecommunications), and open source projects also focus on certain uses cases along the same lines.

Before you build a Linux distribution from scratch (that's the next chapter—skip ahead if you're so inclined), it makes sense to see what's available elsewhere. As Linux has become more common, many projects have sprung into existence to build Linux in one form or another. This chapter looks at build systems that you can use to create an embedded Linux distribution and the offerings of commercial vendors that supply ready-to-use Linux distributions with training and support.

Although Linux is an open source project and the source code is generally available, having somebody else handle the engineering details particular to the selected board make sense because it relieves your schedule of some tasks in exchange for money. Even very technically adept engineers choose to make this trade-off, because frequently time is more valuable than the amount of money required to get a completed Linux platform in the can. Toward that end, this chapter examines the commercial alternatives for Linux so that if you're interested in purchasing, you can approach the transaction as an informed customer. Some commercial embedded products track closely to what's available in open source, whereas others are quite different. For projects that have strict requirements around hardware or software support, the commercial product meeting the requirements is the best choice.

You can obtain a Linux distribution three primary ways:

- *From company that sold the board:* There's a feeling of confidence when you purchase from a board vendor. Chances are overwhelming in favor of the Linux distribution working for the board in question. The cost is usually much less than it would be from a commercial vendor. On the downside, many hardware companies aren't in the software business and don't have the expertise or motivation to support a software product.

- *Via an open source distribution build:* Several open source projects exist to build Linux. The software necessary to build something as complex as a Linux isn't a simple undertaking. Because these projects are open source, the processor support is usually narrow; and the likelihood that the build will work for a specific board (that is, your board) is dicey. Plus, you must overcome a learning curve to use the distribution building software, on top of any learning curve involved in building the software.

- *From a commercial vendor:* A variety of companies offer Linux products and services. These companies do much the same job as the first two alternatives but offer support and mean less risk than trying to build on your own. In addition, these companies offer Linux features like graphics, quick boot-up, and realtime, which the board vendor may not. The support offered by a commercial vendor is also usually more attentive and focused that that available via open source.

Obtaining Linux from the Board Vendor

Board vendors frequently include a Linux distribution with a board so that users can start up the board and see that it works, exercise critical peripherals, and otherwise make sure the board performs as expected. Embedded projects frequently start on a development board that's a proxy for the production board that hardware designers are creating for the device. The completeness of a Linux distribution supplied with the board varies greatly from vendor to vendor and sometimes from board to board.

A development board contains every peripheral possible and has ports that make it easy to attach off-the-shelf components to the board when you're doing development. The development board contains LEDs and sometimes a small LCD to report on the internal board state. During the hardware design process, another team creates a board that fits the industrial design of the device, with the connectors in the right places and the subset of peripherals for the device. This board operates just like the development board from a software perspective, but it doesn't resemble the development board from a physical perspective.

■ **Note** Many board vendors have been switching to established Linux distribution building projects or commercial partners as a way of providing Linux. They've realized that creating, maintaining, and supporting a Linux distribution for their customers is more difficult and time consuming than anticipated.

This section outlines what you need to know to decide about the usefulness of the distribution bundled with the board. In many cases, engineers use the Linux included with the board out of a combination of complacency and fear: complacency because the software works, and fear that getting some other Linux kernel or distribution working would be a waste of time and effort. With that in mind, let's jump in.

Questions You Should Ask Your Board Vendor

The point of these questions is both to assess whether the product offered by the vendor is good enough for the project and to see how committed the vendor is to creating providing a complete solution that will be supported throughout the project:

- *What devices does the kernel support?* You'd think that the devices on the board would be supported, but that isn't always the case! Make a checklist of the devices that will be on the production board so you don't forget any when querying the board vendor. Some board vendors support the most commonly used devices, like network or serial ports, but don't have proper support for a video-out port or audio device.

- *Where are the source code and patches for the kernel?* Open source means you're entitled to the source code, any patches, and instructions explaining how to use those patches. Patches sometimes need to be applied in a certain order, because one patch makes changes on the assumption that some other patch has been applied first. The fact that patches are interrelated isn't indicative of poor engineering, but rather that the company has been carefully tracking the changes it makes to the main kernel.

  If you're aware of other patches that need to be applied, you should test to be sure they're compatible with what the vendor has supplied. For example, the patches for a project like Linux-tiny[1] may make changes throughout the kernel, and those changes may collide with other changes from the vendor. Not all of these issues can be identified or solved before purchasing, but you should address as many that are known.

- *How compatible are patches with the current Linux kernel?* This is important. In the Linux project, changes happen to the *head of line* (old-school speak for the version that will be released next) and are rarely back ported. That means if there's a change to the kernel—say, to address a security issue—that change is made to the current kernel and not to the one included with the board, unless that kernel happens to be the head of line.

  The answer to this question is a function of how old the patches are in combination with how many other changes they contain. For some boards, the changes, although extensive, are limited to the parts of the kernel that deal specifically with the hardware and can be transferred easily to a newer version of the kernel if necessary. Even if patches can't be applied to the newest kernel, you many never need to switch to a newer kernel, making this a moot point.

- *What level of testing has been performed?* One of the things a commercial vendor knows is the state of the software being delivered. Sometimes, the answer is that no testing has occurred. Depending on the project, that may or may not be sufficient. The internal testing done by your company may trump what ever testing the board vendor has or hasn't done.

- *Where's the toolchain?* Getting the sources with the binaries is part of the GPL. There's no provision to ensure that the tools and software necessary to transform those sources into binaries are part of that equation. The toolchain supplied should be the same one used to build the kernel and the root file system (see the next item), and the supplier should include instructions on how to rebuild the toolchain as well.

---

[1] More on this later in the book. Linux-tiny is a set of patches for reducing the size and memory footprint of the kernel.

The GNU toolchain is a group of related projects: a compiler, libraries, linker, utilities, and a debugger. The vendor should understand this notion and be able to describe the version and patches applied to each. As a user, the chances of rebuilding the toolchain completely are fairly low, but you're likely to need to add libraries or use a newer version of the debugger. Knowing how the toolchain is configured helps you determine compatibility with any additional or updated software.

In addition, getting the answer to this question serves as a way to gauge the competency and level of engagement of the vendor with respect to their Linux efforts. Some board vendors put a great deal of care and effort into supplying a top-notch distribution, whereas others do the minimum to claim Linux support.

- *What's in the root file system?* This is a deliberately broad question, mostly because it's a broad topic. A root file system, as explained later in the book, is a complex project that involves several related projects coming together. A root file system can be anything from one file to the contents of an enterprise Linux server. The vendor should be able to describe the version for each software component used in the root file system.

  If you plan to use shared libraries, make sure the shared libraries in the root file system match those in the toolchain. This is a critical detail! When you're cross-compiling applications that use shared libraries on the desktop, those binaries dynamically link to the shared libraries with the toolchain; however, when those same binaries are put in the root file system on the board, they attempt to link with those shared libraries. If there's a mismatch between the libraries used for the compilation and those used for execution, the software may refuse to load or, even worse, may fail unpredictably. If you're linking statically, the shared libraries aren't important, because the code that would reside in the shared library is included in the compiled binary.

- *Do the devices supported on the board have their complementary userland supporting packages?* This is another semi-trick question to gauge the level of care that went into creating the root file system. Devices have become more complex and, for lack of a better word, interactive. For example, supporting USB devices requires support in the kernel and complementary packages in the root file system. The Linux USB software stack includes programs in the root file system that are executed when a user plugs in or unplugs a USB device.

- *Where are the root file system sources and patches, and how do I build it?* Like the toolchain, the root file system is a confederation of packages that work together. Packages included in the root file system are typically licensed under the GPL, so you're due the source under that license agreement along with the build instructions. The build instructions need to explain how to apply any patches along with the information necessary for compilation.

  Because the root file system is a collection of packages, the vendor should explain how to assemble all the packages into something that you can use for booting the board. (This isn't part of the GPL, but it's knowledge you're paying for as part of the purchase.)

- *How often does the company plan to upgrade the kernel?* The Linux project (both the kernel and the collection of projects that make up the root file system) doesn't rest: changes are continually occurring, and that's certainly a good thing. As a customer, understanding how the board vendor reacts to this change helps you understand how you'll be kept up-to-date with the changes in the open source community. Will the software be updated as kernel and package updates occur? Is there a regular release cycle during which the vendor collects changes and validates and tests them before release? Or is the Linux distribution a snap-shot of the current state of the projects and never updated, leaving updates to you? All of these are valid approaches, and as the buyer, it's important for you to know what the board vendor is supplying.

- *What support do you provide? What sort of questions will you answer?* The answer to these questions reveals the amount of in-house expertise the vendor has at its disposal; in general, the more resources the vendor has, the more they're willing to share those resources with their customers.

  You should also ask yourself what level of support required. If this is the first embedded Linux project undertaken at your company, the type and level of support required will be different than if the company already has a high degree of Linux expertise. Some support agreements explicitly say that consulting services aren't offered, where *consulting* means providing advice related to how to use the software. From the vendor's perspective, the support contract exists to limit the support offered, so the vendor doesn't make a commitment it can't fulfill.

Now That You're a Customer…

After signing the check and taking delivery of a Linux distribution included with the board, it's important to assess what was delivered. Plan to spend at least a working week to do the following:

1. Build the kernel.

2. Build the root file system.

3. Boot the board with the newly built root file system and kernel.

4. Compile and debug a small application on the board.

The first three tasks on the list should be done with the tools and advice offered by the vendor. The goal of this exercise is to immediately perform the tasks that will eventually happen in the project, to validate the quality of the delivered software. Even though the distribution includes a kernel that's ready to boot for the board, rebuilding a kernel or re-creating the root file system shouldn't be tasks you approach with trepidation, but rather as a natural part of the project.

At a minimum, if the binaries (kernel and root file system) delivered by the vendor can't be reproduced, the distribution is defective and should be returned for a refund. Likewise, if you can't build and debug a small application, the vendor hasn't supplied you with a set of tools adequate for a project.

Open Source Embedded Distributions

An ever-increasing number of projects build Linux distributions, to the point that building a Linux distribution is a rite of passage for engineers, like building a text editor was in years past. Linux distribution builders all work on the same basic principles: a kernel and group of packages are built according to a specification into a completed set of binaries suitable for deployment. Some distribution builders create a toolchain as part of the process, and others download a binary toolchain from a known location.

When you're classifying these systems, the type of packaging system is a good first-order differentiator, because no matter how the system tries to shield you from the particulars, you eventually need to get familiar with this underlying technology. The most common packing system is a compressed tar file; that's fortunate because this packaging technology is the lowest common denominator and is familiar to most engineers, Linux and otherwise.

Why Embedded Linux Distribution Builders Exist

These distribution-building tools exist due to a catalyst such as supporting a particular usage scenario (for example, as small as possible or rescue disks) or a certain hardware platform (such as a cell phone). These aren't mutually exclusive concepts, because cell phone Linux distributions are frequently small—resource consumption is very important for that hardware platform. The concept of a distribution builder isn't limited to embedded Linux; the same concept exists for desktop Linux systems, the output being an ISO and collection of packages (think RPMs or debs)

In the case of hardware platform–specific distribution builders, the vendor isn't interested in selling the Linux distribution, but rather sees the Linux distribution as an enabler for hardware sales and also as a way to potentially harm the revenue stream of a competitor that sells a Linux distribution as an add-on product. Linux is a way to help sell hardware, plain and simple. As time progresses, the distribution-builder project begins to support a larger variety of hardware, because adapting an existing code base makes for smart engineering.

Several embedded distributions are package system based. The distributions are embedded in terms of the packages, target platform, and size that use an underlying packaging technology to achieve this aim. Although some projects use the same packaging system but have a focus on a particular technology or hardware, these projects are focused on the packaging system.

Should You Use One?

You should certainly try! If the hardware is close to what you'll be using, or you need the technology supported by the distribution, there's little to lose by getting the software and giving it a try. Due to the open nature of the projects, plenty of documentation is available, and probably someone has tried to solve a problem similar to yours and has posted a question or five.

These distribution-building systems build (most) of their components from scratch. That's both an asset and a liability, in that frequently a great deal of configuration is required in order to have the build work successfully. However, as distribution-building projects have improved, they do a better job of detecting and sometimes even fixing configuration-related problems before building starts. But in writing this book, I encountered problems with all the distribution-building projects: none "just worked." LTIB (Linux Target Image Builder) required the least amount of cajoling and twiddling with the machine configuration.

Distribution-building software works by layering software over a packaging system. This layer of software allows configuration settings, among other things, to be placed in a centralized place so that all the software is built using the same general settings. For instance, if the distribution is built without dynamic linking, that is set once and the software then communicates that information to each package as it's built. This means you encounter a learning curve while learning how this works—and that learning curve can be steep, because the software that controls the build process is typically nontrivial. Distribution systems that use make files have a learning curve in that you need to understand the structure of the files and macros. Given the obtuse nature of make, this curve can be larger than you expect. All distribution-building system include a known working configuration that is used to create a build; that configuration serves as the best learning aid when you're modifying the build to fit the needs of your project.

Popular Open Source Embedded Distributions

Following, in no particular order, is an inventory of popular distributions designed for embedded projects. All of these distributions are targeted for embedded engineers, but each may be worth a try for the project at hand.

LTIB (http://www.bitshrine.org)

The Linux Target Image Builder (LTIB) user interface is much like the kernel configuration tool, which, although familiar to systems-level engineers, can be confusing if you're new to Linux. LTIB is accommodating in that it does its best to verify the environment before starting a build and lets you know about corrective actions before starting a 3-hour build process.

One of the complaints about LTIB is that the first time it runs, it downloads the entire set of packages that it could use in a distribution. This is a mixed blessing in that after the packages are on the system, the host doesn't need to be attached to the network in order to get a build running. Another advantage of the big download is that you can put the entire directory into a code librarian and check it out on a build machine for easy platform scripting.

The second complaint is that the software doesn't build toolchains but downloads the binaries and installs them on the system. This is also somewhat advantageous in that building a toolchain requires at least an hour on a very fast computer and, due to the patches and configuration dependencies, is an operation that frequently fails. LTIB provides the sources for the toolchain it downloads; it just doesn't build the toolchain during the build process running on the host machine.

One great advantage of LTIB is that it builds a JFFS2 image containing the root file system, ready to be burned on to a flash partition, as part of the build. Along with the self-contained nature of the project, LTIB is a great tool if you want or need to automate your platform build.

■ **Note** The examples in this chapter are run from the command-line prompt of a terminal. All Linux systems have a terminal program where you can get to a shell prompt. In Ubuntu, that program is under the Applications ➤ Accessories menu and is called Terminal. In Linux, you can get a command prompt several different ways. The examples work equally well no matter what sort of terminal program you used.

LTIB is an RPM-based system. This means it uses source RPM files to do the build, and integrating a package into LTIB means learning how to create RPM packages. Creating a source RPM build for an application isn't difficult; but for some reason, it scares some users away from fully taking advantage of LTIB. Instead of having the software build your application from an RPM as part of the LTIB build, you can post-process the file system, adding the application and making any final changes.

Using LTIB

If you're running a Debian-based system, you need the RPM tools. Open a command shell; Ubuntu users, look for the Terminal program under the Accessories menu. The following commands install the RPM package manager, fetch a release of LTIB, and run it:

```
$ sudo apt-get install rpm
$
```

```
$ tar xzf ltib-8-1-2a-sv.tar.gz
$ cd ltib-8-1-2-sv
$ ./ltib
```

When this book was written, the current version of LTIB was 8.1.2a, but by the time the book makes it to press, the version number will likely be different. You'll probably see this error message complaining that the current user doesn't have proper sudo user permissions to run RPM without asking for a password. To configure this, use the command

```
$ sudo /usr/sbin/visudo
```

Add the following line in the User privilege section:

```
<username> ALL = NOPASSWD: /usr/bin/rpm, /opt/ltib/usr/bin/rpm
```

<username> is your login name on the system. Follow the instructions, and update the sudo file as requested. Running ltib again produces the following message:

```
Installing host support packages.
```

You only need to do this once per host, but it may take up to an hour to complete. This is a frustrating aspect of LTIB for new users. It's a slow process, even if you have a fast connection to the Internet, because of the volume of data being downloaded. If an error occurs, you can find a log file with the full output in /ltib-8-1-2-sv/host_config.log in the directory where LTIB was unpacked. The LTIB directory matches the version you used, which is likely to be different than the one in this book.

After this process completes, a menu appears with the options for the build (see Figure 5-1).

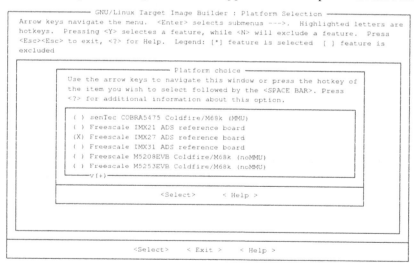

Figure 5-1. *Selecting the target platform in LTIB*

It's a matter of picking the platform (pressing Enter opens in a menu you can choose from) and some additional tools. The LTIB project is the vehicle Freescale uses to distribute Linux, explaining why you're free to pick any platform as long as it's Freescale's.

After you selecting the target platform, the software asks to save the current configuration. Another configuration program is launched, containing the options to set for the build. LTIB does a great job of selecting a minimal system from the start. To create something quickly, change the Options under Target Image Generation to produce a RAM disk. This is the easiest output to manipulate after the build.

The LTIB program provides options to prune the root file system of directories that typically aren't necessary for an embedded system (see Figure 5-2). Without sounding sappy, that's a great feature and tells you the project was designed by a company that knows what embedded Linux engineers do on a daily basis.

```
─────── LTIB: Freescale IMX27 ADS reference board ───────
Arrow keys navigate the menu. <Enter> selects submenus --->. Highlighted letters are
hotkeys. Pressing <Y> selectes a feature, while <N> will exclude a feature.  Press
<Esc><Esc> to exit, <?> for Help.  Legend: [*] feature is selected  [ ] feature is
excluded

    --- Choose the target C library type
        Target C library type (glibc)  --->
        C library package (from toolchain only)  --->
        Toolchain component options  --->
    --- Toolchain selection
        Toolchain (ARMv5te gcc-4.1.2,Multi-lib,gnueabi/glibc-2.5-npt1-3)  --->
    (-O2 -fsigned-char -msoft-float) Enter any CFLAGS for gcc/g++
    --- Choose your Kernel
        kernel (Linux 2.6.22-mx)  --->
    [ ] Build the kernel out of tree?
    [ ] Always rebuild the kernel
    [ ] Produce cscope index (NEW)
    (linux-2.6.22-mx27ads.config) kernel preconfig
    [ ] Include kernel headers
    [ ] Configure the kernel
    [ ] Leave the sources after building
    --- Package selection
 ─v(+)─

            <Select>    < Exit >    < Help >
```

Figure 5-2. *Options for pruning the root file system in LTIB*

After you exit, the build starts. A few hours later, the software will have produced the files and directories listed in Table 5-1, in the directory when LTIB ran.

Table 5-1. *LTIB directory contents after the build*

File or Directory/	Contents
`rootfs/`	The directory created as a result of installing the RPM package created during the build process.

`rootfs.ext2.gz`
 	
`rootfs.ext2.gz.uboot`
	The compressed ext2 image of the `rootfs` directory. If another type of file system was requested, ext2 is replaced with that file system type. The file with the extension `uboot` is properly formatted to be used with that boot loader.

`rpm/`	The collection of RPM files used to create the build.
`rootfs/boot/bootable_kernel`	The kernel that's ready for the boot loader. This file is a link to another file in the same directory. Copy the file that this points to into the `/tftpboot` directory to boot with this kernel.
`rootfs/boot/linux.config`	The kernel configuration file. To later rebuild just the kernel, you can use this file as the configuration.
`/opt/freescale/usr/local/gcc-4.1.2-glibc-2.5-nptl-3/arm-none-linux-gnueabi/bin/`	The location of the toolchain (for this build). Depending on the selected board, the directory varies slightly but resides under `/opt/freescale/usr`.

LTIB Tricks

LTIB is incredibly powerful and easy to use. One of its thoughtful features is the reporting built into LTIB. When LTIB first starts, it downloads a set of packages. To see a nicely formatted listing of those packages, use

```
$ ./ltib -m listpkgs
```

This command produces the following output (snipped)

```
----------------------  ---------------        -------  -------     ------------
----------------------  ---------------
Package                 Spec file              Enabled  License     Summary
----------------------  ---------------        -------  -------     ------------
----------------------  ---------------
DirectFB-1.1.0-1        DirectFB                  n     LGPL        DirectFB is a
graphics
library for embedded syst
alsa-lib-1.0.11rc2-0    alsa-lib                  n     LGPL        A libraries
for ALSA
(Advanced Linux Sound Architecture)
```

```
alsa-utils-1.0.11rc2-0    alsa-utils                    n    GPL         Utilities for
ALSA
(Advanced Linux Sound Architecture)
apptrk-1.37-1             apptrk-ppcbin                 n    Freescale E Userspace
debug
agent for Codewarrior
```

This output shows the version, spec file (what RPM uses for a build), and license for the file along with a brief summary. You can pipe this information to a file and keep it as a basis of comparison when the packages are updated.

The next useful feature is the dry-run mode. This works exactly like the dry-run feature in `patch` and `make` (use the `-dry-run` parameter for both): all the commands are echoed to the console, but nothing is executed. Because some operations take a while, having the system print out what it would be doing is very helpful in deciding whether the configuration changes have the desired effect before you wait several hours to find out they didn't work as expected.

Try the dry run with the `-m clean` parameter to see what the software will do for this command:

```
$ ltib -m clean -dry-run
```

Getting Help

The LTIB project is hosted on a site that's the GNU equivalent of SourceForge. It has mailing lists (and archives) and a bug-tracking system. The mailing list is more heavily trafficked than the bug-tracking system, so a mailing list posting is the fastest way to get help. To subscribe to the mailing list, visit the page http://savannah.nongnu.org/mail/?group=ltib. This page has a link to the mailing-list archives so you can see if another user has posted a similar question.

Buildroot (http://buildroot.uclibc.org/)

Buildroot is a project that helps you create root file systems and toolchains that use uClibc and BusyBox, a small C Library, and basic set of root file system tools. Buildroot grew out of the BusyBox and uClibc projects, two of the most commonly used pieces of software for embedded projects. Because this tool integrated both of these projects, it serves as a great starting point for creating a Linux distribution for a project.

Like LTIB, Buildroot uses an interface that's similar the tool used to configure the kernel. Although this is comforting for a system-level engineer, the tool can be confusing if you're a new engineer. The primary problem with this tool is that you have to keep track of where you are; after you use the software for a few minutes, nearly every page looks the same, and picking the correct options becomes tedious.

Buildroot configures an entire development environment—kernel, root file system, and toolchain— which means you need to configure the options for these complex projects before starting a build. There are literally hundreds of options to configure, and the sheer number of items makes the process mildly tedious. For some boards, default configuration files configure the build with the right settings. Unfortunately, there aren't many of these default configuration files, so the chances of one matching the board you're using are fairly low.

Buildroot uses tar files as its package system and uses a collection of make files to configure the software before building. This implementation is easy to understand if you've used make in the past for moderately complex projects. Each package has a `.mk` file containing the make rules necessary to download, configure, build, and clean the package and a `Config.in` that is used by the configuration tool.

After you select the configuration options, you invoke make, and the build process starts running.

Using Buildroot

Buildroot is packaged as a tar file. Download the file from the downloads page at
`http://buildroot.uclibc.org/download.html`, and uncompress it. The following example code
fetches a version using `wget` that will likely be out of date when this book is published. After the file is
uncompressed, change directories, and run the configuration program (see Figure 5-3):

```
$ wget http://buildroot.uclibc.org/downloads/buildroot-2009.02-rc1.tar.bz2
$ tar xjf buildroot-2009.02-rc1.tar.bz2
$ make menuconfig
```

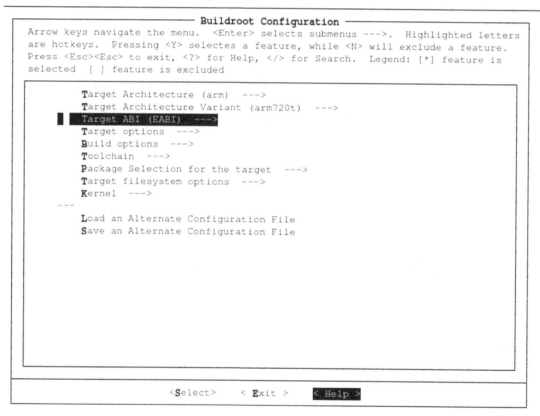

Figure 5-3. *The top-level Buildroot menu, which looks similar to LTIB*

It's worth pointing out that the configuration tool supports rudimentary searching: press the / key,
and a search dialog appears (see Figure 5-4). The dialog asks for a `CONFIG_` symbol, but it searches for
both the `CONFIG_` symbol and the corresponding prompt text that appears in the dialog. If you're new to

this configuration program, the output is a series of lines defining the value of variables, all of which start with `CONFIG_`. If you're familiar with the content and structure of the output file, you know the config var to be changed. But if you're just get starting, the search on the prompt string is more useful.

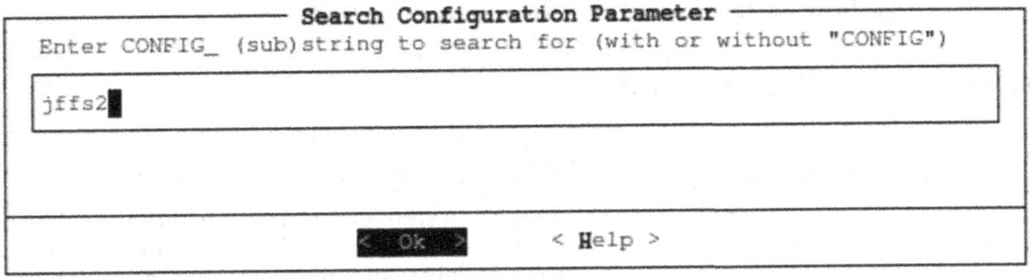

```
──────────── Search Configuration Parameter ────────────
Enter CONFIG_ (sub)string to search for (with or without "CONFIG")

jffs2█



       < Ok >          < Help >
```

Figure 5-4. *The search dialog*

The output of the search is a list of the items that match. Unfortunately, it's just a list—you can't go to one of the items in the list. The best way to use the output is to scan the list for potential matches and record the location of the desired items on a scratch pad, unless your memory is good enough to recall the menu paths of the interesting items.

The easiest way to quickly start a build is to use one of the default configurations stored under the ./target/device directory. To get a quick listing of the configurations, do the following:

```
# find ./target -name "*_defconfig"
./target/device/x86/i386/i686_defconfig
./target/device/KwikByte/kb9202/kb9202_defconfig
./target/device/Atmel/atngw100/atngw100_defconfig
./target/device/Atmel/atstk100x/atstk100x_defconfig
./target/device/Atmel/atstk100x/atstk1002-no-mplayer_defconfig
./target/device/Atmel/at91sam9260dfc/at91sam9260dfc_defconfig
./target/device/Atmel/at91sam9g20dfc/at91sam9g20dfc_defconfig
./target/device/Atmel/atngw100-expanded/atngw100-expanded_defconfig
./target/device/Atmel/atngw100-base/atngw100-base_defconfig
./target/device/Atmel/at91sam9260pf/at91sam9260pf_defconfig
./target/device/Atmel/at91rm9200df/at91rm9200df_defconfig
./target/device/Atmel/at91sam9263ek/at91sam9263ek_defconfig
./target/device/Atmel/at91sam9261ek/at91sam9261ek_defconfig
```

There are several default configurations under this directory for a variety of boards. Try using a basic ARM processor configuration to test things:

```
# make at91sam9261ek_defconfig
```

Several hundred lines scroll by in the terminal window as the configuration program reports what is being set as a result of using this configuration file. You may be prompted to press Enter a few times to accept the default options. All that output offers reassurance that the system is busily working to configure the project as requested. Next, kick off the make process:

```
$ make
```

The build now runs. This process takes a while as the software downloads what's necessary for the build and starts the compilation process. At the end, the system will have built a kernel, a root file system, and a toolchain. Table 5-2 lists the locations of the key files and directories. These examples are specific to the choices used to create the configuration in the example; following each is an example with some placeholders so you can see how the files would look for your configuration.

Table 5-2. *Files and Directories Crucial for the Build*

File or Directory/	Contents
`./project_build_arm/at91sam9261ek/root/` `./project_build_<architecture>/<board>/root/`	The root file system created as a result of the build. This is the layout of the file system before it's processed into the image requested during the build.
`./binaries/at91sam9261ek/at91bootstrap.bin` `./binaries/<board>/<kernelfile>.bin`	The ready-to-boot kernel. This file is a symlink to another file in the same directory whose name contains additional information about how the kernel was built.

`./binaries/at91sam9261ek/ rootfs.arm-`
`20090310.ext2`
`./binaries/<board>/ rootfs.<architecture>-`
`<serialno>.<filesystem type>`
	The root file system image that's been processed into the requested image format. In this case, the format was ext2. If another format was selected, the extension would reflect that choice.

`./build_arm/staging_dir/usr/bin` `./build_<architecture>/staging_dir/usr/bin`	The directory in which the toolchain resides.
`./dl`	The directory to which the files used to build the software have been downloaded. This directory contains the packages in compressed (either gz or bz2 format) tar files for each of the packages used in the toolchain and root file system build.

Curious about the contents of the root file system created by the build? You can mount the root file system image via a loopback:

```
# mkdir -p /mnt/arm-rfs
# mount -t ext2 -o loop rootfs.arm-20090310.ext2 /mnt/arm-rfs
```

■ **Note** Loopback mounts work by associating a block device with a file. A *block device* has semantics that allow random access to the underlying data and reads and writes in terms of a fixed-size data unit. The –o loop option in mount is shorthand for the command necessary to associate the file with the loopback device. After you mount the file system, if you're curious, you can do a losetup –a to see what mount did behind the scenes.

Listing this directory shows what appears to be a regular root file system. Check that the files are appropriate for the ARM processor by doing the following:

```
# file /mnt/arm-rfs/lib/libc.so.0
/mnt/arm-rfs/lib/libc.so.0: symbolic link to `libuClibc-0.9.30.so'

# file /mnt/arm-rfs/lib/libuClibc-0.9.30.so
/mnt/arm-rfs/lib/libuClibc-0.9.30.so: ELF 32-bit LSB shared object, ARM, version 1,
stripped

# file /mnt/arm-rfs/bin/busybox
/mnt/arm-rfs/bin/busybox: setuid ELF 32-bit LSB executable, ARM, version 1,
dynamically↵
 linked (uses shared libs), stripped
```

To run the toolchain, change directories into the `./build_arm/staging_dir/usr/bin` folder, and get a directory listing to see what files have been built. The files follow one of two patterns:

- `arm-linux-*`: These are the tools that use the glibc libraries.
- `arm-linux-uclibc-*`: These tools use the uClibc libraries.

In practice, the only difference between these files is that they use different C libraries when linking. To use one of these compilers in a project, you can add this directory to the path or copy the parent directory `build_arm/staging_dir/usr` to another location.

Buildroot Tricks

Buildroot has the concept of a project that contains all the settings necessary to build the packages into a distribution. After you go through the effort of configuring the kernel and root file system exactly as desired, you can save this information so that you can check it into a version control system or send it to a customer or another party to reproduce the output. To save the state of the project, use the following command from the Buildroot directory:

```
$ make saveconfig
```

This creates a `local/<project name>` directory containing the configuration files.

Buildroot downloads files when necessary as part of the build process. Some users, due to security restrictions or rules regarding how software is built, can't download from the Internet during the build process. Buildroot offers a target that results in the packages necessary for the build being downloaded to the local cache of packages:

```
$ make source
```

After this command runs, the `./dl` directory is populated with all the packages necessary for the build process.

Getting Help

Buildroot, like most embedded projects, conducts support through a mailing list. The page `http://buildroot.uclibc.org/lists.html` has a subscription link and a handy search box so you can look through the history. The mailing list is active, with postings daily, and has a mix of newbie and superuser messages, so there's no need to be shy about asking a question (or lending a hand). You can find well-written documentation at `http://buildroot.uclibc.org/docs.html`. The same documentation is in the `docs` directory in the project, if connecting to the Internet is difficult.

OpenEmbedded (http://wiki.openembedded.net/)

The OpenEmbedded project got started as the build infrastructure for the Sharp Zaurus hand-held computer that ran Linux. The OpenEmbedded system uses the BitBake (more on that later) system for describing packages patches and their interrelationships. Formally, the project views the BitBake system as the build infrastructure for metadata supplied by the OpenEmbedded project.

OpenEmbedded, like the other distribution builders, builds a kernel, toolchain, and root file system. The BitBake software has the notion of *recipes* that it uses to download and cross-build packages; you can use this software to build other software as well.

Unlike many project, OpenEmbedded recommends that you check out the project from a source code repository. To get updates, refresh the project's files from source control. You may find this disorienting; or it may leave you with the impression that the software isn't "done." Because of the rapid changes to OpenEmbedded and the fact that it's implemented in Python plus shell scripts (meaning there's no separate compilation step for you to perform), this model works well.

The BitBake model requires an earnest learning commitment. The software ships with an example configuration file that you can use to create a simple build. However, the software doesn't have a UI, so figuring out what it can do requires that you read the documentation. The OpenEmbedded site contains quite a bit of information, but it seems to operate under the assumption that you're already familiar with the technology.

The OpenEmbedded software models the software build into the following parts:

- *Distribution:* This distribution contains a list of packages for the root file system and the kernel to use for the build. It also contains the settings for the root file system type.

- *Machine:* The machine data describes the hardwarethe distribution will be running on: for example, the size of the flash partitions or the name device for the serial console. The machine also has an associated set of packages that address features specific to that machine.

- *Package recipe:* The metadata part of the OpenEmbedded project is a library of BitBake recipes. A recipe specifies where to download a package, what patches to apply, and when and how to install the package in the target machine's root file system.

OpenEmbedded is very different from other build systems since it's object-oriented in nature. At its core, BitBake uses the recipe to instantiate the appropriate class necessary to build a package. The object-oriented approach makes sense when you're building packages because the overall steps are the same for every package, but the particulars for any step for a given package may be unique. By using classes intelligently, the authors don't repeat code when a group of packages all have the same processing for certain steps in the process.

The notion of inheritance is also writ large on the configuration files used by OpenEmbedded. A file for a distribution likely includes many other files shared by other distributions. This structure has benefits in that one change can be easily applied to many distributions, but it also means the details are hidden if you're a novice user. If you've slogged through other class libraries, you'll have the same feeling when learning the ins and outs of OpenEmbedded's data files.

> ■ **Note** Open Embedded uses two different source-control systems, which are sometimes called *code librarians*: Subversion (SVN) and Git (no known aliases). Both of these systems provide the same sort of functionality, keeping track of code changes from developers over time, but in very different ways. OpenEmbedded is actually two projects that work together, and each project is selected a different source-control system; that's OK, but it may be a little disorienting to new users.

Using OpenEmbedded

The first step in using this software is to obtain the BitBake software. The recommended method is to download the software from the Subversion archive. Subversion may not be installed on your system, so the first command installs it on an Ubuntu system. If you're using an RPM-based system, substitute yum for apt-get:

```
$ sudo apt-get install subversion
$ mkdir -p ~/oe/conf
$ cd ~/oe
$ svn co svn://svn.berlios.de/bitbake/branches/bitbake-1.8/ bitbake
```

Lots of data scrolls past, showing the data that's being downloaded from the Subversion repository. Next, use Git to fetch the OpenEmbedded metadata. When you run this command, there is an uncomfortable delay before data appears on the terminal; be prepared to wait a minute or two, which can seem like an eternity. Be patient:

```
$ git clone git://git.openembedded.net/openembedded
Initialized empty Git repository in /home/gene/oe/openembedded/.git/
remote: Counting objects: 274805, done.
remote: Compressing objects: 100% (85039/85039), done.
```

Add OpenEmbedded's tools to the path, and the system will be ready:

```
$ export BBPATH=~/oe/build:~/oe/openembedded
$ export PATH=~/oe/bitbake/bin:$PATH
```

The documentation recommends doing the following:[2]

```
echo 0 > /proc/sys/vm/mmap_min_addr
```

If you're running an Ubuntu system, you may need to install these packages as well:

```
$ sudo apt-get install diffstat texi2html cvs gawk
```

---

[2] This sets the minimum physical memory address the kernel will accept when mapping memory. It's more a security setting than anything else, because a program that can map into such an address could gain access to kernel data or control structures.

If you're running an RPM-based system, use this command:

```
$ sudo yum install diffstat texi2html cvs gawk
```

OpenEmbedded includes an example file that you can use to start a build of the software at `openembedded/conf/local.conf.sample`. This file contains an explanation of many of the options you can set to configure an OpenEmbedded build. You can use this file as the basis for starting a project by making a copy of it like so:

```
cp openembedded/conf/local.conf.sample build/conf/local.conf
```

Open `build/conf/local.conf`, and read it. A warning at the top of the file says to read everything and includes a passive-aggressive requirement that you delete the last line (otherwise an error is generated), to prove that you at least read the header of the file. Sigh.

This file is complex. For learning purposes, create a much smaller `build/conf/local.conf` containing just the following:

```
BBFILES = "<install dir>/oe/openembedded/recipes/*/*.bb"
DISTRO = "minimal"
MACHINE = "qemuarm"
ASSUME_PROVIDED += "gcc3-native"
ENABLE_BINARY_LOCALE_GENERATION = "0"
ASSUME_PROVIDED += "qemu-native"
```

Make the `<install dir>` in `BBFILES` equal to the directory where OpenEmbedded was installed. The last three lines are critically important. On several systems, the QEMU package refuses to build due to system compiler configuration problems. The last line tells BitBake that QEMU is present, even though it may not be; thus this package isn't built, thereby avoiding the problem. You can do this because QEMU isn't used during the build, but the set of rules says it's necessary. By telling the build process not to check for QEMU, it doesn't try to build it and therefore doesn't cause the build to fail. Yes, this is a little bit of a hack.

Next, kick off the build by doing the following from the oe directory:

```
bitbake bootstrap-image
```

The target `bootstrap-image` builds the minimal set of packages to get the machine up and running. The software automatically finds the `local.conf` file, reads the distro and machine files, and starts the build process.

The distributions defined by OpenEmbedded also define the targets listed in Table 5-3. Not all distributions define all of these targets. The easiest way to determine whether the target is supported is to try it out and see if an error message appears. This seems clunky, but this approach is ea:er than digging through the distribution and machine configuration files.

Table 5-3. *Build Targets Defined by OpenEmbedded*

Target	Purpose
console-image	A distribution without any of the graphics libraries or X11
x11-image	Contains a complete X Window environment and supporting libraries
opie-image	Open Palmtop Integrated Environment (OPIE), which has the tools and graphics environment for a palm-top computer like a PDA
Kernel	Builds only the kernel; doesn't build any of the user packages

The BitBake software downloads the source files necessary for the build according to the instructions in the recipe file as the builds run. The downloaded files are stored in a local cache for reuse. When the build completes, the following appears:

```
NOTE: build 200903122216: completed
```

As you can see, the build serial number is the current date and time. The process puts the build into the ./tmp directory. Table 5-4 lists the locations of the critical build components.

Table 5-4. *Locations of Critical OpenEmbedded Build Componentsn*

File or Directory/	Contents
./tmp/cross/bin	The cross-compiler for the project. Add this directory to your path to easily invoke the cross-compiler.
./tmp/rootfs	The root file system before it was put into the final image. This is the layout of the file system before it's processed into the image requested during the build.
./tmp/deploy	The kernel and root file system image suitable for booting the board.
./tmp/downloads	The source files used in the build. Each file has an md5 sum file (same file name with an .md5 extension) to verify the contents of the file.

Getting Help

The OpenEmbedded project has several mailing lists that you can view at http://wiki.openembedded.net/index.php/Mailing_lists. If you're trying to use OpenEmbedded to build a distribution, the openembedded-users list is the most appropriate mailing list for questions. OpenEmbedded also keeps an archive of messages, using a nice forum-style manager to keep them organized. If you prefer Internet Relay Chat (IRC), the project has several channels at freenode; a complete list is at http://wiki.openembedded.net/index.php/IRC. Like mailing lists, the OpenEmbedded project keeps a log of the IRC traffic.

You can find the user manuals for both OpenEmbedded and BitBake at `http://docs.openembedded.org/usermanual/usermanual.html` and in the `openembedded/docs` directory. The OpenEmbedded site is a wiki; however, the user manual is the best source of information to learn about and understand the project.

Getting Linux from Commercial Vendors and Consultants

Commercial vendors and consultants are different from board vendors in that they make Linux solutions for several different board vendors or processor manufacturers. Chances are, the distribution being sold or supplied with the board was created by one of these consultants under a contract arrangement.

There's nothing wrong with deciding to turn a technical problem (some portion of getting Linux up and running for a target board) into a financial problem. Often, because open source software is available for the taking, people believe they can get it working for a project if the resources are available. Just like any other mutually beneficial exchange, buying from a vendor is the right choice if the product delivered is at the right price and clears your schedule for higher-valued activities.

Vendors in the commercial Linux space focus on creating Linux distributions from a functional level. Customers come to these vendors looking for higher-level features such as quick boot-time, realtime, or graphics, and expect the vendors to get these components up and running on one or more target boards being considered for the project.

Do You Need a Commercial Vendor?

Many companies that examine their budgets, time lines, and resources decide that even though Linux could be built in-house, it makes sense to purchase. The driving element behind many embedded vendors is how the companies view working with Linux: is the operating system part of the core product value?

For example, a company that creates point-of-sale (POS) terminals has core product features like the user interface that increase user productivity or improved ways of capturing signatures that require less storage. This is very different than a company that makes a network-attachable device that aids in system backup. The POS company may be almost indifferent to the operating system used in the product, and people buying their products may care even less. In this case, purchasing Linux is probably the right choice because it allows the company to focus on features that matter to its customers.

Contrast this with the storage device company, for example. This type of device is purchased by very technical people who need to integrate the device into an existing network structure; for them, knowing what operating system the device is running is essential. Some of the work done by engineering at the storage company may give it an edge over its competitors, and the company's management may be reluctant to help those changes make their way back to the main kernel project. In this sense, Linux is a feature of the product and part of its value proposition. This company should consider building Linux from scratch in order to have the greatest amount of control over this critical aspect of the product.

■ **Note** Some software engineers, knowing that Linux is available in open source, bristle at the idea of purchasing it. The thinking is as follows: the source is available for everything that's being sold. With some effort, what the vendor is selling can be produced at zero cost. However, that thinking doesn't account for the cost of the engineering time required to build and create the distribution. In short, without being a shill for the embedded Linux industry, purchasing embedded Linux isn't an unqualified bad decision.

Or, consider a company that builds industrial machinery. In this company, realtime performance is a requirement that must be met. Customers who purchase the machinery may program units in the field, so having an open operating system like Linux is important. This company is another candidate where contracting with a vendor that is responsible for monitoring and understanding realtime on Linux has much to offer.

Getting a Linux environment up and running can also be a research as well as an engineering project. Some products must get to market or be delivered by a certain date, and variance isn't acceptable. In this case, going the route of getting something ready out of the box makes perfect sense, because certainty has higher value than money.

Finally, a vendor does system configuration work that can be of very high value. Some vendors specialize in certain industry hardware protocols, like CANBus, and can supply a Linux distribution that has these drivers in working order for the project.

What You Should Expect

Commercial vendors come in two basic flavors: product-oriented and service-oriented. Product-oriented vendors sell a base product along with additional services. Service-oriented vendors do work on a time and materials basis; after an interview, the vendor returns to you with a price for the services that match your requirements. The product-oriented vendors also include a set of tools wrapped in an Integrated Development Environment (IDE) that work with the software provided. Service-oriented vendors don't have an IDE product or toolset; rather, they expect the customer to use open source tools for development work.

The development tools offered by product-oriented companies are all based on the (admittedly open source) Eclipse IDE project and are much more advanced than what is available for free in open source. For example, the hardware debugger integration in Wind River's toolset is an excellent piece of software engineering that makes low-level debugging much easier. However, this feature isn't valuable if your project schedule doesn't include that sort of work.

Service-oriented vendors have newer versions of the Linux kernel and root file system packages and toolchains. This is a side-effect of how they do business: for each customer, the vendor picks what's available from open source and uses it as the basis of the work the company delivers. When you're working with this type of vendor, it's essential that the changes made to the delivered software be delivered as patches so that you can make additional updates with less difficulty.

Independent of the type of vendor, the software delivered is a Board Support Package (BSP). Unfortunately, vendors have all adopted a different name for this deliverable, but it's still a kernel, root file systemm and toolchain. Along with the BSP, the sources for all of the GPL software delivered must be included. Many vendors also include detailed instructions on how to rebuild the kernel and root file system but don't provide the same level of detail for the toolchain. With a little prying, you can get this from the vendor; but for reasons unknown, some are less than forthcoming with this information.

Roundup of Vendors

The following, in no particular order, is a list of vendors and consultancies for embedded Linux and a summary of what the companies provide. The Linux market is both dynamic and growing, so by the time this book makes it onto the shelf, there are likely to be additions and updates.

Wind River

Wind River is what's called the *incumbent* vendor in marketing speak. Wind River has been in the embedded business since before Linux existed and has a business built on delivering everything necessary for embedded development. In this case, "everything" means software, training, services, legal advice for open source, professional services, development tools for Linux, as well as the company's other embedded operating system, VxWorks.

Wind River's Linux business model consists of supplying a version of Linux and the root file system that have been thoroughly tested and verified for the target boards, along with packages for supporting use cases like consumer electronics and industrial control. Wind River's strong suit is its development tools: Workbench. Workbench is a soup-to-nuts development environment that has excellent debugging and system-building tools to help with development.

To provide a Linux distribution that's been tested and validated, the distributions from Wind River usually run a year or so behind the head of line development of the kernel or patches. But not all projects need the latest Linux.

Wind River's product offerings are the most expensive of the lot. For budget-constrained companies, the pricing may take this company out of the running, the value of the services notwithstanding.

Because Linux competes with Wind River's closed source VxWorks operating system, the company has had a mixed view of Linux and open source, to the point of running a "seven levels of open source hell" campaign complete with gargoyles. Over the years, Wind River has warmed to Linux, but it's still viewed as a secondary offering to VxWorks.

MontaVista

MontaVista's Linux operating system started as Hard Hat Linux that offered realtime performance. The company has branched out into serving the general embedded Linux market and has extended its product offerings through the addition of an IDE and other tools.

MontaVista's value proposition is around delivering a well-tested Linux distribution paired with support and tools. MontaVista has two targeted distributions: one for carrier grade for telecommunications applications, and the other Mobilinux for handsets. The company also markets a general-purpose Linux distribution, Professional Edition.

Unlike Wind River, MontaVista's focus is entirely on embedded Linux, and the company has embraced open source from its inception. The company regularly contributes to the Linux kernel (and, using number of changes contributed as a metric, is one of the top contributors to the Linux kernel project) and other open source initiatives, such as power management and special-purpose file systems. Although the software offered by MontaVista may lag behind that of the general Linux community by a year to 18 months so it can be tested and validated, the company has proven that it's always working on the next version of Linux for its customers.

A transaction with the company involves purchasing a subscription that gives you the right to a certain number of software updates, the use of tools, and support during the length of the engagement. During the sales process, it's typical for MontaVista to sell services and training as well.

Embedded Alley

Embedded Alley is a Linux consultancy house that supplies customers with a mix of off-the-shelf software and services. The typical engagement with Embedded Alley begins with an interview during which the company finds out what you need; it then produces the software that matches your requirements along with support and training services.

Embedded Alley doesn't offer IDE tools like MontaVista or Wind River. Instead, the company expects that customers will use open source tools for their development process.

DENX

DENX is a Linux consultancy based in Germany that does business worldwide and focuses on PowerPC architecture. The company's deep knowledge in kernel engineering for emerging hardware means that people seek out DENX for hardware-related development.

The company got its start by doing boot loader work, creating a widely used boot loader for embedded systems called U-Boot. Getting a boot loader up and running on a system is a tricky bit of engineering that's essential to making the board able to run an operating system. In addition to creating the boot loader, DENX also does the early boot-time work necessary to get Linux running after the boot loader hands execution off to the kernel.

This deep knowledge of the Linux kernel means that DENX distributions frequently support new hardware sooner that what's available in the general Linux kernel. DENX isn't withholding code from the open source community; rather, it takes time for a patch to wend its way through the process for inclusion in the main Linux kernel.

Unlike many companies, DENX makes available its commercial product through the Embedded Linux Development Kit (ELDK). The ELDK is a remarkably complete embedded Linux distribution that includes a root file system, kernel, and tool chain. Because DENX is focused on PowerPC, the company's web site lists only PowerPC processors as supported; however, there are builds that aren't officially supported by DENX for other architectures.

Free Electrons

Free Electrons started as a Linux training house by providing some of the best training materials freely available for embedded Linux engineers. The company has since branched out into providing embedded Linux consulting and training, along the lines of Embedded Alley. With its training heritage, Free Electrons focuses on helping its customers be good embedded Linux engineers, providing additional services where necessary.

Free Electrons is very aggressive about making material and development work available to the open source community. Most of the training materials offered by the company are available for download free of charge. The materials include slides with comments and lab practice sessions. This wealth of information is offered without registration, which is refreshing and relieves you from using a throwaway e-mail address and fake phone number.

Another interesting service that Free Electrons offers is taking the changes that your company may have made to Linux and supporting projects and getting them in shape for submission into the main development projects. Getting changes into the mainline of projects means that code will be supported with future releases of the software, so you won't have to figure out how to get patches to apply when the base software has updated. This reduces the time and efforts involved in keeping patches synchronized with the larger open source community.

Code Sourcery

Code Sourcery's genesis was writing the low-level code to get toolchains running for new hardware architectures. Hardware vendors contracted with this company to create or patch GCC and GDB so that it would work with the new features offered by these processors. Several other commercial embedded Linux vendors use Code Sourcery toolchains in their product offerings; most don't reveal this information, and Code Sourcery is tightlipped about its customer list.

Branching out from toolchains, this company offers an IDE based on Eclipse that works with its toolchains and debuggers. But Code Sourcery remains focused on toolchains and doesn't offer the complete line of services and products that other companies do. If all you require of a vendor is a toolchain, then this company has the right product.

What's Next

This chapter talked about ways to obtain Linux through projects that build Linux through a series of scripts that as a user you influence through configuration files and picking options from menus. This is a fine way to get a Linux system up and running. You may find that what Buildroot produces is perfect, with no further changes or adjustments necessary. However, not all users fall into that category; you may need to make so many changes to the prepackaged scripts that they're more of a hindrance than a help.

In that case, Chapter 6 covers building Linux from scratch, starting with source files and working your way to a complete Linux distribution. This process is the best way to have the most control over the project and fully understand how all the different parts of the project work together. The process starts with a toolchain and then progresses to build the kernel and root file system. Not only do you learn about how to get an embedded system running, but the chapter also demystifies how your desktop system works.

CHAPTER 6

■ ■ ■

Creating a Linux Distribution from Scratch

Creating a Linux distribution from scratch is viewed as a daunting task, and it shouldn't be. The process involves creating a toolchain, using that toolchain to create a root file system, and then building a kernel. The process isn't complex, it just requires you to carefully follow many steps to build the proper tools. After you go over the instructions for building a toolchain and understand how it works, the smartest route may be to use a tool that builds a toolchain, such as crosstool-NG, to build the root file system and kernel.

In prior years, before Linux's popularity with board vendors and chip makers hit its stride, support for any hardware platform other than Intel's X86 was spotty; however, with Linux becoming the platform of choice for embedded devices, support for most embedded hardware platforms is part of the Linux kernel and toolchain.

Chapter 5 discussed getting a Linux distribution from another source, such as the vendor that sold you the board, a commercial vendor, or one of the several open source distribution building project. These are fine approaches to getting a Linux distribution, but building from scratch gives you the most control over the composition of the distribution and how it works. The learning curve to create a distribution from scratch is also about the same (at least for me) as learning a distribution-building tool, and the skill is more transferable.

Making a Linux distribution involves these steps

1. Build a cross-compiler.

2. Use the cross-compiler to build a kernel.

3. Use the cross-compiler to build a root file system.

4. Roll the root file system into something the kernel can use to boot.

A cross-compiler is the Rosetta stone (the flux capacitor, if you will) of embedded development. Until this tool has been built, the kernel can't be built—nor can the root file system's programs be built.

This chapter goes over how to create a toolchain for an ARM board and then build the kernel and root file system. Because the Linux kernel has matured, the sources in the main projects don't need the level of patches they once did in order to support common embedded targets The hunting and gathering step snares many who build distributions from scratch, because there is no canonical place where you can locate the patches for a certain revision of the tools used in the build.

Building the toolchain is still one of the more complex bits of the process, and a reasonable tool is available that just builds a toolchain: crosstool-NG. After you build a toolchain from scratch, the chapter has you create one with crosstool-NG to compare the two processes. If possible, the best approach is to use crosstool-NG or one of the distribution builders to create a toolchain. Because a toolchain involves so many software packages, getting a set that works together is a great value that these projects provide.

Another slightly confusing part of the process is that the kernel sources are used in the build process. One step in building the cross-compiler is to build the corresponding C Standard Library. In order for the C Standard Library to build, it needs to know some information about the target machine, which is kept in the kernel. For the uninitiated, this seems to be a circular dependency; but the parts of the kernel that are used don't need to be cross-compiled.

When you have the cross-compiler in hand, you create the root file system with the BusyBox project. Linux requires a root file system and refuses to boot if one can't be found. A root file system can be one file: the application program for the device. Most embedded Linux systems use additional libraries and utilities. The root file system in this chapter is linked with the GNU C Library at runtime, so these files must be on the target as well.

BusyBox is a program that provides limited-functionality implementations of most command-line tools found on a Linux system. Although a root file system doesn't need to contain all these tools, having them available when the system boots is a convenience. When you understand what tools are necessary (frequently, it's a very small set), you can remove the rest to economize on space and make the system more secure.

How does a small root file system make a system more secure? The fewer programs, the smaller number of possible exploits. A root file system containing just the functionality necessary to execute the application on the target doesn't present an attacker with any more opportunities than absolutely necessary. A small number of programs also reduces the maintenance required to keep current with changes happening in the open source community.

The kernel is the last component in this process. The kernel is a self-contained system that doesn't have runtime dependencies. Being a very mature project, the cross-build of the kernel works very well. The kernel build process is by far the easiest process in this chapter.

Cross-Compiler Basics

A *cross-compiler* is a tool that transforms source code into object code that will run on a machine other than the one where the compilation was executed. When you're working with languages that execute on virtual machines (like Java), all compilation is cross-compilation: the machine where the compilation runs is always different than the machine running the code. The concept is simple in that when the compiler generates the machine code what will eventually be executed, that code won't run on the machine that's doing the generating.

Architecturally, from a compiler designer's perspective, the target machine is a few steps removed from the code-generation process, because the intermediary steps in compilation produce output that's designed to be easy to optimize rather than run on hardware. After the optimization steps, the compiler then produces code intended to run on an actual processor. Thinking about the compiler's operation in this way makes it easy to understand that the final step of turning the optimized pseudocode into the machine code for the target can produce arbitrary machine code and not just code that executes on the host machine.

In this section, the focus is on creating a GNU GCC cross-compiler as the first step to creating an embedded Linux platform. First you build the supporting binutils, then a cross-compiler suitable for compiling glibc, and then the final compiler. For the purpose of illustration, the steps are broken out into several sections. In a real project, all the steps are combined into a script that can be run without intervention.

Some basic terminology is used to describe the players in the process of building the compiler:

- *Build machine:* The computer used to compile the code

- *Host machine:* The computer where the compiler runs

- *Target machine:* The computer for which GCC produces code

The concept of *target* throws many people for a loop. Table 6-1 shows two examples that should make clear the distinction between build, host, and target machines. This table also contains the Canadian cross-compiler case, which is explained in the following paragraph.

Table 6-1. Standard Designations for Cross-Compilers

Machine	Standard Cross-Compiler	Canadian Cross-Compiler
Build	Linux x86	Linux x86
Host	Linux x86	Apple MacOS X86
Target	Linux ARMv7l	Linux ARMv7l

A *Canadian*[1] cross-compiler build is one where the build, host, and target machines are all different. You probably aren't configuring the compiler to run on anything other than an x86 Linux host, but you may need to support development groups running on Windows or Mac OS and want to build the software on a Linux host. It's possible that the build is running an a 64-bit Linux host, producing a compiler that runs on a 32-bit host that generates code for an ARM processor, so it pays to understand the mechanics of cross-building.

The notion of a Canadian cross-build is generally reserved for compiler building. For most other projects, the build and host machines are equal, and only the target changes.

A Note about Building Software

Building open source software like the toolchain involves using a piece of software called Autoconf. This software (which itself is quite complex) creates a make file after running a script called `configure` that inspects the system where the build occurs. When running `configure`, you pass in parameters describing how to build the software for which the `configure` script can't use a reasonable default.

Some of the most confusing parameters passed into `configure` are the values for host, target, and build. These parameters are called *configuration names*, or *triplets*, despite the fact that they now contain four parts. When you're building a toolchain, the triplet describing the target machine is the four-part variety: for example, `arm-none-linux-gnueabi`. This unwieldy string prefixes the name of the toolchain executables so it's clear what the cross-compiler is targeting. It's possible to change this prefix, but the best practice is to leave it be.

Table 6-2 shows a breakdown of the different parts of the configuration name.

---

[1] This describes a certain parliamentary configuration in Ottawa. I had a Canadian buddy explain what this meant, but I lost interest after about the first 30 seconds and pretended to listen for the remaining time before excusing myself to use the bathroom. Canadian politics aren't as interesting as I expected.

Table 6-2. *Configuration Name Values*

Part	Description	Common Values
CPU	The processor label. Use the manufacturer of the CPU, not the board where the CPU resides.	arm, mips, i686, i486, x86_64, ppc, powerpc.
Manufacturer	This can be any value; it's here for informational purposes. For example, the ARM CPU design is built by any number of manufactures, so this could be the ARM licensee that built the silicon.	Free form. none is the most popular. pc is a common value for Intel systems.
Operating System	Operating system	Linux.
Kernel	This describes the libc running on the system. When you're building a toolchain, use gnuabi as the value.	gnuabi, gnueabi, gnulibc, uclibc.

Many users get flustered about what to pick for their processor. The acceptable values for this field are always in flux, and experimentation is a reasonable approach to verify that the triplet is acceptable.

Another thing that is different from other open source packages is that the glibc and libc configuration steps must be done from a directory other than one where the source code files reside. Although the directory can be any one other than where the source resides, the best practice is to create an empty directory and run the configuration program from the newly created directory. One of the great advantages of this practice is that creating a clean build environment is just an rm -rf <build directory> away. Given the experimental nature of building toolchains, being able to start from scratch when building is a great convenience.

Get Comfortable with the Command Line

The examples in this chapter are all executed from a command-line environment. The engineers who build and maintain the kernel, compiler, and libraries work from the command-line, because it's the *lingua franca* of the Linux world. This doesn't show a bias against using IDE tools; years, and in some cases decades, of time and effort have gone into making the command line efficient and productive. After these tools have been built, several graphical environments know how to use them, so time spent at the command prompt is minimized.

These examples use the bash shell. Nearly all distributions use this shell by default. The vast majority of users have graphical desktops, and you run the shell by selecting it from the menu; for example, in Ubuntu, you can start the shell by selecting Applications ➤ Accessories ➤ Terminal from the main menu. If you can't locate the shell on the menu, press the Alt+F2 key combination. On both Gnome and KDE, you're prompted for a program to run (see Figure 6-1; you want to use /bin/bash. Also, be sure to select the "Run in terminal"[2] check box (or the equivalent for your window manager); otherwise, you won't see your shell.

---

[2] It seems odd that you must select "Run in terminal" to ... run a terminal, but that's what necessary. It seems to be tempting a total protonic reversal.

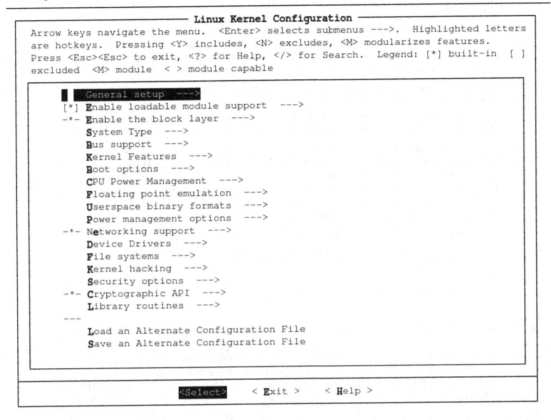

```
.config - Linux Kernel v2.6.29 Configuration
```

Figure 6-1. *Run Application dialogs*

If you're new to the command line, a great hint is to open several command-line terminal windows. This makes it easy to experiment in one window and use another check on the results. A terminal window requires very few resources, so there's no need to economize on the number open at any one point as long as confusion is kept at bay.

Overview of Building a GCC Cross-Compiler

Building GCC involves fetching the sources for several projects, getting them ready for compilation, and then running the compile. The entire process with a reasonably fast computer takes an hour or and requires about 500GB of disk space. In the process, GCC is built twice. An overview of the steps follows:

1. Gather the sources. There are two ways to get the source code for a project: get the sources from version control, or fetch source snapshots created when the software is released. If you're planning to contribute to the development efforts of the projects used in the construction of a toolchain, using source controls is the route you should take; otherwise, you should use the source snapshots. No matter how you plan to get the sources, fetching the source code over a slow connection can sometimes require an hour.

2. Build the binutils. The binutils (binary utilities) provide low-level handling of binary files, such as linking, assembling, and parsing ELF files. The GCC compiler depends on these tools to create an executable, because it generates object files that binutils assemble into an executable image.

3. Build a bootstrap GCC. You build GCC once with minimal settings so that it can be used to then build the C Standard Library—in this case, GNU C Standard Library (glibc). The bootstrap compiler has no such library: it can be used to compile C code, but the functions that most C programmers depend on to interact with the underlying machine, such as opening a file or printing output, don't exist for this compiler.

4. Use the bootstrap GCC to build the glibc library. With the C library, you have a tool you can use to build an executable that runs on the target system. It has the code that opens files, reads, writes, and otherwise functions as you expect when you're using C.

The C Library

In this chapter you build a Linux toolchain with the GNU C Library. This is the library running on the vast majority of desktop Linux machines, and it's the most complete implementation of the C Library for Linux systems. You may even say it's the canonical implementation. Other options for the C Library that are commonly used in embedded systems are addressed later in the book. The process for building a toolchain that uses a different library, like dietlibc, newlib, or uClibc, follows the same pattern of creating a bootstrap compiler, then building the libraries, and then rebuilding the compiler.

The GNU C Library (glibc) is the most ornery to build and get working. After you pass the glibc trial, getting newlib or another library built is much easier. Later in the book, the libraries are discussed and compared to help you select the best one for your project.

Gathering Sources

There are two ways to get the sources: download distribution tars or get the source directly from source control. If you're planning to participate in the development of these projects, get the files from source control, because this is the easiest way to contribute patches and stay current with the development process. If you're planning to use the sources to make a build, and you aren't interested in contributing to the projects, skip the section where the files are fetched as tar archives.

Before you download a bunch of open source projects in your home directory, create a new directory to hold these files so you can stay organized. This directory is known as the *source directory* and is referred to as $SRCDIR later in the chapter:

```
$ export $SRCDIR=~/xtools/src
$ mkdir -p $SRCDIR
```

Getting Sources via Source Control

A *toolchain* is a collection of tools that work together. Each of these tools is a separate project that is maintained by a different group of people. Each project has selected a version-control system and a source-management system that work best for it, and that means not all the projects use the same systems. The following sections outline the commands to fetch the code necessary to build a toolchain from the various projects.

If you don't plan to develop this code, or you don't need the most recent version, skip ahead to the next section, where the release snapshots are downloaded.

Binutils

Binutils is stored in a CVS repository that you can access as an anonymous user by doing the following:

```
$ cvs -z 9 -d :pserver:anoncvs@sourceware.org:/cvs/src login

(use anonymous when prompted for the password)
$ cvs -z 9 -d :pserver:anoncvs@sourceware.org:/cvs/src co binutils
```

As an anonymous user, you can download the code, get updates, and, if you make changes, easily generate diff files that you can send to the project maintainer for inclusion into the project.

GCC

The GCC sources are kept in a subversion source control system. Subversion (SVN) is a successor to Concurrent Versions System (CVS) and shares many of the same commands and semantics of CVS. To get a project, you perform a checkout; when you want to take a snapshot of the source code—say, to get the state of the files for a release—you can tag the sources. The implementation is very different than CVS and in many cases an improvement.

Each release of GCC is tagged with the format gcc_*A_B_C_release*, where *A*, *B*, and *C* are the major, minor, and revision numbers, respectively. Tags in SVN pin the version of the file at a certain point; every time a tag is downloaded, the files are the same. To get a listing of the release tags for the GCC project, do the following:

```
$ svn ls svn://gcc.gnu.org/svn/gcc/tags | grep _release/$
(clipped)
gcc_4_2_4_release/
gcc_4_3_0_release/
gcc_4_3_1_release/
gcc_4_3_2_release/
gcc_4_3_3_release/
```

This command says, "List all the files in the tags directory, and filter to find the lines ending in release/." The tag tree contains many other entries, as you can imagine for a complex project like a compiler. To see a complete listing of the tags, drop the grep filter at the end of the line. To identify the latest release, visit http://gcc.gnu.org and look at the Status section; the version number of the release is clearly displayed as a link to a page with more detail about the release and a link for downloading the source.

There is also a branch where active work occurs for each version, formatted gcc-*A_B-branch*: *A* and *B* are the major and minor versions, respectively. A branch's files, unlike a tag's, aren't immutable. Use a branch to stay abreast of the changes in a certain version of GCC; use a tag if your goal is to get the same files for each checkout, which may be necessary to create a repeatable build process. The branch where the newest work goes is the *trunk* branch. All the newest, not yet officially released code goes into the trunk branch; when it's ready, the trunk becomes the next release.

To get a listing of the current branches, do the following

```
$ svn ls svn://gcc.gnu.org/svn/gcc/branches | grep  "gcc-*[0-9]_*[0-9]-branch"
gcc-3_4-branch/
gcc-4_0-branch/
gcc-4_1-branch/
gcc-4_2-branch/
gcc-4_3-branch/
```

If you're more comfortable getting the sources the old-fashioned way, they're still available as tar files. The easiest way to fetch a tar is using wget, which connects to a remote server and fetches the URL.

Glibc

Next, get glibc. This is a little more complex because in order get support for the ARM architecture, you must download two things: glibc and the special ports project. Some architectures aren't supported directly by the glibc team, with ARM being one of them:

```
$ cvs -z 9 -d :pserver:anoncvs@sources.redhat.com:/cvs/glibc login
$ cvs -z 9 -d :pserver:anoncvs@sources.redhat.com:/cvs/glibc co -r glibc-2_9-branch
libc
$ cd libc
$ cvs -z 9 -d :pserver:anoncvs@sources.redhat.com:/cvs/glibc co -r glibc-2_9-branch
ports
```

GMP and MPFR

The Gnu Multiple Precision (GMP) library uses Mercurial for source code management. Most systems don't have this installed by default; you can install it through the package-management system. Use this for Debian-based systems:

```
$ apt-get install mecurial
```

Or use this for RPM systems:

```
$ yum install mercurial
```

After Mercurial is installed, you check out a project much as in other source code control systems:

```
hg clone http://gmplib.org:8000/gmp
```

This command checks out the sources of the project into the gmp directory. Mercurial is a distributed source control system like Git and works the same, in principle.

MPFR uses SVN for source control. You access the repository with the following command:

```
svn checkout svn://scm.gforge.inria.fr/svn/mpfr/trunk mpfr
```

A Linux Kernel

The Linux kernel project is stored as a Git repository. To get this from source control, you need to clone Linus's Git tree by doing the following

```
$ git clone git://git.kernel.org/pub/scm/linux/kernel/git/torvalds/linux-2.6.git
```

This tree has quite a bit of data, and the cloning process can take upwards of 45 minutes on a slow Internet day. The GCC (and most other GNU sources) are available for download from GNU's FTP server at ftp://gcc.gnu.org/pub. In the case of GCC, the project is located at ftp://gcc.gnu.org/pub/gcc/releases/gcc-<release>. You can navigate this FTP server using your browser: just type the URL into the web address control. For example, to download the GCC 4.3.3 source tarball, do the following:

```
wget ftp://gcc.gnu.org/pub/gcc/releases/gcc-4.3.3/gcc-4.3.3.tar.bz2
```

This command fetches the file at ftp://gcc.gnu.org/pub/gcc/releases/gcc-4.3.3/gcc-4.3.3.tar.bz2 and puts it in into the current directory as gcc-4.3.3.tar.bz2.

■ **Note** bz2 or gz? In this chapter (as well as the rest of the book), open source software is frequently offered as both .tar.gz and tar.bz2 files. Both of these extensions are compression systems. The newer bz2 compression algorithm does a better job making a smaller file, but gz is more widespread. In both cases, the compressed file is in tar format, which is supported by every system.

Getting via Source Archives

You'll fetch files from a variety of places. Although the examples have specific version numbers, there will probably be something newer by the time this book makes it into your hands. These files are kept at FTP servers, and you can easily download them using wget. Following is a brief section describing how to get the sources for each. After you download the files, you can uncompress them with tar.

Binutils

This archive is fairly small and downloads quickly. For this example, you use version 2.20. If you want a different version, change the name of the file to the version number to download. If you're curious about what versions are available, point your browser to http://ftp.gnu.org/gnu/binutils for a directory listing:

```
$ wget http://ftp.gnu.org/gnu/binutils/binutils-2.20.tar.gz
```

Then, unpack the file using the following command.

```
$ tar xzf binutils-2.20.tar.gz
```

Glibc

Glibc is a little more complex, because you must download both the sources for the project and the add-ons, and you need to uncompress the add-ons into the glibc directory:

```
$ wget ftp://ftp.gnu.org/gnu/glibc/glibc-2.9.tar.bz2
$ wget ftp://ftp.gnu.org/gnu/glibc/glibc-ports-2.9.tar.bz2
```

Unpack the files as follows:

```
$ tar xjf glibc-2.9.tar.gz
$ cd glibc-2.9
$ tar xjf ../glibc-ports-2.9.tar.bz2
```

■ **Note** The `ports` code is necessary only if glibc is being built for the following architectures: MIPS, ARM, and PowerPC. Other architectures are supported in the main glibc project.

GCC

The source code is located at `ftp://gcc.gnu.org/pub/gcc/releases`, where you can pick your release tar file. This example uses 4.3.3; you can download this file by doing the following:

```
$ wget ftp://gcc.gnu.org/pub/gcc/releases/gcc-4.3.3/gcc-4.3.3.tar.gz
```

Each GCC release is in its own directory, where there are archive files for each release and a test suite. In this example, you download the tar file with the complete GCC sources.

GMP and MPFR

Like the other projects, these projects create source snapshots for each release. You get both with these commands:

```
$ wget http://www.mpfr.org/mpfr-current/mpfr-2.4.1.tar.bz2
$ wget ftp://ftp.gmplib.org/pub/gmp-4.3.1/gmp-4.3.1.tar.bz2
```

Now you have all the files necessary to build GCC.

A Linux Kernel

You need not just any random Linux kernel, but the one you'll be using on the board. The build process uses some of the headers from the kernel sources to build the compiler and the standard library. This doesn't mean the standard library has to be rebuilt when you switch kernels, because the software interfaces presented by the kernel are stable at this point. Here, you fetch Linux kernel 2.6.28; you should get the kernel that you plan to use with your board:

```
$ wget http://www.kernel.org/pub/linux/kernel/v2.6/linux-2.6.28.3.tar.bz2
$ tar xjf linux-2.6.28.3.tar.bz2
```

Building GCC

The build process for this (and most other) open source software follows the configure/make/install pattern to build the source code. The configure step runs a script that inspects the system, ensuring that the necessary tools are present and interrogating the compiler's support features. The result of the configuration script is a file with the system settings, files necessary to build the project, and a make file. The make file is a complex but standard GNU make file and is run from the command line to actually build the software. When that's complete, you use make again to install the software.

■ **Note** During the process of building a toolchain and libraries, you may want to experiment with the options you send to configure to get a different toolchain for your specific target architecture. Experimentation is good. Always start with an empty build directory! The debris from the prior configure can result in some very unpredictable problems. Because the configuration occurs in a separate directory from the source code, you can unceremoniously delete the contents with rm -rf *.

None of these packages let you build from the source directory, so you need to create another directory for the purpose of running configure and running the build. You may find this confusing at first, because the directory where make runs doesn't have any files to make, such as in other projects. But rest assured, the projects will build.

The Build Environment

After you download all those files, it's easy to get confused about what is where. In this example, all the source files are in $SRCDIR, with a directory for each of the projects. So that this section is easier to follow, it introduces some additional environment variables to make the examples clearer (see Table 6-3). Because the source code may have been downloaded from release snapshots or checked out from version control, the directory on your system will be different for each.

Table 6-3. Environment Variables Used for Toolchain Build

Shell Variable	Definition
$SRCDIR The base source directory. All the sources for the build should reside underneath this directory.	~/xtools/src
$BINUTILS_SRC The sources for the binutils project.	$SRCDIR/<binutils source directory>
$KERNEL_SRC The sources for the kernel.	Location of the kernel used with the target

`$GCC_SRC` The sources for GCC.	`$SRCDIR/<gcc source directory>`
`$GLIBC_SRC` The sources for glibc. The decompressed ports archive is in this directory.	`$SRCDIR/<glibc source directory>`
`$GMP_SRC` The sources for GMP.	`$SRCDIR/<gmp source directory>`
`$MPFR_SRC` The sources for MPFR.	`$SRCDIR/<mpfr source directory>`
`$BUILDDIR` The directory where the binaries are built.	`~/xtools/build`
`$TARGETMACH` The machine that is executing the code built by the toolchain.	The triplet for the target machine. In this case, it's `arm-none-linux-gnueabi`.
`$BUILDMACH` The machine where the build is running.	Set this to `i686-pc-linux-gnu`. The configure scripts usually guess the right value for this field; specify it here to be pedantic.
`$INSTALLDIR` Where the toolchain is installed on the build machine.	Where the toolchain binaries are installed. This can be any directory. You need write privileges to this directory. In this example, use `/opt/arm`.
`$SYSROOTDIR` The location where the target system's libraries and header files belong.	Needs to be under the toolchain installation directory. It can be any name that doesn't conflict with a directory that the toolchain creates. In this example, use `$INSTALLDIR/sysroot`.

For each of the steps, a little code deletes the prior build directory, if it exists, and re-creates the build directory. This ensures that the configuration and build environment are completely clean and aren't affected by prior builds:

```
[ -d $BUILDDIR/<build directory> ] \
        && rm -rf $BUILDDIR/<build directory>
mkdir $BUILDDIR/<build directory>
```

The first line performs an `rm -rf` if the directory already exists; otherwise, the command is skipped. The next line creates the directory so that the output of the `configure` script has someplace to go.

Binutils

The first project to build is binutils, which supplies common routines for handling Executable and Linkable Format (ELF) based executable files. ELF is the format that Linux uses for binary executable files. The GCC compiler relies on binutils to provide much of the platform-specific functionality. Binutils provides the following utilities:

- as: The Gnu assembler. Transforms mnemonic assembler code into opcodes for the target processor.

- ld: The linker. It takes as input a group of object files and creates a binary file such as an executable or shared library or other object file. The linker lays out the file in its final format.

- ar: The archive program that packages a group of object files into a single library file to make using the object files more convenient.

- objdump: Prints out the contents of an ELF file. Can be used as a disassembler.

- objcopy: Makes a copy of an ELF file, allowing you to control what is copied in ELF terms, such as selecting certain sections of the file or removing debugging symbols.

- c++filt: Demangles a C++ symbol. The compiler generates internal symbols to handle classes, namespaces, and overloaded functions; this undoes the process to make finding problems in source code easier.

- size: Prints the size of sections in the file. This is an important tool that's used when minimizing a system's size.

- strings: Prints the null-terminated string constants in a program.

- strip: Removes debugging and other bookkeeping information.

Building binutils is a nice place to begin building a toolchain, because it's very straightforward and rarely fails. Look at Table 6-4 to analyze the build options:

```
$ [ -d $BUILDDIR/binutils ] && rm -rf $BUILDDIR/$binutils
$ mkdir $BUILDDIR/binutils
$ cd $BUILDDIR/binutils

$ $BINUTILS_SRC/configure \
        --disable-werror \
        --build=$BUILDMACH \
        --target=$TARGETMACH \
        --prefix=$INSTALLDIR \
        --with-sysroot=$SYSROOTDIR
```

Table 6-4. *Build Values and their Explanations*

Configure Parameter	Meaning
`--build = $BUILDMACH`	The type of build system. The `configure` script can guess this, but it's a good habit to tell it what system is being used.
`--target=$TARGETMACH`	What machine is being targeted for the build. The value here follows the same format as the `build` parameter. In this case, you're building for an ARM processor that is running Linux.
`--prefix=$INSTALLDIR`	The installation directory of binutils. This is called `prefix` because it's tacked on to the front of the normal installation directory.
`--disable-werror`	The compiler builds with the flag that considers warnings as errors. This version has a few warnings; using this flag allows the build to continue running in spite of the one or two warnings that appear.

The `configure` script runs and produces output showing what it's inspecting. When it's complete, run the make:

```
$ cd $BUILDDIR/binutils
$ make
```

The software builds; this takes about 20 minutes on a typical machine. When the build completes, put the newly built binutils in the installation directory:

```
$ make install
```

Kernel Headers

The next step is getting the headers for the kernel that is used on the target board. This involves using the kernel sources to create some header files and then copying those header files into a directory that the other tools will use. This may seem a bit confusing, but these files are necessary because the kernel has the machine-specific information (such as the number of bytes in an integer) that the remainder of the programs need to build code for the target. Furthermore, these files have information about how to call kernel services that the C libraries use to access kernel functionality, because much of the C Standard Library is a layer over the operating system, providing a uniform API or accessing files for the heap.

To get these files, the kernel must be configured for the target machine. In this case, the target is the ARM Integrator board. This is a board that ARM, Ltd. uses in its developer kits and is therefore well supported in the kernel.

Unlike other steps, this step uses the `make mrproper` command to clean up the environment before the build. Running this command puts the kernel source directory in the same state as when the directory was unpacked:

```
$ cd $KERNEL_SRC
$ make mrproper

$ make ARCH=$TARGETARCH integrator_defconfig
```

The screen fills with output as the system tells you that it's first building some tools that will run on the host platform and then sets the configuration for the kernel build to the settings in the `integrator_defconfig` file. The *integrator* is a device created by ARM for doing development work and is the closest thing in the ARM architecture to a generic device. If you have a specific ARM board in mind for your project, you can select that board's `defconfig` now. Of course, if you're building for a non-ARM architecture, select the appropriate `defconfig` for your board. A `defconfig` is the kernel's way of storing the default set of build settings and is discussed in "Building the Kernel" section later in this chapter.

If you're new to building the kernel (also covered in detail later in the chapter), the first step is putting the source tree in the right state to build for the target. It's not necessary at this point to configure the particulars of the kernel; you just need to get the architecture and processor correct.

Now that the kernel source tree is ready to build for the intended target, this command results in the proper headers being generated and then installs them to the toolchain:

```
mkdir -p $INSTALLDIR/sysroot/usr
    make ARCH=$TARGETARCH headers_check
    make ARCH=$TARGETARCH \
INSTALL_HDR_PATH=$INSTALLDIR/sysroot/usr \
headers_install
(clipped)
  INSTALL include/linux/wimax (1 file)
  INSTALL include/linux (349 files)
  INSTALL include/mtd (6 files)
  INSTALL include/rdma (1 file)
  INSTALL include/sound (9 files)
  INSTALL include/video (3 files)
  INSTALL include (0 file)
  INSTALL include/asm (31 files)
```

Bootstrap (Stage 1) GCC

You're ready to build the bootstrap GCC. Building GCC for a production system is done in several steps, where each steps builds a compiler with more capabilities. The first step is creating a compiler that can then be used to build the Standard C Library (in this case, glibc, but it could be another library). The compiler without a Standard Library is functional, but it doesn't have the bits necessary to produce an executable on a Linux platform. You replace the bootstrap compiler with the final compiler later in the process.

■ **Note** Although a compiler without the standard libraries isn't that useful for producing applications, it's a perfectly good tool for building a Linux kernel, which itself has no dependencies on a Standard C Library.

The build for this is more complex than for prior packages, because you're sending more information into the `configure` script and the make targets aren't standard. In addition, after running the build, you need to create a symlink so that other components can build properly:

```
[ -d $BUILDDIR/bootstrap-gcc ] && rm -rf $BUILDDIR/bootstrap-gcc

mkdir $BUILDDIR/bootstrap-gcc
cd $BUILDDIR/bootstrap-gcc

$SRCDIR/$GCC/configure \
    --build=$BUILDMACH \
    --host=$BUILDMACH \
    --target=$TARGETMACH \
    --prefix=$INSTALLDIR \
    --without-headers \
    --enable-boostrap \
    --enable-languages="c" \
    --disable-threads \
    --enable-__cxa_atexit \
    --disable-libmudflap \
    --with-gnu-ld --with-gnu-as \
    --disable-libssp --disable-libgomp \
    --disable-nls --disable-shared

make all-gcc install-gcc
make all-target-libgcc install-target-libgcc

ln -s $INSTALLDIR/lib/gcc/arm-none-linux-gnueabi/4.3.3/libgcc.a \
    $INSTALLDIR/lib/gcc/arm-none-linux-gnueabi/4.3.3/libgcc_sh.a
```

Table 6-5 explains the purpose of each of the command-line parameters passed to `configure`. Most of these parameters disable some feature that's not necessary to do what this compiler is meant to do: build the standard libraries. A few parameters tell the software what type of machine is being targeted so the proper code is generated.

Table 6-5. *Bootstrap GCC Configuration Parameters*

Configure Parameter	Meaning
--build=$BUILDMACH	The type of build system. The `configure` script can guess this, but it's a good habit to tell it what system is being used.
--target=$TARGETMACH	What machine is being targeted for the build.
--prefix=$INSTALLDIR	The installation directory of binutils. This is called `prefix` because this value is tacked on to the front of the normal installation directory.
--enable-languages="c"	Only the C language is necessary at this point.
--disable-threads	Disables thread support. Thread support comes from the libc library that this bootstrap compiler is building.

--enable-__cxa_atexit	Another C++-related configuration command describing how to implement the atexit() function call.
--disable-libmudflap	Library for runtime bounds checking. It isn't necessary.
--disable-libssp	Supplies protection from buffer overflow or stack-smashing attacks.
--disable-libgomp	Disables the inclusion of the OpenMP programming API for parallel programming. A parallel execution framework is unnecessary to build the full C library, and it also depends on the thread library, which isn't built at this stage.
--disable-nls	Removes internationalization.
--disable-shared	Specifies that the compiler doesn't have support for shared libraries. Shared library support is something else that is implemented with the yet-to-be-built C library.
--enable-arch=armv4	Gives the compilation process a hint about the target processor, so it can generate the right code.
--with-gnu-as, --with-gnu-ld	Instructs the configure script to use the GNU assembler and linker, as opposed to some other linker or assembler on the system.

The make targets all-gcc install-gcc create the base compiler and install it in the prefix directory. The next parameters all-target-gcc install-target-gcc build a library that GCC uses during code generation, such as exception handling and floating-point emulation routines. This needs to be built before the Standard C Library, because this build relies on libgcc.

Last, there is a bit of trickery, when a symlink is created. The toolchain wants to link to the libgcc_sh file, which is for shared libraries, even when doing static linking. If your toolchain build is targeting a different platform or uses different software versions, you need to adjust this command appropriately.

Creating Glibc Headers

The glibc headers are the used by the target system's compiler to get the definitions for the functions created by glibc. The GNU C Library, like others, isn't completely written in C; some of the code is written in the C preprocessor. There are also some circular dependencies: in order for glibc to compile, it needs some of the headers it generates that describe the host system.

Creating the headers involves configuring glibc and then running a portion of the build. You configure glibc now and then use the same configuration in the next step; you use the environment variables CC, LD, and AS to use the bootstrap cross-compiler, because you want to build code for the target machine:

```
[ -d $BUILDDIR/libc ] && rm -rf $BUILDDIR/libc
    mkdir -p $BUILDDIR/libc
    cd $BUILDDIR/libc
```

```
echo "libc_cv_forced_unwind=yes" > config.cache
echo "libc_cv_c_cleanup=yes" >> config.cache
export PATH=$INSTALLDIR/bin:$PATH

export CROSS=arm-none-linux-gnueabi
export CC=${CROSS}-gcc
export LD=${CROSS}-ld
export AS=${CROSS}-as

$LIBC_SRC/configure \
    --build=$BUILDMACH \
    --host=$TARGETMACH \
    --prefix=$SYSROOTDIR/usr \
    --with-headers=$SYSROOTDIR/usr/include \
    --config-cache \
    --enable-add-ons=glibc-ports-2.9,nptl \
    --enable-kernel=2.6.0

make -k install-headers \
    cross_compiling=yes \
    install_root=$SYSROOTDIR

ln -s $INSTALLDIR/lib/gcc/arm-none-linux-gnueabi/4.3.3/libgcc.a \
    $INSTALLDIR/lib/gcc/arm-none-linux-gnueabi/4.3.3/libgcc_eh.a
```

This is more convoluted than the others so far. First, the file config.cache is created with the following lines:

```
libc_cv_forced_unwind=yes
libc_cv_c_cleanup=yes
```

These lines prevent the configuration process from trying to run code compiled with the cross-compiler on the host system. Because the compiler generates code that runs on an ARM computer (and the compiler doesn't have the library support to create executables on Linux, which is why you're building glibc in the first place!) it won't run on the host system. By putting the results of these configuration parameters in a file and telling the configure script to use the cache, the code isn't executed, and the cached values is used instead. Table 6-6 lists the configuration values for glibc.

Table 6-6. *Configuration Values for glibc*

Configure Parameter	Meaning
--build =$BUILDMACH	The type of build system. The configure script can guess this, but it's a good habit to tell it what system is being used. Unless your computer has a big red switch on the side, this is the correct identifier.

`--target=$TARGETDIR`	What machine is being targeted for the build.
`--with-sysroot=$SYSROOTDIR/usr/include`	The root directory of the newly built system. When the toolchain is being built for an embedded system, this contains the files that are installed relative to the / directory.
`--enable-add-ons`	Tells the configuration script to see the `ports` directory (remember, your processor's support is in that directory) and all other glibc add-ons. The one add-on you're concerned with is nptl (native POSIX thread library); the rest are harmless at this point.
`--with-tls  --with-__thread`	Options that work together to support the nptl feature by enabling thread local storage.
`--cache-file=config.cache`	Instructs `configure` to read the information in `config.cache`. Doing this results in your configure process skipping some problematic tests, because `configure` checks its cache before running code in order to execute faster.
`--with-headers=/opt/arm/include`	The location of the system headers to use with the build. These headers are used by glibc because many glibc functions rely on kernel system calls; these header files contain the necessary code to enable those calls. In addition, the headers include architecture-specific information used by glibc.
`--enable-kernel=2.6.0`	Instructs glibc that this software is running on a kernel that's 2.6 or later.

The symlink that is created is due to the bootstrap toolchain attempting to link to the `libgcc_eh` file in all cases. This file contains routines for executables that use shared object and shouldn't be included, because you've built a static bootstrap compiler. The `libgcc.a` file has all the symbols you need; creating this symlink is a maneuver to satisfy the linker, because it insists that it can link to `libgcc_eh.a` even though no symbols are used from this file.

Building Glibc

At this point, the directory `$INSTALLDIR` contains a toolchain that's complete enough to build the GNU C Standard Library. As with the other tools, this step involves a configuration and an installation step. But it has some differences in that the compiler used is the newly created cross-compiler, not the host compiler as in the prior steps:

```
[ -d $BUILDDIR/$LIBC ] && rm -rf $BUILDDIR/$LIBC
mkdir -p $BUILDDIR/$LIBC
cd $BUILDDIR/$LIBC
```

```
echo "libc_cv_forced_unwind=yes" > config.cache
echo "libc_cv_c_cleanup=yes" >> config.cache
export PATH=$INSTALLDIR/bin:$PATH

export CROSS=arm-none-linux-gnueabi
export CC=${CROSS}-gcc
export LD=${CROSS}-ld
export AS=${CROSS}-as

$SRCDIR/$LIBC/configure \
    --build=$BUILDMACH \
    --host=$TARGETMACH \
    --prefix=/usr \
    --with-headers=$SYSROOTDIR/usr/include \
    --config-cache \
    --enable-add-ons=glibc-ports-2.9,nptl \
    --enable-kernel=2.6.0

make -k install-headers cross_compiling=yes install_root=$SYSROOTDIR
ln -s /opt/arm/lib/gcc/arm-none-linux-gnueabi/4.3.3/libgcc.a \
    /opt/arm/lib/gcc/arm-none-linux-gnueabi/4.3.3/libgcc_eh.a

make
make install_root=${SYSROOT} install
```

The build for the glibc can take an hour or two on a reasonably fast computer. After the build completes and the software is installed, it's time for the final build of GCC. This produces a compiler that includes a complete Standard Library and is ready for use to build the kernel or an arbitrary user program.

Building the Next GCC

With glibc compiled, you can now build a cross-compiler that has enough code to build an executable for the target; you need also build the GMP and MPFR libraries. These libraries use some of glibc and expect more than a bootstrap compiler installed on a system. This step builds a cross-compiler with all the dependencies necessary for these libraries. In addition, this cross-compiler has everything necessary for building static applications, so you can stop after this step if you're just building static libraries:

```
$ [ -d $BUILDDIR/final-gcc ] && rm -rf $BUILDDIR/final-gcc
$ mkdir -p $BUILDDIR/final-gcc
$ cd $BUILDDIR/final-gcc

$ echo "libc_cv_forced_unwind=yes" > config.cache
$ echo "libc_cv_c_cleanup=yes" >> config.cache
$ BUILD_CC=gcc
```

```
$ GCC_SRC/configure \
        --build=$BUILDMACH \
        --target=$TARGETMACH \
        --prefix=$INSTALLDIR \
        --with-sysroot=$SYSROOTDIR \
        --enable-languages=c \
        --with-gnu-as \
        --with-gnu-ld \
        --disable-multilib \
        --with-float=soft \
        --disable-sjlj-exceptions \
        --disable-nls --enable-threads=posix \
        --enable-long-longx

$ make all-gcc
$ make install-gcc
```

Table 6-7 lists the GCC build configuration options.

Table 6-7. *GCC Build Configuration Options.*

Configure Parameter	Meaning
--enable-languages=c	This cross-compiler is built with C support for now.
-disable-sjlj-exceptions	This is specific to C++ exception handling and means "set jump, long jump." GCC's C++ uses a table-driven exception-handling system that's more reliable.
-enable-__cxa_atexit	This is another C++-related configuration command describing how to implement the atexit() function call.
-enable-threads=posix	This instructs the glibc to include the POSIX threading API. The other option for this (aside from no thread support), LinuxThreads, is considered obsolete.

Building GMP and MPFR

The GMP library performs arithmetic on integers, floating-point, and irrational numbers. When the language needs to add multibyte numbers (and there's no opcode in the processor to handle such a task), GMP does the work. MPFR is a library that handles floating-point operations with high precision, greater than that of the processor.

GMP

This library must be built first, because MPFR depends on it to build. This library builds much like the others. Notice how the CC, LD, and AS environment variables are set, because this code is cross-compiled for the target. There is one additional trick—because the cross-compiler doesn't have shared library support, you need to pass in the -static flag as an argument to the compiler and request a static GMP library:

```
$ [ -d $BUILDDIR/gmp ] && rm -rf $BUILDDIR/gmp
$ mkdir -p $BUILDDIR/gmp
$ cd $BUILDDIR/gmp

$ export PATH=$INSTALLDIR/bin:$PATH

$ export CROSS=arm-none-linux-gnueabi
$ export CC=${CROSS}-gcc
$ export LD=${CROSS}-ld
$ export AS=${CROSS}-as
$ export CFLAGS=-static

$ $SRCDIR/$GMP/configure \
        --build=$BUILDMACH \
        --host=$TARGETMACH \
        --prefix=$INSTALLDIR \
        --disable-shared
$ make
$ make install
```

This code builds quickly. The parameters passed in to configure have been covered already in this chapter.

MPFR

This toolkit for floating-point arithmetic is built next. The parameters for building it are as familiar as those for GMP, with the difference being that you must pass in the location of the GMP library:

```
$ [ -d $BUILDDIR/mpfr ] && rm -rf $BUILDDIR/mpfr
$ mkdir -p $BUILDDIR/mpfr
$ cd $BUILDDIR/mpfr

$ export PATH=$INSTALLDIR/bin:$PATH
$ export CROSS=arm-none-linux-gnueabi
$ export CC=${CROSS}-gcc
$ export LD=${CROSS}-ld
$ export AS=${CROSS}-as
$ export CFLAGS=-static

$ $SRCDIR/$MPFR/configure \
        --build=$BUILDMACH \
        --host=$TARGETMACH \
        --prefix=$INSTALLDIR \
        --with-gmp=$INSTALLDIR
```

```
$ make
$ make install
```

Like GMP, MPFR builds quickly, this process shouldn't take more than a few minutes.

Building the Final GCC

Now that all the necessary libraries are in order, you can build the final toolchain. This is the final step in the process; after it's complete, the $INSTALLDIR directory contains a complete toolchain you can use for building applications for the target.

Configuring this toolchain is much like configuring the bootstrap toolchain. Notice that the configure statement points to the newly built GMP and MPFR libraries during the configure step and that the CC, LD, and AS variables aren't overridden because you want to use the compiler on your build system. The executable that is produced runs on the build machine, but you're producing code for the host machine:

```
$ [ -d $BUILDDIR/final-gcc-2 ] && rm -rf $BUILDDIR/final-gcc-2
$ mkdir -p $BUILDDIR/final-gcc-2
$ cd $BUILDDIR/final-gcc-2

$ echo "libc_cv_forced_unwind=yes" > config.cache
$ echo "libc_cv_c_cleanup=yes" >> config.cache

$  $GCC_SRC/configure \
        --build=$BUILDMACH \
        --target=$TARGETMACH \
        --prefix=$INSTALLDIR \
        --with-sysroot=$SYSROOTDIR \
        --enable-languages=c \
        --with-gnu-as \
        --with-gnu-ld \
        --disable-multilib \
        --with-float=soft \
        --disable-sjlj-exceptions \
        --disable-nls --enable-threads=posix \
        --disable-libmudflap \
        --disable-libssp \
        --enable-long-longx \
        --with-shared \
        --with-gmp=$INSTALLDIR \
        --with-mpfr=$INSTALLDIR

$  make
$  make install
```

This build runs for about an hour, even on a reasonably fast machine. When it's complete, your computer has a cross-compiler installed at $INSTALLDIR.

Building Toolchains with Crosstool-NG

Creating a toolchain from scratch, as you can see, is tricky. The architecture and processor used in the example were chosen because of their widespread support in the Linux community. Some processors aren't as well supported and require patches or other non-obvious changes in order for the tools to build. The cross-compilation process, although completely open, is complex to the point that understanding it well enough to diagnose problems and keep abreast of the changes to the tools requires a serious time commitment.

A tool like crosstool-NG exists to encapsulate the knowledge about building toolchains and keeping the process up to date as the software advances. Crosstool-NG (the *NG* stands for "next generation," a nod to a television show of which you may have heard) grew from the efforts of Dan Kegel, who created a collection of scripts (the original crosstool) to build cross-compilers by changing some configuration files.[3] This script was later improved and morphed into the crosstool-NG project.

Using crosstool-NG reduces the effort for building a toolchain to a matter of choosing items from a menu. To get the tool, visit this URL for the latest version: `http://ymorin.is-a-geek.org/dokuwiki/projects/crosstool`. The following example uses version 13.2. By the time this book is published, the newest version will certainly be newer, given the amount activity on the project and the frequency of changes to the projects used by crosstool-NG.

Here are the steps necessary to create a toolchain using crosstool-NG. First, download the tools and extract them:

```
$ wget http://ymorin.is-a-geek.org/download/crosstool-ng/crosstool-ng-1.3.2.tar.bz2
$ tar xjf crosstool-ng-1.3.2.tar.bz2
```

Crosstool-NG has a short configure and installation process:

```
$./configure -prefix=~/ct
```

During the configuration process, crosstool-NG checks to make sure all the necessary utilities are installed, producing an error message if some are missing:

```
$make install
```

You can configure crosstool-NG to run from the directory where it was unpacked using the `-local` option when configuring. However, having the software installed in a separate directory is good practice. It includes samples that contain the typical tool settings for a processor and architecture. The samples in the distribution have been checked and should yield a toolchain without error. To list the samples, use the following command:

```
~/ct/bin/ct-ng list-samples
(clipped)
armeb-unknown-linux-uclibc
armeb-unknown-linux-uclibcgnueabi
arm-unknown-eabi
arm-unknown-elf
arm-unknown-linux-gnu
arm-unknown-linux-gnueabi
(clipped)
```

The toolchain you created earlier in this chapter, `arm-unknown-linux-gnueabi`, can also be created with this tool, which is what you do in the following few steps. To get additional information about any

---

[3] As somebody whose first job in embedded Linux was building toolchains, I was amazed how well this tool worked.

one of the toolchains listed, prefix any of them with show-. Here's the command for arm-unknown-linux-gnueabi:

```
$ ./bin/ct-ng show-arm-unknown-linux-gnueabi
    arm-unknown-linux-gnueabi  [g  ]
    OS        : linux-2.6.26.8
    GMP/MPFR  : gmp-4.2.4 / mpfr-2.3.2
    binutils  : binutils-2.19
    C compiler: gcc-4.3.2 (C,C++,Fortran,Java)
    C library : glibc-2.7
    Tools     :
```

You need to make a few additional changes in the configuration program, such as removing sstrip (a tool for reducing a program's size by a few bytes, which causes frequent compilation problems) and turning off the Fortran and Java compiler front ends, because these frequently fail to compile the intended target. You access the configuration program for crosstool-NG by doing the following. The configuration program interface should be familiar at this point:

```
$./bin/ct-ng menuconfig
```

To configure the build process using the arm-unknown-linux-gnueabi sample, do the following:

```
$./bin/ct-ng
```

The software does some work and outputs a message indicating that the build is ready. This process takes an hour or so. When it's complete, the toolchain is installed at ~/x-tools/arm-unknown-linux-gnueabi/bin and is ready for use. The build log, stored in the ~/x-tools directory as build.log.bz2, is verbose. Every file that's created, unpacked, or copied, along with each command executed, is kept in the log.

Considering that crosstool-NG builds completely from source and is largely implemented as bash scripts, using it to generate a toolchain is a better alternative than maintaining the code necessary to build a toolchain yourself. As the open source community updates and improves GCC, glibc, and its family of tools, the code around building this software also remains in flux, creating a maintenance task that crosstool-NG completes nicely.

Creating the Root File System

Every Linux system has a root file system. On a desktop machine, the root file system is stored on a magnetic disk; but on an embedded system, the root file system may be stored on a flash device, packaged with the kernel, or, for some larger embedded systems, stored on a disk drive. During the bootup process, the kernel always looks for an initial RAM disk. The initial RAM disk comes from a file attached to the kernel during the build process that is uncompressed into RAM memory when the kernel starts. If a file to boot the system (initrd) is present, the kernel attempts to use the initial RAM disk.

Because the initial RAM disk is built during the kernel build process, it's being built before the kernel. When the root file system is completed, the kernel build process points at the root file system created during this step.

Although a fully functional root file system can be just one executable file or a few device files, for this example the root file system consists of a complete set of command-line tools typically found on a desktop system—compliments of the BusyBox project. BusyBox contains minimal implementations of the commands found on a desktop system, and all the utilities in BusyBox are compiled into one executable and the file system. The file system is then populated with symlinks to the BusyBox executable. In the `main()` of BusyBox, a switch uses the name of the file (which is the name of the symlink used to invoke the program) to figure out what code to execute.

Configuring the Environment

Before you build the root file system, create an installation folder for the executables, libraries, and other files that go into the root file system. From the perspective of the machine that eventually uses the root file system, the contents below this directory are the / of that machine. This is referred to as `$RFS` in the remainder of this section, because the directory can be in any arbitrary location:

```
$ export RFS=$RFS
$ mkdir -p $RFS
```

Building and Installing BusyBox

Start by downloading and unpacking the source code

```
$ http://busybox.net/downloads/busybox-1.13.3.tar.bz2
$tar xjf http://busybox.net/downloads/busybox-1.13.3.tar.bz2
```

The method for configuring the tool should now be familiar. For example purposes, use the `defconfig` option that enables just about every BusyBox option except debugging:

```
$ make defconfig
$ make menuconfig
```

In the `menuconfig` interface, do these two things:

1. Set the Cross-Compiler Prefix under the build options to point to the newly created toolchain. This option is under BusyBox Settings" ➤ Build Options Menu. Set this value to the entire path and name of the cross-compiler. For example, using the cross-compiler built in this chapter, the value is `/opt/arm/bin/arm-none-linux-gnueabi-`. The trailing - is important!

2. Change the BusyBox installation to $RFS. Look for this option under BusyBox Settings ➤ Installation Options. This is where BusyBox will put its executable and symlinks after the build process.

    After you've made these changes, the next step is starting a build:

```
$ make
$ make install
```

The folder $RFS contains the start of a root file system:

```
bin
linuxrc -> bin/busybox
sbin
usr
```

This root file system isn't yet complete. It's missing some critical components such as the libraries, device files, and a few mount points. The next sections cover how to gather the rest of the components from the toolchain.

Libraries

The BusyBox project was built with shared libraries—the glibc shared libraries in this case. These libraries need to be in the root file system when the board runs; otherwise the program will refuse to load. In addition to the shared libraries, the system needs the program that loads the program and performs the dynamic linking of the program and the shared libraries, usually called ld.so or ld-linux.so. Just like everything else in Linux, this program doesn't have a fixed name—it can have any arbitrary name, so long as all parties agree on the label.

On a desktop Linux system, to find the name of the library loader, use the ldd command to show the libraries loaded by a program:

```
$ ldd `which ls`
        linux-gate.so.1 =>  (0xb7f6c000)
        librt.so.1 => /lib/tls/i686/cmov/librt.so.1 (0xb7f4f000)
        libselinux.so.1 => /lib/libselinux.so.1 (0xb7f36000)
        libacl.so.1 => /lib/libacl.so.1 (0xb7f2f000)
        libc.so.6 => /lib/tls/i686/cmov/libc.so.6 (0xb7de0000)
        libpthread.so.0 => /lib/tls/i686/cmov/libpthread.so.0 (0xb7dc8000)
        /lib/ld-linux.so.2 (0xb7f6d000)
        libdl.so.2 => /lib/tls/i686/cmov/libdl.so.2 (0xb7dc4000)
        libattr.so.1 => /lib/libattr.so.1 (0xb7dbf000)
```

Look at the list, and find the program that starts with an absolute path. In this system, the file is /lib/ld-linux.so.2. When running a program linked with shared libraries, the operating system runs /lib/ld-linux.so.2 and passes the name of the program to run (along with its parameters) to the loader.

To generate this output, ldd runs the program in question. This can't be done with the cross-compiled BusyBox, because it contains binary code for an ARM processor, and the build was likely done on an Intel PC. The alternative to using ldd is the much cruder but effective solution of looking for strings in the executable that start with lib:

```
$strings $RFS/bin/busybox | grep lib
/lib/ld-linux.so.3
libm.so.6
libc.so.6
__libc_start_main
/lib/modules
/var/lib/misc/udhcpd.leases
/lib/firmware
/var/lib/hwclock/adjtime
```

The files you're interested are /lib/ld-linux.so.3 (the loader), libm.so.6, and libc.so.6. These files are symlinks stored under the $SYSROOT directory using during the toolchain build. To get them in the root file system, create the directory and copy the files:

```
$ cd $RFS
$ Mkdir lib
$ pushd $SYSROOT/usr/lib
$ cp libc.so.6 libm.so.6 ld-linux.so.3 /home/gene/build-gcc/rfs/lib/
$ popd
```

To avoid the problem of shared libraries, BusyBox can be linked directly to the libc libraries (static linking) so that the .so files aren't needed on the target. As an experiment, try static linking: use the search in BusyBox's menuconfig to find the menu item, rebuild the root file system, and see how the size changes.

Creating Device Nodes and Directories

Linux requires that two devices be present in order to work correctly: console and null. A device node is a way for a user program to communicate with a kernel device driver. These are created on the file system so the kernel build can gather them into the RAM disk it uses to boot the file system:

```
$cd $RFS
$mkdir dev
$cd dev
$sudo mknod console c 5 1
$sudo mknod null c 3 1
```

This is one of the few commands during this process executed as root. Be careful and make sure the commands are executed in the right directory. Later, the book discusses a way to do this without being root, when more time is dedicated to the kernel build process.

A root file system also needs a few extra directories: root, tmp, and proc. The proc directory isn't strictly necessary, but many programs rely on the proc file system being mounted at /proc to operate correctly:

```
$cd $RFS
$mkdir tmp root etc proc
```

The system will start without these directories, but having them present prevents some error messages from appearing when the kernel loads. If you're fretting over every byte in the root file system, you can leave these out to save a little space (even empty directories consume a few bytes).

Finishing Touches

The system requires a few additional files that are read by user programs: the user and group files and the inittab. You can create these files from the command line:

```
$ echo "root::0:0:root:/root:/bin/sh" > $RFS/etc/passwd
$ echo "root:x:0:" > $RFS/etc/groups
$ echo "::respawn:/sbin/getty -L ttyAMA0 115200 xterm > $RFS/etc/inittab
```

The first two lines create a group and user for the root user. The third line creates an inittab that starts a terminal login when the system starts. When a Linux system boots, it reads the inittab file to figure out what to run. In this case, the inittab instructs the system to run /sbin/getty at the start and to restart the program when it stops.

In a deployed Linux system, this file contains references to additional scripts that start programs necessary for the system, such as an HTTP server, or perform housekeeping tasks like configuring network adapters. The most important aspect of the inittab is that one program is configured for respawn: when init no longer has anything to run, it stops, and so does the kernel.

This system is built using an initial RAM disk. This is part of the kernel and is loaded into memory during boot time. The kernel attempts to run the file /linuxrc; if this file isn't present or can't be loaded, the kernel continues the standard booting process by mounting a root file system and as specified on the kernel command line. This is covered in the next section.

Building the Kernel

Now that the toolchain and root file system builds have been completed, the next step is to compile the kernel for the target machine. By now, the kernel configuration program should be familiar, because several of the projects in this chapter have adopted it as their configuration interface. In addition, the process of configuring a project so that the source tree is in the correct state before building should also be familiar. Early in the chapter, to get the header files necessary to build the toolchain, you configured the kernel for an ARM processor running on one of ARM's development boards using this command executed from the top-level kernel directory:

```
$ make ARCH=arm integrator_defconfig
```

This command results in the kernel finding the file integrator_defconfig under the ARM architecture directory and copying those settings into the current configuration, stored at .config.[4] This file was contributed by ARM to make it easier to build a Linux kernel for this board and isn't the only defconfig present. To see a list of all the defconfig files, do the following:

```
$make ARCH=arm help
```

This lists the make targets and the _defconfig files for the architecture. ARM has by far the largest count of defconfig files. This command doesn't have any side effects, so feel free to view the support for other architectures by passing in other values for ARCH. You can find the population of acceptable values for ARCH by looking at the first level of subdirectories in the kernel sources under the arch directory. For example:

```
$find ./arch -type d -maxdepth 1
```

Because the kernel has already been configured to build for the target device, only a little extra configuration is necessary: updating the kernel command line to boot up using some parameters specific to this build of the kernel and root file system. The kernel command line is like the command line on a utility run from a shell: the parameters get passed in to the kernel at bootup time and let you change how the kernel works without recompilation. In this case, make the kernel command line this value:

```
console=ttyAMA0
```

---

[4] The file .config is a hidden file. To see it in a directory listing, use the -a argument to ls, which shows all files in the directory.

You set this value through the kernel configuration tool by running the following:

```
$ make ARCH=arm menuconfig
```

The following appears before the configuration menu, during compilation of the software that draws the configuration menu. This happens the first time the kernel menu configuration programs runs:

```
(clipped)
  HOSTCC   scripts/kconfig/lxdialog/inputbox.o
  HOSTCC   scripts/kconfig/lxdialog/menubox.o
  HOSTCC   scripts/kconfig/lxdialog/textbox.o
  HOSTCC   scripts/kconfig/lxdialog/util.o
  HOSTCC   scripts/kconfig/lxdialog/yesno.o
(clipped)
```

Look for Boot Options in the Linux kernel configuration top level screen, as shown in Figure 6-2

```
.config - Linux Kernel v2.6.29 Configuration
```

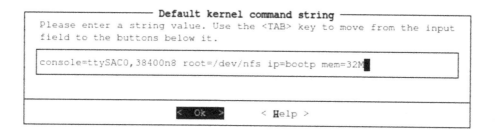

Figure 6-2. The Linux Kernel Configuration top level menu

The settings for the kernel command line are at the following menu location: Boot Options ➤ Default Kernel Command String. To change the settings, highlight the item in the menu, and press Enter. The window shown in Figure 6-3 appears on screen.

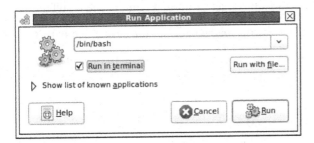

Figure 6-3. Setting the value of the kernel command line

The user interface for entering strings in the kernel configuration program is frustrating. You can't use the cursor keys to navigate to some character and begin typing. Instead, you must make changes by backspacing and replacing text. The easiest way to make changes is to compose them in an editor and paste them into this control. After you update the boot parameters, select OK and Exit on the subsequent menus. The software asks to save changes, which you should affirm. The kernel is now ready to build.

When you run make from the command line for the kernel, you need to pass in the cross-compiler prefix and the architecture:

```
$ export PATH=$PATH:/opt/arm-tools/bin
$ ake zImage ARCH=arm CROSS_COMPILE=arm-none-linux-gnueabi-
```

This command line requests that a zImage be built and prefixes the compiler name (GCC) with `CROSS_COMPILE`. How do you know the right target—not xImage or ouiejsdf, for example? Table 6-8 lists the common build targets for Linux.

Table 6-8. Commond Linux Target Build Options

Target	Explanation
zImage	This is a zlib compressed image of the kernel, ready to boot on a board.
uImage	This is a zlib compressed image, ready to boot on a board that's running the U-Boot boot loader. It's much like the zImage but contains additional data that makes booting with U-Boot more efficient.
bzImage	This is a big zImage—the type of image used with the boot loaders on x86 hosts.
vmlinux	The vmlinux target builds the Linux kernel executable image. This closely resembles what's in memory for the Linux kernel and is frequently used for debugging.
srecImage	Very few board use S-records. For those that do, this is the target. An S-record is a format where each line in the file starts with *S*.
xipImage	XIP stands for Execute in Place. This image is formatted so that it can be put into a flash partition and run from there, without getting loaded into RAM first.

If you've built the kernel for an Intel x86 architecture, the target bzImage is familiar and is still the right value when you're building for x86 embedded boards. The target in question in an ARM board, which expects a zImage. The documentation for a board's boot loader specifies the format of binary it requires.

The kernel compilation takes about 30 minutes, give or take. The last few lines of the kernel build show what file was created:

```
Kernel: arch/arm/boot/Image is ready
Kernel: arch/arm/boot/zImage is ready
```

Congratulations! The kernel is completed, and the root file system has been built as part of kernel an initial RAM disk. When this kernel boots, it will start a command shell and wait for a login. The root file system has been built into the kernel, and the kernel has a copy of what was include in the ./usr directory under the kernel root with the name initramfs_data.cpio.gz.

Note Don't have an ARM integrator handy? Yes, you do. The kernel and root file system that you've built can be booted using QEMU. Use the qemu-system-arm command with the -kernel and -initrd of the initramfs_data.cpio.gz created during the build.

Troubleshooting Booting Problems

What if it didn't work? The software built in this chapter is remarkably resilient and is configured to do the right thing with minimal input. Still, after all this work, more often than not, you may have skipped a step, or some other problem may require debugging. In general, systems don't boot for one of the following reasons:

- The kernel isn't properly configured for the board.

- The root file system can't be mounted.

- The root file system init program doesn't run.

- It's booting, but the serial connection parameters are wrong.

The easiest way to diagnose board-booting problems is to have a running Linux for the board. Because nearly every board vendor includes a Linux distribution of one sort of another, this is a less unreasonable statement than in years past. When Linux is up and running, you can use it as a test-bed for the code that's not.

Improperly Configured Board

This occurs when the following output appears, followed by nothing.

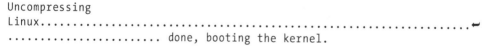

```
Uncompressing
Linux...............................................................
..................... done, booting the kernel.
```

This can be confused with the kernel actually booting but the configuration parameters are incorrect. Double-check that the cables are connected and that the communication parameters are correct. Then, check this item again. If the kernel is indeed stopping here, check the kernel configuration program to ensure that the board and processor are correct. Next, check that that the toolchain is correct; some users with several toolchains mistakenly use the wrong one when compiling the kernel.

If all seems well at this point, look at the distribution of Linux included with the board and diff the configuration file against the one used to build the kernel. If the configuration file isn't present, it's sometimes built into the kernel and resides at /proc/config.gz. The kernel includes a utility that can extract this information from a kernel file called ./scripts/extract-ikconfig. This file writes the output to the console, so it's best to redirect the output to a file:

```
cd $ <kernel directory>
./scripts/extract-ikconfig <path to kernel zImage>  > ~/kernel-config
```

After it's extracted, you can use this file to configure the kernel by making a copy of it named .config in the top-level kernel directory. After making the copy, issue a make oldconfig command to have the build reread the configuration file and configure the environment:

```
$cp ~/kernel-config <kernel directory>/.config
$make ARCH=arm oldconfig
```

When the kernel builds again, it may ask for default values for configuration parameters added because the oldconfig was created. The best thing to do is accept the defaults, unless you know otherwise. When the kernel finishes building, it's configured close to how the booting kernel was built.

The Root File System Can't Be Mounted

The kernel looks for an initial RAM disk root file system and then for the root file system as instructed on the command line. If the kernel can't use the initial RAM file system, it probably doesn't have the linuxrc file in the root directory or this file isn't executable. Checking for its existence isn't difficult, but making sure it can run is more of a trick. This is where having a running kernel and RFS comes in handy, because you can copy the files to the board and execute them to see if they run, or you can mount the file system via NFS and test over the network.

Most problems with the file system not being mounted come from not entering the correct directory for the root file system in the kernel configuration program. The kernel build fails silently if it can't find the directory or file containing the root file system.

The Root File System init Program Doesn't Run

This problem is generally a result of not having the libraries and other supporting files in the root file system. If BusyBox was linked with shared libraries, make sure they're all present in the /lib directory and that the linker file (ld-linux.3) is present as well. This error is difficult to find because the kernel produces an error like the following if this is indeed the problem, and it doesn't seem to have anything to do with the init file not working:

```
Root-NFS: No NFS server available, giving up.
VFS: Unable to mount root fs via NFS, trying floppy.
VFS: Cannot open root device "<NULL>" or unknown-block(2,0)
Please append a correct "root=" boot option; here are the available partitions:
Kernel panic - not syncing: VFS: Unable to mount root fs on unknown-block(2,0)
```

What really throws people new to Linux is the message about no NFS server being available. This appears even if there's no attempt to use an NFS server. When you're chasing down library dependency problems, using `ldd` on the running Linux host is the best way to go. On the build system, you can't run `ldd` because it tries to execute the program in question and its instruction set is probably different than the host system, resulting in an error. If the problem is still mysterious, copy all the `.so` files from the toolchain's `sysroot` directory into the `/libfolder` of the target, and begin eliminating files one at time. This is a crude but effective method.

Distributing the Distribution

The Linux distribution created for a project needs to be bundled up and transmitted to people working on the project. Because most Linux developers work for companies with small teams, the most common practice is to create archives with the toolchain binaries and a snapshot of the root file system in binary form. The sources for these projects are then checked into source control along with the build scripts. For this project, you create the toolchain tar file like so:

```
$ tar cjf arm-tools.tar.bz2 $INSTALLDIR
```

This archive can then be unpacked on a developer's machine in any location and used to compile programs.

You can archive the root file system in the same manner:

```
$ tar cjf arm-tools.tar.bz2 $RFS
```

The user can then unpack this root file system and use it to boot the board or add it into a kernel build.

Getting the kernel ready for packing is a little more complex. The zImage file used to boot the system can be stored and given to people working on the project; however, those doing kernel work need to rebuild the kernel and should be do so with the same configuration used to create the distribution.

The kernel configuration process creates a `.config` file to hold the user's selections. You can copy this file into the appropriate `arch/configs` directory with the name *<something>*_config, where *something* is an arbitrary identifier. In the case of this project, the command looks like

```
$ cp .config arch/arm/configs/example_defconfig
```

After the configuration is saved, you should clean the kernel directory of all output using this command:

```
$ make ARCH=arm distclean
```

This command does a complete clean of the kernel tree, even deleting files that look like editor backup files. When this is finished, you can archive the kernel tree into a compressed tar file, ready for distribution. When users receive the file, they need to uncompress it and do the following to re-create the build environment:

```
make ARCH=arm exmaple_defconfig
```

Then they're ready to do their development and build the kernel.

Wrapping Up

Creating a Linux distribution from source files isn't terribly difficult. It's a task that's complex by virtue of the number of steps you must follow and the amount of detail at every step. Perhaps the biggest problem is the large cycle time between experimentation and seeing results. Many times, a toolchain or kernel build requires 30 minutes of compilation to test just a small change, and that latency makes experimentation unwieldy.

CHAPTER 7

■ ■ ■

Booting the Board

Booting a Linux System Is a Three-Act Play

The performance opens with a boot loader that sets the groundwork for the board to be able to load the kernel. Just like an opening, the boot loader paves the way for the kernel, going as far to load it from a remote server into memory so it can be executed. After it's in memory, the boot loader hands execution to the kernel and exits. The kernel then has its own bootstrapping process (which duplicates what the boot loader did in some cases) that readies the hardware, loads drivers, and starts its processes to manage the system. When it's in a running state, the kernel hands off control to an init program. The kernel and init then share the stage until you shut down the system; when the system restarts, the performance begins again.

This chapter walks through the process of a board running Linux from power-up to the first program being executed. Understanding this process is essential to understanding how to optimize the time necessary to start Linux. For example, a consumer device like a cell phone can't take as long as desktop system to become available to make a call; likewise, a high-availability network device will have reduced uptime if it can't route packets for three minutes while it's booting.

The Boot Loader

A boot loader isn't unique to Linux or embedded systems. It's a program first run by a computer so that a more sophisticated program can be loaded next. In a Linux system, two boot loaders usually run before the Linux kernel starts running.

The program that the boot loader runs can be anything, but it's usually an operating system that then starts additional programs so the system can be used by a user. The interesting question is, how does the processor know to run the boot loader? At power-up, the processor goes to a certain memory address (put there by the processor designer), reads the content of that address, and performs a jump to the address stored at that location. This address is hard-coded into the processor so the chip maker doesn't have to change the silicon design for each customer or when the boot loader changes. This little bit of code is referred to as the *first-stage boot loader*.

The code that runs next is what is commonly viewed as the boot loader in a Linux system. This may be a program like U-Boot, RedBoot, or something else (don't worry, they get detailed treatment later in the chapter) smart enough to then load the operating system. After Linux has been loaded into memory, the boot loader is no longer needed and is discarded; any evidence of the code in RAM is overwritten by the operating system. Any device configuration done by the boot loader—for example, setting the speed of the serial port or an IP address assigned to the network adapter—is also lost. Linux reinitializes these devices during its startup process.

Boot loaders can be configured either to automatically run a sequence of commands or to wait for user input via a serial connection or console. Because embedded systems traditionally lack monitors and keyboards, you interact with the boot loader over a serial connection using a terminal emulator like minicom. The serial port is the favored way of presenting a user interface because the programming necessary to interact with a universal asynchronous receiver/transmitter (UART) that manages a serial port is an order of magnitude simpler than code to use a USB device or start a remote console over the network. The boot loader's user interface looks a little like a terminal shell in Linux, but it lacks the bells and whistles you normally find, like auto-completion and line editing.[1]

Boot loaders also act as an interface to the flash devices on the board. *Flash memory* (named so because the reprogramming process was reminiscent of a flash camera to the designer) is a type of Electrically Erasable Programmable Read-Only Memory (EEPROM) where individual areas (called *blocks* or *erase blocks*) can be erased and written; before the invention of flash memory, EEPROMs could only be erased and rewritten in their entirety. With no moving parts and low power consumption, flash memory is an excellent storage medium for embedded devices. Flash support in the boot loader gives you the ability to manage the flash memory by creating *segments*, which are named areas of the flash memory, and to write data, such as a root file system or kernel image, into those areas.

Boot loaders have been getting increasingly sophisticated over the years. Early boot loaders only accepted one-letter commands and positional parameters and were very unforgiving. Incorrect input resulted in an unrecoverable error, and the board had to be power-cycled (or the reset button pressed, if it had one) to return to the boot loader. Help was non-existent or so minimal that it was equivalent to non-existent. The board usually included a manual explaining how to use the boot loader, or a live person showed up and helped with the boot process, depending on the value of the account.

■ **Note** The boot loader for a PC running Linux is either GRand Unified Boot loader (GRUB) or Linux Loader (LILO). Running Windows? The boot loader for that system is NTLDR; it works as a second-stage boot loader, and the Phoenix BIOS is the first-stage boot loader.

Boot loaders on a desktop system run in two steps: a first- and a second-stage boot loader. The first-stage boot loader does just enough to get the second-stage boot loader running. On a desktop system, the boot sequence reads one sector of data into memory and begins executing that code. The first-stage boot loader contains a driver so that it can access a file system on a fixed drive or possibly download the kernel from a remote source, like a TFTP server or an NFS share. On a PowerPC or ARM system, the first-stage boot loader is the code the chip runs after power-up instead of code that is loaded from the hardware.

After the boot loader does its job of getting Linux into memory, the Linux boot-up process starts. Sometimes the kernel is compressed, and the first code decompresses the kernel and jumps to an address that's the kernel's entry point. This code runs and performs processor-level configuration, such as configuring the memory management unit (MMU—the part of the processor that handles virtual memory addressing) and enabling the processor's cache. The code also populates a data structure that you can view by doing the following after the system is up and running:

```
$ cat /proc/cpuinfo
```

Next, the kernel runs its board-level configuration. Some boards have peripherals like PCI controllers or flash-management hardware that must be initialized so they can be accessed later during the kernel startup process. When it's ready, the code jumps into the processor-independent startup code. Linux is now in control of the system; the software starts the kernel's threads and process management, parses the command line, and runs the main kernel process. The kernel first runs what you indicated on the command line (via the `init` parameter) and then attempts to execute `/sbin/init`, `/etc/init`, `/bin/init`, and, finally, `/bin/sh`.

---

[1] Early boot loaders even lacked support for backspace. Being a terrible typist, I found that composing the lines in a text editor and then pasting them into the terminal emulator was the best way to proceed. Now that backspace is well supported, that's something I don't have to do anymore, but old habits die hard.

When the kernel starts the main user process, that process must continue running, because when the process stops the kernel panics and stops as well. A kernel panic is the worst sort of kernel error, because this sort of problem results in the system coming to halt. The following illustration describes the booting process from power-on until the first program runs.

Figure 7-1 shows the boot process in detail. The following reviews the previous discussion and explains what happens each step of the way:

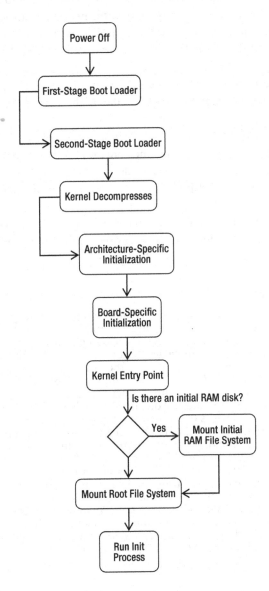

Figure 7-1. *Linux boot process*

1. The first-stage boot loader is the code in the processor that reads a location in memory and may put a message on the console or screen.

2. The second-stage boot loader is responsible for loading what the system will run. In this case, that is Linux, but it could be any program.

3. If the kernel is compressed, it's now uncompressed into memory. A jump instruction follows the decompression step that places the instruction at the next executable instruction.

4. Processor and board initialization runs. This low-level code performs hardware initialization. The code then reaches the kernel's entry point, and processor-independent code runs to get the kernel ready to run the init process.

5. The kernel entry point is the code that's in the architecture-independent part of the kernel tree. This code is located in the `start_kernel` function in the `init/main.c` file in the kernel source tree.

6. The system mounts the initial RAM disk, sees if it contains an `/init` program, and if so, runs it. If this program doesn't exist or isn't found, the boot process moves to the next step.

7. One of the parameters passed to the kernel is the device containing the root file system and the file system type. The kernel attempts to mount this file system and panics if it isn't found or isn't mountable.

8. The program that the kernel first attempts to run is the value of the kernel parameter `init`. In lieu of this parameter, the system looks for an `init` executable by attempting to run `/sbin/init`, `/etc/init`, `/bin/init`, and finally `/bin.sh`.

Kernel-Land vs. Userland

In Linux, a bright line exists between the kernel's execution context and that of the programs being run. The kernel's context is called *kernel-land* or *kernel space* and encompasses all the device interaction, threads, interrupt handlers, data structures, and memory. When a program is executed, the kernel creates a virtual memory address, configures resource descriptors (like those for files, timers, and semaphores), loads the program into memory, and configures the processor's registers to start execution. All of this activity occurs in *userland*. These two execution contexts can communicate under controlled circumstances but are otherwise separate and distinct.

Although the kernel and userland are separate and distinct, they're very much related. When the kernel boots, it initializes (and registers) devices that can be used later in the startup process or when the system is up and running. For example, when a board boots that has a USB host controller, the driver for that device initializes in the kernel; in userland, programs can run that interrogate the devices attached to the USB bus and load corresponding drivers.

Understanding the hand-off from the kernel to the first userland process helps when you're debugging startup problems and trying to reduce startup time. From a diagnostic perspective, knowing that the kernel started successfully means booting problems have been automatically narrowed to something in the root file system or initial RAM disk. From a performance perspective, knowing that a configuration step can be done in the kernel or userland (such as assigning an IP address to a network adapter) means certain activities can be deferred until later and scheduled such that system appears to boot faster, or when you can more readily control the configuration process.

Boot Loaders

Many boot loaders are available for Linux, all of which are open source. The boot loader included with the board is the best choice to use for shipping the board, because it's proven to work; getting another boot loader working is a combination engineering and research project that can be difficult to schedule. The maker of the board has likely paid for the development of a working boot loader so that engineers can easily use the board for development. Because the boot loader is open source, the source code should be included or available for customization.

Boot loaders have matured over the past few years to have the functionality of a minimal operating system: they can run video devices, serial ports, flash memory, USB devices, and even IP networking over Ethernet. Boot loaders have also become less agnostic and have additional features built in for supporting Linux—for example, U-Boot has the ability to uncompress the kernel rather than have the kernel decompress itself.

Getting the source code for a boot loader and building it works much like any other open source project. The part that's very different is getting the code on the board so that it can be run. In some cases, the boot loader supplied by the board can access the flash memory to write the new code; in other cases, you must place the code on the board with a Joint Task Action Group (JTAG) device. JTAG is a communication mechanism, akin to serial or parallel. The software that runs in a JTAG debugger can usually program flash memory on the board. Some vendors, like Atmel, have flash programming tools that use USB instead of JTAG.

The following sections contain detailed information about the boot loaders found on most systems.

RedBoot

This boot loader is built on the hardware abstraction layer of the eCos embedded operating system. The result is a very robust boot loader with a wide range of architecture and device support. As you can guess from the name, this software is part of the Red Hat family of projects.

You can obtain the sources for RedBoot from sourceware like so:

```
$ mkdir ~/redboot
$ cd ~/redboot
$ wget --passive-ftp ftp://ecos.sourceware.org/pub/ecos/ecos-install.tcl
$ cd ecos-install.tcl
```

The file downloaded is a script that downloads the rest of the RedBoot's code. This script is written in Tcl (it was first TCL, for Tool Command Language, but now it's frequently referred to as "tickle"). The code first prompts for a download mirror; select one close to your current location. Next, the software prompts for the installation directory; you can accept the default.

The next question asks what prebuilt tools to install. The RedBoot loader is picky about the configuration of the compiler used to build it. The cross-compiler created earlier works fine under most conditions; however, the best practice is to download the toolchain offered by the installation program:

```
Available prebuilt GNU tools:
[1]     arm-eabi
[2]     arm-elf (old)
[3]     i386-elf
[4]     m68k-elf
[5]     mipsisa32-elf
[6]     powerpc-eabi
[7]     sh-elf
[q]     Finish selecting GNU tools
```

The menu lets you select several tool chains. Each architecture has one toolchain (except ARM; in that case, choose the first), After the installation process finishes, you rebuild by running `ecosconfig` to configure the source tree and then `make` to run a build. For example, to do this for an ARM Integrator board, you need the following commnds:

```
$ cd <redboot installation directory>
$ source ./ecosenv.sh
$ ecosconfig new integrator redboot
$ ecosconfig import ~/ecos/ecos-3.0/↵
packages/hal/arm/integrator/v3_0/misc/redboot_ROMRAM.ecm

$ ecosconfig tree
$ make
```

The first two lines configure environment variables for eCos based on the installation script. The next line creates a skeleton project for the ARM Integrator board, and the next two lines import a configuration file for that board and create the source tree for the build. The build product is in the `install/bin` directory. The correct values for the parameters passed into `ecosconfig` for the configuration steps are contained in the http://ecos.sourceware.org/docs-latest/redboot/installation-and-testing.html file. This example builds two binaries: one to be loaded into RAM and executed and the other suitable to be written into flash.

After it's built, you can write the new boot loader into flash using RedBoot. This is platform specific. The basis process involves uploading the image on the board into RAM and then writing the data to flash. An example of the commands to perform these steps follows; again, the exact instructions vary for each board. You issue these commands d on the board using the existing `redboot` program:

```
redboot> fis init -f
redboot> load -r -b <address> redboot_ROM.bin
redboot> cksum
redboot> fiscreate redboot
```

When the board is reset, the new version of RedBoot is running.

Using RedBoot

The general process for using RedBoot is to load the kernel into memory and run it. A kernel comes from either flash storage or from a TFTP server. To load a kernel from flash, use these commands:

```
redboot> fis load -b 0x1000000 kernel
```

This command loads the data from the kernel flash partition named `kernel` and loads the data starting at address `0x100000`. A flash partition is a logical division of the flash memory space that's been assigned a name.

From TFTP, use these commands:

```
redboot> ip_address -l <ip address>  -h <address of tftp server>
redboot> load <kernel_image_file>
```

The first command configures the first adapter on the board to have the IP address *<ip address>* (remember to use an acceptable address for your network or hardware configuration; duplicate IP addresses summon an IT staff member who won't be impressed) and looks to address *<address of tftp server>* when performing a TFTP download. The TFTP server IP address should be the one of the host configured earlier in the book. After it's loaded into memory, you can run the kernel by doing the following:

```
exec -b 0x100000 -l 0x80000 -c "init=runme root=/dev/mtdblock2"
```

This command runs the kernel loaded into memory at 0x0100000 that's 0x80000 bytes long with the parameters sent to the kernel following the -c parameter. The kernel is now off and running.

RedBoot has support for mounting, reading, and writing Journaling Flash File System (JFFS) partitions, a handy feature because reading these file systems usually requires starting Linux. However, because RedBoot is built on a very small embedded operating system, eCos, this feature isn't surprising. In addition to being able to perform operations like listing directory contents and reading files, you can also create files. You do so by loading the file into memory and then writing it out into a flash partition. For example:

```
redboot> fs mount -d /dev/flash1 -t jffs2 /rfs
redboot> fis cd /opt
redboot> load <file> -b 0x80000000
redboot> fis write -b 0x80000000 -l <length> <file name>
```

<file> is a file loaded from the TFTP server. After it loads into memory, RedBoot returns the length of the file and uses that length in the next command when writing the data from the RAM into the flash file system using the fis write command.

■ **Note** TFTP stands for Trivial File Transfer Protocol. TFTP is used by boot loaders because it's a very simple protocol that runs over User Datagram Protocol (UDP), the least demanding of the IP protocols. TFTP also doesn't perform authentication or other security checks, further reducing its complexity. TFTP is related to FTP in name only; FTP is a considerably more sophisticated protocol that uses Transmission Control Protocol (TCP) sockets, a much more resource intensive protocol, to transport data. Because TFTP is relatively easy to implement (even I wrote a TFTP server!) and doesn't require a full IP stack, it was adopted as the way to send files over the network to boot loaders, which need to use something simple. Now that boot loaders and the boards they run on have become more sophisticated, using a complete IP stack would be reasonable, but technological inertia may keep TFTP around for a while.

YAMON

YAMON is the boot loader used on MIPS development boards and is created and maintained by MIPS. Because YAMON is specific to MIPS development boards, it's rarely rebuilt. The best thing to do is download the required binary from http://www.mips.com/products/system-software/yamon/. On this page is a link for the sources; to download them, you must register.[2] YAMON is different in that it primarily uses S-records (frequently called SRECs) as its input format. An S-record file contains lines starting with the letter S (for "Start"), a number indicating the type of line, and the payload followed by a

---

[2] Consider using http://mailinator.com for registration so you're not bugged with spam.

checksum. All the data in an SREC file is ASCII characters, making this format very easy to examine in a text editor.

To download and run a kernel, do the following:

```
YAMON> load tftp://<tftp server ip address>/<file>
YAMON> go
```

`<tftp server ip address>` is the IP address of a host running TFTP, and `<file>` is the SREC to download. Notice that the there's no load address in this command; that information is encoded into the SREC file.

Das U-Boot

U-Boot (which means "the submarine" in German) is a popular boot loader for ARM and PowerPC boards. This tools is maintained primarily by DENX Software is part of this company's embedded Linux suite of products. This company contracts with hardware manufacturers to keep U-Boot up to date for their hardware, which means U-Boot is frequently the first boot loader ready for a large number of boards.

The sources are available via Git or using the FTP site. To download with Git, do the following:

```
$ cd ~
$ git clone git://git.denx.de/uboot.git u-boot
```

If you want to use a specific release of the software, download via FTP and unpack the compressed tar file. Substitute the version number for `<version>` in the commands:

```
$ wget ftp://ftp.denx.de/pub/u-boot/u-boot-<version>.tar.bz2
$ tar xjf u-boot-<version>.tar.bz2
```

After you download the sources, the building software works using the configure/build model. The project has configurations stored in the `include/configs` directory; to use the configuration, strip off the path, remove the training `.h`, and append `_config` to the remaining text. The `include/configs` directory contains this file:

```
MPC8260ADS
```

To configure a U-Boot build for this board, do the following:

```
$ make MPC8260ADS_config
```

The software works a little while and shows a confirmation message indicating that the project was configured. If you're working with several boards, be sure to clear the environment between configurations by doing the following to empty the build directory of any leftovers that could cause errors:

```
$ make distclean
```

Using U-Boot

U-Boot works like other boot loaders in that you load a kernel into memory and then run that image. The image loaded into memory can be stored on a server running TFTP or on a flash partition. You configure

IP information in U-Boot by setting environment variables to configure the board's and TFTP server's address. To set the board's IP address to 10.0.0.2 and the address of the TFTP server to 10.0.0.1, use the following commands:

```
=> setenv ipaddr 10.0.0.2
=> setenv serverip 10.0.0.1
```

The device is now configured so that it can communicate over the Ethernet adapter. To download a file from a TFTP server, use the tftpboot command

```
=> tftpboot 0x80000000 kernel
```

This loads the kernel into memory at the specified address and starts the booting process. The bootargs environment variable controls what kernel command-line parameters are sent during boot-up. Setting bootargs works like setting the board's IP address:

```
=> setenv bootargs root=/dev/mtd1 rootfstype=jffs2 init=theapp
```

To save the values of the environment variables, use the saveenv command. It writes the values of the current set of environment variables to flash so they're present the next time U-Boot runs on the board.

LILO

You're probably familiar with LILO as a boot loader for desktops and x86 systems; in the early days of Linux, this was the only boot loader. LILO has been surpassed in popularity by GRUB, which has more features, but the minimalistic nature of LILO is what makes it ideal for embedded systems.

Recall from the first part of the chapter that LILO is a second-stage boot loader for an x86 system. It's loaded from the Master Boot Record (MBR) of the first bootable device the BIOS locates.

LILO gets its marching orders from the lilo.conf file. The contents of this file are written to the device's MBR by LILO as part of the configuration process. In this file, you can specify several different boot-up configurations, setting one as the default. You can also set parameters for all configurations; LILO calls these *global* parameters. The structure of lilo.conf is such that the global options precede the image section, where you tell LILO what kernel to load. A typical lilo.conf file for an embedded system looks like the following:

```
boot=/dev/hda
root=/dev/hda1
read-only
default=theapp
#  kernel image to boot
image=/boot/zImage
label=theapp
```

This tells the software to load the kernel located in the /boot directory for the root device (in this case, dev/hda1). default= isn't necessary, because the file contains just one configuration; but being explicit is a good habit, because if this file is changed, LILO will prompt you for an image label—and that could be problematic if the device doesn't have traditional input like a mouse or keyboard.

GRUB

GRUB is the boot loader commonly used in desktop systems, having supplanted LILO in the past few years. GRUB performs the same job as LILO: after the first-stage boot loader has run, GRUB finds a kernel, puts it into memory, and lets the system start.

GRUB divides booting into three stages: 1, 1.5, and 2. The stage 1 boot loader fits into the MBR of the device; its job is to mount the devices necessary to run the stage 2 GRUB boot loader, which reads a configuration file and presents a user interface. The 1.5 boot loader is necessary when the code required to find the stage 2 boot loader doesn't fit into the 512 bytes of the MBR.

GRUB is controlled by the /boot/grub/menu.lst file stored on the boot partition configured when you install GRUB This file is divided into one section (at the start of the file) with global options and a second section containing a list of kernels to boot. A typical menu.lst file for an embedded system looks like the following:

```
title           Linux

root            (hd0,1)

kernel  /zImage root=/dev/hda2 ro
```

The root parameter indicates that the / should be mapped to the device hd0's first partition. The next line tells the system to get the kernel at /zImage. Because there's only one entry, grub doesn't display a menu. This root parameter doesn't have an effect on the root file system that the kernel eventually mounts; it's the root file system for the boot loader itself.

The root device format is different than Linux, which can result in confusion. In GRUB, a device has the following format:

```
(device[bios number][,partition])
```

Device can be one of the following values: hd for fixed disks, fd for floppy disks, or nd for network drives. The number that follows is the identifier assigned by the computer's BIOS. You can find this in the BIOS setup for the computer; the assigned numbers start at 0 and work upward. The partition is the logical division of the drive. To find the partitions on a drive, use the sfdisk command:

```
$ sudo /sbin/sfdisk -l
```

GRUB allows you to load the kernel from a TFTP server. To do this, you need to configure the IP parameters and use (nd) instead of (hd0,1) as the root device. For example:

```
ifconfig –address=10.0.0.1 –server=10.0.0.2
kernel (nd)/bzImage
```

This results in GRUB configuring the adapter to have an IP address of 10.0.0.1 and use the default netmask (255.0.0.0) and contact 10.0.0.2 to download the kernel file bzImage via TFTP to boot the system.

About Flash Memory

Flash memory resembles other types of memory in that it's one large array of bytes. The starting address is at 0 and the ending address is one less than the total number of bytes on the device. In order to make this pool of memory more manageable, the concept of flash partitions was added a few years back; these are analogous to partitions on disk drives. With flash partitions, a small amount of flash is reserved and populated with a start address, length, and name. You can refer to the starting address using a name rather than a hex number; and when partitions change in size or location, code that refers to the names of partitions doesn't need to change.

The kernel also uses the partition table to manage the flash memory. In Linux, the device used to access flash is /dev/mtd*N*, where *N* is the ordinal of the flash partition, starting at 0. The first flash partition is 0, and the number increases for each entry subsequent partition. *Memory technology device* (MTD) is the generic term for EEPROM storage devices in Linux.

Flash memory comes in two flavors: NOR and NAND. Although the MTD software interface presents a uniform interface to these flavors, they're very different. The differences between NAND and NOR from a functional perspective are that because NAND memory can't be read and written in a random manner, each block within a NAND device (where a *block* is a subdivision of the device's memory) must be accessed sequentially. On a NAND device, the driver can't write to byte 5 on block 100 without first writing to bytes 0 through 4. NOR memory also has a different tolerance for errors: the device can have some number of bad blocks that the driver software must be able to work around, as opposed to NOR memory, which is designed to have no bad areas.

■ **Note** You can't use NAND memory to execute in place because it isn't random access like RAM memory. Execute in place works by mapping a flash memory address into what would otherwise be RAM memory, because NAND doesn't permit random access to individual bytes the way NOR memory does.

When booting, the kernel needs to know what device contains the root file system. If the kernel uses a flash-based root file system, one of these partitions contains the root file system; looking at the flash partition table tells you the location of the root file system so the proper device name can be sent to the kernel.

Kernel Startup

Getting the kernel loaded into memory isn't even half the fun of starting a Linux system. The boot loader's job is to get the operating system from storage (flash, TFTP) into a place where it can be executed (RAM) and then go away. Most of the time, the kernel is stored as compressed data. To uncompress the data, the kernel build process tacks a decompression code on the front of the kernel image, so the first output visible to you is like this:

```
Uncompressing
Linux.......................................................................
done,
```

This isn't really the kernel running; it's the decompression program for the kernel. These dots are quickly followed by

```
booting the kernel.
```

That output means the kernel has finished going through the processor and board-specific initialization code and is now in the kernel_start or main entry point for the kernel. It's important to know what happens in this area, even though you'll probably never touch this code.

After decompression, the next code that runs is in the head.S used to build the kernel. For example, if you use a PowerPC 32-bit processor, you find this code at

arch/powerpc/kernel/head_32.S

The processor family is the one selected during the configuration of the kernel. If you're building an ARM-based system, the entry-point file later links to a file containing the processor-specific initialization:

arch/arm/kernel/head.S

Both of these files do the same thing; they perform processor-specific configuration:

1. Initialize the MMU.
2. If the processor is multicore, get the second processor ready to run.
3. Get the kernel command line from the boot loader (before it's overwritten), and copy the command line into memory where it can be safely passed to the kernel's entry point.
4. Configure hooks for hardware debuggers.
5. Flush the processor's cache.

Looking in the directory for the architecture reveals many more files than those mentioned. The kernel type you choose during the configuration step specifies what additional files are linked into the final initialization object code. No matter what initialization code happens to run, all initialization programs end by jumping to start_kernel.

The Kernel Entry Point

The kernel's entry point is located in init/main.c in the routine start_kernel. The architecture-specific code jumps to this address after the hardware setup is complete.

The sure way you know you've arrived at this step is when the following appears:

Linux version 2.6.17 (built@by.you) (gcc version 4.2.1)

The code here starts the interrupt handlers, process scheduler, virtual memory management system, and power management; it also scans the PCI bus for peripherals, enables networking, and performs other housekeeping tasks. While this activity is occurring, the device drivers print out information that documents the current state of the system:

```
CPU: ARM926EJ-Sid(wb) [41069265] revision 5 (ARMv5TEJ)
Machine: ARM-IntegratorCP
Memory policy: ECC disabled, Data cache writeback
CPU0: D VIVT write-through cache
CPU0: I cache: 4096 bytes, associativity 4, 32 byte lines, 32 sets
CPU0: D cache: 65536 bytes, associativity 4, 32 byte lines, 512 sets
Built 1 zonelists
Kernel command line: console=ttyAMA0 mem=128M ip=192.168.20.100:::::eth0:off
```

The kernel command-line printing is an important milestone: if the kernel has made it this far, then the *scheduler* (the part of the kernel that decides what software should be running) has started and is ready to handle threads started by the kernel itself as well as the initial user process. The output from the kernel startup process is available from the command line by using the dmesg command immediately after the kernel boots. dmesg prints out the contents of the kernel's temporary buffer, which is overwritten with newer data as the system runs. For example, on a desktop machine, try

```
$ dmesg | less
```

That command sends the results of dmesg to the less program, which lets you control the file's scrolling.

Hardware initialization continues, ending with the configuration of the network adapter:

```
eth0: link up
Sending DHCP requests ...... timed out!
IP-Config: Reopening network devices...
eth0: link up
Sending DHCP requests ., OK
IP-Config: Got DHCP answer from 10.0.2.2, my address is 10.0.2.15
IP-Config: Complete:
     device=eth0, addr=10.0.2.15, mask=255.255.255.0, gw=10.0.2.2,
     host=10.0.2.15, domain=, nis-domain=(none),
     bootserver=10.0.2.2, rootserver=10.0.2.2, rootpath=
```

These messages show an adapter that attempts to get an address via Dynamic Host Configuration Protocol (DHCP) and succeeds on the second attempt. DHCP is a protocol in which the board sends out a packet to the entire network requesting an address and waits for a reply. Because the board doesn't know if it will get a reply, it makes several attempts before giving up.

The kernel initialization of the hardware interface is necessary for kernels that will attempt to mount a root file system over the network using NFS or PXE, both of which were covered earlier in the book. If the kernel doesn't need to mount a remote file system as root, it doesn't need to configure the network adapter at this point, because this may happen later in the boot process; doing so results in the system getting to userland slightly faster, and you have more control over the assignment of the IP address if the operation is deferred until a userland scripting language can be used.

Sysfs and Device Management

As devices initialize, the practice is to use a certain data structure, a *kobject*, to track its existence. Kobjects aren't objects in the Yourdon and Coad[3] sense of the word; they're data structures used throughout the kernel that are exposed through the sysfs file system mounted at /sys. If your desktop is

---

[3] The book *Object-Oriented Design* by Peter Coad and Edward Yourdon (Prentice Hall, 1991) remains one of the most lucid explanations of how to approach object-oriented system design.

running a 2.6 kernel and doesn't have a file system mounted at /sys, do the following to make this file system available:

```
# mkdir /sys
# mount -t sysfs none /sys
$ cd /sys
```

One of the purposes of kobjects when they were introduced was creating a uniform, dependable way for a process in userland to see the device drivers loaded by the kernel. Their use has been expanded over the years to include keeping track of more types of kernel-level data. The notion of kobjects makes it very easy for devices to register and be queried from userland in order to create the device nodes files in the /dev directory, and that is why kobjects are important in the boot-up process.

■ **Note** Device nodes are an interesting concept if you're new to embedded Linux. Linux has a Unix heritage, in that a file establishes the semantics for how things communicate. A hardware device like a USB drive, mouse, or serial port uses a file for communication as well; however, these aren't real files but rather placeholders in the file system (device node files) that look like files. They serve as proxies for communicating with device drivers in the kernel. By writing or reading these things that look like files, the device driver calls functions that handle getting data from userland (the result of a write) or sending data to userland (the result of a read).

The typical desktop machine has a Linux distribution designed to work on some computer, but not necessarily your computer. During the boot-up process, the kernel probes the hardware and attempts to load drivers for that hardware. When those drivers load, they create a kobject in their tracking data structures that is registered by the kernel. The kobject is a data structure exposed in the sysfs file system. In user space, another process runs, called udevd, which inspects the sysfs file system to create the necessary entries in /dev for the device drivers that have been loaded. This is how the /dev file system gets populated with all those device nodes without your direct intervention. This process ensures that the /dev directory has device nodes for all the drivers—and that means the hardware is accessible to the system for use.

Most embedded systems have a fixed set of devices that doesn't change; the overhead of the sysfs file system and udevd is wasteful, because the set of device nodes necessary could be created once and stored on the root file system. This is worth mentioning at this point because it's important to understand what happens during the startup process. When the book discusses reducing boot time and root file system size, udev and the /dev and /sys directories are low-hanging fruit.

Finding a Root File System

After the hardware has initialized, the kernel searches for something to run. The first thing the kernel does is unpack the initial RAM files system, initramfs. Every kernel has one of these file systems, stored as a compressed cpio archive. If you didn't tell the kernel to create one, there's a very small, empty archive.

The purpose of initramfs is to have a failsafe way to load device drivers early in the boot process. Depending on the hardware, for example, the device driver for the device boots the system may not be known when the kernel is compiled and thus must be loaded so the kernel can use the device to continue the booting process. The kernel loads the initrd file system by using a file system that's a layer on top of the disk cache, with the small modification that changes are never written to the disk. How the initrd works is a clever hack. With very little overhead, the Linux system has a RAM disk that supports all the functionality of a disk-based file system.

After the initramfs is in memory, the kernel attempts to run /linuxrc. There is no way to specify another file—it's that or nothing. If this file exists, the kernel runs it and waits for it to finish before continuing the boot process. It's common practice for embedded systems to use initrd as the primary file system on the board, and this is perfectly acceptable. The BusyBox project built in the last chapter created a /linuxrc file in the root or installation for this purpose. If no /initrd file exists, or when it returns, the kernel continues its regular booting process.

After not finding an initrd, the kernel mounts the root file system. The kernel knows what to use because of the root and rootfstype kernel parameters. For example:

```
root=/dev/mtd0 rootfstype=jffs2
```

This line instructs the kernel to mount the file system at /dev/mtd0 and says that the file system type should be jffs2. But if no file system has been mounted at /, how can the kernel use a file /dev/mtd0 to mount the root file system? There seems to be a circular dependency. The answer is that during the startup process, the kernel maintains its own in-memory file system for the /dev file system that's disposed of when you mounts the real root file system.

If the device specified by root doesn't exist and isn't created in the temporary /dev file system created by the kernel, you must use the initial RAM disk root file system to load the appropriate driver and ensure that the proper entries exist in the /dev directory of the initramfs file system.

After the root file system has been mounted, the kernel needs to execute the userland init program. The kernel first uses what was specified as the init= parameter on the kernel command line. If you didn't provide an init argument, the kernel attempts to run the following commands, stopping at the first one that works:

```
/sbin/init
/etc/init
/bin/init
/bin/sh
```

If none of the above can run, the following error appears on the console:

```
No init found. Try passing init= option to kernel.
```

And the system stops.

NFS Root File Systems

Systems using Network File System (NFS) root file systems have an additional twist in the booting process. Because NFS file systems require a working network stack, one adapter must have an IP address. You set the IP address with the IP kernel parameter, which has the following format:

```
ip=host-ip:server-ip:gw-ip:netmask:hostname:device:auto-configure
```

A typical line looks like the following when you specify an IP address

```
ip=10.0.0.1:10.0.0.2:10.0.0100:255.0.0.0:theboard:eth0:off
```

or like this when you use DHCP to obtain IP information:

```
ip=:::::eth0:dhcp
```

Table 7-1 breaks this down and explains each parameter.

Table 7-1. *Parameters to the IP Kernel Argument*

Argument	Notes
Host IP	The IP address to assign to the board. This isn't required. In its absence, the kernel doesn't assign an IP address but still attempts to initialize the adapter.
Server IP	The IP address of the host with the NFS file system that will be mounted as root. Optional, because a server IP address can be supplied in the nfsroot parameter in the following section.
Gateway IP	The network's gateway IP address. Optional. When absent, the kernel doesn't attempt to route packets that aren't on the local network.
Netmask	Indicates what parts of an address are network and which identify a machine. In the example, the first 8 bits identify the network, and the remaining can be used to identify a machine. When not supplied, the kernel attempts to calculate a netmask based on the IP address. If the network address fits into the class A, B, or C range, it picks the right netmask automatically.
Hostname	The text name given to the host. A synonym for the IP address. Optional.
Device	The device name that is autoconfigured. No \dev is necessary. Required. This tells the kernel the hardware device to which to apply the prior parameters.
Autoconfigure	When off, the kernel doesn't attempt to use BOOTP or DHCP to get IP address information. This doesn't turn off the adapter. Optional. Default is BOOTP, which can result in the other parameters being overwritten with data from a BOOTP or DHCP server.[4]

After the system has an IP address, the next step is telling the kernel the IP address of the NFS server and what export to mount for the root file system. That information appears in the nfsroot kernel parameter, which follows this format:

```
nfsroot=nfs-server-ip-address:export-name,options
```

A typical NFS root parameter looks like the following:

---

[4] Get into the habit of putting something here. Many hours have been wasted trying to figure out why the IP address parameters aren't working either because they're being overwritten by a DHCP server that was forgotten about or because the kernel was run on a customer's network that was serving DCHP addresses while the development network wasn't. Not that any of this has happened to me.

```
nfsroot=10.0.0.2:/opt/boardrfs
```

Table 7-2 explains each parameter in detail.

Table 7-2. *NFS Root Parameters*

Argument	Notes
NFS server IP address	The IP address of the server that's exporting the NFS information. Optional. If the server is specified in the IP parameter, it's used by default. It's permissible for this to be different than the IP supplied in the IP parameter.
Export name	The directory on the NFS server to mount as the root file system. Required.
NFS options	Any option to control the NFS connection. The default parameters are sufficient; however, a table follows that describes GRUB's different values.

For the record, Table 7-3 lists the NFS options. When you're booting a board, the default NFS parameters are usually adequate. For a production system, you're likely to change the rsize and wsize parameters, because most devices perform better with higher numbers However, in some situations on a production, an NFS server is used as a data-sharing tool, and in that case, the parameters that control caching are of utmost importance.

Table 7-3. *NFS Mount Options*

Parameter	Default	Notes
Port	Returned by the port map daemon	Default value is usually 2049. To find out what the value is on your system, look in the /etc/services file.
Rwize	4096	The number of bytes in a read packet.
Wsize	4096	The number of bytes in a write packet. Setting this higher means the network generates fewer handshaking packets, thereby increasing the effective bandwidth.
Timeout	7	The number of seconds the server should wait before it considers the server as not responding.
Retrains	3	The number of times the client should retry a transmission before considering the connection inoperable.
Acregmin	3 (seconds)	The minimum amount of time the server can cache file-attribute information.

Acregmax	60 (seconds)	The maximum amount of time the server can cache file-attribute information. A lower number decreases performance in exchange for more current data.
Acdirmin	30 (seconds)	The minimum time directory attributes can be cached.
Acdirmax	60 (seconds)	The maximum time directory attributes can be cached.
soft/hard	soft	If a communications timeout occurs, using the soft timeouts results in the system producing a message for the system log and retrying indefinitely. Hard timeouts result in the program receiving an error. You should use hard timeouts in production systems so that errors can be properly handled.
posix/noposix	noposix	Mount the file system with POSIX semantics. This is important if the client mounting the server needs to query properties like the maximum name length.
cto/nocto	nocto	Stands for "close to open," meaning that when one NFS client closes a file, the next user opening the file sees all the changes from the prior close. This is important for NFS servers that have a large number of clients changing a few files.
ac/noacl	noacl	Indicates whether the system uses access control lists instead of UIDs/GIDs to grant file access.
lock/nolock	lock	Some very old NFS servers don't support locking. The default is the acceptable value, but dropping locking results in a slight performance gain.
Nsfvers	3	What NFS protocol to use. The other valid value is 2.
udp/tcp	tcp	What networking transport to use. UDP is lighter weight and faster, but it doesn't have the packet-delivery guarantees of TCP. Use UDP only if you really know what you're doing.
ac/noac	ac	Set (ac) to cache file attributes. Turn off (noac) so the NFS server doesn't keep a copy of the file attributes between system calls. Set to noac when several machines are writing to the same NFS share.
sync/nosync		Set to sync to wait for the data to be written to disk before returning from the write routine. Using nosync results in the server caching several writes and replying that the write completed as soon as it's queued, rather than when it was written.

Userland Startup

At this point, the system kernel is up and running, the root file system is mounted, and the system has found something to run. On most desktop systems, that something to run is usually init, but it could be any program. To find out, do the following:

```
$ ps aux | head -5
USER       PID %CPU %MEM    VSZ   RSS TTY      STAT START   TIME COMMAND
root         1  0.0  0.0   3056   128 ?        Ss   Apr19   0:01 /sbin/init
root         2  0.0  0.0      0     0 ?        S<   Apr19   0:00 [kthreadd]
root         3  0.0  0.0      0     0 ?        S<   Apr19   0:00 [migration/0]
root         4  0.0  0.0      0     0 ?        S<   Apr19   0:00 [ksoftirqd/0]
```

The process with the PID of 1 is the init process, in this case /sbin/init. On a desktop system, this file is either SysV init or Upstart (from Ubuntu, the binary name is called init, but it's nothing like the SysV init). For an embedded system, both of these solutions are overkill.

SysV init, the most common init, works by running certain programs based on a runlevel. A *runlevel* is an integer that represents what tasks the system should be running. The *level* part of runlevel may cause you to think that runlevels are scalar; however, this number is just an identifier. Thus runlevel 1 isn't "less than" runlevel 4. Systems with a graphical environment typically start in runlevel 5. Table 7-4 lists the conventions for assigning programs that should be run for a given runlevel

Table 7-4. *Run Level Descriptions*

Runlevel	Mode
0	System shutdown.
1	Single-user mode. The system doesn't start the network adapter or services. Uses a text console for login.
2	Not used.
3	Multiuser mode. The system starts the networking services. Log in through a text console.
4	Not used.
5	Multiuser mode with X Window login.
6	System reboot.

The parameters controlling how init works are stored in /sbin/init. The format for this file is cryptic; it's composed of lines in this format (see Table 7-5).

id:*runlevel*:*action*:*process*

Table 7-5. Runlevel Parametersn

Field	Explanation
Id	Some identifier for the row. This can be any value that contains letters and numbers, but it can't be longer than 4 characters.
Runlevel	The runlevel at which this command should be run. Because runlevels are one character long, there's no delimiter for multiple runlevels. Some actions ignore this field.
Action	What action should be taken for this line.
Process	The program to execute. Depending on the action, this can be empty.

There are many potential actions for each line. Most are unused, but it's helpful to know what's available. The order of Table 7-6 is the order in which init executes the actions.

Table 7-6. Runlevel Actions

Action	Explanation	Uses Process Field	Uses Runlevel Field
Initdefault	Specifies the default run level.	No	Yes
sysinit	Runs during system startup.	Yes	No
boot	Runs during system startup. Init spawns this task and runs the next task.	Yes	No
bootwait	Like boot, but init doesn't run the next command until this command finishes	Yes	No
respawn	Runs the process and restarts the process when it stops running.	Yes	Yes
wait	Runs the process and waits until it completes to run the next process.	Yes	Yes
once	Runs the process once during the runlevel.	Yes	Yes
ctrlaltdel	Executes a process when you press the Ctrl+Alt+Del key combination, triggering a SIGINT.	Yes	No
powerwait	Triggered by a UPS device when the commercial power is interrupted. Init waits for this to complete running.	Yes	Yes

powerfail	Like powewait, but init doesn't wait for this command to finish running before running the next command.	Yes	No
powerokwait	Means commercial power has been restored. Waits until this command finishes before running the next command.	Yes	No
powerfailno w	Means the UPS has exhausted battery backup and the system must be shut down.	Yes	No

The sysinit file can be very difficult to parse. Table 7-7 breaks down a sample inittab file and explains each part in detail.

Table 7-7. Example inittab lines

inittab line	What It Does
id:2:initdefault:	Instructs init that this system starts at runlevel 2. This means that in the following scripts, init executes the lines with runlevel 2 in the second field.
si::sysinit:/etc/init.d/rcS	This tells init to run the script /etc/init.d/rcS the first time init runs. Init waits for this command to finish running before looking for a runlevel-specific command to execute.
l0:0:wait:/etc/init.d/rc 0 l1:1:wait:/etc/init.d/rc 1 l2:2:wait:/etc/init.d/rc 2 l3:3:wait:/etc/init.d/rc 3 l4:4:wait:/etc/init.d/rc 4 l5:5:wait:/etc/init.d/rc 5 l6:6:wait:/etc/init.d/rc 6	This block of commands tells init what to run for each runlevel. During system initialization, init looks for the lines with the sysinit runlevel.
ca::ctrlaltdel:/sbin/shutdown -t1 -h now	The system runs the /sbin/shutdown command when you press Ctrl+Alt+Del. Removing this line disables this behavior. Even if the system doesn't have a keyboard, you should remove this line from production systems unless it's necessary.
1:23:respawn:/sbin/getty tty1 VC linux 2:23:respawn:/sbin/getty tty2 VC linux 3:23:resawn:/sbin/getty tty3 VC linux	The respawn command means these commands are reexecuted when they die. Each of these lines produces a login prompt. respawn ensures that when the command exits, it's rerun, so kernel doesn't die for the lack of something to execute.

This /etc/sysinit results in the following commands being run in the following order:

```
/etc/init.d/rcS
/etc/init.d/rc 2
/sbin/getty tty3 VC linux
```

Init continues to execute the last command any time it stops. The init command doesn't indiscriminately reexecute this command. If the command fails quickly a few times, init waits a few seconds before attempting to run it again.

■ **Note** You should configure at least one command for the system's starting runlevel as respawn. Otherwise, the kernel will panic and the system will stop running the when the command exits.

What an Init Program Needs to Do

When the kernel hands control to the init program, some things should happen to make the system usable. None of these steps are required; however, if they aren't done, commands that expect to be running on a regular embedded system will find that random problems occur. The following is a list of the housekeeping chores you should perform:

1. Mount the proc file system. This file system isn't required, but so many programs read it that it needs to be configured.

2. Ensure that /tmp exists and is read-write. The /tmp directory is a requirement: programs attempt to write to this directory, and not having it will result in errors that are very difficult to find.

3. Set the system $PATH to the location of the binaries on the system.

4. Run any daemons (background tasks like web servers or disk-sharing tools) necessary for the application.

Mysteries of the /etc/init.d Directory

The second command that runs in the startup sequence, /etc/init.d/rc 2, runs a script that's responsible for running a series of other scripts in the directory /etc/init.d/rcN.d, where N is the runlevel. This folder contains a series of symlinks that follow this format:

K|S##command

The K or S character means "Kill" or "Start"; ## is a number that's used to sort the entries, and command is an identifier (usually the name of the command to be run). Start means this command should be executed when entering the runlevel. The Kill command is run when leaving the runlevel. The command portion is informational, because the number controls how commands are executed.

The target of the symlink (that *target* is what the symlink points to) in the `/etc/init.d/rcN.d` directory is a file in the `/etc/init.d` directory. This level of indirection minimizes the amount of duplicated code: if you want to start the HTTP server in several runlevels, the commands to start this service reside in `/etc/init.d/http server`, and several symlinks reside in the `/etc/init.d/rcN.d` directories of the runlevels where the commands should run.

This set of scripts is perfect for a server or other enterprise-type system. It has terrific flexibility, and the different levels let you configure with a fine degree of control. This system isn't efficient with respect to time or storage space and isn't the best for a system where both are at a premium. The next two sections cover alternatives that are more appropriate for embedded systems.

BusyBox Init

BusyBox's `init` implementation is a common replacement for the SysV `init`. The BusyBox `init` program works much like the original, with the following exceptions

- *There are no runlevels:* The only runlevel supported is 0. If a runlevel is supplied, it's ignored.

- *Only the following actions are supported:* `sysinit`, `respawn`, `becausekfirst`, `wait`, `once`, `restart`, `ctrlaltdel`, and `shutdown`. The action `askfirst` provides a prompt asking that a key be pressed before running the command; it then works like `respawn` with respect to restarting the task.

- *The first field isn't an identifier:* This field is used to indicate what TTY device to use when running the program. This value is appended to `/dev/` when supplied, so the following lines run login processes on ttyS0 and ttyS1:

      ttyS0::respawn:/sbin/getty -L ttyS0 9600 vt100
      ttyS1::respawn:/sbin/getty -L ttyS1 9600 vt100

- If no `/etc/inittab` file is found, BusyBox uses this as a default:

      ::sysinit:/etc/init.d/rcS
      ::askfirst:/bin/sh
      ::ctrlaltdel:/sbin/reboot
      ::shutdown:/sbin/swapoff -a
      ::shutdown:/bin/umount -a -r
      ::restart:/sbin/init

The default `init` file is usually good enough to quickly get a system running. A production system needs to define something different.

Your Init

The program run for `init` can be anything that the system can execute: a binary, shell script, Perl script—the only requirement is that it can be run. Like any other `init` process, when this program stops, the kernel panics and halts. That means the program must be coded so that it works something like the `respawn` command in `init`. The typical strategy for implementing this sort of protection is to spawn the program such that the system runs in a separate process and restarts when it fails.

The code for this sort of program follows this pattern:

```c
#include <sys/wait.h>
#include <stdlib.h>
#include <unistd.h>
#include <stdio.h>

#define THE_APPLICATION "somebinary"

int main(int argc, char **argv)
{
    pid_t app, appstatus;
    int status;

    while (1) {
      app = fork();
      if (app == -1) {
        perror("could not fork, application not run");
        exit(EXIT_FAILURE); /* this is a panic */
      }

      if (app == 0) {
        execl(THE_APPLICATION, "");
        sleep(3);
      }
      else {
        appstatus = waitpid(app, &status, 0);
        printf("process exited with %d status, restarting\n", status);
      }
    }
}
```

The code is very simple in that when the program fails, the controlling program prints out a message, and the loop restarts. This code is basic enough that the opportunity for bugs is low; the simplicity means the resulting binary is small as well. The execution time for this approach is very low, because this init program doesn't need to open and parse a file in order to run the application.

What's Next

The next section of the book covers getting a development environment together to build an application. You pair the cross-compiler with other tools for debugging and development that embedded engineers use to be productive. Linux is very flexible, and you can code a project in any number of languages—maybe to two or three. In years past, C was the only language considered for embedded development, but now choices abound.

■ ■ ■

## CHAPTER 8

Configuring the Application Development Environment

Pick the Right Tool for the Job

Using Linux grants a great degree of freedom when you're selecting an approach to use when implementing a project; the same tools available on a desktop are available for an embedded project. The great variety of tools is very liberating for engineers who could only code in C in years past—now you can use C++, Perl, C#, shell scripts, Python, or Java to build an application. Picking the right tool for the job is an important decision that involves knowing the nature of the application and the hardware constraints.

Not only does Linux give you great freedom in selecting development tools, but the environment also doesn't limit the selection to one. Using a mix of C and Java is a perfectly good idea if the device will be communicating with an enterprise server that's running Java. It's also entirely practical to use C++ as the tool for the UI development while using a mix of shell scripts and Perl to process data. When you're selecting what to use for application development, the key isn't to focus on picking one right tool; the important part is to identify what the application is doing and then choose the correct development tools for different parts of the job.

This chapter starts by discussing the importance of understanding requirements: many projects get off on the wrong foot and never recover because the goals are never well understood by all involved. That results in the wrong choices being made. Embedded development can have some interesting twists and include requirements not found in other projects. Knowing about those twists before you start helps you identify risky parts of the project sooner. To paraphrase a random U.S. politician, "There are unknowns and unknown unknowns." This chapter makes both less mysterious.

Know Your Application

Knowing your application means understanding the requirements of the project. The *requirements*, in the software world, specify what the application must do. The process behind requirements is a book in itself;[1] however, the Zen of requirements boils down to the following:

1. Requirements are written.
2. Changes are tracked.
3. Project participants understand the requirements.
4. The requirements explain *what* and not *how*.

---

[1] I recommend reading the excellent *Managing the Software Process* by Watts Humphrey (Addison-Wesley Professional, 1989).

When you're an engineer working on the project, items 3 and 4 are very important. Many times, the product manager responsible for the project doesn't supply sufficient detail: for example, "The device must boot quickly" as opposed to "The device must be ready to process data in 10 seconds or less." Or you may get conflicting items like "The device must store 10,000 audio files" and "The device must have no more than 64MB of flash." The last requirement brings up the most obvious difference in embedded development: the additional constraints introduced by the hardware itself.

Hardware Constraints

When you're starting on the requirements for an embedded project, divide the list into hardware versus software constraints. Hardware requirements represent the most constraining items because they reflect equipment already in the field that can't be replaced, hardware that has been designed, or market expectations where users won't accept any other solution.

Some hardware constraints are easy to spot (touch screen, wired network connectivity, CANbus support), whereas others are more subtle. For example, the following place hardware constraints on the project that may not be intuitively obvious (some are real-life examples and others are made-up—see if you can tell):

- *The device will operate for 6 hours once disconnected from commercial power:* This was an actual requirement. It was later refined to include a statement about what sort of battery would be attached to the device. This requirement could be solved by attaching a car battery to the device, which was not the intent. After clarification regarding the type of backup power that could be accommodated and the notion of "operate," it was clear that the device needed to be a low-power chip with power management and not that much RAM memory, because that's a drain on power. This influenced the language selected (C, due to the low amount of memory) and the kernel (power management was key), which had a cascading effect throughout the project.

- *The unit will emit no more than 15 BTUs per hour:* Some equipment has a power budget, and the corollary to that is a heat budget. This is another requirement that affects the amount of RAM, CPU MHz, and type of power management that must be available. These sorts of requirements appear in all sorts of projects, and it's no accident that cell phones don't get too warm in your hand. This was a real customer requirement.

- *The product will produce 0 decibels of sound at 3 feet:* This means a couple of things: no fans for cooling, and no hard drive. The device must use flash memory. Home entertainment systems have requirements like this because nobody wants to hear a fan whirling during the favorite parts of their movie. Automotive devices fall into this category too, because background cabin noise is a competitive factor.

- *The system will make a routing decision in no more than 2 microseconds:* This is a sneaky requirement, because this is really a realtime system. *Realtime* means that if a deadline isn't met, the output of the system is incorrect. Realtime systems need to have software that works deterministically; but in order for the software to function as expected, the underlying hardware must also work in a deterministic manner. In this example, at a minimum, the system clock must have a minimum amount of drift and the hardware interfacing with the peripherals must also work accurately. *Drift* occurs when the system clock is running ahead or behind the real-world clock. This is not a traditional wall clock but the hardware clock used to drive the processor. When this clocks ticks at an irregular rate (as some do), it drifts out of time compared to a more accurate clock.

Left out of this list are additional requirements for interacting with special devices, like analog to digital converters or peripherals attached to the device via USB. These requirements impose needs on the operating system and supporting software as well. After you identify constraints that are hardware related, the next step is understanding the impact on the software that's selected for the project.

Software Constraints

Requirements also limit the possible choices for the development environment. Certain processing activities can only be achieved with lower-level software, and some hardware devices have libraries that work better in one language than another. Most software constraints appear in these areas:

- *Realtime:* Realtime, in the computer science sense, means predictable behavior, not fast or timely behavior. Some languages or tools don't offer predictable behavior because of garbage collection or a lack of control when accessing system resources such as peripheral devices. Other languages don't allow you to specify how memory is accessed, which can also result in unpredictable performance.

- *Graphical user interfaces:* Many devices have a user interface more complicated than a few LEDs and a power switch. In a device like a cell phone or GPS device, the user interface *is* the device from the user's perspective and largely determines the device's overall success. Picking a GUI library means picking the underlying technologies used for that library and using them for other parts of the project as well.

- *Throughput:* Throughput measures how many units of work a system can perform in a given amount of time. Code that is compiled to run directly on the machine is faster than code that runs on a virtual machine or inside an interpreter. Faster still is the code that runs without an operating system, because the operating system introduces overhead. The flexibility and extensibility offered by an OS pays for itself for most applications.

- *Interoperability/Extensibility:* Requirements around interoperability impose constraints because some libraries that support communication with databases or remote procedure calls (such as SOAP and CORBA) only function with select languages. Although you can use any general-purpose language to create the infrastructure necessary to communicate with some other program, the time necessary to do that work may not be permissible in the project's schedule. Plus, the bespoke implementation will be more buggy than a solution that's been running for years.

  In other cases, the device needs to be field-upgradeable or otherwise changed by the user in the field. In order to accomplish this, the device's software must be able to load and execute arbitrary code. Some languages have the concept of *late binding* built in (like Java and Python); with others (like C), loading and executing arbitrary code is more difficult.

- *Legacy:* Many project have code that's years old, that works, and that is kept because it performs a complicated algorithm too risky to attempt to port to another language. In some cases, the company shares code across projects in order to reduce testing and debugging overhead. This existing code may force you to select a certain language.

- *System size:* Devices that have very little memory or storage require you to select a development language that creates minimally sized programs. The language also needs to work with other libraries and code that is also designed to be small if system size is important. Most languages are small with runtime libraries that are large and monolithic; others have modular runtime environments that you can reduce to include only the code used by the application.

Requirements that affect what can be used for development should be marked as such, so that when you're deciding what to choose for development, you understand how the business requirements affected the technical decisions of the project. When you're selecting development tools, some business requirements may be subject to change, depending on the tools selected.

What to Use for Development

Linux gives you much more freedom when selecting development tools. Although C is still a reasonable choice, it shouldn't be the default choice; Linux offers an incredible selection of tools, from shell scripting to C. With that in mind, the primary dividing point is interpreted versus compiled languages. Compiled languages perform better and are generally smaller that interpreted languages. The most commonly used compiled language, C, is used because a C compiler is available—it was used to build the kernel. This chapter brings to light other tools and languages that embedded engineers frequently overlook. But first, C and C++.

C

The C language and Linux go hand in hand (going further back, Unix and C were developed at the same time, with Unix being a platform for C while C was one of the development tool for Unix). Because the Gnu C compiler (GCC) is necessary to compile the kernel, this tool is already running and known to be in a working state. This takes much of the technical risk out of using C, which usually makes managers and engineers happy.

C is a language where you have a great deal of control over the machine's resources via high-level constructs. When used properly, the type checking available in C results in code that can be checked at compile time for a vast array of errors that aren't found until much later with other languages. Because C is one step removed from assembler language, it makes working directly with the underlying hardware and processor as easy as possible. The variables in C map directly to the word length of the machine where it's running, and an array is nothing more than an alias for a block of memory.

With C, you have the most direct access to the functionality supplied by Linux: file handling, interprocess communication, threading, and process control. For example, other languages have the notion of starting a thread, but with C you can control the thread's stack size, its scheduling policy, whether the thread starts running after it's created, and even whether the parent process is able to wait on the thread to finish.

But the C language has limits for application development. It's a low-level, procedural language that gives you just enoughto shoot yourself in the foot. Type checking can be circumvented though type casts, and directly accessing the computer's memory can result in defects that aren't immediately obvious. The threading and process control can result in *race conditions* (a defect where the order of execution matters) and *deadlocks* (where threads are waiting on each other to complete an operation). The procedural nature of C also makes interacting with databases and other higher-level data structures difficult.

C's direct-access, laissez faire memory access can also result in the dreaded *memory leak*, where a program allocates memory and doesn't release it. Memory leaks can cause a system to fail at unpredictable times in very unpredictable ways. Later, the book discusses tools that help you locate memory leaks; but no software outperforms a person's ability to find and repair these problems.

If you need low-level control and performance, C is an excellent choice. However, if the application spends most of its time moving data around or querying a database and presenting the data to you, other choices can reduce the amount of time you spend in development and debugging.

C++

C++ is more than C with classes, but the object-oriented features in C++ are hugely differentiating. The C++ language has the notion of a class. A *class* is a data structure for which you define properties and methods. The properties in a C++ class look much like the members of a struct in C. *Methods* are function declarations that are also members of the class and that have as their scope the other members and properties of the class.

Working with classes are *templates*, which are language constructs that let you specify the type of something as a parameter. A C library uses typecasts (usually to void*) for handling arbitrary types, whereas a C++ library uses a template. The advantage of using the template is type-checking at compile time. The code can't add a real to a list of integers without generating an error.

Type checking goes beyond templates. As far as C++ is concerned, there's a difference between a char and an int, and trying to use these interchangeably results in an error at compile time.

Using C++ means using the C++ standard library, which is much more extensive than C's. C++ has the standard collection of I/O and math routines and adds features like containers and iterators.

For all of C++'s advantages, it still has some of the disadvantages of C in that you can have direct control over memory resources and can write programs that leak memory. Although the type checking is substantially better than C's, you can still use type casting to circumvent the type checking. C++ code also runs a little slower than C code, and the templates result in a larger image size. In addition to the technical reasons for using C++, you have a learning curve if you've spent years working in C: the similarities in syntax may lull you into thinking the languages are more similar than they really are.

Java

Java (neé Oak, as it was called by its inventors) is a language created with the idea of freeing you from the hardware platform. It's a combination of language, runtime environment, and standard library. As a language, Java has a syntax similar to C++ and many of the same constructs. Java is completely object oriented. To start a program, for instance, you need to create a class with an entry point; C++ still starts by calling a procedural entry point.

Java is a compiled language that is strongly typed. The compilation process, in all cases, produces code called *byte code* that executes on a Java Virtual Machine (JVM). At a stretch, this process can be thought of a cross-compilation. As long as the target hardware is a JVM, it's able to run Java byte code. *Strong typing* means the language requires variables to be declared before use and there is very little automatic conversion between types. For example, Java allows an assignment of an integer to a long integer, but it doesn't allow the assignment of an integer to a character variable.

With the addition of generics in Java 1.6, the language has functionality similar to that of templates in C++. This is a welcome addition, because, for example, the code for handling arbitrary list objects required you to cast objects into Object types (the base type for all objects in Java), reducing the ability to check for type problems at compilation time.

Java Runtime Environment

Java byte code runs on a JVM, which is fairly small—just a few hundred KB on a Linux system. Built on the Java language is a library of code for higher-level activities, like creating and handling files, thread synchronization, lists, and other utilities. This code is rather large—close to 100MB for the Java 1.5 library. You can reduce this when deploying Java by leaving out the locale data and only including the jar files (the equivalent of libraries for a compiled system) necessary to run the program on the target device.

Embedding Java: Using GCJ

Because Java is a compiled language, why not change the compilation output from Java byte code to machine language? GCJ, part of the GCC compiler set, does exactly that by being a *front end* for the GCC compiler. This means development can be done and tested in Java and then deployed on any machine that has a GCJ compiler, not just machines that have a JVM. You can have the development conveniences of Java and the performance of a natively compiled language.

Inside GCC, the process for compilation has steps that involve converting the input into a data structure that GCC can then use for optimization and eventual conversion into machine code for the target platform. So, GCJ parses the Java input for processing the same way the C compiler handles C code.

GCJ is part of the GCC compiler suite and can be built at the same time as the toolchain, but adding Java to the list of enabled languages when building the final compiler. Crosstool-ng has an option to build GCJ as well, and this is the recommended option as the GCJ front end; it usually requires patches to cross-build, and cross-tooling does an excellent job of keeping track of the source patches necessary for the target machine.

Compiling Java Code with GCJ

Compiling Java code with GCJ is like compiling any other code with GCC. Consider the following simple Java program:

```
class simpleProgram
{
    void hello() {
        System.out.println("Hello");
    }
    public static void main(String args[])
    {
        simpleProgram program = new simpleProgram();
        program.hello();
    }
}
```

To compile it, do the following:

```
<cross-compiler>-gcj simpleProgram.java -o test-java –main=simpleProgram
```

The –main parameter indicates what class contains the entry point. Java allows for multiple classes to have this function, so the compiler can't guess what class's main should be used as the entry-point for the program. The authors have made compiling with GCJ similar compiling a C program.

Embedded GCJ

After you compile the program in to a binary, it looks like any other binary that needs to be placed on a target system. Any libraries used by the file must be put in the target's /lib directory. All programs compiled with GCJ link to the libgcj.so library by default, so that must be copied to the target.

If you want to link statically, use the following command for the previous example:

```
<cross-compiler>-gcj simpleProgram.java \
        -static-libgcj -o test-java –main=simpleProgram
```

Depending on the size of the program, static linking may make sense. For example, the simple example program, when statically linked, is about 12KB in size, which is a much smaller footprint than the size of libgcj.so.

Non-Traditional Embedded Languages

Most embedded development has been done in C/C++ and Java. These languages can be configured to produce very resource efficient programs. However, when you're designing a board, the cost differential between 512MB and 1GB of RAM is just a few pennies, and flash memory is priced the same; saving a few 100KB here and there isn't as important as it used to be. In combination processors that are much more powerful, wringing the most out of every processor cycle also isn't as important. The engineering time value involved in optimizing code is much greater than adding a little more processing power, memory, and storage. One of the ways to make the best out of your time is to pick the highest-level language for the job and let the underlying language or runtime environment handle the details.

The following languages fall into the high-level category in that you don't need to worry about the underlying machine much when you're coding. Several commercial embedded systems use these languages as their primary development tool, so the information in this section isn't to illustrate that these can possibly be used but to let you know that these are practical alternatives to C/C++/Java.

Python

Python is a high-level, object-oriented, compiled language that runs on a Python virtual machine. The code runs anywhere a Python virtual machine is available. Python is a language that isn't high performance: the goal is to make code that is easy to read and debug. For applications where performance isn't paramount, Python is a great approach for development.

Python's core language is very simple with an extensive library, built from Python code. You can find the library of Python code at /usr/lib/python<version>. This directory contains both the source code and the object code; if you're new to python, it's an excellent educational tool. Python structures its code into many small library files, making the language adaptable for embedded development; you can put just the libraries used for the project on the target.

Embedding Python

To use Python in an embedded project, you must build the Python virtual machine for the target. That virtual machine is built with a cross-compiler. To build Python, you need a cross-compiler built as explained in the previous chapter with the glibc library, but you can't use the uClibc C library to build the Python virtual machine. First, obtain and download the source code:

```
$ wget http://www.python.org/ftp/python/<version>/Python-<version>.tgz
$ tar xzf Python-<version>.tgz
```

You can find the list of current Python releases at http://www.python.org/download/releases/. The latest version of Python is 3.2.1. The 3.0 line of Python contains enough new features that some older code written for Python 2.x won't compile or run, and this has stopped users from switching. Because the 2.x line of Python is more popular, version 2.6.2 is used as the example version.

After unpacking the code, change directories into the source directory and use the `configure` command to set up the build environment:

```
$ cd ./Python-<version>
$ CC=<compiler> ./configure -prefix=<board-rfs>
$ make
$ make install
```

Change *<board-rfs>* to the directory containing the board's root file system, because this is a directory on the development host before it's readied for deployment on the board. The build process chugs along and produces a working Python virtual machine.

Code development can occur on any machine, even one without Python, because Python binary on the target machine can be used to compile the code. The best practice, however, is to use a Python runtime on the development machine to test the code for logic and syntax errors. The object code produced by Python can then be put on the target machine. Take the following example program:

```
import sys

def main(argv = None):
    for arg in argv:
        print arg

if __name__ == "__main__":
    main(sys.argv)
```

There isn't a compile utility in Python proper; you produce object code by importing the module and having interpreter compile the code as a side effect. Helper modules make this easy, such as the `compileall` module that can be pointed at a directory or path and that imports the files. For example, this simple script compiles all the code in the current directory:

```
import compileall
compileall.compile_dir(".");
```

After compilation, you can move the `pyc` files to the target's root file system. When Python sees an `import` command, it finds the compiled python program in the path (or current directory) and loads it for execution.

Debugging

Python's debugger is a module that's imported before a module is run, but it doesn't support remote debugging in the same way that GCC does. To debug the code on the target, put the debugger module, `pdb`, on Python's import path on the target machine, and do the same process from a console. A debugging session looks like this:

```
>>> import pdb
>>> import hello
>>> pdb.break('hello.main:1')
>>> pdb.run('hello.main()')
```

This series of commands loads the pdb debugger and then the module to debug. A break point is set for the first line in the hello.main function, and then main runs, tripping the breakpoint. The debugger module is only 40KB, so there should be space for it on any system. The debugger doesn't require much in the way of RAM resources, so it's practical to run on systems without much free memory.

TCL

TCL is an interpreted scripting language that is procedural with object-oriented language extensions. TCL (rhymes with "pickle") doesn't run in a TCL virtual machine similar to the way Python or Java works; instead, it's read by an interpreter and executed. The nature of the language is such that each line starts with a declaration or function name. The TCL interpreter uses the name of the TCL function to locate a C symbol and then calls that with the parameters as an array.

What makes TCL such an inviting language to use for embedded systems is how well it interfaces with C. It lets you write timing-critical or low-level code in C and do the remaining development in TCL.

TCL also has a windowing library, Tk. Tk provides a TCL interface over the X Window environment and uses the object-oriented features in TCL to represent the windowing system elements. Tk is designed to be a thin layer over the underlying windowing kit to keep a small and light library.

Embedding TCL

You can obtain the software for TCL at http://www.tcl.tk/software/tcltk/download.html. Download the source, and perform a cross-build using these steps:

```
$ tar xzf tcl<version>-src.tar.gz
$ cd tcl<version>/unix
$ export tcl_cv_strtod_buggy=1
$ export ac_cv_func_strtod=yes
$ CC=<cross-compiler> ./configure -prefix=<board-rfs>
$ make
$ make install
```

This compiles TCL with the cross-compiler and puts the resulting code in the board's root file system. These two commands

```
$ export tcl_cv_strtod_buggy=1
$ export ac_cv_func_strtod=yes
```

compensate for incorrect assumptions made when cross-compiling; in this case, the configuration script assumes that the cross-compiler's library doesn't have strtod, and it creates this function as part of the build. If these are forgotten, an error similar to this appears during the build process:

```
fixstrtod.c:(.text+0x0): multiple definition of `fixstrtod'
```

TCL with its libraries consumes about 1MB of disk space. Most of TCL's functionality is contained in the libtcl<version>.so library, and there isn't a way to reduce the size of this file by removing functionality when building. Because most TCL programs are small, this overhead is tolerable.

A simple TCL program looks like this:

```
puts "Here are the arguments"
foreach i $argv { puts $i }
```

To run this code, save it in a file such as `aprogram.tcl` and do the following:

```
$ tcl<version>  aprogram.tcl
```

Generally, you'll put the following at the top of a TCL script and mark the file as executable:

```
#!/usr/bin/tclsh
```

Use this command to make the file executable:

```
$ chmod +x aprogram.tcl
```

When the file is marked as executable, Linux examines this first line, \ runs the program following the #! (called *hash bang*), and then changes the standard input of the following program to the rest of the current file. That means you can execute the program by running it from the command line like a binary:

```
$ ./aprogram
```

It's worth noting that this trick isn't limited to TCL, and this is a common practice in Linux.

Debugging

You debug in TCL through the incredibly powerful (or primitive) `puts` statement. The language doesn't have a built-in debugger, so several tools have come into being to support debugging. The most commonly used tool is ActiveState's Komodo debugger, with RamDebugger a close second. Komodo supports remote debugging, which is handy for embedded development. Even so, the best practice is to do as much debugging on the development host as possible, because remote debugging has communication and resource overheads that can overwhelm some hardware platforms. Plus, debugging locally is quicker even if the target device is a powerful computer with fast communication.

To get the open source version of Komodo, visit `http://downloads.activestate.com/Komodo/releases` and select a release. If you're the daring sort, pick the latest release and download it. The file is large, about 50MB, so be prepared to wait depending on the speed of your network connection.

Shell Scripting

The shell used on most Linux system is Bash. It's a powerful language for development in and of itself. As with all of Linux, there are many choices for a shell, including ash, nash, dash, and tcsh. Each shell has its merits and drawbacks, and all offer the same core features with respect to executing files and redirecting input through pipes and files. This book uses Bash to illustrate the concepts of shell scripting because you probably have it available on your development host, and it may be the default shell.

Bash works primarily by executing commands in the file system and using piping to move data between programs. In this way, Bash is easily extensible and can work with existing programs with ease, because the data output to the console can be filtered through a text-handling program (like `awk`) to be parsed before being sent to another program.

The glue that holds shell scripting together as a language is the simple notion of pipes (|) and redirection (>, <). When you use a pipe, the output of one program is attached to the input of another. The concept of attaching input and output works because Linux programs follow the convention of reading input from a *standard in* file and writing output to a *standard out* file. These files are opened for programs automatically, and most programs stick to using them for input and output. The redirection symbols write the standard output of a program to a file (>) or read a file and pass the data to the standard input.

Shell scripts don't execute code quickly, but it's easy to write code in C or another language that does run quickly. Thus programs are rarely written as 100% shell scripts, but rather use the shell scripting language as a way to integrate various programs. One of the nicest things about shell scripting is that each program can be independently tested and verified easily; reuse is also more practical, because the program as a whole can be placed in another project wholesale.

Embedded Shell Scripting

Embedding the shell on an embedded device isn't a demanding activity. The Bash shell is statically linked (so it runs under most circumstances); and all distributions come with a shell or some sorts, because this is necessary to run the startup scripts for the system. Using what comes with the distribution is usually a good approach, unless you need a shell other than the default.

PHP

Seasoned embedded engineers gasp in disbelief when PHP is mentioned as a possible language, mostly because PHP has been so strongly associated with web development. The language is interpreted and weakly typed, which reduces the amount of development effort, but it can produce write-only code and makes testing a little more challenging. PHP has the concept of *types*, but the software may coerce a variable into another type of when necessary with no warning. Even uninitialized variables return a type of null; when used in a calculation, they have the value 0.

PHP is a good language for embedded development for the same reasons it's popular for web development: it's a stable, feature-rich environment that's very easy to use. PHP has mix of object-oriented and procedural idioms, and you're free to pick a mix of what's best for your project and your personal preferences.

PHP has an extensive list of built-in functions, and these are a prime reason to use the language. The standard library for PHP contains functions for networking, handling arrays, and parsing regular expressions and also has great support for MySQL and PostgreSQL. This makes it an ideal tool for applications that interact with a database. PHP is a well-supported language with a large and growing number of extensions.

Nothing in the PHP language disallows it from being used outside of a web server; this was made easier with the introduction of the php program, which runs a PHP script like any other scripting language. To experiment with PHP from the command line, install the PHP command-line client by doing the following:

```
$ sudo apt-get install php5-cli
```

Use this if your system is RPM based:

```
$ sudo yum install php5-cli
```

This installs a program on the system that you can use to run PHP scripts in the following fashion:

```
php hello.php
```

The PHP script can also begin with a #!/usr/bin/php so you can run the program directly from the command-line. For example, this code

```
#!/usr/bin/php
<?php
function info($something='') {
        print $something;
}

print "Hello there";
?>
```

can be executed by doing the following to make the file executable

```
$ chmod +x ./test.php
```

and then running it from the command line:

```
$ ./test.php
```

Embedding PHP

You can cross-compile PHP by obtaining the source code from http://www.php.net/downloads.php. This page contains a list of mirrors to pick from; use the mirror closest to your location:

```
$ wget ftp://xmlsoft.org/libxml2/libxml2-2.6.30.tar.gz
$ tar xzf libxml2-2.6.30.tar.gz
$ CC=powerpc-405-linux-gnu-gcc ./configure --host=powerpc-linux-gnu
 --disable-all --enable-cli
```

PHP is highly configurable. Although this example shows a configuration that builds on most systems, running `./configure -help` shows the number of things you can set. When you're enabling additional functionality, the build must include a library that enables that extension; that is something that must also be built before you build PHP. If you disable the extensions, the build requires the least number of dependencies and is easiest to compile. As more about the application becomes known, you can rebuild PHP with additional features. After it's built and installed, you can use the command-line PHP interpreter to run scripts.

Performance and Profiling Tools

Even after your code is running and formally works, it usually isn't finished. There can be defects that aren't easily spotted or that don't appear until after the code has run for days or weeks. In order to find these problems, you can use a wide range of tools, with each looking at a different aspect of the code. Profiling tools look at what runs when, static analysis tools examine code and find problems based on how the code is written, and memory-leak checkers run code and check for places where memory is being reserved but never properly released.

Profiling

Profiling tools show how a program is spending time and are invaluable in helping you understand where to spend time to optimize performance. GCC includes an excellent profiling tool, gprof. It's a two-part tool: one part builds the application so that it collects the performance data, and the other parses the data and displays the results.

To build a program with instrumentation, add the -pg and -g flags to the compilation step. For example, suppose you have the following code for a bubble sort:

```
#include <stdlib.h>
#include <stdio.h>
#include <time.h>

#define ELEMENTS 25000

void swap(int* first, int* second) {
  int t;

  t = *first;
  *first = *second;
  *second = t;

}

int main() {
  int i, j, vector[ELEMENTS];

  srand((unsigned int)time(NULL));

  for(i = 0; i < ELEMENTS; vector[i++] = (int)rand() % 100);
  for(i = 0; i < ELEMENTS; i++)
    for(j = 0; j < ELEMENTS-1; j++)
      if(vector[j] > vector[j+1]) {
              swap(vector + j + 1, vector + j);
      }

  printf("Done sorting %d elements\n", ELEMENTS);
}
```

Store this code in a file called bubblesort.c, and compile it with the -g -pg options:

```
$(CC) bubblesort.c -g -pg -o bubblesort
```

$(CC) is the cross-compiler for the board. Or, if you're experimenting with this on your desktop machine, use GCC. Running the program produce the gmon.out file in the directory where the program was run. The gmon.out file contains the runtime information for the file, which gprof then uses to produce output using the following command:

```
$(GPROF) bubblesort gmon.out
```

For $(GPROF), substitute the gprof included with the toolchain. The output is something close to the following:

```
Each sample counts as 0.01 seconds.
  %   cumulative   self              self    total
 time   seconds   seconds    calls  ns/call ns/call  name
 75.85     3.58     3.58                              main
 24.15     4.72     1.14 155384964     7.34    7.34  swap
```

(output clipped to save the trees, you'll see some documentation when running this on your computer)

                        Call graph (explanation follows)

granularity: each sample hit covers 4 byte(s) for 0.21% of 4.72 seconds

```
index % time    self  children    called     name
                                                <spontaneous>
[1]     100.0   3.58      1.14                 main [1]
                1.14      0.00 155384964/155384964     swap [2]
-----------------------------------------------
                1.14      0.00 155384964/155384964     main [1]
[2]      24.2   1.14      0.00 155384964        swap [2]
-----------------------------------------------
```

 This table describes the call tree of the program, and was sorted by
(output clipped to save even more trees, you'll see some documentation when running this on your computer)
   [1] main   [2] swap

The output is about as self explanatory as you could ever want. The first few lines make it clear that the program spends the majority of its time in the main() function and a much smaller portion in the swap() function:

```
  %   cumulative   self              self    total
 time   seconds   seconds    calls  ns/call ns/call  name
 75.85     3.58     3.58                              main
 24.15     4.72     1.14 155384964     7.34    7.34  swap
```

However, this doesn't give you insight into how the time is spent in main. Using the -l parameter outputs profiling data on a line-by-line basis, as follows:

```
  %   cumulative   self              self    total
 time   seconds   seconds    calls  ns/call ns/call  name
 31.04     1.47     1.47                              main (bubblesort.c:38 @
804865e)
 25.85     2.69     1.22                              main (bubblesort.c:37 @
80486a8)
```

15.25	3.40	0.72				main (bubblesort.c:39 @ 8048679)
7.63	3.77	0.36				swap (bubblesort.c:21 @ 804859f)
6.14	4.05	0.29				swap (bubblesort.c:22 @ 80485a7)
5.08	4.29	0.24				swap (bubblesort.c:23 @ 80485b1)
4.03	4.49	0.19	155384964	1.22	1.22	swap (bubblesort.c:18 @ 8048594)
2.44	4.60	0.12				main (bubblesort.c:37 @ 8048655)
1.27	4.66	0.06				main (bubblesort.c:27 @ 80485bb)
	4.72	0.06				swap (bubblesort.c:25 @ 80485b9)

From this, it's obvious that you should examine lines 38-39 of main() in bubblesort.c to see whether the code can be optimized to run faster. The code in question is the following:

```
for(j = 0; j < ELEMENTS-1; j++)
  if(vector[j] > vector[j+1]) {
    swap(vector + j + 1, vector + j);
```

On inspection, it seems that you can make some optimizations. Because this program was compiled without any optimization, the easiest thing to do is let GCC do the optimizations by compiling with the -03 flag, which instructs the compiler to build the most optimized code possible:

```
$(CC) bubblesort.c -03 -g -pg -o bubblesort
```

After you run the program, gprof reports the following:

30.48	0.45	0.45	main (bubblesort.c:38 @ 8048668)
26.37	0.83	0.39	swap (bubblesort.c:23 @ 8048675)
19.18	1.11	0.28	swap (bubblesort.c:21 @ 804866f)
11.99	1.28	0.17	main (bubblesort.c:37 @ 804867a)
11.99	1.46	0.17	swap (bubblesort.c:22 @ 8048672)

This shows a huge performance increase over the unoptimized code.

What the profiler doesn't tell you directly is when the program is taking the wrong approach to solve a problem. The bubble-sort system doesn't scale and isn't the fastest way to sort a medium-sized list, but it does work well for smaller lists. Instead of investing effort in making the code go faster, the smarter approach is to consider replacing poorly performing sections with code implemented to best handle the expected use cases.

Gprof Option Reference

The previous example shows a few output options for gprof. Table 8-1 contains a complete reference for gprof command-line parameters.

Table 8-1. *Gprof commandline reference*

Parameter	Explanation
-a	Don't include private functions in the output.
-e <*function*>	Exclude output for a function <*function*>. Use this when there are functions that won't be changed. For example, some sites have source code that's been approved by a regulatory agency, and no matter how inefficient, the code will remain unchanged.
-E <*function*>	Also exclude the time spent in the function from the percentage tables.
-f <*function*>	The opposite of -e: only track time in <*function*>.
-F <*function*>	Only use the time in <*function*> when calculating percentages.
-b	Don't print the explanatory text. If you're more experienced, you can appreciate this option.
-s	Accumulate samples. By running the program several times, it's possible to get a better picture of where time is spent. For example, a slow routine may not be called for all input values, and therefore you maybe mislead reading where to find performance problems.

Leak Detection

Most leaks are memory leaks, where a program allocates memory from the heap (or free store) and then never properly releases that memory. Thus the memory can't be reallocated until the process stops running and the operating system then frees all resources. Memory leaks are dangerous because they're latent problems that don't affect a system until it has been running for some time. When a system needs to be running for days or weeks, even a small memory leak can consume all the memory allocated to a process.

The concept of leaking can be applied to any limited resource that a program reserves for use and never relinquishes. A program can just as easily leak file handles as memory. The nature of programming usually results in memory being leaked, so tools focus on that problem. All memory-leak tools tell you where the allocation occurred that wasn't released; they don't show you what you'd like to find, which is where the memory wasn't released.[2]

---

[2] This makes perfect sense. How can the computer show where something should have been released? Nonetheless, some users expect to run a leak-detection tool and have it figure where the memory is leaking. They're disappointed when they get a list of the mallocs that somewhere down the line aren't released properly.

Many leak-detection tools are available; however, dmalloc and mpatrol are the most commonly used in embedded because they demand the least amount of resources on an embedded target where memory is at a premium.

dmalloc

This tool is part of the GNU standard library and works well. It works by logging the calls to free() and malloc() and seeing when a pointer delivered by malloc() isn't returned via a corresponding free(). Engineers frequently use this tool for three reasons: it's there and available with little or no extra effort, it works well on a large number of platforms, and it has low overhead. Because it's part of glibc, using this isn't an option for systems running uClibc or another C library.

Suppose you have the following program (called leak.c) that does nothing but leak memory:

```
#include <stdlib.h>
#include <mcheck.h>

int main() {
  int i;

  for(i=0; i< 10; i++) {
    malloc(i+1);
  }
return 0;
```

You need to do the following to build the program for use with dmalloc:

1. Add calls to mtrace() and muntrace() as the first and last executable lines in the program. This turns tracking on and off. If the program was larger and was suspected to be leaking in a small area, you could enable for just that subset of the program, reducing the resource overhead of the profiling.

2. Compile the program with -g, where $(CC) is your cross-compiler:

   ```
   $(CC) leak.c -g -o leak
   ```

3. Put the program on the target computer, and set the environment variable MALLOC_TRACE to a file that can be opened for write:

   ```
   export MALLOC_TRACE=/tmp/leak
   ```

4. Run the program.

5. Use the mtrace file to view the results.

The mtrace program is a Perl script that produces output like the following:

```
Memory not freed:
-----------------
   Address      Size      Caller
0x09f98378       0x1   at 0x8048461
```

```
0x09f98388     0x2  at 0x8048461
0x09f98398     0x3  at 0x8048461
0x09f983a8     0x4  at 0x8048461
0x09f983b8     0x5  at 0x8048461
0x09f983c8     0x6  at 0x8048461
0x09f983d8     0x7  at 0x8048461
0x09f983e8     0x8  at 0x8048461
0x09f983f8     0x9  at 0x8048461
0x09f98408     0xa  at 0x8048461
```

The program predictably leaks an increasing amount of memory each time the loop iterates, as shown by the increasing value in the size column, so the output from mtrace matches expectations. This case shows when mtrace can't resolve the caller address into a line, which is common for embedded systems where the source code isn't in a location that can be correlated to an address. In this case, use addr2line in the toolchain to get the offending line:

```
$ $(ADDR2LINE) -e<path to binary>/leak  0x8048461
/home/gene/code/leak.c:8
```

This shows that the address is line 8 in leak.c:

```
malloc(i+1);
```

And this was expected.

Mpatrol

Mpatrol is a lightweight memory-leak detection tool that's been around for nearly ten years. It works the same way as dmalloc: the malloc and free functions are overridden, and the system tracks what's been requested versus what's been relinquished. Mpatrol supported on x86 and some PowerPC platforms. The lack of support for ARM means that many embedded engineers can't use mpatrol.

To obtain mpatrol, visit this site, download the source tar file, unpack it, and do the following:

```
$ cd mpatrol/pkg/auto
$ ./setup
$ export ac_cv_func_setvbuf_reversed='no'
$ CC=powerpc-405-linux-gnu-gcc ./configure --build=powerpc-linux-gnu -
prefix=/tmp/board-dev
$ make
$ make install
```

The mpatrol library is installed into the /tmp/board-dev directory. To compile a program with mpatrol support, you need to add some additional libraries to the command line. These libraries are part of a glibc installation:

```
$(CC) -I/usr/local/include -L/tmp/board-dev/lib -lmpatrol -lbfd
 -liberty -lintl
```

Static Analysis

Static analysis means finding defects in code without executing the code. Static analysis is helpful for embedded systems because you can run the analysis code on a development host and not worry about the overhead on an embedded target that may be low on resources. The most commonly used tool for static analysis on Linux is passing the correct -pedantic -Wall flags into GCC so that it's very verbose about warnings. For example, compiling the bubble-sort code produces the following errors:

```
bubblesort.c:33:3: warning: C++ style comments are not allowed in ISO C90
bubblesort.c:33:3: warning: (this will be reported only once per input file)
bubblesort.c: In function (main)
bubblesort.c:43: warning: control reaches end of non-void function
```

This little bit of code has several errors that aren't reported with the regular compiler settings.

■ **Note** the -pedantic -Wall flags are your friends. Consider always compiling with these settings, because they flag problems at compile time that frequently result in runtime problems.

What GCC doesn't find, a program called splint does. Splint is a free implementation of the static analysis tool lint that's been around since the dawn of Unix. You can install splint by doing this

```
$ sudo apt-get install bubblesort.c
```

or this

```
$ sudo yum install bubblesort.c
```

Using splint with this code produces the following output:

```
$ splint bubblesort.c
bubblesort.c: (in function main)
bubblesort.c:43:2: Path with no return in function declared to return int
  There is a path through a function declared to return a value on which there
  is no return statement. This means the execution may fall through without
  returning a meaningful result to the caller. (Use -noret to inhibit warning)
bubblesort.c:18:6: Function exported but not used outside bubblesort: swap
  A declaration is exported, but not used outside this module. Declaration can
  use static qualifier. (Use -exportlocal to inhibit warning)
    bubblesort.c:25:1: Definition of swap
```

Of all the static analysis tools, perhaps the best one is located behind your eyes. You should engage in regular code reviews, where you explain the code to your peers and get feedback. No matter how well these tools work, they can't understand the program to the point necessary to spot truly complex defects.

IDE

Integrated Development Environments (IDEs) are nothing new. Several embedded vendors tout that they have a set of tools wrapped in an IDE that's been created with the embedded developer in mind. In reality, most of these tools become shelfware when you find that the tools available in open source are just as good, if not better, for embedded development chores.

This section covers several different approaches for getting the tools in place for an IDE that's productive for embedded engineers. These projects are all mature and ready for use in a production environment. Like any tool, each of these has limitations that you should consider before making your selection as well as great functionality that reduces the drudgework involved with embedded development.

Your Editor + Make + Shell

This is the most popular IDE by far. Using these tools gives you the most control over the development environment in exchange for more work on your part. You create and maintain make files for the project and interact with the code librarian on the command line. Using the shell has the very tangible benefit of a ready-to-use set of scripts for building the software in a separate build system, as long as the engineers have been disciplined enough to put all the settings in make files or shell scripts.

You can choose from hundreds of editors. Sometimes, an editor is almost a religious preference, and this book makes no effort to pick one over another. If you're new to Linux, I advise you to try a few to see which ones you're comfortable with. Table 8-2 lists some popular editors, in no particular order.

Table 8-2. *Selection of editors available on Linux*

Editor	Pros	Cons
Vi (really vim or nvi) `www.vim.com` or `http://www.bostic.com/vi/`	Excellent syntax highlighting for a wide range of files. Fast and small. Implementations exist on nearly all operating systems.[3]	Steep learning curve. Editing modes are very confusing to new users.
Emacs `www.gnu.org/software/emacs/`	Integrated with a wide range of tools. Runs on Windows. Highly configurable. Interfaces well with the C debugger.	Easy to start using. Steep learning curve for advanced features. Default set of keyboard shortcuts is disorienting to new users.
Nano `www.nano-editor.org`	Fast and small. Keyboard shortcuts are always displayed; easier to learn.	Terminal based, with hard-to-configure font faces. Doesn't contain the same depth of features as other editors.

---

[3] This editor also has a gang sign: `http://www.homebrew.net/visign/`.

Joe
`http://joe-editor.`
`sourceforge.net`
	Great syntax highlighting. Easy to configure for new languages.
	Built-in key bindings for WordStar and Emacs.
	Contains extra features like a hex-editor and scientific calculator.
		No built-in macro language.
		Can't edit files side-by-side.

Using Make

Although using make is worth a book in itself,[4] this section looks at make through the lens of a user who is already a little familiar with the tool. Make is a tool that looks at a target and dependencies and figures out what steps are necessary to create the target if it's out of date with its dependencies. The notion of *out of date* means the file system has a date on a dependency that's newer than the target file. Make then looks to see if there's a rule to rebuild the dependency, first by name then by file extension.

A make rule looks like this:

```
output-file: input1.o input2.o input3.o
       $(CC) $^ -o $@
```

This line is read, "output-file is made from input1.o input2.o and input3.o" and means that make attempts to be sure that on the file system, the dependencies are up to date before running this rule. To help you be more productive, make has a large number of predefined rules; the author of a make file doesn't need to write much in the make file to get something built. This has disadvantages in that a make file seems to work by magic, because you haven't specified much of anything but make still seems to have enough information to build something.

One of the most confusing aspects of make files is the usage of environment variables and how those affect make. When make starts, all environment variables become make variables. Make sets defaults for some variables so that the predefined rules work on most targets. Make's rules then use these variables to execute tools to build dependencies. In the previous example, the tool $(CC) defaults to the value of cc, which is a symlink to GCC on most systems.

For embedded projects, you can still use the standard make file rules, but some make variables need to be changed so that they point to the cross-compiler and not the native tools on the system. Table 8-4 lists the most frequently reset variables.

Table 8-3. *A Selection of Make Variables*

Variable	Default Value	Purpose
CC	cc	Default C compiler.
LD	ld	Linker.

---

[4] *Managing Projects with GNU Make* by Robert Mecklenburg (O'Reilly, 2004) is a great book to get your head around this tool, but it's for more advanced readers. If you're a beginner, consult the make documentation at `http://www.gnu.org/software/make/manual/`.

CPP	cpp	C preprocessor.
CXX	g++	C++ compiler. The Xs are +s on their sides.
AR	ar	Archive tool for creating static libraries.
OBJCOPY	objcopy	Copies a binary file, respecting the internal format.
OBJDUMP	objdump	Reads and prints out sections of an ELF file. You can use Objdump to see what shared libraries, if any, a file uses.
STRIP	strip	Removes sections from an ELF formatted file. Frequently used to discard debugging information, it can be used to remove any section of a file.

Each of these variables has a corresponding FLAGS variable in the format <*variable name*>FLAGS that's used to pass parameters in for that tool. The FLAGS variable makes it so that you don't need to alter the built-in rules to change how the programs work.

In most projects, the LDFLAGS (flags for the linker) are updated to include references to additional libraries and link instructions, such as when you want to build without shared libraries.

When you're cross-building, you should set these in the environment or in the make file so that the right tools are invoked. The kernel's make file appends the default value to a prefix to the tools that you supply—for example, from the kernel make file:

```
AS              = $(CROSS_COMPILE)as
LD              = $(CROSS_COMPILE)ld
CC              = $(CROSS_COMPILE)gcc
CPP             = $(CC) -E
AR              = $(CROSS_COMPILE)ar
NM              = $(CROSS_COMPILE)nm
STRIP           = $(CROSS_COMPILE)strip
OBJCOPY         = $(CROSS_COMPILE)objcopy
OBJDUMP         = $(CROSS_COMPILE)objdump
```

When you run the make file, the value of $(CROSS_COMPILE) is passed via the environments:

```
export CROSS_COMPILE=armv4l-linux-
make zImage
```

Or it can be passed in the value CROSS_COMPILE when make is run:

```
make CROSS_COMPILE=armv4l-linux-
```

No matter which way make is invoked, the result is the same. When you're working on embedded projects, all you need to do is use the built-in make variables and tools. The rest of the software adjusts to the project.

Eclipse

Eclipse has quickly become the IDE of choice, and not just for embedded engineers. This project was released by Object Technologies (a unit of IBM) more than 5 years ago as a general-purpose coding platform with very strong support for Java.[5] Shortly after the introduction of the Java-oriented Eclipse release, the C Development Toolkit (CDT; the Java IDE was called the JDK early on) was released; it provided rudimentary C support. Over the years, the CDT has become much more robust and feature-complete.

Installing Eclipse and Plug-ins

Eclipse is designed to be highly extensible. Its extensions are known as *plug-ins*, and the CDT is such a plug-in. To use Eclipse, the easiest thing to do is get the version from the package manager:

```
$ sudo apt-get install eclipse
```

Here's the command for RPM systems:

```
$ sudo yum install eclipse
```

And then you wait. An Eclipse installation is about 350MB and takes at least 15 minutes to download with a reasonably fast Internet connection. After you download it, run Eclipse and install the CDT by pointing Eclipse at the CDT plug-in update site. To do so, select Help ➤ Software Updates ➤ Find and Install (see Figure 8-1).

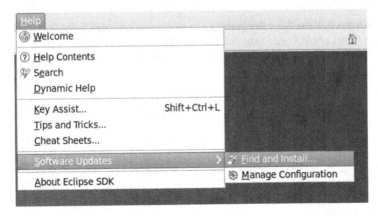

Figure 8-1. *Finding Eclipse updates*

---

[5] There was a bit of a fad going on at the time, with IDEs written in Java all but springing from the earth like summer annuals; many have since withered away. I think Eclipse succeeded because the IDE is a strong tool for creating Eclipse IDE extensions and the authors were smart enough to use a GUI library other than the hideous and slow AWT/Swing.

Doing so displays the dialog shown in Figure 8-2. Choose "Search for new features to install." This is a misnomer because it doesn't search for the features: you need to tell it a URL that contains the binaries for the plug-in that the wizard should download and install into the current Eclipse configuration.

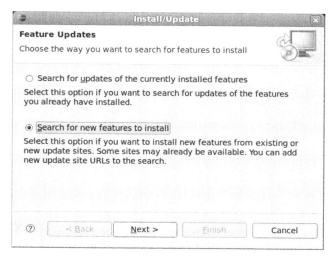

Figure 8-2. *Choosing Plugin Search Method*

On the next page, shown in Figure 8-3, click the New Remote Site button and enter the following URL: http://download.eclipse.org/tools/cdt/releases/callisto. The name can be any value. Then, click OK. The name appears in the list with a check mark to the left of the value. Click the Finish button to start the update process.

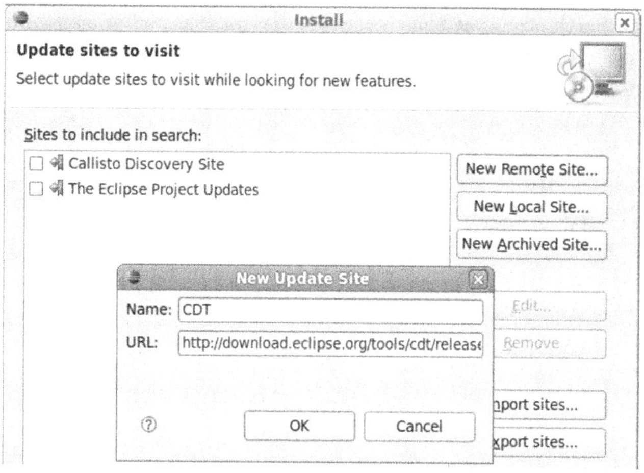

Figure 8-3. *Eclipse plugin mirror selection*

A list of mirrors appears. Select the mirror closest to you, or navigate to the bottom of the list and select the canonical site, CDT. The software churns for a few seconds and then displays the dialog shown in Figure 8-4.

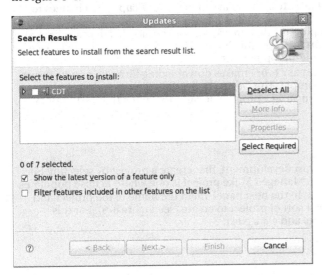

Figure 8-4. *Eclipes Plugin Selection*

Check the box next to CDT, and click Next. The next panel shows a license agreement. After you agree to the terms of the license (you read every word, didn't you?), click Next. The panel in Figure 8-5 shows exactly what will be installed as part of this update.

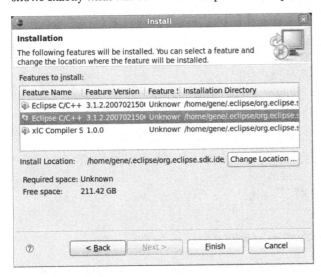

Figure 8-5. *Confirmation of Eclipse Plugin Installation*

Clicking Finish begins the installation process. The Update Manager displays a dialog that shows the progress of the download. Depending on the proximity of the mirror, the number of users doing an upgrade, and how many of your kids are watching streaming videos while downloading new kernel source tarballs, this process could take up to 30 minutes. You're asked to restart Eclipse for changes to take effect.

Along with the CDT project, the next set of plug-ins that are essential to embedded development are in the Device Software Development Platform project, specifically the Target Management and Device Debugging plug-ins. The Target Management plug-in (update site: `http://download.eclipse.org/dsdp/tm/updates/3.0/`) makes downloading files to a remote target, such as a board running embedded Linux, very simple. The Device Debugging plug-in is designed to make remote debugging in Eclipse as easy as debugging a program locally. Installing these additional plug-ins is left as an exercise for you.

Using Eclipse

In Eclipse, the organizing entity is a project. To start development, first create a project by selecting File ➤ New and selecting Managed Make C project. A Managed Make project is one where Eclipse populates the make file based on the contents of the project. In the next panel, fill in the name of the project and click Next. In the next panel, the wizard asks what sort of project to create (see Figure 8-6). For this example, select the Executable (Gnu) project type, and click Next.

Figure 8-6. *Configuring Projects and Compiler Settings in Eclipse.*

A *configuration* is a set of compiler settings used to build the source code. The Debug configuration builds the code with no optimizations and debugging symbols turned on, whereas the Release configuration builds with the highest optimization level and no debugging symbols. Click Finish to create the project.

The default project settings are appropriate for the native compiler and not for cross-compilation. Only a few changes are necessary to make the project invoke a different compiler in the project's property page. Open the property page by selecting the project and pressing Alt+Enter. The dialog in Figure 8-7 appears.

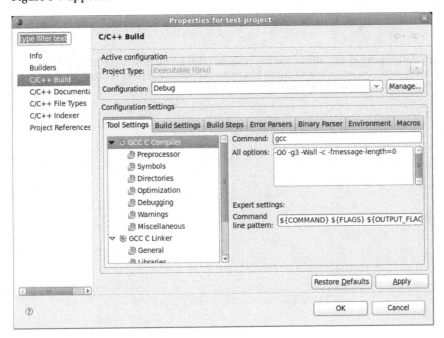

Figure 8-7. *Choosing Development Tools in Eclipse*

In the Tool Settings panel, change the GCC C Compiler and Linker command to the cross-compiler, and the assembler command to the cross-assembler. In this example, the compiler is /home/gene/x-tools/powerpc-405-linux-gnu/bin/powerpc-405-linux-gnu-gcc and /home/gene/x-tools/powerpc-405-linux-gnu/bin/powerpc-405-linux-gnu-as, respectively.

Next, add a file to the project by selecting File ➤ New ➤ File and creating a file with the extension .c—for example, test.c. The software adds this file to the make file and attempts to build the project, resulting in an error. Automatic project builds are great for Java but irritating for C or C++ projects. Disable this feature by choosing Window ➤ Preferences and then choosing General ➤ Workspace on the menu at left. In the panel on the right, unselect Build Automatically.

For each build configuration, Eclipse creates a directory of the same name to contain the project make files generated by the project. To allow for maximum flexibility, the make file optionally includes three make files that you can further customize:

- makefile.init: Use this file to add initialization instructions to the make file. This file is included first, before anything else.

- makefile.defs: This is the best place to define any variables used later in the file.

- `makefile.targets`: In this file, add any additional targets, where *targets* are the things that the build creates.

That's all you need to do to create a working environment in Eclipse. As new files are added to the project, the make file automatically adjusts.

What's Next

The next chapter dives into developing applications for the remote target. You now have quite a few different tools up and running, and you use a few of them to create the classic "Hello World" application and test your work on both live hardware and simulators.

CHAPTER 9

■■■

Application Development

Getting Started on Your Application

Embedded development on Linux is similar enough to desktop development that you may be lulled into thinking they're the same. There are some important differences, which this chapter covers as you go through the mechanics of setting up a project from scratch. Although several IDEs perform this for you with varying degrees of success, they all end up creating make files, executing them, and interpreting the results. Learning what's happening behind the scenes isn't a character-building exercise; it is, however, a way to make sure you understand what's happening when you need to get the tool to do something that's not on the IDE's menu or when the tool does something contrary to your expectations or needs.

Knowing and being comfortable with the steps for getting a project running and building from the command line also gives you an important leg up when it's time to make a repeatable build for your project. Most project plans include time for making the build and shell scripts to have the software build from the command line. Too often, that time is spent in a scramble trying to figure out how to get the software to build, because prior to that point in the project, nobody bothered to properly document the steps for building the software (let alone create a nice make file). By getting into a good habit at the start, you can avoid the build scramble.

This chapter includes a section about getting your code ready for debugging. Chapter 10 is dedicated to debugging, but debugging and development overlap and you can do some things to make the process a little easier.

Desktop vs. Target

The target where an application runs is remarkably similar to your desktop machine: it has a file system that is about the same and roughly the same set of device nodes. These similarities make it possible to use your desktop machine as a reasonable emulator for your target board. Yes, the processor is different; but between the kernel and the development language, the difference apparent to you is small to nonexistent, depending on the nature of the application. There are some key differences, however, which fall into two large categories: language and system related. Language-related differences appear as a result of the development language used to build the code; system-related differences have to do with the Linux kernel and root file system.

The target is slower than, has less memory than, has smaller fixed storage than, and probably doesn't have the same input and output features as the desktop. However, the interface to those resources is identical to what's on a desktop system. Because the interfaces are the same, the software can reasonably be run on both systems with similar results.

The Linux kernel provides a uniform interface to resources that stays the same even if the kernel is running on a different processor. Similarly, when programming in C, you use the same function calls for printing, reading input, interprocess communication, and process control. Compiling the C code with a cross-compiler outputs different object code, which, when run on the target, should work the same as the code run on the development host.

Coding for Portability

C isn't absolutely uniform between a desktop system and an embedded target. Its creator referred to the language as a framework for creating assembler code; when you view it in that light, C leaves many differences exposed, not because of flaws in the language but because that's how it was designed. Most users don't encounter these problems unless they're programming at a low level, but you should nonetheless understand them for the times they become an issue. For example, a system that transmits data over a TCP network must translate this data to big endian (*endian* is described in the next paragraph); if the target machine is big endian, this could be inadvertently skipped and the code would still run, but it would break on a little endian machine. There are, however, some factors that have to be taken into account almost every time we code portably in C, and on occasions, in other programming languages.

- *Endianess:* This concept describes how multibyte data is stored. In a *big-endian* system, the highest byte is stored first, with low-order bytes stored in the memory locations following in memory. *Little endian* is the opposite: the lowest byte is stored first, and high order bytes follow. Arabic numbers are big endian: 78,123,456 puts the highest byte first (78 millions) following by the bytes 123 and 456. If Arabic numbering was little endian, this number would be represented 456,123,78. If the code is written to get the first byte, the results are very different on big- versus little-endian machines, but the code is formally correct and compiles without complaint.

- *Word alignment:* This is a way of storing data so that bytes are stored in memory locations evenly divisible by the size of the word on the system. In most systems, a word is 4 bytes, meaning that addresses fetched from memory must be evenly divisible by 4. This allows the processor designer to optimize the design of the processor so that it can access memory more quickly. In order to make data structures align nicely, the compiler inserts some padding into data structures so they line up nicely. No standard exists, however, to set up padding.; it's possible to have code that once worked fail from an overrun or underrun bug that now corrupts data. During an *overrun*, code writes outside the upper limits of its memory; an *underrun* happens when code accesses memory that's below the lower limits.

- *Capacities:* An integer is two byte long, and that byte represent numbers of up to 56535; but as the numbers get larger, there's no standard as to how they're stored. A PowerPC system may store long integers with 12 bytes, but an x86 system may use 16 bytes. Developing on an x86 system may result in code that fails on a PowerPC because you may need to store a value larger that what's supported.

- *Symbol locations:* This is less of a problem, but sometimes toolchains put symbols in different files; during compilation, errors are generated. These problems are easy to find.

When you're doing application development, the best strategy is to compile the code for execution on your development host and work out coding problems that aren't architecture-specific before you test the code on the target. In order to do this, you must do some work to compile the code so it runs on the host and the target. Although the code won't be running on the target right away, it's a good habit to regularly compile it for the target so that any problems the compiler can spot can be fixed as you go instead of having to fix them all at once.

Higher-level languages don't have these incompatibilities because they run on a virtual machine or interpreter (written in C) that hides these differences. The fact that C has these differences isn't a flaw or feature but rather an artifact of the design philosophy of the language itself.

System Differences

These relate primary to the differences in the target's hardware and the software that serves as the interface. The primary way a userland program (that is, an application) interacts with the Linux kernel is through device nodes, which operate with the same set of rules as a file.

Device nodes can be anywhere on a system. The practice is to put them in the /dev directory. Writing data into the device node passes that data into the waiting device driver running in the kernel, which can then react to the input. Reading from a device node results in the device driver supplying data; the exact sort of data depends on the device driver.

Other device drivers supply an interface via *system calls* (also known as *syscalls*). Frequently, syscalls are supplied as well as a file interface. These are functions that register with the kernel to provide an interface that's a function call. When you make a system call, the parameters passed into the function are passed to the kernel, which then passes them along to the device driver that registered the syscall. After the device driver's call completes, any return data is passed back to you. Many device drivers that have a syscall type of interface supply an executable program that makes executing syscalls more convenient for you.

A syscall interface and a device-node interface are both acceptable ways to provide access to system resources. What matters as an application developer is what's necessary to make those resources available on the development host. Many times, the development host can be populated with the same device drivers as the target machine. If that's not possible, you can construct the application code with a wrapper around the bits of code that read from and write to the device driver or make syscalls. This extra bit of code introduces additional overhead and code size, but the amount is inconsequential.

FIFO

It's worth mentioning FIFOs, which are handy ways of emulating /dev/$(*something*) files that report the state of some hardware. As you recall from your data structures class, a FIFO is a First In First Out queue of data. In real life, it resembles a line at the bank: the order which the data is entered is the order in which it comes out the other side of the queue.

In Linux, a FIFO is a special sort of internal data structure that has a file interface. Write to the FIFO, and it accumulates data so that when the reader asks for data, the queue is reduced. Create a FIFO by doing the following (you don't need root access to do this):

```
$ mkfifo ~/test-fifo
```

You open the file with a program called tail that prints out the contents of the file as soon as data becomes available. Call this terminal one:

```
$ tail -f ~/test-fifo
```

In another terminal window (terminal two), you can write to this file by doing the following:

```
$ echo something > $/test-fifo
```

On terminal one, "something" appears. You can pass as much data as desired; for example:

```
$ ls / > $/test-fifo
```

The FIFO has a limited amount of resources to store the data after it's been written but before it's read. The current limit is one page size, or about 4KB.

The wonderful thought about FIFO is how it lets you read from it from the command line. This makes creating a simple fake device easy. A real-life example of this feature's usefulness is a board with a device driver for some digital IO buttons and a potentiometer. The buttons have a device driver that updates a file /dev/buttons with a new line of data when the button changes state. The device has six buttons, and the contents of /dev/buttons when none have been clicked is

```
0 0 0 0 0 0 <newline>
```

The corresponding 0 changes to a 1 while you hold down the button:

```
0 1 0 0 0 0 <newline>
```

It changes back to a 0 when you release the button. The code that reads from this device driver does so in a loop with scanf(). To test the code on a desktop machine, I created a FIFO /dev/buttons and ran a script that wrote into the FIFO to simulate the buttons being clicked:

```
echo "0 0 1 0 0 0" > /dev/buttons
```

That's all the code necessary to emulate the device on a desktop. This interface also makes it much easier to test the code before deployment. When you're thinking about how a device will interact with other parts of the system, put some thought into using what Linux already has in terms of interfaces, especially a file-type interface—doing so lets you leverage a host of other features.

Hello World

Most programming books that explain programming languages and techniques start with a "Hello World" example. There's no need to break with tradition. You use the command prompt as the IDE; this is important because all IDE tools available for Linux create make files like the one you create here, based on the project's contents. Eventually, you must figure out how they work when a problem surfaces.

Before getting started, you need the following:

- *A cross-compiler:* There are several places to get a cross-compiler, or you can build your own.

- *A target to run what's been compiled:* This can be the board or an emulated board on your development host.

- *A way to get the code on the target:* After the code is compiled, you can't run it on your target machine, so you need a way to get the binaries to the target.

- *Basic make tools:* You're only using make in these examples. It's found on every Linux system by default.

- *GCC for your development host:* GCC is the GNU C Compiler. Unlike the cross-compiler, this compiler produces code that can run on the target machine.

Getting the Tools

The prior chapters cover getting a cross-compiler for your system. If you've managed to build a cross-compiler from scratch, using `crosstool-ng` or a distribution builder tool, your system contains the necessary tools for this part of the book, because they were necessary to build the distribution.

If you've paged ahead, or if you received a toolchain in binary form and you aren't interested in rebuilding the sources given to you with the binary (you got the source code, didn't you?), your system may not have the right set of tools. If you're not sure, run the following command anyway; the software informs you whether the most recent versions are installed and quits. If you're an Ubuntu user, use this command to fetch the host tools necessary for development:

```
$ sudo apt-get install build-essential gcc make
```

If you're running a system that uses RPM, do the following:

```
$ sudo yum install gcc make kernel-devel
```

In both cases, you're asked to confirm the installation. These commands fetch a version of GCC and make. As for the editor, there are no restrictions: you can even use OpenOffice Writer, as long as the files are saved as text. For a practical suggestion, use the text editor that's available on your system in the Accessories menu. Linux has no shortage of text editors.

Making Make Work

What makes embedded different than other systems is the notion of cross-compilation and remote execution and debugging. In Chapter 8, you looked at several programming languages; this example uses C because it's widely used and does a great job of demonstrating the tools. You use other tools throughout the chapter as well. One tool you use no matter what the language is make, which is used to build software. There are alternatives to make (like ant and CBuild), but make is by far the most commonly used tool for building software and will stay that way for decades for come.

If you're comfortable with make, you use it here in a slightly different way than you may be accustomed to. One of the goals of creating this project is an environment where it's easy to cross-compile the code for the target and compile it for execution on the host. Doing this means creating some additional directories to contain the make file, source files, and results of the build.

To get started, create a new, empty directory in your home directory. All the files will be stored in that directory. For this example, use the directory ~/embedded-project:

```
$ mkdir -p ~/embedded-project/src ~/embedded-project/host \
        ~/embedded-project/target
$ cd ~/embedded-project
```

The first command creates a directory structure that looks like this:

```
~/embedded-project
        src/
        host/
        target/
```

The src directory contains the C source files for this example, and the ~/embedded-project directory contains the make file. Building will be done from the host or target directory. This way, your object code stays separate from your source code, and building for different architectures is more reliable. If the object files were stored with the source files, you'd need to rebuild the entire set of source files when switching from host to target. When the example gets more complex, I revisit and explain this point.

Use an editor to create the classic program that prints something out and then quits:

```
#include <stdio.h>

int main(int argc, char** argv) {
        printf("I'm here\n");
        return 0;
}
```

Save this file as src/hello.c.

You can use make to build any software, not just C; but to start, you use it to build C files. This file starts by building the executable with a simple rule:

```
VPATH=../src
hello: hello.c
```

That's it! Store this file as makefile. The first line tells make to find the source code in the ../src directory. This second says, "the file hello is made from hello.c." Ensure that there's an empty line at the end of the file, or make will complain that the file. To build the software, invoke make in the same directory as the makefile:

```
$ make -C host CC=<your cross compiler>
```

For <your cross compiler>, substitute the fully qualified path to the compiler. For example:

```
$ make -C host -f ../Makefile \
        CC=/home/gene/x-tools/powerpc-405-linux-gnu/bin\
        /powerpc-405-linux-gnu-gcc
```

This appears as the output:

```
  <your cross compiler>    ../src/hello.c    -o hello
```

What just happened? The -C host parameter told make to switch to the host directory immediately after startup. -f ../Makefile told make to execute the make file in the parent directory. After the make file was loaded, how did make know to execute the cross-compiler to build the code? Make has built-ins that handle most use cases. In this case, make used this rule:

```
LINK.c = $(CC) $(CFLAGS) $(CPPFLAGS) $(LDFLAGS) \
        $(TARGET_ARCH)
%: %.c
        $(LINK.c) $^ $(LOADLIBES) $(LDLIBS) -o $@
```

In make, variable names are enclosed in $( ). Recall that at make's invocation, the variable CC was set to your cross-compiler. The %: %.c part of the rule says, "any target build with files ending in '.c'"— when this matches, the rule following is executed. One of the other peculiarities of make is that the input file requires not only whitespace before the command executes, but a tab and only a tab. Use the space key, and you're headed for trouble. The other variables in this command don't have a value assigned, so they expand to nothing, resulting in the build command. If you're curious about all the default make rules, use this command to print them out:

```
$ make -p -f /dev/null
```

Still, even if make finds a default file and has a default rule for building the file in question, how does it know what to build? In make, the first rule in the file is the default rule; so, if you don't specify a target on the make file, the default rule is used. In this case, the one and only rule is the default rule.

You can verify what sort of file was created by using the file command (part of every Linux distribution):

```
$ file hello
```

In this case, it produces

```
hello: ELF 32-bit MSB executable, PowerPC or cisco 4500,
version 1 (SYSV), dynamically linked (uses shared libs),
for GNU/Linux 2.6.27, with unknown capability 0x41000000 = 0x11676e75,
with unknown capability 0x10000 = 0x90402, not stripped
```

This tells you that the code is built for a PowerPC processor, uses shared libraries, and isn't stripped of debugging information.

The convention for make files is that they have three targets: all, clean, and rebuild. You can add that functionality so this make file looks like the standard. Here's the make file you have now:

```
.PHONY: all clean rebuild

VPATH=../src

all: hello

clean:
        -rm -f $$PWD/hello

rebuild: clean all

hello: hello.c
```

This file has three additional targets: make, clean, and rebuild. Make looks for the files all, clean, and rebuild on the file system to decide whether they need to be rebuilt. Because these files are never created, the rules always execute. Using the .PHONY target tells make that these targets don't exist on the file system and to just build the dependencies. Executing the rebuild target results in the clean target and then the all target being built:

```
$ make -C target -f ../Makefile CC=<cross compiler> rebuild

rm -f <directory>hello
```

```
<cross compiler> hello.c   -o hello
```

This make file is good enough to build the program for the host machine as well as to cross-compile it for the target. There's one more change: modifying CC so the make file builds for the cross-compiler by default. You do so by setting CC in the make file, resulting in the following:

```
CC=<cross-compiler>
.PHONY: all clean rebuild

VPATH=../src

all: hello

clean:
        -rm -f $$PWD/hello

rebuild: clean all

hello: hello.c
```

An oddity in this make file requires explanation. First, assigning CC to the cross-compiler works because you're passing in the assignment of CC as part of the make command line. Second is the $$PWD variable. In all shells, an environment variable PWD is set to the current directory. To expand variables in a shell, you use $ in front of the symbol. For example:

```
$ echo $PWD
```

In this make, you use the $ symbol to expand variables by doing the following from the ~/embedded-project directory:

```
$ make -C host -f ../Makefile rebuild
$ make -C target -f ../Makefile CC=<cross compiler> rebuild
```

On your system, you now have the following file system:

```
~/embedded-project
        src/
                hello.c
        host/
                hello
        target/
                hello
```

The file host/hello will execute on the development host (try it!), and the file target/hello will run on the target machine. Running target/hello on your host produces the following error message:

```
bash: ./target/hello: cannot execute binary file
```

This is what the bash shell prints when an executable file isn't the proper format, which makes sense because the binary is built to run on a PowerPC processor. The next step is running the code on the target machine.

Running the Code on the Target

One key metric of being productive as an engineer is the speed of the edit/compile/run loop. You've created a make file that makes building for the target a one-line step, and the next thing is to be able to quickly run the program on the board. The fastest way to get this done is to mount the ~/embedded-project directory via Network File System (NFS) from the board. Configured this way, there's nothing extra to do in order to run the application. If an NFS server isn't installed on the host, do the following to get it on your system:

```
sudo apt-get install nfs--kernel-server
```

Or do this for Red Hat systems:

```
sudo yum install nfs-server-kernel
```

To check whether NFS is available on the target as a root file system, look at the contents of the /proc/filesystems directory:

```
$ grep nfs < /proc/filesystems
```

In most cases, the board has support for NFS as part of the standard kernel. To make the directory available to be mounted, add this line to the /etc/exports file on the host machine:

```
<your home dir>/embedded-project               *(rw,no_root_squash)
```

Then, restart the NFS server so the changes take effect:

```
$ sudo /etc/init.d/nfs-kernel-server restart
```

At the board, mount this file system by doing the following:

```
# mkdir -p /mnt/nfs
# mount -t nfs -o nolock \
        <hostip>:/<your home dir>/mnt/embedded-project/target \
        /mnt/nfs
```

Now, the NFS file system is mounted and ready for use on the target machine. On the target machine, run the code by doing the following:

```
# cd /mnt/nfs
# ./hello
I'm here
```

Congratulations! You've run the program on the target. If you don't have NFS support on the target, the next best thing is to use ssh or FTP to copy the file to the device.

More Complex Projects

Most projects contain more than one file.. In the simplest case, this is a matter of adding the source file to the list of targets. For example, assume the project had a library file, lib.c, that performs a calculation:

```
hello: hello.c lib.c
```

When you compile this command, the following appears:

```
/home/gene/x-tools/powerpc-405-linux-gnu\
        /bin/powerpc-405-linux-gnu-gcc  \
            ../src/hello.c ../src/lib.c   -o hello
```

However, most engineers like shared libraries because they can change them independently from the application they're linked against or because the company has a standard library of code that's used across all projects. It is a fact, though, that shared libraries in embedded projects frequently don't make much sense, because they contain code that may not be used by the binary and that therefore consumes space in storage and memory unnecessarily. You should use shared libraries when the device has several programs that may possibly load the library or when the device may be running arbitrary programs.

Building libraries for an embedded system is much like building them for a desktop system. The make file is altered a little to include support for a shared library, libzed. The "Hello World" program uses this library to print an integer. The library also has another function that returns a character. The make file for this project looks like this:

```
CC=/home/gene/x-tools/powerpc-405-linux-gnu/bin/powerpc-405-linux-gnu-gcc

.PHONY: all clean rebuild

VPATH=../src:../src/lib

all: libzed.so hello

clean:
        -rm -f $$PWD/hello $$PWD/libzed.so*

rebuild: clean all

LDFLAGS=-L. -lzed
hello: hello.o lib.o
```

Create a file lib/file1.c that contains the following function (as described earlier):

```c
#include <stdio.h>
void a(int b) {
  printf("this is the %d\n",b);
}
```

Create another `file2.c`. It can contain any code, because it's here so you can see how to get several files built into a shared library. For example:

```
int b(int c) { return c++; }
```

Now, add this rule to the make file to compile the shared library:

```
libzed.so: file1.c file2.c
        $(CC) -fPIC -shared -Wl,-soname,libzed.so.1 -o libzed.so.1.0.1 $?
        -ln -s ./libzed.so.1.0.1 libzed.so.1
        -ln -s ./libzed.so.1.0.1 libzed.so
```

The interesting part is the last line, where the shared library is created from the source files `file1.c` and `file2.c`. These files are stored in the `~/embedded-project/src/lib` library. In order for make to find them, you update the VPATH variable to include the `./src/lib` path. The last line creates a shared library by passing the parameters listed in Table 9-1.

Table 9-1. *GCC Parameters to Create Shared Libraries*

Parameter	Purpose
`-fPIC`	Generates position-independent code or code that has addresses listed as an offset from a base address. When this is loaded into memory, those addresses are reduced into memory addresses.
`-shared`	Instructs the linker to create a shared library
`-Wl,-soname,libzed.so.1`	The identifier from the linker's perspective. When programs are linked with `libzed`, they look for the library `libzed.so.1`, making it easier to have multiple versions of this library.

Running make the way you did before

```
$ make -C target -f ../Makefile rebuild
$ make -C host -f ../Makefile rebuild
```

results in the following directory structure:

```
~/embedded-project
        Makefile
        src/
                hello.c
                lib/
                        file1.c
                        file2.c
        host/
                        hello
                libzed.so
```

```
        libzed.so.1

        libzed.so.1.0.1
        lib.o
    target/
            hello
        libzed.so

        libzed.so.1

        libzed.so.1.0.1
        lib.o
```

Verifying that the file runs means you have to log in to the target machine and try to run the program:

```
# cd /mnt/nfs
# ./hello
```

This results in the following output:

```
./hello: error while loading shared libraries: libzed.so.1:
        cannot open shared object file: No such file or directory
```

This isn't the expected output. Looking at the directory, libzed.so is certainly there. Use the file command to check that these files are the right ones for the target architecture. The reason this isn't working lies in the way Linux handles shared libraries, which for embedded systems can cause some problems.

When you ask Linux to run a program with shared libraries, it runs a shared library loader, making the program you invoked from the command line a parameter. In the example, the following is run:

```
/lib/ld.so.1 ./hello
```

The program /lib/ld.so.1 does the following:

1. It reads what shared libraries are associated with this program. This information is stored in the header of the executable file; the loader knows what section to read because part of the ELF file-layout standard determines whether the program uses shared libraries and what files it needs.

2. It locates the shared libraries on the file system. The address for the shared library loader is fixed. For the libraries themselves, the loader looks in your specified location and then in the default location, as described later in this section.

3. It requests that the shared libraries be loaded.

4. It fixes the addresses of calls to shared objects to point to the actual address of the code. The code contains references to the symbols in the shared object's code. The linker changes those placeholders to point to the memory address of the now-loaded shared library.

On a desktop system, you can see what libraries are used by the program by using the `ldd` command:

```
$ ldd ./host/hello
        linux-gate.so.1 =>  (0xb8021000)
        libzed.so.1 => not found
        libc.so.6 => /lib/tls/i686/cmov/libc.so.6 (0xb7eae000)
        /lib/ld-linux.so.2 (0xb8022000)
```

This shows you that the file `libzed.so.1` can't be found, which matches your observations on the target. The next question is, how does the binary know to use `/lib/ld-linux.so.2`? And how can you make the library you built visible to the loader?

When the toolchain was built, you specified the location and initial configuration of this file, so ldd knows to look for files in `/lib` by default. Through a configuration file, you can point the loader at additional directories. This file is `/etc/ld.so.conf`, and on a desktop system it usually includes another file that eventually includes a list of directories. Many embedded systems eschew using this file in favor of putting the libraries directly in `/lib`.

When you're doing development, copying the files to another directory adds a step and can result in confusion if the files aren't copied due to computer or human error. The best way to handle this is to use the environment variable `LD_LIBRARY_PATH` to point to additional directories where the files can be loaded. On the target,

```
LD_LIBRARY_PATH=/mnt/nfs ./hello
```
produces the following output:
```
Hello, world
this is the 1
```

By using the `export` command, you can set this variable once, and it doesn't need to be present on the command line:

```
export LD_LIBRARY_PATH=/mnt/nfs
```

This approach has the benefit that you don't need to put the variable on the command-line. But this setting goes away when the board reboots or after logout, which can cause confusion when the program doesn't run and you forgot that this needs to be set.

One last note: if the shared libraries are in several directories, separate them with a colon, just like you do for the Linux path. For example:

```
export LD_LIBRARY_PATH=/mnt/nfs:/some/other/directory
```

The last question is figuring out how to see the libraries used by a cross-compiled executable. You can't do so using `ldd`, because that program wants to run the file. The graceful way, using the `readelf` program, inspects the binary's header and prints out relevant sections. You're interested in seeing the dynamic section:

```
<toolchain dir>/<prefix>-readelf -d ./target/hello
Replace <toolchain dir>/<prefix> with the correct values for your toolchain. That
will↵
 produce the following output
(this is the top few lines, the rest has been clipped)
```

```
Dynamic section at offset 0x1f30 contains 21 entries:
  Tag          Type                        Name/Value
0x00000001 (NEEDED)                Shared library: [libzed.so.1]
0x00000001 (NEEDED)                Shared library: [libc.so.6]
0x0000000c (INIT)                         0x100013c4
0x0000000d (FINI)                         0x100018b8
0x00000004 (HASH)                         0x100001a4
0x00000005 (STRTAB)                       0x10000c90
```

The first few lines show the names of the libraries that are imported. The value in [ ] is the name given to the shared library with the -Wl,-soname,libzed.so.1 parameter when it was compiled. This is the name that the system will always look for when loading the library; when the next big release comes out, a system can have both libzed.so.1 and libzed.so.2 and still load the correct library.

If the endianness of your computer and the target match, you can use the native readelf, because no code in the files under inspection is run. When the endianness doesn't match, readelf fails to recognize the file a valid ELF file and stops.

The less elegant way of getting this information is with the strings command. This program returns all the null-terminated strings in a file. Using strings produces a lot of noise data, so the output is passed through grep to reduce increase the signal-to-noise ratio. For the example program, do the following:

```
<toolchain dir>/<prefix>-strings ./target | grep so
```

Even with the filtering, there's a little stray text—a surprising result for such a small file. Just like the readelf program, if the endianness of the target and host are the same, you can use the host program. Here's an example:

```
$ strings ./hello | grep lib
/lib/ld.so.1
libzed.so.1
libc.so.6
__libc_start_main
```

The main advantage of using strings is that the program is on nearly every computer's root file system, making it one less thing to install when you're configuring your desktop for embedded development with Linux.

Not to be forgotten are static libraries. *Static libraries* (or *archives*) are collections of object files that the linker knows how to search and include in a binary. For an embedded system, static libraries aren't included on the target system because in order to use them, you must run a linker—and that's a highly unlikely use case.

Linking with the -static flag causes the debugger to search for static libraries and then combine the code from the libraries into an executable file. This means the resulting file has no dependencies, which is one less potential problem.

Using the example, this adds the following to the make system:

```
libzed.a: file1.o file2.o
        $(AR) r $@ $
```

This command combines the files file1.o and file2.o into an archive libzed.a. During static linking, the linker can use either object files or archive files. Archive files can have any name, but the convention is to start the file name with the prefix lib and end it with the extension a.

The important thing to remember is that a shared library can't be used for static linking. When linking with the -static flag, the compiler looks for a different file rather than use the contents of a shared library differently. If you plan to link statically and with shared libraries, the project must build both sorts of libraries.

Getting Ready for Debugging

The limited resources on an embedded system mean you need to begin thinking about application debugging while you're doing the application development. This section contains some best practices that help make debugging easier when the target machine lacks a keyboard, mouse, or monitor. If you're accustomed to debugging an operating system that included the application as a process within the OS (hint: this OS begins with the letters *vx*), Linux works differently, and this requires a change in practice.

The project you created earlier in the chapter performs one of the critical steps in preparing to debug: creating a build for the software that runs on the development target. If you can run and debug the code on the target, that's the most effective way to root out gross defects. Finer defects, like those surrounding timing or handling the input from a device, must be done on the board. Intelligently configuring the project so that it's isolated enough from its hardware offers a handsome return, because debugging on the development host is much more productive than remote debugging.

Next, no matter what the target, you should compile the program being built with no optimizations by the compiler; you do so by using -O0 (capital *0*, number zero) to compile the program. High optimization levels make it so that the program flow doesn't match that of the language; stepping through code with a debugger can be very confusing because there's little association between a line of source code and the machine code generated by the compiler.

The most popular tool for debugging code running on a target is printf(). This unobtrusive, low-resource tool has the flexibility to handle most anything. But if you're new to the craft, it seem stodgy and downright primitive. Because most of the debugging happens while the code is running on the host, using printf() is more reasonable that you may initially think.

When you use printf, the best practice is to print all debugging output on standard err (stderr) and leave standard out (stdout) for regular, nondebugging messages. When a program starts, both stderr and stdout are associated with the application's console, so it appears that they're the same. When output appears on the console, you may assume it's data from stdout, but it may be from either stdin or stdout. Take the classic "Hello World" program, and modify it a bit so that it prints to stderr:

```
#include <stdio.h>
int main(int argc, char** argv) {
  fprintf(stderr, "Hello, world\n");
  return 0;
}
```

Store this in a file (hello.c), compile, and run it. The following appears:

```
$ gcc hello.c -o hello
$ ./hellow
Hello, World
```

211

Now, try to direct the output into a file:

```
$ ./hello > hello-out
Hello, World
```

The > symbol results in stdout being sent to the file hello-out. To redirect stderr, do the following:

```
./hello 2> hello-out
```

This works because stderr is opened at file handle two. It also separates the diagnostic output from program output, as the program could be run to send all of the output into a file that the program will throw away:

```
$/hello 2> /dev/null
```

The next approach is to use the *system log*, or *syslog*, as a place to write debugging data. The syslog is a buffer in memory that is monitored by a process that fetches the data and writes it to a file. On most systems, that file is /var/log/messages, but it can be any file. Consider this sample code, saved in log.c:

```
#include <syslog.h>
int main(int argc, char** argv) {\
        setlogmask(LOG_UPTO(LOG_INFO));
        openlog(argv[0], LOG_CONS | LOG_PID | LOG_NDELAY, LOG_LOCAL1);
        syslog(LOG_NOTICE, "Notice message");
        syslog(LOG_INFO, "Informational notice");
        closelog();
}
```

Compile this with the following command. Cross-compiling this isn't important right now, because this code behaves the same way on a target machine:

```
$gcc log.c -o log
```

Run the code; nothing appears on the console. However, look at the contents of /var/log/messages, which has the following output:

```
May 10 12:04:23 sony-laptop ./log[32056]: Notice message
May 10 12:04:23 sony-laptop ./log[32056]: Informational notice
```

The setlogmast() function changes the messages that are sent to the syslog. This function accepts a bitmask for an acceptable messages, and the helper macro LOG_UPTO means that messages less than the argument to LOG_INFO aren't displayed. Table 9-2 lists the possible message codes and when they should be used, from highest to lowest.

Table 9-2. Error Message Catalogue

Priority Code	Meaning
LOG_EMERG	The software has failed completely.
LOG_ALERT	An event has happened that must receive immediate attention.
LOG_CRIT	Failure isn't immediate, but corrective action should be taken.
LOG_ERR	An error condition was encountered and properly handled.
LOG_WARNING	Something out of the ordinary has happened.
LOG_NOTICE	Like LOG_INFO, but slightly more important.
LOG_INFO	An informational message.
LOG_DEUG	A message pertaining to debugging.

Using this facility means you don't need to change or recompile the code to change the chattiness of what's kept in the log file. Using this approach also results in more flexibility, because you can change the log mask on the fly to track down a problem that can be produced in the field. The syslog facility also has some interesting remote-access capabilities that are covered in Chapter 10.

What's Next

Now that you have a grasp of what's involved in creating a build for a target, Chapter 10 covers remote and other debugging techniques. When you're working on a project, the majority of your time is spent debugging, so you want to make the process as predictable as possible.

■ ■ ■

Debugging Applications

Getting Started on Your Application

Debugging consumes the lion's share of time in a project. Peeling away the wrapper around programming methodology fads usually exposes methods and practices for minimizing the time spent debugging, usually via planning and adding help during the debugging phase. Part of this chapter is dedicated to practices that reduce debugging, but mostly it focuses on tools to use when you're debugging. The information is mixed, because it's sometimes difficult to separate one topic from the other.

This chapter covers debugging both C/C++ and Java programs in detail, using remote debuggers. Engineering projects using these languages do a fair amount of debugging remotely, and knowing how to get this debugging setup running is an important part of the project. As you've seen so far with Linux, there are at least three different ways to do everything, and debugging provides more of the same.

The techniques for instrumentation transcend language; they just have implementation differences. Embedded engineers fall back on instrumentation because you can't find defects that are timing related by stepping through the code. Even though remote debugging technologies have improved vastly over the years, the favorite debugging tool for embedded engineers remains `printf()`.

Types of Debugging

There are a few different ways to look at application debugging: interactive, post mortem, and instrumentation. This chapter focuses on the first and last debugging types with the most detail, because they're the most commonly used and productive techniques. Due to the space limitations on embedded systems, getting a core dump for post-mortem debugging isn't that common, but the concept does merit mention for systems that are less memory constrained. Following are descriptions of the three approaches:

- *Interactive:* This is what comes to mind first for debugging. The process consists of stepping through the code a line at a time (so called *single-stepping*) and examining the state of memory as well as observing program flow. When single-stepping gets tedious, you use break points to stop execution on certain lines. Interactive debugging is great at finding logic problems, but the act of debugging makes it impossible to find timing bugs: single-stepping through the code doesn't change the sequence of the code but does change what else in the system gets a chance to run while the current program is being debugged. As such, this is a small example of the Heisenberg uncertainty principle, where the act of measurement affects what is being measured.

- *Post mortem:* This means "after death," and it involves looking at the state of the application or system after it has stopped. GDB includes the ability to examine core dump files for your target platform. Post-mortem debugging gives you the ability to see the state of the system right before the program stopped working, because it's forensic in nature; you work backward from the point of death to determine how the system died. This type of debugging is made easier when the code has some instrumentation, because you get a clearer picture of how the system arrived at its current state.

- *Instrumentation:* This method means debugging by adding statements to the code that print out information; you examine that information after the program runs, or maybe while the program is running, depending on how the code was instrumented. Instrumentation works best for bugs that are timing related, but even low-overhead instrumentation causes timing problems. What are timing problems? Essentially, they're a general way of describing race conditions, where the order of execution of two or more threads of code can result in an incorrect result or where two threads of execution need to use a resource in a coordinated fashion. Timing problems can also be introduced when code relies on the passage of time in order to be accurate: for example, a timer that must work every 10 milliseconds or a process that must complete work within a certain time interval.[1]

The goal of debugging is, of course, to root out problems. However, many times engineers use debugging as a learning aid. No matter how well the documentation describes how a function call works, being able to see the results first hand and perhaps change the parameters interactively is a great technique for those who learn by experimentation. All of these debugging methods are well-supported in Linux.

Remote Debugging Overview

Debugging when the debugger and the program being debugged run on separate hosts is called *remote debugging.* Whereas regular debugging involves two major components (the debugger and the program being debugged), remote debugging adds one more item to the list: the debug monitor. The debug monitor is a stand-in for the debugger that's running on a different machine; during debugging, the debugger and the monitor exchange messages over a communications link, and the monitor handles the mechanics of settings the breakpoints and fetching the contents of memory when you ask to see a variable's value.

When you use the GNU debugger (which is really the only C/C++ debugger for Linux), the debug monitor is gdbserver. For a Java program, the debug monitor is built into the virtual machine: when you run the program with the java executable, you pass in a few extra parameters. The way Java is structured, debugging on the machine where the program is running and from a remote machine use nearly the same communication mechanism.

---

[1] A true story: A buddy was debugging code that was mysteriously failing but that always worked when instrumented. The code contained a hash map that used a timestamp as its key. When not instrumented, the code occasionally produced timestamps that were in the same microsecond, because the code ran faster than the system clock was updated; when this happened, the hash map had two entries with the same key and happily deleted the older one. There's a lesson here: don't depend on a timestamp to be unique.

Debugging C and C++

In order to debug C and C++ code, you must compile the code with debugging information. On a Linux system, that debugging information is in DWARF 2 format, the successor to the original Debugging With Attributed Record Formats (DWARF)[2]. DWARF 2 describes a format for storing information about line numbers and symbols as additional data in the file. With this information, a debugger can understand how the data is stored in memory and has an idea of what instructions belong with one line.

When the code is compiled correctly, if it's to be debugged remotely, two programs are necessary: the debugger (GDB) and the debug monitor (gdbserver) The GDB binary runs on your development host computer, and gdbserver runs on the target. The rationale for having two programs is simple: gdbserver is much smaller and requires very few resources in order to work, whereas GDB needs quite a bit of memory, which the target machine may lack.

If you're using a toolchain built with crosstool-ng, you can find the gdbserver component at `<cross-tool>/debug-root/usr/bin/gdbserver`. This program is linked without shared library dependencies, so all you need to do is copy it to the /bin directory of the target system. If your system doesn't have gdbserver or GDB, the next section covers building GDB so you can begin debugging.

Building GDB

Like any open source project, GDB is built by downloading the source, using configure, and then compiling the program. If you built the toolchain yourself, building GDB is substantially easier. In order to do remote debugging, you also need to build a GDB server on the target that serves as the controller program with which GDB communicates.

The process begins by creating a directory that holds GDB source files and the build directory. Like the toolchain, the best practice is to build in a different directory than the sources. When you build GDB, it's best to start with the most recent version; in this example, replace `<version>` with the current version, which is currently 6.8:

```
$ mkdir ~/gdb ; mkdir ~/gdb/build
$ cd ~/gdb
$ wget  ftp://sourceware.org/pub/gdb/releases/gdb-<version>.tar.gz
$ tar xjf gdb-<version>.tar.gz
```

Like the projects you've build so far, there's a configuration step. Before you run configure, make sure the cross-compiler that will be used with GDB is in the path. The configure script looks for these tools, and the build won't work properly if they can't be found. The other thing that's a little different is that the -target flag is passed into configure script because you're building GDB to run on your host machine but work with code that runs on the target architecture:

```
$ export PATH=$PATH:<tool chain bin directory>
$ cd ~/gdb/build
$ export CFLAGS="-Wno-unused"
$ ../gdb-<version>/configure --target=<system> --prefix=
```

---

[2] DWARF is a play on ELF, the format for Linux programs, which means Executable and Linkable Format. Officially, DWARF has no meaning.

What should ⟨*system*⟩ be? This is the four-part "triplet" that's the prefix for the GCC cross-compiler. If you invoke GCC by doing the following

```
powerpc-405-linux-gnu-gcc
```

The argument to `target` could be `powerpc-405-linux-gnu`. Configure scripts are very forgiving in what they accept for a system identifier.

When the `configure` script completes, run the build. The first thing the build does is run another `configure` script and then begin compiling the program.

Setting `CFLAGS` to `-Wno-unused` suppresses the warning generated if the code doesn't check the return value of a function. Depending on what system the compilation is run on, this warning may be generated, in which case the build treats the warning as an error and stops. This flag suppresses that warning and therefore the build continues. The adventurous/motivated can fix this in the code instead of suppressing the warning; suppressing the warning is equally as good and more expedient:

Once GDB is build, the next step is to build `gdbserver`.

```
$ mkdir ~/gdb/build-gdbserver
$ cd ~/gdb/build-gdbserver
$ export LDFLAGS=-static
$ export CFLAGS-Wno-unused
$ CC=powerpc-405-linux-gnu-gcc ../gdb-6.8/gdb/gdbserver/ \
configure --host=powerpc-405-linux-gnu –prefix=<board rfs>/bin/gdbserver
$ make
```

Depending on the toolchain, a supporting library for handling threads (such as `libthread_db`) may not be present when linking with `-static`. If you'll be debugging programs with several threads, you must link gdbserver with shared libraries. If you want to create a static gdbserver, do the following when configuring the project, before running make:

```
$ LDFLAGS=-static CC=powerpc-405-linux-gnu-gcc \
../gdb-6.8/gdb/gdbserver/configure --host=powerpc-405-linux-gnu \
--prefix=<board rfs>/bin/gdbserver
```

The disadvantage of using shared objects is that gdbserver is a little more complex to put on the target, because the libraries it needs must be present on the target as well. The installation directory ⟨*board rfs*⟩ is on the file system on the development host; it's either an NFS mount or is transformed to be placed on the target.

GDB Front Ends

GDB is a command-line debugger, and most users are accustomed to a graphical debugger or at least one with some menus. Several tools work with GDB to provide a GUI that displays the code that's currently being debugged and lets you set breakpoints by clicking a line. The design of GDB is such that it can work in the background with a front end; there also happen to be several excellent choices for GDB front ends. This section covers a few of the more popular solutions that work well during remote debugging:

- *Data Display Debugger (DDD):* This tool works well when you're debugging remotely because it has a great mix of point and click and command-line oriented features. The command-line interface makes it easy to start a remote session, and the UI features make normal debugging features accessible.

- *Emacs:* The Emacs GDB debugger works very well, even if you aren't inculcated with the Emacs tradition. As with DDD, you can access the command line and need to do so to start a remote debugging session, but the rest of the functionality is more or less a point and click interface.

- *Eclipse:* This tool can also be used as a debugger front end. However, unless it's being used as the IDE as well, the overhead for using it as a debugging tool may outweigh what it has to offer. For example, in order to debug a project, you must import the project into Eclipse; that process alone is time consuming enough to suggest looking elsewhere.

There are probably more front ends for debugging, but these are the most frequently used in embedded development. After you see how to start a remote debugging session, your favorite GDB debugger front end, if not named here, may be perfectly suitable for remote debugging.

The next few sections cover the mechanics of compiling a program for debugging and starting a remote debugging session. The chapter also covers how to obtain and configure the tools mentioned here to make them suitable for debugging in an embedded environment.

Compiling for Debugging

To compile a program with debugging information, add the -g parameter to the command line used to compile the program. For example, given the program hello.c, this compiles it with debugging information:

```
$ <cross-compiler>-gcc hello.c -o hello -g
```

Nothing will be different other than the size of the file, which will be larger because of the additional debugging information. Most users don't compile from the command line a file at a time. Considering the example project from the last chapter, the best approach is to modify the make file so that all the code is built with debugging information. For example, adding this to the make file

```
ifeq ($(D),1)
            CFLAGS += -g
endif
```

causes -g to be appended to the CFLAGS variable that holds the extra command-line variables passed to GCC during compilation, when the D variable has been defined by passing D=1 on the make command line. Taking this approach is better because later, you can add more meaning to the notion of debugging, as you see later in this section. Making this change to the make file created in chapter 9 and compiling the program with this command line produces a set of binaries:

```
$ make -C host -f ../Makefile clean all   D=1
make: Entering directory `/home/gene/embedded-project/host'
rm -f $PWD/hello $PWD/libzed.so* $PWD/*.o
```

```
/home/gene/x-tools/powerpc-405-linux-gnu/bin/powerpc-405-linux-gnu-gcc -fPIC -
shared⏎
 -Wl,-soname,libzed.so.1 -o libzed.so.1.0.1 ../src/lib/file1.c ../src/lib/file2.c
ln -s ./libzed.so.1.0.1 libzed.so.1
ln -s ./libzed.so.1.0.1 libzed.so
/home/gene/x-tools/powerpc-405-linux-gnu/bin/powerpc-405-linux-gnu-gcc -g   -c -o⏎
 hello.o ../src/hello.c
/home/gene/x-tools/powerpc-405-linux-gnu/bin/powerpc-405-linux-gnu-gcc -L. -lzed⏎
  hello.o  -o hello
make: Leaving directory `/home/gene/embedded-project/host'
```

The code is now ready for debugging. It needs to be downloaded or otherwise made available to the target along with the supporting libraries. If the target board has NFS mounted as a root file system on the development host, you can copy the files to the appropriate directory; otherwise, you must copy the files to the target.

For many projects, the procedure for getting the code on the board can be put in the make file as well, making the debugging process easier. One of the steps involved in getting the code on the board is putting the libraries used by the executable somewhere that the dynamic linker can find them. You can also set LD_LIBRARY_PATH to the directory containing the shared libraries.

To debug with GDB on a remote machine, follow these steps:

1. Start the program with gdbserver on the target machine.

2. Start GDB on the development host, connect to the remote machine.

3. Set the initial breakpoint.

4. Run the code.

Because this process involves a few different machines, in order to make the instructions clear, the host machine has the command-line host$ and the target's command line us target$:

```
target$ cd /path/to/project/files
target$ export LD_LIBRARY_PATH=`pwd`
target$ gdbserver x:12345 ./hello
Process ./hello created; pid = 7168
Listening on port 12345
```

This little example program uses a shared library. Linux only uses shared libraries that are in a well-known place on the system or that reside in directories specified in the LD_LIBRARY_PATH. The first few commands switch to the directory where the application and libraries reside and set LD_LIBRARY_PATH to the appropriate value so the program will run.

The first parameter to gdbserver is the connection parameter. It can be either a serial device or a host and port number. In the example, x is used as the host; but you can use any value, because it's ignored, meaning any machine can connect. At first glance, it seems that you need to supply the hostname or IP address of the machine that will be connecting, but this isn't the case. The next parameter is the program to run; any following parameters are passed to the program.

■ **Note** Debugging over a serial connection is possible, but the amount of data sent using the GDB remote protocol is so voluminous and the connection so slow (even at 115200 baud) that debugging in this fashion is very tedious. If you only have a serial connection, consider instrumenting your code.

Start GDB on the development host machine, and load the file to be debugged. Then, connect to the remote machine using the same port number used to start gdbserver:

```
host$ <cross-compiler>-gdb
(gdb) file ./hello
Reading symbols from /home/gene/embedded-project/host/hello...done.
(gdb)   target remote 192.168.10.22:12345
Remote debugging using 192.168.10.22:12345
[New Thread 7168]
0xb7f31810 in ?? () from /lib/ld-linux.so.2
```

On the remote machine, the following message appears to show that remote debugging has started:

```
Remote debugging from host 192.168.10.26
```

Now you're cooking with gas! The next step is to create an initial breakpoint. You do so from the command-line interface of GDB with the following command:

```
(gdb) b main
Breakpoint 1 at 0x8048515: file ../src/hello.c, line 5.
```

Run the program, and it meets the first breakpoint, resulting in this output from GDB:

```
(gdb) c
Breakpoint 1, main () at ../src/hello.c:5

5           fprintf(stderr, "Hello, world\n");
```

You're remotely debugging your program with GDB using the command-line interface. The c means *continue*. When you make a connection to a remote target running gdbserver, it's already running the program; gdbserver puts a breakpoint in the first few instructions to stop the program as it waits for a connection. Using c after connecting resumes the execution to the next breakpoint. That's why the b main command is necessary—otherwise, the program would continue to run.

GDB Command Line Survival Guide

The vast majority of users don't debug from the command line. The following sections are devoted to GDB front ends that provide a GUI exposing all of GDB's functionality in a more accessible manner. However, in some instances, the GDB command line is the only tool available; and even GUI-oriented tools require an occasional trip to the command line to get things working when you're doing embedded work. Table 10-1 is a quick reference to the most commonly used commands when you debug with GDB.

Table 10-1. *GDB Debugging Commands*

Command	Purpose
target remote <*comm*>	Sets the debugging target to a serial device or remote IP address and port.
b <*where*> [thread <*thread #*> bt	Sets a breakpoint at <*where*>. This can be a function name (thankfully, tab completion works), a line number, or a file and line number in the format *file*:*line*. If the program has many threads, the code stops when <*thread #*> reaches the breakpoint. The bt variant of this command sets a temporary breakpoint that is deleted after it's encountered.
C	Continues program execution until the next breakpoint has been encountered.
l <*what*>	Lists 10 lines of source code around <*what*>. <*what*> can be a line number in the current file, a *file*:*line* number, a function name, a *file*:*function* name, or an address. Because GDB prints the current line, you can use l to see additional context around the current line.
bt	Means Back Trace; prints out the current call-stack along with any parameters passed to that function. Use this command to answer the question, "How did I get into this function?"
info threads	Shows the current list of running threads. Useful when you're setting a breakpoint in a thread.
n	Moves the instruction pointer to the next source line, stepping through function calls.
s	Moves the instruction pointer to the next line, stepping into functions.
Help	Obviously, provides help. GDB has an incredible amount of built-in help that explains the commands in detail. There are so many commands that the GDB developers thoughtfully put them in functional groups.

Remote Debugging with DDD

The Data Display Debugger is a commonly used front end for GDB, remote debugging or otherwise. DDD started as a debugger for C and C++ code but now can be used to debug Python or Bash scripts as well. Visit http://www.gnu.org/software/ddd to download the sources, view bug information, read support cases, and see what's on deck for the next release. DDD is very stable and actively supported.

DDD isn't installed on most systems; the easiest way to get it on your system is to use your package-management software to do the work of installing the program and its dependencies. To accomplish this, do the following on a system using the Debian package manager:

```
$ sudo apt-get install ddd
```

Or do this, if you're using a system with an RPM-based package manager:

```
$ sudo yum install ddd
```

To run DDD for remote debugging, you need to start it from the command line with the name of the debugger to use, because picking DDD from the menu results in it running using the system's debugger:

```
$ ddd -debugger <cross-compiler>-gdb
```

The DDD welcome screen appears, along with the "tip of the day" dialog. You're responsible for getting the code to the target machine before you start a debugging session. The next step is to open the binary file you want to debug, by selecting File ➤ Open Program. After the program load, use the same steps you used earlier to connect to a remote machine to now start a debugging session. After making the connection, use the tools in the GUI to set breakpoints and watch variables (see Figure 10-1). DDD has the ability to track the value of variables over time and plot them in a graph; this is handy when you're debugging a timing-sensitive program and single stepping would interfere with the program's operation, or when you're tracking infamous Heisenbugs.[3]

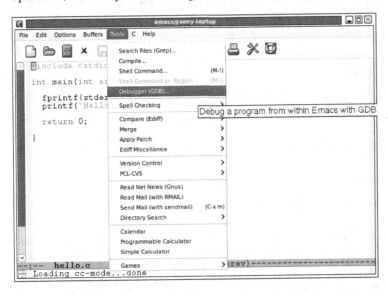

Figure 10-1. *DDD Display after a GDB Trial Run.*

One note about DDD: it produces quite a bit of output on `stderr`, which is visible on the console used to run the program. This output isn't anything to be alarmed about and can be safely ignored. To get rid of this output, you can redirect `stdout` and `stderr` to `/dev/null` by doing the following when running DDD from the command line:

```
$ ddd -debugger <cross-compiler>-gdb &> /dev/null
```

---

[3] The Heisenberg Uncertainty Principle says that you can measure the position or velocity of a body but not both, because the measurement of one affects the other. Applied to programming, sometimes the act of debugging alters the operation of the program, usually in such a way that the bug no longer occurs or causes some other, more complex bug.

When you're working on a project where this program will be a launched frequently, the best idea is to create a small script that runs DDD with the correct debugger and sends the output to the bit bucket.[4] For example, if the project is targeting an ARM processor, create a script called `arm-linux-ddd` that does the following:

```
#!/bin/bash

ddd --debugger /path/to/toolchain/armv4l-linux-gdb $@ \
        1> log.stdout 2> log.stderr l
```

This script runs DDD with the correct debugger and passes along any additional command-line arguments to DDD using $@ while sending the output of the program to the files `log.stdout` and `log.stderr`. By storing this data in files, you can review the output if you have instrumentation in your code. Put this script in your home or project directory or some place that's on the path. Now, getting the debugger running is as easy as

```
$ arm-linux-ddd your-program
```

Remote Debugging with GNU Emacs

Emacs is a great all-around tool for software development. If you haven't already installed it, use one of the prepackaged Emacs distributions available through the package manager with your Linux distribution. If you're running a system using the Debian package-management system, do the following:

```
$sudo apt-get install emacs
```

Or do this, if you have an RPM-based system:

```
$sudo yum install emacs
```

Emacs is available at `http://www.gnu.org/software/emacs` in source form if there are no prebuilt binaries for your platform. If possible, use the prebuilt distributions of Emacs.

Emacs contains a Lisp interpreter that provides a widely used mechanism for developing extensions. One extension included with the standard Emacs installation is for C and C++ development, as mentioned earlier in the book. This extension has a front end for the GDB debugger and works well for remote debugging because it provides you with a mix of access to the GDB command line and point-and-click debugging. Access to the command line is important when you're starting a debugging session; afterward, you can use the GUI as the primary way to interact with the debugger.

When you're debugging C or C++ files, Emacs loads some software that adds menu entries appropriate for the file type. To open the debugger, select Tools ➤ Debugger (GDB). In the mini-window at the bottom, enter the command to launch the GDB for the target platform. The debugger loads and presents a command prompt for the GDB you just loaded (see Figure 10-2).

---

[4] A colloquialism for /dev/null. This file is present on every Linux system and is essentially a write-only file. Data goes into this file and is discarded.

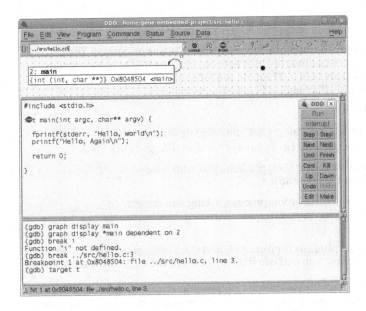

Figure 10-2. *DDD with GDB Commandline Enabled.*

When you're In this mode, the method for setting up a remote connection is exactly the same as the command-line GDB. You're responsible for getting the code to the target machine before debugging. After you establish the connection to the remote machine, you can set breakpoints by clicking in the gray area to the left of the line. To step through code, use the icons under the menu. If you've used Emacs to debug local programs, there is virtually no difference after the program has started running.

Emacs stores the last state of the debugger at the beginning of the project, so the next time a debugging session starts, you won't need to type as much to start a debugging session. Emacs also keeps track of breakpoints between debugging sessions.

Remote Debugging with Eclipse

Eclipse contains interesting tools for remote debugging that are part of the Eclipse platform: CDT and DSDP. Because the embedded development parts of Eclipse are leading edge, you need to download the latest Eclipse distribution and packages for embedded development and debugging.

Unlike the other tools in this section, Eclipse isn't a debugger—it's an entire IDE. In order to use just the debugging features, you must import your project into Eclipse and possibly restructure how the project builds. If you're starting a new project and use Eclipse from the beginning, this isn't a factor. If you have an existing project and just want to use the debugging features of Eclipse, you may want to consider using one of the other tools in this chapter.

To get Eclipse for embedded, visit http://www.eclipse.org/downloads/packages/eclipse-ide-cc-developers/ganymedesr1 and click the Download Package link. This takes you to a page containing a link for a mirror that's usually close to your physical location. Download the software, and unpack it. For example:

```
$ wget http://www.eclipse.org/downloads/download.php?
file=/technology/epp/downloads/release/ganymede
/SR1/eclipse-cpp-ganymede-SR1-linux-gtk.tar.gz
```

225

```
$ tar xzf eclipse-cpp-ganymede-SR1-linux-gtk.tar.gz
```

After it's unpacked, the software is ready to run in the directory where it was unpacked. You can relocate this directory to your /opt or /usr/bin directory; but Eclipse runs just fine in any directory. When you have Eclipse in the desired directory, run it. Then, do the following to install the Target Management and Device Debugging plug-ins that extend Eclipse functionality:

1. Select Help ➤ Software Updates.

2. In the Software Updates and Add Ons dialog, click the Add Site button, enter http://download.eclipse.org/dsdp/tm/updates/ for the URL, and click OK.

3. The software churns for a little while and then presents you with a list of software to install. Select all the items in the list.

4. The wizard walks you through the installation process, asking you to agree to license terms and confirm your selections. After installation, the software asks you to restart.

Eclipse is now updated with the correct plug-ins for remote C and C++ debugging. The first package installed is a tool that manages a remote target; you can use it to copy files to the target without resorting to going to the command line.

To start a remote debugging session, select Run ➤ Debug Configurations, and double-click the C and C++ Remote Application item to create a new empty Debug Configuration. This example assumes you've created a simple "hello" project in Eclipse in the earlier chapters and are reusing that code. The program that's being debugged is less important that the process of configuring Eclipse for remote debugging. You see a dialog that looks like Figure 10-3.

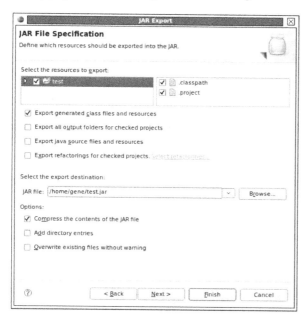

Figure 10-3. *Debugging a C/C++ applications remotely via Eclipse.*

Supply a name for the configuration (it can be anything). The next thing of interest is the connection: this is where you tell Eclipse how to communicate with the remote target when starting a debug session or downloading files. Click the New button to start the wizard.

You're asked the type of system, with Linux being an obvious choice. Don't be tempted, because this configures Eclipse to communicate with an agent, dstore, that hasn't been installed on most systems; instead, select Ssh Only, because most embedded systems have small versions of SSH installed (see Figure 10-4).

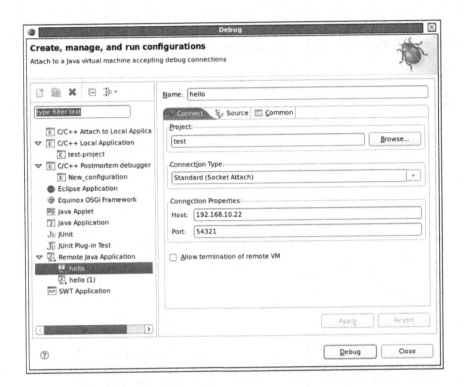

Figure 10-4. *Enabling SSH under Eclipe.*

The next panel asks you for the IP address or host name of the remote machine (see Figure 10-5). In this example, the IP address is 192.168.10.21, but it will likely be different for you. The connection name defaults to the host name or IP address; the Description field is optional. The last two panels in the wizard define how Eclipse opens a shell on the target and transfers files.

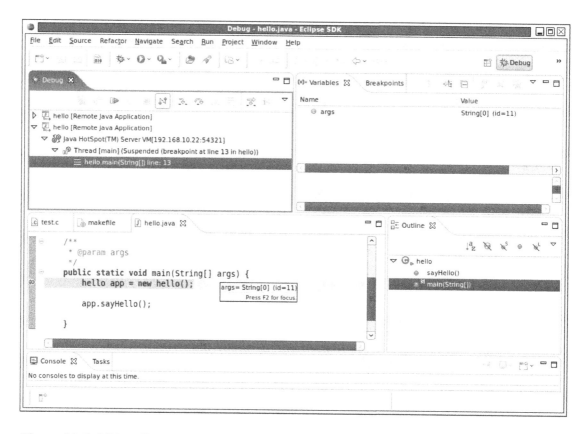

Figure 10-5. *SSH configuration under Eclipse.*

Back at the Debug Configuration panel, fill in the name of the project containing the sample program. Next, click the Search Project button, and select the binary for your project. Make the remote path /tmp/remote the place to download the binary to the target machine. You must have write privileges for this directory or the download will fail.

The next step is to switch to the Debugger tab and select a debugger. The default value for this field is GDB, which is the debugger residing on the host system, not on the target. Click the Browse button next to the field, and select the debugger you built earlier in the chapter or the one that was built with the toolchain. If you're curious, there's a drop-down for selecting the protocol where you can select Default, mi1, mi2, or mi3. This field means the version of the machine interface protocol that Eclipse should use when communicating with the debugger. You only need to set this if the debugger in use is older and must use one of the older protocols. For the most part, Default is an acceptable value.

Now, you're ready to debug. Click the Apply button, and then Debug. A small dialog appears, asking for a user name and password for the remote host, to be used for transferring the file and opening the shell. The application file is downloaded, and the debugger starts. The debugging works the same as if you were debugging locally.

Debugging Java

This section discusses how to remotely debug Java using the tools offered by Eclipse. Remotely debugging Java is much like remotely debugging a C program: you make a connection with a remote target that is running some software that lets you control program execution and inspect values from memory.

Java isn't that much different from a lower-level language like C. Java source code is compiled into byte code for a Java Virtual Machine that runs on top of a host machine. The way Java has been engineered, that host machine should have no effect on how Java runs; and this is how things work, to a great degree. When you think about it, all development done in Java is like embedded development, because the code is cross-compiled.

■ **Note** Remote debugging is always less efficient than debugging locally. Because the Java language produces code that be run on a development host, make it a point to do most of your debugging on your host machine: it's faster and easier.

When you run code for a debugging session, you start the virtual machine in a state where it waits for a connection from a remote machine, similar to the way gdbserver waits for a connection to start debugging. After you make the connection with the debugger, the remote virtual machine waits for commands to step through the code and return the values of variables.

You can do this from the command line, but the most practical and common way of creating and debugging code is with Eclipse. This section focuses on using Eclipse to create the code and start the remote debugging session. Fortunately, with Java development and debugging, there are no additional packages to download or install—everything necessary for remote debugging is included with the standard Eclipse installation or download.

The remote debugging protocol is an extension of the standard JVM. Make sure you're using a Sun or IBM JVM, because these implementations contain the code necessary to support debugging. To see what version is installed, do the following:

```
$ java -version
java version "1.5.0"

gij (GNU libgcj) version 4.3.3
```

If you see this output, you need to install either Sun's or IBM's java. The GNU implementation of Java is frequently installed by default, but it doesn't have the code necessary for remote debugging. Visit http://sun.java.com, and install the correct version of Java; or use your package manager to install the correct versions. After installing Java from your preferred source, update the path so that the first entry is for the location of the java executable you want to use.

When you install Java on Ubuntu, it doesn't override the GNU Java path. Put the path to the Sun or IBM Java first in your path. When you use the GNU Java, you can start the Java JVM, and it will accept the parameters for starting a remote debugging session; but when you start the remote debugging process with Eclipse, it just runs the program, ignoring any breakpoints and not presenting any error or warning messages. The lack of error or warning messages can make figuring out what is wrong a frustrating process.

To start a remote debugging session, you need to run the Java VM with some special parameters in order for it to wait for a debugging connection. For example, let's say you create a very simple class (hello) packaged in a jar file (test.jar) and put it on a remote machine. The class hello contains the following code:

```
public class hello {

        public void sayHello() {
                System.out.println("hello");

        }

        public static void main(String[] args) {
                hello app = new hello();
                app.sayHello();
        }
}
```

Create this class with the standard Eclipse class wizard. Then, use the File ➤ Export wizard to create a `jar` file in your home directory. Figure 10-6 shows the jar file export page.

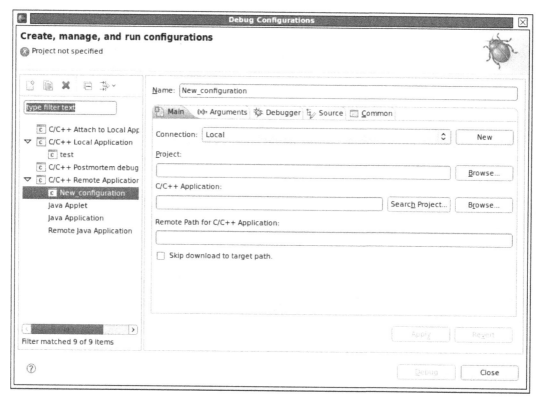

Figure 10-6. *Creating a jar file using Eclipse.*

You need to copy this jar file to the target for execution. For your system, the home directory is likely something other than /home/gene. After this jar file has been created in your home directory, ensure that it can be executed by running it from the command line:

```
$ cd ~
$ java -cp test.jar hello
hello
```

■ **Caution** When you're remote debugging Java, make sure you're using the Sun or IBM Java implementation. The GNU version starts a remote debugging session, but breakpoints aren't honored and the program runs to completion after you connect from the development host.

This test ensures that the jar is runnable and the export was done properly. To test debugging, run the class from the command line again, this time using some extra parameters to start the debugging process on the target machine:

```
$ java -Xdebug -Xrunjdwp:transport=dt_socket,server=y, \
suspend=y,address=54321↵
 -cp test.jar hello
Listening for transport dt_socket at address: 54321
```

The target now waits in this state for a connection. Table 10-2 provides a rundown of what these parameters mean (see Figure 10-7).

Table 10-2. *Java debugging parameters.*

Parameter	Meaning
-Xdebug	Starts the VM in debugging mode.
Xrunjdwp	Runs JDWP, the communication scheme use for remote debugging. The items following this parameter, which are separated by the colon (:) in the command line, are arguments that affect how this runs.
dt_socket	Indicates that communication will be over a network socket. The other option is shared memory, which is used when you're debugging code locally.
server=y	Means this instance of Java will wait for a connection from a remote machine.
suspend=y	Tells the Java VM to suspend immediately. When N, the code runs and the remote machine attaches to the running process for debugging.

`address=[host:]por` `t`	Indicates what port to listen on when in server mode. This should be a value above 2000. `host` is optional and can be used to restrict the host that starts a debugging session.

To start the debugging session from Eclipse, create a Remote Java Application Debug Configuration by selecting Run ➤ Debug from the menu and double-clicking Remote Java Application at left. This creates a new debug configuration that you can populate with the right values to begin debugging:

- *Project:* The Project field is filled in with the current project in the workspace. If you've been following along, that should default to `test`; otherwise, use the Browse button to select the project with the test code.

- *Connection Type:* The default value is Standard (Socket Attach). There's no need to change this value.

- *Host:* This is the host name or IP address of the machine where Java was run, waiting for a connection. The default value is `localhost`; change this to the IP address of the machine where `test.jar` is being run.

- *Port:* Use the same value as the argument to `address=` when running the program. In this example, the value is 54321

Figure 10-7. *Creating New Java Debug Configuration Using Eclipse.*

After you complete the page, click Apply and then Debug. The connection happens very quickly, and Eclipse switches to the debugging perspective by default. Remote debugging looks much like local debugging; if you're observant, you'll notice the IP address and port number in the call stack (two lines above the highlighted line in Figure 10-8) that shows that Eclipse is remotely debugging the class.

Remotely debugging a complex Java application is essentially the same as doing so for this small example class. The arguments sent to the Java VM are the same for controlling the debugging session; the class path and initial class are, of course, different.

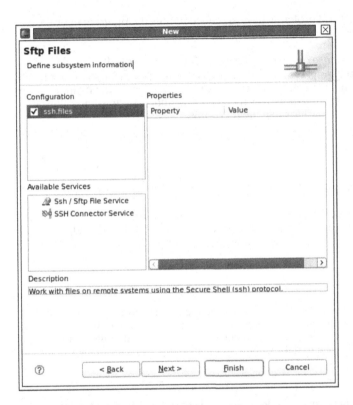

Figure 10-8. Stepping through a Java Application via Eclipse.

Instrumentation

Instrumenting code is something that almost everyone has done and is a very effective way of debugging on machines with limited resources; the code for printing out something to the console is probably already part of the application. Adding a few more lines of output doesn't demand much in terms of memory or resources. Instrumentation is as simple as putting a `print` statement in the code, running the program, and watching the results. Some target machines don't have the resources necessary to run even a small program like gdbserver to host a debugging session. Instrumentation is also the best way to find bugs that appear at odd intervals or to solve timing-related problems, where interactively debugging skews the results of the program.

The biggest drawback of this approach is that the code itself contains debugging statements that should be removed for production builds. There isn't a "strip" command for removing debugging print statements like there is for removing debugging symbols. For this reason, many QA departments want to retest the code after instrumentation has been removed, because it does require a rebuild of the software. Minor drawbacks include the fact that you may mistakenly write instrumentation code that has a side effect on the program; for example:

```
printf("value of a=%u\n", a++);  // changes the value of a!
```

When this is removed from the code, it will probably have an effect on how the program operates because it changes the value of a in the print statement. Most engineers know not to do something like this, but everyone makes mistakes.

Instrumentation in C is very simple because of the preprocessor. Consider the small example project that uses a symbol D to enable debugging. When the symbol D is set to 1, extra flags are set to enable debugging. You can use the same mechanism to define a preprocessor symbol that includes code in the C files when the symbol is defined. *Defining* directives means the symbol is set to some value; any value will suffice. For instance, the make file may look like the following:

```
ifeq ($(D),1)
        CFLAGS += -g
        CPPFLAGS +=-DDBG_OUT
endif
```

CPPFLAGS aren't additional flags for the C preprocessor C++, even though the CPP in the name may lead you to that conclusion. The source files in the project may contain source code like the following:

```
#ifdef DBG_OUT
fprintf(stderr,"a=%u\n", a);
#endif
```

This sort of code is peppered through the project, which causes a readability problem if you don't regularly remove the debug output that you know is no longer used. This is a matter of how the company manages the source code: some companies forbid checking in code containing any debugging print code but support the technique as a way for you to debug code on the desktop.

■ **Note** CPPFLAGS is a variable used in the standard make rules when building a C file. When you set this variable to a value (or append data), it's automatically used when appropriate if the standard rule hasn't been overridden. Most makefile authors prefer to use the predefined make rules, so setting this variable and rebuilding results in the right thing happening.

Notice that the output is sent to the stderr file. A program has two output handles, stdout and stderr. Reserve stdout for output that's always intended for a user and stderr for errors (obviously) and debugging information; that way, you have a method of getting to debugging data in the field without rebuilding the application, You can also open an additional file handle just for printing debugging messages if the regular output to `stderr` contains information that's used elsewhere and the instrumentation would interfere.

Debugging messages don't usually go to the console; instead, you can send them to the *system log*, which is a buffer of memory that the kernel maintains. When the buffer fills, new data goes into the top, overwriting the oldest data. This structure is called a *circular buffer* and is used when the system can afford to lose old data in an overflow situation. Chapter 9 contained code for producing system log messages that can also be wrapped in a macro so they aren't included in the final product. For example:

```
#ifdef DBG_OUT
        syslog(LOG_INFO, "Informational notice");
#endif
```

This has the effect of logging the code in a location such that even if it's accidentally sent out with debugging information, the result isn't as bad because the debugging output is hidden from most users. On a low-resource system, the system logger is off and the buffer is small, so not much memory or processing time is wasted. The point isn't to plan on software going out with debugging instrumentation. If the code is being sent out even though it hasn't been compiled properly, the consequences aren't as dire as when you write a large amount of data to the console.

The output of `syslog()` can also be sent to another machine by the daemon handling the syslog buffer, if it's running. By starting this program with the `-R` option, you can send the output to another machine that is configured for listening. For example, on the embedded device, BusyBox's `syslogd` is started like this:

```
$ syslog -R <ip address>
```

On the machine at `<ip address>`, `syslogd` needs to be configured to accept remote syslog information; you do so by adding the argument `-h` to `syslogd` and restart the service. If you're running Ubuntu, the file where this option is set is at `/etc/default/syslogd`. After this is configured, the syslog output appears in the development host log. When you're testing a device that is memory constrained, being able to send the debugging data to a machine with more storage makes this debugging practical.

Java Instrumentation

Java doesn't have a preprocessor. You could run Java code through the C preprocessor and use roughly the same instrumentation techniques as for C and C++ programs, but Java has something that's close enough that it doesn't run roughshod over the language. To get the same effect, create a class like so:

```
class dbg {
        public static boolean print = true;
        private void dbg();
}
```

and use it through the application code:

```
if (dbg.print) {
        System.err.println("message");
}
```

■ **Note** Many Java programmers who did J2EE work and find themselves doing Java embedded programming may be tempted to use one of their favorite tools, log4j, for system logging. Unless your embedded target is a powerful x86 class machine, this tool isn't the right one for the job, because it has a memory footprint tipping several megabytes and imposes a large performance premium on a lower-resource machine.

When you're getting ready for production, set the `print` property to `false`. The javac compiler is smart enough to factor out the code that won't be reached because the value of `print = false`. The effect is the same as in C: the instrumentation code isn't included in the final binary, so space isn't wasted with text that isn't of use to the program.

Instrumentation in Scripting Languages

The same theory used for Java instrumentation can be used for any language, the primary difference being that scripting languages don't have C's notion of preprocessing or Java's compilation step to remove unwanted code. This has some advantages in that the instrumentation can be turned on in the field easily for debugging, but it has the disadvantage of consuming space with messages and other information that is essentially dead weight. Most systems that use scripting languages aren't economizing for space and can afford the few extra KB of text.

What's Next

This chapter winds up the application-development focused part of the book. The next chapter looks at the kernel and how to get it ready for your application. Most kernel work nowadays involves configuring it so that it has the right features for the application and less engineering work is required to get the kernel to boot.

CHAPTER 11

■■■

Kernel Configuration and Development

Embedded Linux development when you're creating applications is much less about kernel development and more about kernel configuration. Because hardware vendors have a vested interest in making sure Linux is ready for their hardware the day it ships, the days of a developer on an embedded project porting a kernel for a board has become a thing of the past. A typical embedded developer needs to know how the kernel project works but doesn't spend time doing in-depth kernel hacking like in the days of yore.

This chapter explains the kernel project layout and how to build the kernel for your board. If you're changing the kernel and want to make your changes part of the Linux project, a section explains the kernel development process, how to make a patch, and the steps necessary to get your changes accepted into the mainline kernel build. If you receive a patch, a section reviews how to apply it to your current kernel code.

The kernel project is complex, but the complexity is tempered with good organization and a well-defined process for building and development. Compared to other open-source project, the kernel is very well engineered for cross-building; you should have very few problems getting the kernel to build for your target platform. As hardware companies have made it their business over the years to fully support Linux, they have been aggressive in making sure their changes make become part of the mainline Linux kernel available from `http://www.kernel.org` and making sure engineers choosing Linux for their operating system can be confident that building a functional Linux kernel for an embedded board will be as simple as building one for a desktop system.

Kernel Project Layout

The Linux kernel is a large-scale C and Assembler project that's held together with GNU Make and GCC. Some additional scripts control the way the project builds, and some additional helper programs are contained in the `scripts` directory and aren't part of the code that goes into the final kernel image.

The kernel has hundreds of active developers. To keep things in order, the project has established its own "a place for everything and everything in its place" policy that's important to understand. Table 11-1 describes the project's directory structure, starting from where the kernel was unpacked or fetched from Git.

Table 11-1. *Kernel Directory Layout*

Directory	Contents
`<top level directory>` The top level directory.	Contains some very basic information about the project. Most notable are the `README` and `REPORTING-BUGS` files that give an excellent overview of the kernel project and how to interact with the community of kernel developers.
`Arch`	Contains a directory dedicated to each architecture that Linux supports. The Linux kernel has very little architecture-specific code; most of what's here focuses on boot-time, power management, and the like. Any assembler code for a given architecture is found in this directory. Under each architecture, the organization varies a little, but each contains folders for architecture subtypes and board-specific code.
`Block`	Contains core code for managing block devices. The driver code resides elsewhere; this is the API the kernel presents to block devices.
`Crypto`	Contains the cryptographic API for the kernel.
`Documentation`	Contains kernel documentation. This is a key part of the kernel: the documentation is well written and well-organized. Use the `00-INDEX` file as the table of contents for the documentation.
`Drivers`	Contains directories for each major type of driver: USB, keyboard, display, and network drivers, to name a few.
`Firmware`	Provides the API For devices that have firmware loaded into memory as part of the device driver load.
`Fs`	Contains the general code for handling file systems in Linux and a directory for each supported file system.
`Include`	Contains header files used throughout the kernel project. The kernel sets the search path this directory when building the kernel.
`Init`	Contains the code that's run as part of the kernel's initialization. The entry point for the kernel (after the assembler parts of the code are executed) is in this directory.
`Ipc`	Contains the API for interprocess communications. This directory contains the code for the semaphores and pipes.
`Kernel`	Contains infrastructure code for the kernel. The scheduler code resides in this directory, as does the timer and process-management code.
`Lib`	Contains helper code that's shared across all other parts of the kernel.

Mm	Contains the memory-management code for handling virtual memory and paging.
Net	Contains the TCP stack and networking infrastructure code. The kernel supports much more than TCP in terms of networking, and each networking technology has a directory with some of the shared code in the top level
Samples	Contains sample code for a few of the newer kernel constructs like kobjects and tracepoints.
Scripts	Contains the kernel configuration and build code. None of the code in this directory is included in the kernel when it's compiled—it's there to make the compilation process happen.
Security	Contains Security Enhanced Linux (SELinux) and smack, an alternate access control system. The top-level directory contains some code shared by both of these modules.
Sound	Contains the drivers and codecs for audio.
Usr	Contains the stub initramfs file system when one isn't included in the kernel during the build process.
virt	Contains the kernel-level virtualization code for the kernel. This isn't code for QEMU virtualization; it's the drivers for the kernel-level x86 virtualization used in server devices.

Downloading the Kernel

You can find the current releases of the kernel at http://kernel.org (see Figure 11-1). This site is the canonical location of the Linux kernel sources and the hub of activity for the kernel project. Present on the site is every Linux distribution released along with links to the various mailing lists you can use to follow and participate in the project.

There are three ways for you to get the kernel sources. Each is described in a brief section following the summary:

- *Download a compressed tar file:* This is the traditional (as much as this term can be applied to open source distributed software development) method of getting the kernel sources. This archive contains a snapshot of the sources during the development cycle. When the kernel is released, a tar file is created with the sources constituting that release. If you want or need to get a certain version of the kernel (say, 2.6.31.2), this is the easiest method.

- *Use Git to clone the repository:* Git is a distributed source code control system used by developers (and by developers of other projects; Git is a general-purpose tool) for the kernel project. If you start from a Git repository, it's much easier to retrieve updates to the kernel release and incorporate them into your kernel tree.

- *Supplied by your vendor:* You board vendor may supply you with some kernel sources. These could be supplied to you in any number of ways; this chapter assumes that sources supplied in this manner also include enough support that you can get them unpacked and in a place where they can be used for a build.

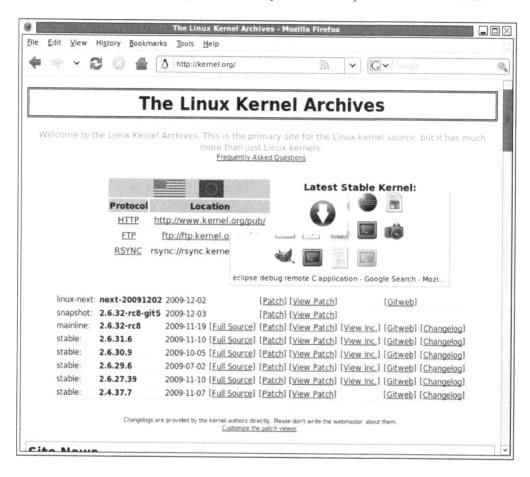

Figure 11-1. *The current releases of the kernel can be found at* http://kernel.org

Downloading a Compressed Tar File

This is the easiest way to get the sources. Just click the link, and wait for the download to complete; the waiting is the hardest part. After the download completes, you can unarchive the file by doing the following:

```
tar xzf linux-2.6.30.1.tar.gz
```

The kernel version you download will likely be something different, but the format will be the same. A directory is created named after the tar file, sans the .tar.gz suffix.

Using Git to Clone the Repository

The Git source code control system is explained in greater detail in chapter 13, so this section just covers the mechanics of getting the Linux sources. When working with Git, you don't check out the sources, as with other source code control systems; you create a copy, or clone, of a repository. For the Linux kernel, you use the following command:

```
$ git clone git://git.kernel.org/pub/scm/linux/kernel/git/stable/linux-2.6.31.y.git
```

You'll likely use a different version of the kernel, so the 2.6.31 in this link will be the version of the kernel that you want to download. Your company may have a firewall that blocks the URL git://; if this is the case, replace git: with http:, and the data will be downloaded over port 80.

Building the Kernel

Building the kernel is frequently viewed as a difficult proposition. There's also the view that building the kernel is risky because the newly build kernel won't work properly even if it does compile. These assumptions are simply false. Building a kernel from source is easy, and the risks of the software not working are minimal—the kernel is tested by thousands of software engineers on a daily basis. Because the project is complex, building the kernel requires a few steps not necessary for other project. The basic steps are as follows:

1. *Configuration:* During the configuration step, you set the parameters and options that control how the kernel is built. There are several different ways of configuring the kernel, but it doesn't matter which one you select because all of them perform the same underlying activities. Configuration is frequently aided by default configuration settings supplied with the kernel for most boards and processors; for many boards, you can use this default configuration as is to build a kernel that will boot on the board.

2. *Building the kernel:* After it's configured, the kernel can be compiled and linked. This process works much like any other project using GNU Make as the build tool. The result of the kernel build is a binary that can be put on the board and booted as well as file suitable for debugging.

3. *Building the modules:* The Linux kernel supports linking code into the image at runtime, similar to the way a program uses a shared library. Kernel modules support hardware components that may not be present when the kernel is started, so having the code in memory is a waste of resources. The code that can be linked into the kernel, in a process called *loading*, is called a *module*; these modules can be built separately from the kernel. Modules can be loaded and unloaded on demand.

The Linux kernel build process involves first priming the kernel source tree so that it's in the right state to be compiled; this process is called *configuration* or *configuring the kernel*. The kernel configuration process grew out of environment variables that were set in the shell, which were then used by the make file to compile certain code or change the compilation method. As the complexity of the kernel project grew, the configuration process advanced similarly and gained a text-based menu interface that is essentially unchanged in the current distribution of Linux.

To start the kernel configuration process using the text-based menu-oriented configuration program (other methods are discussed later), do the following from the command prompt while in the kernel's top-level directory:

```
$ make menuconfig ARCH=<your architecture>
```

If the kernel has never been configured before (or has been *cleaned*—more on that later), the programs used to configure the kernel and display the text-based menu are compiled, after which the screen shown in Figure 11-2 appears on your console.

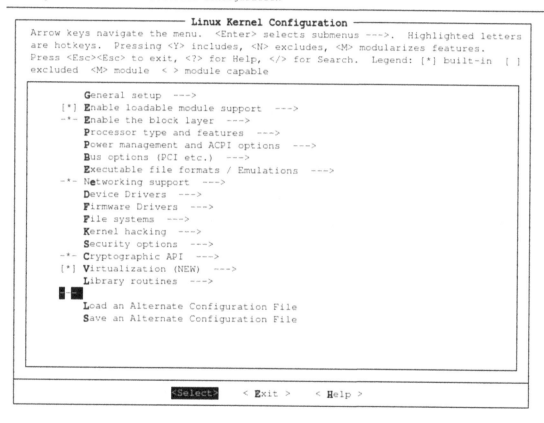

Figure 11-2. Kernel Configuration Options Window.

The value for ARCH is one of the entries in the kernel's arch directory and is always in lowercase. To see a list of the supported processor architectures, do the following from the top of kernel's source tree:

```
$ ls arch
alpha   blackfin  h8300    m32r      mips     powerpc  sparc  xtensa
arm     cris      ia64     m68k      mn10300  s390     um
avr32   frv       Kconfig  m68knommu parisc   sh       x86
```

If you're uncertain what to pick for the architecture, run `uname -m` on the target machine. If you're still uncertain, get in touch with the technical support department or FAE for the board. The most popular targets for embedded (in alphabetical order) are `arm`, `mips`, `powerpc`, `sh`, and `x86`.

Many people prefer to use GUI tools that can work with a mouse, as opposed to the text-oriented configuration program. For the kernel, there are two different graphical kernel configuration systems: one that uses the QT graphics library and the other that uses GTK libraries. Table 11-2 describes the configuration programs, the packages you need to install in order to build them, and why you would want to use one over another. GTK and QT use different GUI widget sets, where a *widget* is a check box or button. Because many systems don't have the proper libraries in place for compiling applications using either of these widget sets, the table also says what extra packages you need to install in order for the configuration build to work.

Table 11-2. Kernel Configuration Programs

Method How	Required Packages	Why Use
Console `make menuconfig`	Ncurses	Fewest requirements. You'll have the least problem getting this method to work on a large variety of computers. Fast and easy to use when you get the hang of it.
QT Based `make xconfig`	qt3-apps-dev	Runs and loads quickly. Friendlier for keyboard users. Excellent search feature.
GTK `make gconfig`	libgtk2.0-dev libglade2-dev libglib2.0-dev	Friendlier for mouse users. Incremental search feature.

No matter what configuration program you use, the program does the same thing, so feel free to experiment with each and pick the one you prefer. Many kernel developers have a preference for the console-based menu configuration tool, so if you're working with a kernel developer, learning and using this tool is a good idea.

The options selected by the kernel configuration program are stored in a `.config` file. Because this file starts with a `.` it doesn't appear when you list a directory's contents in Linux and use the default parameters for `ls` (hint: use the `-a` argument to `ls` to see files starting with a dot); that confuses users who look for the file containing their configuration information. After you run the configuration program, take a peek at the contents of the file using the `head` command or by opening the file in an editor:

```
$ head -50 .config
#
# Automatically generated make config: don't edit
# Linux kernel version: 2.6.29.4
# Tue  Jun 2 23:08:27 2009
```

```
#
CONFIG_MIPS=y

#
# Machine selection
#
# CONFIG_MACH_ALCHEMY is not set
# CONFIG_BASLER_EXCITE is not set
# CONFIG_BCM47XX is not set
# CONFIG_MIPS_COBALT is not set
# CONFIG_MACH_DECSTATION is not set
```

Notice that some of the comment lines show variables that aren't set to a value. This is a vestige of when this file set environment variables; having the line commented out was a trick to show that the variable wasn't being set while keeping a record of the variables that weren't being set. The configuration system now relies on the pattern

```
# CONFIG_VARIABLE_NAME is not set
```

to determine if a variable is not set, even though this line appears to be a comment. Don't change lines that follow this pattern, because doing so will confuse the kernel configuration program.

How Kernel Configuration Works

The kernel configuration process works when the kernel configuration program reads a kernel configuration specification file, called the kconfig file. This file resides in the arch directory, as specified with the ARCH=<*your architecture*> parameter when you run menuconfig. The kconfig file for the architecture contains the settings specific to the architecture and then includes configuration files for the rest of the kernel. For example, the MIPS kconfig file contains the following:

```
config MIPS
        bool
        default y
        select HAVE_IDE
        select HAVE_OPROFILE
        select HAVE_ARCH_KGDB
        # Horrible source of confusion. Die, die, die ...
        select EMBEDDED
        select RTC_LIB

mainmenu "Linux/MIPS Kernel Configuration"

menu "Machine selection"

(many, many lines clipped)

source "net/Kconfig"
source "drivers/Kconfig"
```

```
source "fs/Kconfig"
source "arch/mips/Kconfig.debug"
source "security/Kconfig"
source "crypto/Kconfig"
source "lib/Kconfig"
```

The kernel configuration program reads in the .config file for the kernel, applies the settings to the kconfig that was just read into the system, and renders the menu. After you select options, the changes are written back out to the .config file. Early in the build process, the file include/linux/autoconf.h is generated: it contains all the settings in the .config file as C preprocessor macros. The autoconf.h file is included in all the files in the Linux kernel; that is how the options you select in the configuration program are made available to the kernel. To see the process in terms of actions and configuration files, have a look at Figure 11-3.

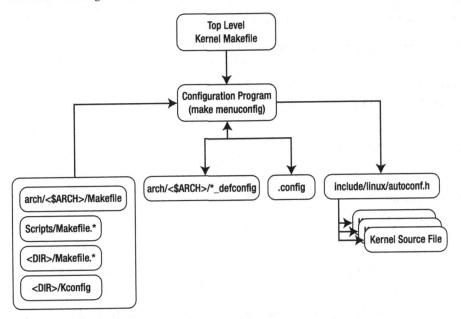

Figure 11-3. How the Linux kernel configuration process works

Default Configurations

The settings for the current configuration session are kept in the .config file in the top level of the kernel sources. Default configuration files (called defconfig files) for boards are stored under their respective arch directories. To get a listing of the defconfig files for a given architecture, do the following from the top-level kernel directory:

```
$ make ARCH=<your architecture> help
```

Some generic help for building the kernel appears, followed by a listing of the defconfig files for <your architecture>. In this case, the value was mips:

```
pnx8335-stb225_defconfig - Build for pnx8335-stb225
pnx8550-jbs_defconfig    - Build for pnx8550-jbs
pnx8550-stb810_defconfig - Build for pnx8550-stb810
rb532_defconfig          - Build for rb532
```

These defconfig files are nothing more than .config files that has been copied to a different directory and renamed. The kernel build system expects these files to be in the configs directory under the selected architecture; when the make target matches a file in the defconfig directory, it copies the file to .config.

If you're not interested in running make to see the default configurations available, or if you want more information than make provides (such as a date, or if you'd like to sort the list), you can locate these files with the find utility:

```
$ find arch/<your architecture> -name "*_defconfig"
```

Using mips for the architecture, the following appears:

```
(clipped)
arch/mips/configs/msp71xx_defconfig
arch/mips/configs/ip32_defconfig
arch/mips/configs/ip27_defconfig
arch/mips/configs/jazz_defconfig
arch/mips/configs/yosemite_defconfig
(clipped)
```

To use one of these files to configure the kernel, use it as a target for make. For example, to configure the kernel to build for the yosemite board, you issue the following command from the top level of the kernel directory:

```
$ make ARCH=mips yosemite_defconfig
#
# configuration written to .config
#
```

The kernel will be ready to compile, targeting this processor. Because a defconfig file is just a renamed and relocated .config file, you can also store the .config file used in your project in the configs directory.

■ **Note** Most board and processor vendors create defconfig files for their boards. The documentation included with the board tells you the correct defconfig file. If you didn't get this information, browse the configs directory for your board to find a match. Having a defconfig file isn't a requirement for building the kernel, but it does make the process less error prone because the creator of the default configuration file has tested that the settings therein are correct.

Editing .config By Hand

Because the .config file is a plain-text file with an uncomplicated format, editing it directly is a temptation and is sometimes the fastest way to change a value that's buried in the configuration's menu system. There is nothing wrong with editing this file by hand, and doing so is common among developers who know exactly what change they want to make. As an example, developers frequently change the value of CONFIG_CMDLINE, the kernel command line; opening the file in an editor and changing the line is much faster than using the existing kernel configuration tools.

After you make a change to the .config file, the best practice is to use the oldconfig target to test the selected options against the current configuration settings. For example,

```
$ make ARCH=arm oldconfig
```

results in the current .config file being processed. Any problems are reported on the command line. For example, some changes to the file result in other dependent options no longer being valid.

Another practical use for oldconfig is when you use the contents of a kernel's /proc/config.gz file. Recall from Chapter 4 that when examining a board, you can get a copy of the configuration used to build the kernel from the kernel itself. If you want to build the kernel with that file, the steps are e as follows:

1. Get the file. On the board is a file /proc/config.gz that is a compressed version of the .config file used to build the kernel. Uncompress it into a regular file by doing the following command on the target:

```
$ gunzip -c /proc/config.gz /tmp/kernel.config
```

This decompresses the file /proc/config.gz and makes a copy in /tmp/kernel.config.

2. Copy to the kernel's source tree. Copy the file from the board using the method you've already established. This could mean using SCP, FTP, or a USB thumb drive. Copy the file to the root of the kernel source tree, naming it .config.

3. Use make oldconfig. This step loads the existing configuration options, checks them against the current .config file, and reports any problems:

```
$ make ARCH=<your arch> oldconfig
```

Building the Kernel

After the kernel is configured, it's ready to be built. The output, or target, of a kernel build is a binary suitable for the boot loader on the target board, because the boot loader is the program responsible for getting the kernel code in memory and ready to be executed. The build also produces some of the tools used to build the kernel itself; unlike other projects, the build does the right thing when compiling programs for the host (such as those supporting programs) and object code for the target, such as the kernel and modules.

Many different targets are available for building a kernel, and the right one depends on the boot loader for the board. The differences between the targets in terms of the overall Linux build is quite small, because the build targets determine what happens in the last few steps of the build to format the object code so that it can be used with the boot loader on the board. Table 11-3 outlines the targets available and their applicability.

Table 11-3. *Kernel Build Image Types*

Target	Description
Zimage	Compressed kernel image. This contains a bit of code in the header that decompresses the rest of the kernel.
bzImage	Big Z image. Although similar in name to the bz2 compression tools, this just means the size of the image is greater than one sector for an x86-based system.
uImage	Image suitable for the U-Boot boot loader. It contains some additional information in the header so that the boot loader can put this file in the right place in memory along with some checksum information. This is the most common format for an embedded system.
srecImage	S-record image. S-records are files that use an encoding scheme so that binary data is represented as printable ASCII characters. This is the least common format for an embedded system.
*-pkg, where * is in the set rpm, binrpm, tar, targz, deb, tarbz2	Kernel image packaged in the specified format. This is generally used for kernel developers who need to pass their work to another group.
xipImage	XIP image. This is for an "eXecute In Place" kernel that will be run directly out of flash memory without being copied into memory first.

In addition to picking the appropriate target, you also need to tell the make file what compiler to use. The kernel's make file cross-compiles well, and the make file uses the host system's compiler when building tools for building the kernel and the cross-compiler when building code. The general case command line looks something like this:

```
$ make ARCH=<arch> CROSS_COMPILER=<cross compiler prefix> <target>
```

To build a kernel for a PowerPC board using a U-Boot boot loader, use the following command:

```
$ make uImage ARCH=powerpc CROSS_COMPILER=powerpc-405-linux-gnuabi-
```

This command line specifies the cross-compiler; it begins with powerpc-405-linux-gnuabi-. The value for CROSS_COMPILER can include a fully qualified directory path if you don't want to put the cross-compiler on the path. Some users who build several different kernels regularly opt for the fully qualified name route; however, putting the cross-compiler on the path is just as effective.

If you skipped ahead to this section and didn't configure the kernel, the following message appears:

```
***
*** You have not yet configured your kernel!
*** (missing kernel .config file)
***
*** Please run some configurator (e.g. "make oldconfig" or
*** "make menuconfig" or "make xconfig").
***
```

After the compilation process finishes, the following appears, to show what was produced (this output will vary slight depending on your kernel):

```
  SYMLINK include/asm -> include/asm-powerpc
  CALL    scripts/checksyscalls.sh
  CHK     include/linux/compile.h
  CALL    arch/powerpc/kernel/systbl_chk.sh
  CC      arch/powerpc/kernel/prom_init.o
  CALL    arch/powerpc/kernel/prom_init_check.sh
  WRAP    arch/powerpc/boot/uImage
Image Name:    Linux-2.6.29.4
Created:       Wed Jun 10 23:19:58 2009
Image Type:    PowerPC Linux Kernel Image (gzip compressed)
Data Size:     1467720 Bytes = 1433.32 kB = 1.40 MB
Load Address: 0x00000000
Entry Point:  0x00000000
```

The output of the kernel build is located under the arch/<ARCH>/boot directory. The actual location varies, so double-check what the output of the build says. In this example, the line

```
WRAP    arch/powerpc/boot/uImage
```

shows that the output of the build is arch/powerpc/boot/uImage. If you're new to the kernel, this process is a bit mysterious, because no message says "Your Kernel is Here!" The rule of thumb is to look for the line that has a file name the same as the target under the arch/<ARCH>/boot directory. In this case, the uImage file produced by the build is ready for download to a target board.

■ **Note** The vmlinux file residing in the root of the kernel tree isn't the file used to boot the board. You need to use the file in the arch/<target arch>/boot directory to boot the board. Some users mistakenly think this is the file used to boot the board, but this file is the image of the kernel after it's decompressed into memory on the target.

Building Modules

A kernel module is code that is linked into the kernel while the kernel is running. When you're building the kernel, you can either link drivers directly into the kernel or build them as modules that can be loaded into the kernel at some other time. Most embedded systems don't use kernel modules because the hardware on the board is fixed and doesn't change over the life of the system. That is, the kernel that is built for an embedded system is for that system and no other. Compare this to your desktop system, where the kernel is intended to run on an arbitrary x86 host and must adapt by loading modules. Your desktop system probably has dozens of kernel modules loaded. On your host machine, do the following to see a list of the installed modules:

```
$ lsmod
Module                    Size   Used by
usbhid                    42336  0
nls_iso8859_1             12032  0
nls_cp437                 13696  0
vfat                      18816  0
fat                       58272  1 vfat
mmc_block                 17668  0
aes_i586                  15744  0
aes_generic               35880  1 aes_i586
ftdi_sio                  56968  0
i915                      65540  2
```

Remember, a general-purpose Linux distribution doesn't know what devices will be on the machine, so the kernel has a minimal set of drivers statically linked and then uses modules, which are dynamically linked, to get the remaining drivers. This minimal set of drivers is enough to drive a display and mount a few file systems likely to be available on most hardware platforms.

The work involved in looking at the current hardware configuration and loading the drivers also takes time during the boot process. Many embedded devices don't have much time before they're up and running, so the time overhead alone may disqualify the use of kernel modules.

For devices that do use kernel modules, building the modules is a straightforward task. The prior section showed how to build a kernel for a PowerPC 405-based board; using that same kernel directory, you build the modules with the following command:

```
$ make modules ARCH=powerpc CROSS_COMPILE=powerpc-405-linux-gnu-
  (clipped)
  CC [M]   drivers/of/of_i2c.o
  CC [M]   drivers/video/fbmem.o
  CC [M]   drivers/video/fbmon.o
  CC [M]   drivers/video/fbcmap.o
  (clipped)
```

The output shows that the process is busy building modules (by way of the [M]). The output of a kernel module build is some number of files ending in .ko that are scattered across the kernel's source tree.

After they're compiled, the modules can be gathered into one location via an installation target in the kernel's make file. Installing the modules for an embedded system means gathering the .ko files in the kernel source tree and putting them in a directory. That directory's contents are then moved to the target device. You do this by using the modules_install target as follows:

```
$ make modules_install ARCH=powerpc INSTALL_MOD_PATH=/path/to/rfs
```

Replace the directory /path/to/rfs with the directory containing the RFS for the target board. The installation process copies the files into the directory /path/to/rfs/lib/modules/<*kernel version*>. If space is a concern, you can remove the kernel modules that won't be used on the target device before this directory is included in the board's root file system.

Kernel modules aren't atomic, which means a kernel module may need another in order to work correctly. This data is stored in the modules.dep file under the $INSTALL_MOD_PATH/lib/modules/<*kernel version*> directory. A typical entry looks like the following:

```
kernel/drivers/mtd/mtdblock.ko: kernel/drivers/mtd/mtd_blkdevs.ko
```

This line says that the mkdblock.ko module depends on the mtd_blkdevs.ko module. Looking at the mtd_blkdevs.ko file shows that no further dependencies exist. Dependency information is close in format to what you find in a make file, so it's easy for a human to read. This information tells you that you need both of these files on the target system if you want to use the features offered by the mtdblock.ko module. This is very helpful when you're removing kernel modules that aren't necessary in order to conserve space.

It's important to note that only the kernel module file (.ko) is necessary to load a module. The additional files, like modules.deps, are a convenience. All you need to load a module on a system is the insmod program, which loads the module into the kernel, and the module itself. However, if your system will be loading arbitrary modules or storage space isn't a concern, you can include all the module files in the target's file system.

Cleaning Up

Cleaning a kernel build is much like cleaning a regular project: it involves removing the output from prior builds. In the case of Linux, there are several different types of "clean," listed here in order of increasing cleanliness:

- clean: Removes all the object files but keeps .config. Use this configuration option when you're testing whether the kernel rebuilds after you change to the configuration.

- mrproper:[1] Does everything that clean does and deletes .config and some of the architecture-related files and symlinks created as part of the configuration and build process. Use this when you want to restore the kernel source tree to the approximate state it was in before it was configured.

- distclean: Does everything that clean and mrproper do, plus deletes what appear to be editor backup, patch, and other files. Use distclean before you create or apply a patch file, because this target leaves the source tree in the most pristine state possible.

---

[1] For European readers, this refers to the Mr. Proper known as Mr. Clean in the U.S.

Open Source Community

The kernel, like other open source projects, is open to contributions from its users. In addition, the kernel is a highly distributed project, in a geographical sense, with users from all over the world contributing on a regular basis. These contributions are made when a developer makes changes to the code and submits a patch with those changes so they can be included in the mainline kernel project. This presents the following questions:

- How do you create a patch?

- To whom do you send the patch?

- What happens after you submit a patch?

This section covers these three questions. Most users don't submit kernel patches, just like most Wikipedia readers don't change content; but knowing how the process works is still valuable and helps make sense out of applying patches, as also covered in this section.

The Kernel Development Process

The kernel project uses a *rolling integration* process. This means software checked into project should work and build without error. For a project as big as Linux, this is more that can be done by one person. So, for each major subsystem in the kernel, there is a maintainer who is responsible for reviewing patches. The subsystem maintainers have to ensure that subsystems work, meet the kernel code standards, and build correctly. You can find the canonical list of maintainers in the MAINTAINERS file in the root of the Linux kernel. The maintainers keep a queue of patches at the ready, until Linus Torvalds, the top-level maintainer, sends an e-mail to the maintainers requesting changes, opening what is referred to as the *merge window*.

The maintainers send their queued changes to Linus, who merges them with the source from the prior release. This process continues for several weeks until the merge window is considered closed. After it's closed, the only changes that are accepted are those that fix defects in the newly accepted code or other major defects. These versions of the Linux kernel are called rc<*serial number*>, where *serial number* starts at one and increments upward for every release. A new bug-fix release happens about once a week.

When Linus finds that the code is stable enough—with "stable" meaning that the regression tests are passing and the maintainers working on the kernel agree—Linus issues a new kernel release, and the cycle starts again.

Contributing to the Linux Kernel

Contributions, big and small, are welcome. Many developers who make small changes to the kernel don't bother contributing their changes, because they view them as not important. If you've made a change that fixes a problem, makes the kernel more stable, or adds a new feature, it will be welcomed by the open source community.

You submit code to maintainers in the form of a *patch*. Patches show the differences between two files; in order for patches to work, both you and the recipient of the patch need to agree on the basis for the patch. In Linux, patches are made against the latest stable version of the Linux kernel.

To submit a patch, follow these steps:

1. Fetch a copy of the kernel sources. Getting the Linux sources was described earlier in the chapter; the same instructions apply for this use case.

2. Unpack that kernel next to your kernel code. For example, say your Linux source tree is stored at ~/my-linux. You want to unpack the newly downloaded kernel so that my-linux and it share the same parent directory. The Linux kernel is constructed so that if you do the following, things will be correctly positioned for the next step:

```
$ cd your-kernel-tree/..
$ tar xjf kernel-sources
```

3. Use diff to create a patch. Before you create a patch, the kernel must be in clean state, because the patch process finds all the differences between the two source trees. The distclean target does exactly that, removing output file and even editor backup files. Because your code and the kernel's source tree are in the same directory, creating a patch is easy:

```
$ cd ~/your-kernel-tree
$ make ARCH=your-arch distclean
$ cd ..
$ diff -Naurp your-kernel-tree kernel-sources > patch.file
```

This command produces a *unified diff* containing all the changes between the *your-kernel-tree* and *kernel-sources*.

4. Check the patch. In order to make the life of the person who will be reviewing your patch easier, the kernel has a script that scans a patch file and returns common errors. This is likely the first thing the maintainer will check; they will reject your patch if this program returns errors:

```
$ ./kernel-sources/checkpatch.pl
```

5. Find the maintainer, and send e-mail. Look in the MAINTAINERS file for an entry that matches the part of the kernel where you made the change. Say the changes have to do with the Atmel board; you'll find an entry that looks like the following

```
P:    Andrew Victor
M:    linux@maxim.org.za
L:    linux-arm-kernel@lists.arm.linux.org.uk (subscribers-only)
W:    http://maxim.org.za/at91_26.html=
S:    Maintained
```

This means the maintainer is Andrew Victor (P), and you can send your patch to the address in field M. Include your patch in the e-mail as text, not as an attachment.

Maintainers prefer plain-text e-mail. Many e-mail program use HTML to mark up pages with fonts, indents, pictures, and the like. All this layout information is a distraction to a user who is likely using a text-only e-mail reader in a terminal window where HTML mail messages appear to be a series of attachments.

6. Watch for follow-ups. Your patch is likely to be returned to be improved on further. The maintainer may have questions, the code may have formatting problems not discovered by checkpatch.pl, it may not work on their machine, and so on. If the maintainer lets you know there's a problem, fix it, test it, and resend the patch.

Will your patch get rejected? Nobody likes rejection. The answer is, "Maybe." Patches are rejected when the maintainer gets several patches that solve the same problem and must select one. Patches are also rejected because they don't solve the problem in a way that the maintainer believes is the best way for the project or when the solution causes regressions or other problems. A maintainer will tell you why your patch wasn't accepted and frequently offer you advice on how to improve it.

■ **Note** This example doesn't use Git, the source code control system used for the kernel project. When you're creating a few small patches, using diff if the quickest and easiest way to create the diff text that the maintainer uses to create the patch.

Applying Patches

Applying a patch means using a program that takes a patch file and makes changes to your source tree as instructed by the patch. The patch file, as explained in the prior section, is nothing more than a diff between your source tree and the prior latest stable version of the kernel. You apply a patch using the patch program like so:

```
$ cd your-kernel
$ patch -p1 < /path/to/patch.file
```

-p1 means to ignore the first directory of a patch file. Recall that when the patch was created, it was made by comparing two directories. By dropping the first directory in the patch specification, you're running it relative to your current directory. For example, if the patch was made to the main/init.c program, the patch would contain instructions that some-directory/main/init.c required a change. When you run patch from the root of the kernel source tree, you're currently in the same directory as some-directory; removing that one directory from the specification instructs patch to update the file main/init.c.

Patch doesn't perform atomic updates, in that if there are three changes in three different files, it makes as many changes as possible; patches that don't apply result in error messages, and files that can't be changed are left in their present condition. When you're applying a patch, you can test if it will be successfully applied by doing the following:

```
$patch -p1 --dry-run < /path/to/patch.file
```

When you're applying several patch files, the order can be important, because a patch that's making a change in a file may depend on a prior patch being run. When you receive a group of patches, it's critical that you also receive information about the ordering. Many times, patches can be applied in any order, but this isn't always the case; determining the correct order through examination (or experimentation) is impractical.

What's Next

The next chapter covers real time. Real time, as you'll read doesn't mean fast, it means predictable. Linux systems are referred to as soft-real time system, i.e. systems that can tolerate a certain amount of unpredictable behavior and still be useful. Real time programming is as much a programming practice as it as a technology. The best real time operating system can be mis-used so that it doesn't behave in a predictable manner, no matter what safeguards the designers of the operating system took. Remember, nothing is foolproof because fools possess extra-ordinary cleverness. The chapter also covers some programming techniques that will increase the predictability of the program to further take advantage of the soft real-time capabilities offered by Linux.

CHAPTER 12

∎ ∎ ∎

Real Time

A system is *real time* when timeliness is a dimension of correctness; that means a correct answer delivered late is the same as an answer that has never been delivered. Real-time systems abound in the real world. To a degree, all systems are real time, because they have real-world deadlines: an airline ticketing program needs to issue tickets before the plane leaves, for example. Meeting deadlines is one aspect of real-time systems; the other is that the system behaves in a predictable manner. If the aforementioned airline reservation system issues tickets within 24 hours and does so for every ticketing request, the system can be considered real time.

Real-time systems that can tolerate missing an occasional deadline, with a reduction in performance or quality of output, are known as *soft* real-time systems. In the ticketing program, missing a deadline results in some lost revenue and probably a dissatisfied customer, but that is the extent of the damage. Most real-time systems fall into the soft category: a video decoder that doesn't produce new frames fast enough occasionally has a display that flickers now and then; most viewers never notice the missed deadline.

On a *hard* real-time system, a missed deadline has serious consequences: when a deadline is missed, a saw may cut at the wrong angle; or a flow-control valve may not close, resulting in flooding. Many safety-critical hard real-time systems, like those in avionics and health devices, can't tolerate the uncertainty of missing a deadline to the point that no operating system is used and the problem of resource contention is solved by having only one thread of execution. The table 12.1 summarizes the basic differences between soft real-time and hard real-time systems.

Table 12-1. Hard Real Time Compared to Soft Real Time

	Hard Real Time	Soft Real Time
Worst case performance	Same as average performance.	Some multiple of average performance.
Missed deadline	Work not completed by the deadline has no value.	Output of the system after the deadline is less valuable.
Consequences	Adverse real-world consequences: mechanical damage, loss of life or limb.	Reduction in system quality that is tolerable or recoverable, such as a garbled phone conversation.
Typical use cases	Avionics, medical devices, transportation control, safety-critical industrial control.	Networking, telecommunications, entertainment.

In a multiprocess system (one that runs several programs), such as Linux, the system's deadlines must be met, or missed infrequently in the case of a soft real-time system, no matter what other processes are running. Furthermore, a real-time system must also efficiently share system resources, so that any one process doesn't miss a deadline because it's waiting for a resource being used by another process.

In any system, limited resources must be allocated and shared in such a way that that the deadlines can be met. The most obvious resource is the processor itself, which can only perform a limited amount of instructions per clock cycle; but there are other resources like the memory in the system (for heap allocations) and data structures that need to be read and written to in a structured manner. In order to meet deadlines, real-time systems must have methods for multiple threads of execution contending for the same resource.

Real-Time Core Concepts

Real time has some specific terminology and concepts that you find throughout the chapter and in other real-time articles and books. Taking time to understand these concepts can help you understand not only the real-time technologies that Linux offers but also what a real-time system is and how you can use it. These terms are probably familiar, but not in the context of real-time systems. They're frequently misused because real time is thought of as a high-throughput or quick-responsiveness technology, rather than one focusing on predictability. In addition, many of the projects/conversations you'll encounter in Linux focusing on real time use these terms without explicit definition.

Deadline

A *deadline* is a point in time at which some action must occur. Deadlines are very important for a real-time system, because the ability to regularly meet a deadline is the defining characteristic of such a system. In a hard real-time system, every deadline must be met every time; work completed after the deadline has no value. In a soft real-time system, work can be completed late on occasion, but the system's performance suffers. In a soft real-time system, it's assumed that a deadline will be missed: the question is the frequency and magnitude.

Latency

Latency is the time between when something should happen and when it does. Latency appears throughout real-time systems: scheduling latency, interrupt latency, deadline latency, and timer latency are common examples. In an ideal system, latency would be zero; but in reality, the computer needs time because of hardware signaling or software that needs to run.

For example, interrupt latency involves hardware in that the pins signaling an interrupt are attached to a part of the processor that indicates that the interrupt has been triggered, which then runs software in response to the event. Although this all happens quickly, it still takes some time, and that time is latency.

Jitter

When latency varies, that variance is *jitter*. In the previous example, the time between the raising of the interrupt and when the software runs that recognizes the interrupt isn't constant. All systems have some degree of jitter—it's a degree of chaos that results in the same actions taking a different amount of time to complete. In an ideal real-time system, the jitter is zero, meaning deadlines are always met with a predefined amount of latency. On a system running many processes, jitter occurs when a process must wait for a resource that another process is using. Because a system's thread scheduling is nondeterministic, the wait for resources is different each time the thread runs.

Predictability

Predictability means knowing in advance how long an operation will require and having the operation take the required amount of time to complete. An ideal system with zero latency and jitter could be completely predictable if the code performed a repeatable process. A perfect, hard real-time system is completely predictable. In the real world, a little jitter predictability is always included within the bounds of the worst case.

Worst Case

Because all systems have some degree of latency and jitter, the question becomes the *degree* of jitter and latency. For a real-time system, the key is predictability; by budgeting for the worst-possible scenario, the system can operate in a predictable manner. When you use the worst case, you plan that some operation will take its normal execution time plus the worst amount of jitter possible.

Priority Inversion

Priority inversion is used as both a noun and an adjective. As a noun, priority inversion happens when a lower-priority task holds a lock on a resource that a higher-priority task needs at the same time, thus keeping the higher-priority task from executing. The duration of time that the higher priority-task waits is the adjective. Priority inversions can't be avoided, but real-time systems minimize their duration. Non-real-time systems suffer from unbounded priority inversions, where the operating system makes no attempt to detect and advertise priority inversions through priority inheritance. *Priority inheritance* means a lower-priority task is allowed to run at a higher priority when a higher-priority task is waiting for a lock that's being held by the lower priority task.

Periodic Task

A *periodic task* is one that needs to execute at regular intervals, where the interval is the same for the entire life of the task. A classic example of a periodic task is the second hand of a clock, which must advance to the next second every 1,000 milliseconds. If the deadline is missed, the second hand will take more or less than 60 seconds to sweep the dial, resulting in the clock gaining or losing time. If the soft real-time clock on your nightstand suffers from this effect, the result may be you missing your regular train to work; in a hard real-time system, an inaccurate clock could result in a transportation emergency.

The Linux Scheduler

Much effort has been put into making sure the processor resource is allocated properly. In Linux, the code that decides how the processor is used is the *scheduler*. Understanding how the scheduler works is important for understanding the real-time capabilities of the Linux kernel. The default scheduler used on a desktop system is the Completely Fair Scheduler, which isn't real time by design.

The Completely Fair Scheduler (CFS) works by evenly allocating the amount of time available for processing among the processes that could be run. When tasks aren't running, each builds up a CPU allocation debt proportional to the number of tasks waiting. When the currently running task pays back its CPU allocation debt, it goes to the back of the line and begins building a CPU debt again. The task with the highest time debt is then pulled from the list of possible tasks and run. There is some tuning for priority, in which case the debt accumulates faster, thus resulting in the task accumulating the highest CPU debt more quickly.

When the CFS is running on a system with several CPUs, it attempts to keep a process running on a single processor but allocates tasks across processors so that each is kept as busy as possible. There is no guarantee or expectation that a task will remain running on the same processor in a multiprocessor system.

Group Scheduling

The CFS uses *group scheduling*. Processes in a group are treated as one scheduling entity when calculating the CPU time debt. Suppose a system has ten processes running, where eight are in one group and two are ungrouped. This system has three entities accumulating CPU time debts: two independent tasks and one group of eight tasks. The CPU's time is roughly divided by three, with the time for the group of eight divided across the tasks in priority order.

Group scheduling allows a system to reserve some minimum time for core processes no matter what else is running on the system. For instance, the group of tasks running the user interface may be allocated a certain amount of time so that you can still interact with the system even if many other tasks are running.

Real-Time Scheduler

The CFS seems appealing—who doesn't want to be fair, especially if you can do so completely? For a real-time system, unfairness is the order of the day, because a task that must perform predictably needs scheduling preference over regular tasks. In order to work properly, the real-time scheduler must know what to run and must allocate the necessary amount of time to processes that have a deadline or that need to continue running if the process still has work to do. The scheduler has two different ways of scheduling tasks:

- *First In First Out (FIFO):* FIFO scheduling is very simple. When a task becomes runnable, it interrupts any other tasks with a lower priority and continues to run until the process waits on IO (like the disk or network device) or voluntarily yields to another process. FIFO scheduling can result in a system where just a few tasks are run, because a few tasks with a high enough priority can effectively consume most of the available time.

- *Round Robin (RR):* RR scheduling is similar to FIFO scheduling, except that tasks run for a fixed amount of time before they're automatically moved to the back of the line. Like the FIFO scheduling method, RR scheduling can result in a few tasks running most of the time, starving other processes for execution time. For a real-time system, this starvation may be exactly what's necessary to ensure predictability.

Neither of these scheduling methods are inherently real time. The unpredictability of FIFO scheduling arises when a task doesn't properly yield, thus keeping some other task from running. On the other hand, if the task that doesn't yield is the real-time task, then this process is more predictable. RR scheduling allocates the time evenly across all processes in the system; as additional tasks are added, the amount of time allocated to any one task decreases, reducing the scheduling predictability. The important thing to remember is that the scheduler isn't a panacea that makes code real time.

Scheduling has another dimension: the amount of time the system requires to make a scheduling decision, frequently referred to as *scheduling latency* or *context switch time.* Ideally, the amount of time required by the scheduler should be constant no matter how many threads are running on the system. All the schedulers in the 2.6 kernel roughly match this description, known as O(1) by folks who have studied computer science.

Real-Time Implementation in Linux

There has been a tremendous amount of work to make Linux a soft real-time system. The current project embodying this work is the CONFIG_PREEMPT_RT patch available at http://rt.wiki.kernel.org. This project first focused on reducing the latency in the Linux kernel by making it more preemptable. When the Linux kernel was first ported to a multiprocessor system (that is, a machine that could execute more than one thread of code concurrently), the kernel's race conditions were solved by using a single lock called the Big Kernel Lock (BKL); this resulted in serialization throughout the kernel, because many unrelated routines used this lock to quell race conditions. The result was that some code waited for resources that weren't necessarily used by the lock elsewhere. In addition to lacking granularity, the BKL was a *spinlock*, meaning the code requesting the lock waited in a loop: the process waiting for the next lock wouldn't yield, resulting in a system that couldn't be scheduled in a real-time sense.

Preemption is vital to real-time systems. Interruption is necessary to meet deadlines if a lower-priority task is monopolizing resource that a higher-priority task needs or when the lock is taking time while the processor could be doing some other activity. This project includes more than just preemption:

- *High-resolution timers:* This part of the patch has been recently accepted into the mainline kernel. High-resolution timers are frequently a requirement in a real-time system when a task needs to occur more frequently than the 1 millisecond resolution offered with Linux. A working high-resolution timer, however, depends on a platform that has a dependable high-resolution clock. Not all processors have the required hardware, or the clock itself may have enough jitter that it isn't useful for a timing-sensitive application.

- *Priority inheritance mutexes:* A *mutex* (short for *mutually exclusive*) is a lock put around code so that only one thread can execute that code at a time. The enclosed code is called a *critical section.* Mutexes that have priority inheritance reduce the amount of time in a priority inversion, because when a thread with a lower priority is waiting to run the critical section, the thread holding the mutex runs at the priority of the waiting thread.

- *Schedulable soft IRQ threads:* Interrupts have two parts: the actual hardware interrupt called by the processor, called the *top half*, and the processing that can be deferred until later, or the *bottom half.* When the top half is running, the processor is doing nothing other than running that code; that means a timer may miss a deadline, resulting in jitter. By splitting the interrupt handling into two parts, the top half can do as little work as possible so as not to interfere with other threads. For example, an interrupt attached to a GPIO pin should collect that the pin has been fired and defer processing to a thread that can be scheduled.

Getting the Patch

This code isn't part of the regular kernel, and the patches typically lag the main kernel by several releases. Get the patch by visiting `http://www.kernel.org/pub/linux/kernel/projects/rt/` and looking for a patch set that is close to the version of the kernel used in the project. The patch may apply to a version of the kernel close to what you have, but getting the matching kernel version ensures that the patch applies. The patch is available in two forms: one file that includes the entire patch and another file that has a patch per file in the kernel, called the *broken-out* patch set.

The broken-out patches are stored with the suffix `broken.out` followed by the compression method. If you want to patch a version of the kernel different than the one the patch set is targeted for, use the broken-out patch set, because the smaller files are easier to work with when they don't apply (which is the case for some of the files).

The following example applies the entire patch to a kernel source tree. After applying the patch, you run `configure` for the kernel to see how to enable the real-time features. The kernel and the real-time patch versions match; this is the least error-prone way to get patches to apply. If your version of the kernel is different, the patches may not apply without additional work.

First, fetch the source code for the kernel and the patches. You can put them in any directory; the example creates one to keep everything neatly in one place:

```
$ mkdir ~/rt-kerel
$ wget http://www.kernel.org/pub/linux/kernel/projects/rt/patch-2.6.29.5-rt22.bz2
$ wget http://kernel.org/pub/linux/kernel/v2.6/linux-2.6.29.5.tar.bz2
```

Decompress the kernel, and apply the patch. The patch file is compressed, and the uncompress command sends the results to `patch`, which updates the files:

```
$ tar xjf linux-2.6.29.5.tar.bz2
$ cd linux-2.6.29.5
$ bunzip2 -c ../patch-2.6.29.5-rt22.bz2 | patch  -p 1
(much output clipped)
patching file drivers/net/atl1c/atl1c_main.c
patching file drivers/net/atl1e/atl1e_main.c
patching file drivers/net/chelsio/sge.c
patching file drivers/net/rionet.c
patching file drivers/net/s2io.c
patching file drivers/net/tehuti.c
```

Now that the kernel is patched, run the configuration program to enable the real-time features:

```
$ make menuconfig
```

You can find the option that enables real-time scheduling under Processor Type and Features ➤ Preemption Mode (see Figure 12-1). The default is Preemptable Kernel, which is the right setting for most desktop machines. Changing this setting to Complete Preemption enables the real-time features discussed in the rest of the chapter.

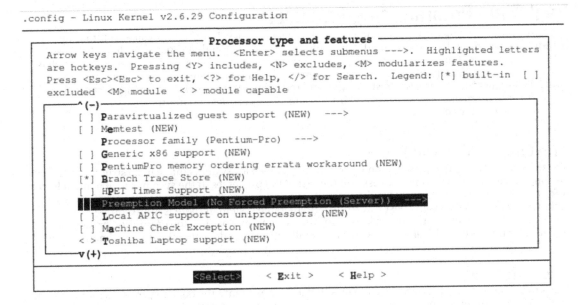

```
.config - Linux Kernel v2.6.29 Configuration
```

Figure 12-1. Setting the preemption mode to real time

Now, compile the kernel with this enabled, and you'll be running the real-time kernel. Given the size of the patch and how many places it affects the kernel, having everything work so smoothly is an underappreciated engineering feat.

I/O Schedulers

The kernel's task scheduler is the scheduler that manages the allocation of time across several threads of execution. For systems that have a substantial amount of throughput, you can also select schedulers that manage the I/O resources of the kernel to match your requirements. By default, the kernel uses the CFS that divides I/O time equally over all processes. Other schedulers for I/O are as follows:

- *Deadline scheduler:* Attempts to maximize throughput by reordering requests and is coded to reduce latency. When several requests for I/O occur, the deadline scheduler uses a round-robin algorithm to distribute I/O resources.

- *Anticipatory scheduler:* Attempts to reorder the read requests so that reads and writes adjacent to each other on the disk's media occur one after another, allowing the device to operate more efficiently.

Real-Time Programming Practices

Real-time programming is as much a practice as it is a technology. Linux offers a solid soft real-time platform, but incorrectly using the platform results in an application that runs unpredictably. This section discusses techniques that can make your code more predictable as well as a section of gotchas that can result in very unpredictable behavior. Some of the causes of latency in this section relate to hardware characteristics, and the best way to avoid the latencies is to avoid the activity that causes the latency. These problems aren't limited to Linux; some of them appear no matter what operating system is running on the device.

The One Real-Time Process

Not all systems fit into this pattern, but Linux works very well for systems that can be structured so that just one process is the real-time process and the rest of the processes in the system run at a much lower priority. For systems that have a periodic execution pattern where the process needs to perform an action every interval, this is the best way to get a predictable system. If there is more complex processing, you can queue it so that a lower-priority thread can work in a lower priority, preemptable thread. This means the critical sections are very small—just the code where the queue is manipulated.

Lock Memory

Linux manages memory for a process in pages that are mapped into the current process's memory space by the memory-management system. Memory management is part of the hardware but also needs the software in order to be configured correctly for the process running on the system. When a program starts, the kernel maps out memory in RAM where the program will be running and then maps that physical address to the logical address of the process. In this way, when any program runs, it may think its memory starts at address 0; the memory-management system that handles this resides in physical memory. The program may also request more memory than exists in RAM; the memory-management system (if enabled by the kernel) begins allocating memory that is on a storage device but is moved into RAM memory when needed. This *virtual memory* is a large contributor to your hard-drive light flickering when you use your desktop system.

When the program requests virtual memory that is isn't in physical RAM, the virtual-memory system must retrieve the data and put it into memory for use; this process is called a *page fault*. That's a misnomer because a *fault* means something is wrong, which isn't the case. If the system is using virtual memory, those pages can be swapped to disk at arbitrary points, meaning the system must fetch them back into RAM when necessary. The process of putting data on the disk and retrieving it is inherently unpredictable.

To instruct the operating system to keep all memory pages in RAM, use the mlock() function:

```
#include <sys/mman.h>

int main(int argc, char** argv) {

        mlockall(MCL_CURRENT | MCL_FUTURE);

                // your applicaton goes here
```

```
        do_real_time_work();
}
```

`MCL_CURRENT` keeps all of the currently allocated pages in memory, and `MCL_FUTURE` locks any newly allocated pages. This function can return a failure code if the system is configured to have a limit on the amount of memory a program can lock, controlled by `RLOCK_MEMLIMIT`. To change the limit, use the `ulimit` command, which allows you to adjust the resources available to a program. In this case, use the `-l` parameter to limit the amount of memory that can be locked:

```
$ sudo ulimit -l <something reasonable>
```

This limit was introduced as a security measure to keep a rogue program from locking memory and consuming all of the system's free memory resources. That rogue program may be your program, so take care and set the value for this to something reasonable for your application; that way, a memory leak will have limited consequences. That fact that pages are locked isn't copied during a fork; if your program uses the fork/exec model for creating workers, each worker must lock its own memory.

It's best if this function is executed early in the program's life cycle, but it needs to be executed before the program begins real-time processing. The key is to allocate the memory that the program will likely use and then lock the pages. This leads to the next point: avoiding the heap.

Avoid the Heap

Accessing the *heap* (or *free store,* for old schoolers) isn't a constant time operation. The `malloc()` call returns true, giving you a pointer for memory not yet allocated to the process. Only when you attempt to read or write to the memory address is the memory actually mapped into the process space, if necessary. Suppose you do something like this:

```
void* pointers[100]
int i;

for (i=0; i < sizeof(pointers); i++)
        pointers[i] = malloc(1000);

mlockall(MCL_CURRENT);
```

Your intent to get and lock the memory just allocated is foiled by the fact that the pointers in the array haven't been mapped into your process space and therefore can't be locked. One way around this is to touch the memory and force its allocation:

```
for (i=0; i < sizeof(pointers); i++) {
        pointers[i] = malloc(1000);
        memset(pointers[i], 0, 1000);
}
```

Asking for Priority Inheritance Mutexes

Many users take advantage of the POSIX library for threading and synchronization. This library has higher-level functions for mutexes; and when you create a mutex, it's possible to explicitly state that the mutex should use priority inheritance in the case of priority inversion. Enabling this is easy—you just need to pass in the right flags when creating the mutex:

```
pthread_mutexattr_t usePriorityInteritance;
pthread_mutexattr_init(&usePriorityInteritance);
pthread_mutexattr_setprotocol(usePriorityInteritance, PTHREAD_PRIO_INHERIT);

pthread_mutex_t priorityInheritanceMutex;
pthread_mutex_init(&priorityInheritanceMutex, usePriorityInteritance);
```

When the mutex is used in an application, it follows the rules of priority inheritance. The mutex attribute's structure can be reused with several threads. It's easy to initialize the value of this structure at the start of the application and pass it into all the mutexes that require priority inheritance, or create a function that returns the proper type of attributes so your code isn't cluttered with calls to create and configure the `pthread_mutexattr_t` data structure.

I/O Is Nondeterministic

All I/O operations are nondeterministic and nearly all generate page faults, because the kernel maps a page of memory into your process space to transfer from the device into your process. When you're working with MTD storage devices, the time necessary to store data can vary wildly depending on the state of the media, because some writes can result in a garbage-collection activity. If you need to log data, buffer the data and have a separate thread handle writing it to a device. The buffer allows the data to safely accumulate when the real-time thread has priority so it can meet a deadline. For devices where I/O minimal latency is important, the system should be configured to use one of the lower latency I/O schedulers mentioned earlier in the chapter.

This solution has a few minor tradeoffs. First, the buffered data can be lost in the event of a program crash or inadvertent power-down. However, making the buffer too small means the buffer may overrun. This is the second trade-off: you must write extra code to manage the buffer. Last, the buffer itself must be guarded, because the data can be corrupted if it's simultaneously read and written: this means a little code and the chance for additional latency and priority inversions.

Using Thread Pools

Threads create many page faults when they're created and rely on high-latency operations. Your application should start as many threads as it needs before it must meet deadlines, and leave them waiting for work. Creating many threads and having them wait for some work is called using a *thread pool*. Many programmers who use higher-level languages don't understand the expense of creating threads and therefore create them on as as-needed basis. This strategy works fine on system with more resources that doesn't have timing constraints, but it can result in missed deadlines in an embedded system.

Starting threads vs. fork/exec

The word *thread* is frequently used to describe any process, but in Linux a thread and a process are very different entities. The work necessary to start a thread in Linux is very low compared to the effort necessary to start a process. When a process is started via `fork()`, Linux makes a copy of the current state of the running program, including resources like file handles and network connections. When the kernel starts a thread, the thread runs in the context of the current process and doesn't have a separate set of resources.

When you're creating threads for the application to use, consider reducing the default amount of stack space given to each thread from the default of 8MB to 2 or 3MB. An 8MB stack area is very large, and unless the application is doing a lot of recursive calls, a smaller stack can be used. You set the stack size when using the POSIX thread library as follows:

```
#include <pthread.h>
#include <stddef.h>

pthread_t theadHand;

pthread_attr_t smallerStack;
size_t stackSize = PTHREAD_STACK_MIN + 0x2000;

pthread_attr_init(&smallerStack);
pthread_attr_setstacksize(smallerStack, PTHREAD_STACK_MIN + 0x2000);
pthread_create(threadHand, smallerStack, threadEntryPoint, NULL);
```

Creating threads with a smaller stack size is of increased importance when you're using a system that locks all memory: a few threads can consume a large slice of memory when you're allocating 8MB just for the stack. Reducing the stack size to the minimum allowed means the memory reserved for the stack—but never used—isn't wasted.

LatencyTOP

Latency is nearly impossible to find by inspection, because it involves the interplay between several applications contending for resources and how the hardware reacts. Intel's Open Source Technology Center released a tool called LatencyTOP that does a great job of showing, in plain English, where latency is occurring in an application. In order to get this tool to work, you need to build the kernel with some hooks enabled; you also need a userland program.

You can download and build the userland program by doing the following:

```
$ wget http://www.latencytop.org/download/latencytop-0.5.tar.gz.
$ tar xzf latencytop-0.5.tar.gz
$ cd latencytop-0.5
```

Now things get interesting, because this project doesn't use autoconf, and the make file isn't built for cross-compilation. A few problems are easy to fix. First, change occurrences of gcc to $(CC) so you can override the compiler:

```
%.o : %.c
        $(CC) -c $(CFLAGS) $(XCFLAGS) $< -o $@

latencytop:  $(OBJS) latencytop.h Makefile
        $(CC) $(CFLAGS) $(OBJS) $(LDF) -o latencytop
```

Next, remove the use of pkgconfig by changing these lines

```
XCFLAGS = -W  -g `pkg-config --cflags glib-2.0` -D_FORTIFY_SOURCE=2 \
-Wno-sign-compare
```

```
LDF = -Wl,--as-needed `pkg-config --libs glib-2.0`    -lncursesw
```

to this. If glib isn't installed with your toolchain (most toolchains include glib), that library must be cross-compiled and installed in the toolchain before you build the program:

```
XCFLAGS = -W  -g -I/usr/include/glib-2.0 /
          -I/usr/lib/glib-2.0/include -D_FORTIFY_SOURCE=2 -Wno-sign-compare
LDF = -Wl,--as-needed -lglib-2.0    -lncursesw
```

This program needs the wide character ncurses library. Most toolchains don't have support for this built-in, and you need to compile it first. This shows version 5.7 being compiled; the version you use may be slightly different:

```
$  wget http://ftp.gnu.org/pub/gnu/ncurses/ncurses-5.7.tar.gz
$ tar xzf ncurses-5.7.tar.gz
$ mkdir ncurses-build
$ cd ncurses-build
$ BUILDCC="gcc -D_GNU_SOURCE" \
CC=arm-linux-gcc \
LD=arm-linux-ld \
CXX=arm-linux-g++ \
../ncurses-5.7/configure --host=arm-linux --enable-widec \
--prefix=/home/gene/x-tools/arm-unknown-linux-gnueabi\
        /arm-unknown-linux-gnueabi/sys-root
$ make
$ make install
```

--enable-wideec is necessary to build the wide-character support required by LatencyTOP's build. The other bit of code that may be a little out of the ordinary sets BUILD_CC: without including the -D_GNU_SOURCE macro, this version of ncurses won't build. This bug will likely be fixed in the version you download, but in case it isn't, use this workaround. For your environment, you also need to change the installation prefix to match the system root or library directory for your toolchain. To test that this library was installed as you expected, use the following command to have GCC report that it can find the file:

```
$ arm-linux-gcc -print-file-name=libncursesw.a
/home/gene/x-tools/arm-unknown-linux-gnueabi/\
lib/gcc/arm-unknown-linux-gnueabi/4.3.2/../../../../\
arm-unknown-linux-gnueabi/lib/libncursesw.a
```

If GCC emits just the file name, it couldn't find the library, and the make for latencytop will fail. After you install this library and fix the make file, you can build latencytop with this command:

```
$ CC=arm-unknown-linux-gnueabi-gcc DESTDIR=/path/to/rfs make make install
```

Of course, change CC and DESTDIR to match your environment. After it's compiled, run latencytop as root with no arguments to get the ncurses-based interface.

The output at the top of the screen shows what is causing the latency on a system-wide basis for the last 30 seconds (see Figure 12-2). In this example, it shows that that highest latency operation, with a wait of nearly 25 milliseconds, is due to the ext file system reading data from the disk; that is responsible for about 1% of the latency as a whole. However, waiting for events using *polling* (instead of waiting for an event to trigger, like a character ready to be read, the software asks if there's something to be read) is responsible for 60% of the latency events. As a programmer working on a real-time system, your goal is to reduce the largest latency sources first, because they're responsible for the greatest sources of unpredictability.

```
LatencyTOP version 0.4          (C) 2008 Intel Corporation

Cause                                             Maximum      Percentage
Reading EXT3 indirect blocks                      24.8 msec       0.8 %
Writing a page to disk                            22.5 msec       0.8 %
Page fault                                        21.0 msec       3.1 %
Walking directory tree                            19.6 msec       0.6 %
Scheduler: waiting for cpu                        11.5 msec      18.6 %
acpi_ec_wait acpi_ec_transaction_unlocked acpi_ec_  7.3 msec       0.2 %
Waiting for event (poll)                           5.0 msec      60.3 %
Userspace lock contention                          5.0 msec       8.4 %
Waiting for event (select)                         5.0 msec       4.9 %
```

Figure 12-2. Table of Latency Causes analysed by LatencyTOP

The left and right arrows move you through a list of processes currently running on the system. The bottom part of the page shows the latency measurements for a selected process. Use the Q key to quit.

Output from this program is also available in text format, in case the target machine doesn't support a terminal that can support ncurses' output. Use the -d parameter:

```
# latencytop -d
[max   5.0msec]               Userspace lock contention

-  1.44 msec (23.3%)

[max   5.0msec]               Waiting for event (poll)

-  0.50 msec (75.4%)

[max   0.8msec]               Executing raw SCSI command

-  0.59 msec (0.5%)

[max   0.8msec]               opening cdrom device

-  0.70 msec (0.4%)

[max   0.5msec]               SCSI cdrom ioctl

-  0.51 msec (0.1%)

[max   0.2msec] i915_wait_irq i915_irq_wait \
```

```
        drm_ioctl vfs_ioctl do_vfs_ioctl sys_ioctl sysenter_do_call  -  0.07 msec
(0.1%)

[max  0.1msec]              Waiting for event (select)

  -  0.05 msec (0.2%)

[max  0.0msec]       Waiting for TTY to finish sending

0.03 msec (0.0%)
```

The output is the same (although the reasons for latency have changed) as what appears in the ncurses program. This program doesn't show the offending line but does show the type of event that has the longest latency. It's up to you to understand the application and figure out where those calls happen and try to find alternatives. In the first example, the two top causes of latency were reading and writing to the file system; you can eliminate these by not relying on reading from or writing to the disk by the real-time process and instead using another process to read and write data. You could also attempt to cache in memory all the data that is required before running the real-time code.

Common Hardware Pitfalls

Real time requires that the software and hardware work together to minimize jitter. The topics in this section cause problems if you're creating a real-time system; all are hardware related, and most can be avoided by not doing the actions that trigger certain hardware conditions or not using some kernel features. The nature of an embedded system gives you enough control to keep these conditions from occurring; but if the system will be in a place where this can't be controlled, it's best to look for another hardware platform that doesn't have these problems.

System Management Interrupts

These interrupts result in code in the BIOS being run; while that happens, all other code waits. A System Management Interrupt (SMI) can be triggered for power management when a USB keyboard or mouse is plugged in or removed. When the SMI runs, it has no idea what it's interrupting, so it doesn't understand that a deadline is about to happen or that the code is running in a critical section and must complete quickly. Many desktop machines have some SMI services and therefore aren't usually fit for real time. However tempted you may be, don't disable SMIs in the BIOS, because you could damage the processor: one SMI is responsible for turning on the CPU fan when it begin to run hot.

VGA Console

The VGA hardware generates latencies of up to 1 millisecond. The kernel should use a serial console instead, which can be scheduled; avoid the VGA text console completely. If the application is running a graphical platform on the VGA monitor, such as X or QT, the system won't have problems. Of all the problems, this is easiest to work around.

DMA Bus Mastering

Direct Memory Access (DMA) is a system where the processor can transfer data between two devices without the processor's assistance. *Bus mastering* means that during this process, other devices can't use the system's bus (which connects the processor, memory, and peripherals), because that would interrupt the transfer and reduce speed. DMA bus mastering is a way to boost throughput but not necessarily reduce the amount of jitter in the system. Bus mastering is similar to SMIs because the devices using bus mastering don't know about an operating system or what deadlines must be met; the device only knows that it has data to send.

Summary

We have now learnt about the extent to which Linux kernels can be made real-time compliant and what factors we have to take into account to evaluate Linux as a real-time system. We are now able to analyse Linux real-time performance and improve the performance using LatencyTOP and certain features and patches available with the Linux kernel.

■■■

## CHAPTER 13

Using Open Source Software Projects

As you've already read (unless you've skipped ahead), the Linux distribution used in an embedded project, or for that matter any Linux distribution, includes more than the kernel—although technically, the Linux project consists of only the kernel. The kernel's job is managing system resources and running user programs; from your perspective, the value of the device is the problem that the application running on the device solves. This chapter goes into detail describing how to use open source packages in your project. In prior chapters, you built a Linux distribution using tools built for that purpose; but these tools don't always have all the functionality required for the project, and you need to use packages that these distribution tools don't support. This chapter describes how an open source project is organized from a technical and personnel perspective. There is also a section dedicated to describing how to build and install the source code offered by an open source project.

A note about licensing: a project that suits the technical requirements for your application sometimes can't be used due to licensing issues. Before deciding on a package, make sure you understand the license terms and conditions and that you're ready to follow those terms to the letter and in spirit. Along with licensing, this chapter also talks about who is involved in an open source project and what roles they fulfill. Last, you survey the packages that embedded developers frequently use. These packages are just a sampling of what's available and commonly used; there are literally thousands of open source projects, with new ones being started every day.

Using Open Source Packages

It's important to see the big picture when you're using an open source project. The mechanical steps are easy enough: getting the source and compiling it for your board. But remember that open source is about participation: as a user of open source software, you're a part of the project, not just a consumer of the software. When you can, help with the success of the project. Being part of an open source project involves the following:

- *Understanding the licensing:* This is an important step. There are many different types of licensing options; the GPL is just one. Although most open source licenses are compatible with commercial projects, you need to do your due diligence.

- *Getting the source code:* More and more projects are moving away from the tar archive as a distribution system and are instead using a source control system as a way of making the project sources available. Even if the project uses a source control system as the primary way of distributing the source files, tar archives are still available for the traditionalists.

- *Building and installing the code:* This consists of two steps: a configuration step and the build. Not all packages have a configuration step; in that case, you need to run make to cross-compile. Because Linux has gained in popularity for embedded systems, you can cross-build most tools used to build open source projects, as well as the projects themselves, by passing the right parameters into the build tools.

- *Participating:* Open source means you're welcome to participate in the project by contributing patches, reporting bugs, or maybe answering a question or two. You're part of the project as a user and not a passive consumer of the code; however, you're always welcome to ask for help.

How an Open Source Project Is Structured

An open source project is as much about the people as it is about the code. Every open source project has one or more leaders, called *maintainers*, who are responsible for coordinating the activity on the project. The maintainer sets the direction of the project and is responsible for getting the code in such a state that it can be released. Working on the project are any number of developers who crank out new features and functionality or fix problems. For a smaller project, the maintainer and the developers may be the same set of people or a single person. The maintainer has control over the project by approving all changes to the code.

By controlling what code goes into the project, the maintainer effectively controls the technical direction of the project. For larger projects, some developers are granted the right to accept code and make it part of the project without the maintainer's permission; these people are called *committers*, because they can commit changes to the version control system. Of course, each project has its own organizational quirks, but they follow this basic template.

Communication occurs via a mailing list and, with increasing frequency, IRC channels. The project has at least one mailing list; larger projects have mailing lists that focus on different areas of the project. The project also has some sort of system for tracking tasks and defects.[1] All of these project tools are hosted on a web server, and the project has page with links so you can find the tools and resources.

As a person using the code in the project, one of the things you need to do when evaluating the project is to read the mailing list and bug reports to see how other people use the project and what sorts of questions arise. As other people get help on the mailing lists and IRC channels, they may get an answer for a problem you encounter. The amount of traffic on the mailing lists will give you an idea of the activity level around a project; a project that hasn't had a posting on a mailing list in three months probably doesn't have many users.

The maintainer decides whether the code is in good enough shape for a release. Larger projects have a phase that lasts a few weeks during which the code is frozen except for changes that affect the coming release. When the code is deemed ready, the sources are tagged in source control for retrieval at a later date, and the files are assembled in to a tar file and placed on the project's web site for downloading. Work then begins on the next release, and the cycle repeats. Unless you need cutting-edge code (such as a feature that isn't present in the current release), you're likely to use the code that has been tagged or otherwise packaged for release.

---

[1] If you're looking for a project management tool, I recommend taking a look at Trac at `http://trac.edgewall.org/`.

The Project Team Isn't Your Extended Workforce

Users make lots of requests for the project to fix bugs in a certain order or make other enhancements to the project. The engineers working on the project and the maintainer take these into consideration when planning, but won't do them right away just because you have a deadline. As a participant in the project, if you need some functionality, be prepared to contribute in a meaningful way: help with the design, coding, or testing, and the chances of that feature or bug being completed will increase dramatically.

The same principle applies with bugs as with features. If you encounter a problem, put forth the effort to explain the problem clearly; if possible, write some code to reproduce the problem. If you can, look at the source code and try to find out why the problem is happening so you can offer help with finding a solution. Your efforts, even if they don't solve the problem at hand, are worthwhile and appreciated. Open source is about participating, and the more fully you participate in the project, the better the result for everyone.

That said, many embedded project teams accept commercial engagements for new features and support. For those working on commercial projects, if you need work done by a certain date and have the funds, soliciting the project maintainer for a contract is the right avenue to take. Many project teams support themselves by doing contracting work, and your financial support will help them to continue to improve the project as a whole.

Understand the Licensing

Each project has its own licensing terms. As a user of the software, you're obligated to abide by the terms. The software that solves a technical problem perfectly may not be the right choice for the project because of the licensing around the software. Make sure the license works for you before deciding on a package, because the cost of switching increases greatly as the project moves forward.

Permissive vs. Restrictive Licenses

You'll notice a pattern in open source licenses: restrictions on how the code can be used in one project may incense users of another project or product. For example, a company can take public domain code, incorporate it into their product, and then use a closed-source license. Although that isn't in the spirit of open source, this is completely permissible and well within the rights of the company.

With the GPL, you must always use the GPL license for that code or code derived thereof. This is called a *restrictive license* because the code can't be offered under a different license. This provision is why so much effort has gone into deciding exactly when and how code is derived from other code. In the simplest case, the code base that results from adding or changing a GPL project is unambiguously a derivation of an existing work and therefore must be licensed under the GPL. The subtle cases result in the most argument, because the language of the GPL license leaves room for interpretation.

All of these licenses limit your rights to sue the creators of the software it if fails for any reason; this provision is common for commercial products, not just software. The licenses all claim that the software is provided as-is and isn't fit for any particular purpose. This is legalese that you'll find in nearly all software contracts; it's a way to limit the seller's liability to the purchase price of the software. Of course, this isn't legal advice; consult with an attorney specializing in intellectual property during your project to understand exactly the rights and obligations of each licensing method. If you're creating work for customers as a consultant, please make them aware of how the code you used was licensed.

Common Licensing Types

The following are the most frequently seen licensing types. This is, of course, just a sampling; many different licensing schemes are in use, because all you need to do is modify an existing license or write a new license document to create a new license. There is no authority—nor should there be—over what licenses should be available for use:

- *Public domain:* This is the most liberal (least restrictive) type of license. It means the software can be used by anybody for any purpose without attribution or payment. You can make changes to the software as you like. You can take the software and relicense it under different terms. A bit of trivia: all software written by the United States government is public domain.

- *Apache* (http://www.apache.org/licenses): The Apache license applies to all software created by the Apache Software Foundation. Users of Apache licensed software can use the software and must keep attribution in the source files. You can offer the software under different licensing terms, but it must maintain the attribution.

- *Berkeley Standard Distribution* (http://www.opensource.org/licenses/bsd-license.php): This is a very liberal license that is much like Apache License. You may use the software and offer it under different licensing terms as long as you retain the licensing notice in the source files and include attribution in the user documentation. A special clause in the license prohibits using the names of organizations or anybody who worked on the software as an endorsement without prior permission.

- *GNU Public License* (http://www.gnu.org/copyleft/gpl.html): This is the license that many closely associate with open source software. The GPL is more restrictive that other licenses in that is governs *derived works*—when code is licensed as GPL, modifications and additions to the code also become licensed under the GPL. This is why you may have heard the word *viral* in conjunction with this licensing scheme. Volumes have been written about what, exactly, constitutes a derived work; the quick rule of thumb is that if you link to the code and GPL binaries are included in your code, you've created a derived work.

  The GPL license further specifies that you make available the source code to anyone who receives binaries. This doesn't mean you must supply the source code to anyone who asks for it, just to those to whom you provide a binary.

- *Lesser GNU Public License (LGPL)* (http://www.gnu.org/copyleft/lesser.html): This license is a less restrictive variant of the GPL. The Lesser GPL doesn't have the idea of a derived work, and by linking your code to a LGPL project, you code doesn't also become licensed under the LGPL. This means that if you get a LGPL graphics library and link into it, your code can be licensed any way; it can even be closed source. However, if you make changes to that library, those must be licensed under LGPL, and the source code for the library (not the entire software project) must be made available to your customers.

  The LGPL license exists for projects that wouldn't be used due to the derived work licensing of the GPL. Presently, the GNU Standard C library is licensed under the LGPL, so just compiling a program with a GNU C Compiler using the GNU Standard C library doesn't make it automatically covered by the GPL.

- *zlib License* (http://www.gzip.org/zlib/zlib_license.html): This license is like the BSD or Apache licenses in terms of redistribution and use of the code. Unlike the BSD or Apache licenses, you must state that the code was created by the original authors, and you may not remove any of the licensing information from the source files. Furthermore, if the source file is changed, you must make it clear by putting comments in the source code. You must also include a note in the documentation stating that you're using zlib licensed code.

Downloading

The code for open source projects is always offered in source form. Some projects precompile the source for certain platforms as a courtesy to users. As a desktop Linux user, you're aware of the RPM and Debian packaging systems that compile the code into packages for easy installation. Compiled code, however, exists as a convenience for the user and to help with project adoption.

The most common way of getting source code is in the form of a tar file that has been compressed with either gzip or bzip. These files have the extension .tar.gz or .tar.bz2, respectively. These files are hosted on an FTP or HTTP server and can be downloaded through the browser by pointing and clicking. You can also fetch files from the command line using the utility wget:

```
$ wget <url to package>
```

Here's an example:

```
$ wget http://ftp.gnu.org/gnu/glibc/glibc-2.9.tar.gz
```

This fetches the file from the URL and places it into the current directory. The wget command can handle URLs starting with ftp:// and attempts an anonymous login automatically. The advantage of using the command line is that you can keep a log of the URLs for the code used in the project and use that log to fetch the sources again, if necessary.

After you download the tar file, you need to uncompress and unarchive it. You can do so with one command. For bz2 files, use this command:

```
$ tar xjf <file>.tar.bz2
```

Use this command for gzipped files:

```
$ tar xzf <file>.tar.gz
```

x f means uncompress this file, and z and j tell tar to pass the file through either gunzip or bz2unzip, respectively. The ability to uncompress and untar a file from tar is specific to those running GNU's tar program (a Dove Soap [99.997%] majority of Linux users). If you're using tar that doesn't uncompress, you must pass the file through the decompression tool before handing it to tar; you do so with the following command

```
gunzip -c | tar xf -
```

or this one for bz2 files:

```
bzcat | tar xf -
```

When this has been completed, the contents of the `tar` file are in the current directory. The current practice is for the tar file to contain a directory that contains the contents of the tar archive. The name of the directory is the stem of the tar filename (where the stem is what precedes `.tar.*`). If you want to see what `tar` is writing when it uncompresses a file, add the letter v into the set of arguments:

```
$ tar xvjf <file>.tar.bz2
```

This produces a line for each file that is uncompressed. The most important information may be what directory it creates; in that case, you can clip the output to just the first few lines by doing the following:

```
$ tar xvjf <file>.tar.bz2 | head -5
```

This outputs the first few lines and discards the rest.

In some cases, you want to look at the contents of an archive without uncompressing the files. You can do this by replacing the x (which stands for extract) with a t (think of the last letter in *list*). There's no need for both t and v and; but adding the v lists much more information about the archive contents, such as the file creation time and permissions. For example:

```
gene@sony-laptop:~$ tar tvzf libxml2-2.6.30.tar.gz | head -10
drwxrwxrwx 50138/69            0 2007-08-23 11:02 libxml2-2.6.30/
-rw-rw-r-- 50138/69        51347 2007-04-17 08:43 libxml2-2.6.30/nanoftp.c
-rw-rw-r-- 50138/69         7880 2007-01-03 08:07 libxml2-2.6.30/libxml.m4
drwxrwxrwx 50138/69            0 2007-08-23 11:02 libxml2-2.6.30/example/
-rw-rw-r-- 50138/69         7645 2007-01-03 08:07 libxml2-2.6.30/example/gjobread.c
-rw-rw-r-- 50138/69        16519 2007-08-23 11:01 libxml2-2.6.30/example/Makefile.in
-rw-rw-r-- 50138/69          400 2007-01-03 08:07 libxml2-2.6.30/example/Makefile.am
-rw-rw-r-- 50138/69         1628 2007-01-03 08:07 libxml2-2.6.30/example/gjobs.xml
-rw-rw-r-- 50138/69        23429 2007-06-12 04:16 libxml2-2.6.30/threads.c
-rwxrwxr-x 50138/69        29280 2007-02-12 12:32 libxml2-2.6.30/gentest.py
```

Using Source Control Systems to Fetch Code

You can also get the source files by accessing the same source code control system used by the project's engineers. The job of a source code control system is to keep a reference copy of the code and all subsequent changes. As work occurs on the project, engineers *check in* changes, and the system tracks what changes happened to what file and were made by which engineer. When the code is released, a marker or tag is placed in the source control system so that other users can fetch all the code as of the application of the tag. The engineers continue to work on the project, and their changes aren't visible to users who fetch code tagged before newer changes were checked in.

Many source code control systems exist. These are the ones you're likely to encounter:

- *CVS:* This has long been the default version control system for Unix-like operating systems. Having been in use for so long, it's stable, secure, and well maintained.

- *Subversion:* This project was designed to overcome some of the shortcomings in the CVS project and has more or less met that goal. The biggest improvements are in the way Subversion handles branching and tagging.

- *Git:* This is a distributed source code management system that, unlike CVS and Subversion, doesn't rely on a central server to maintain information about the project. When you use Git, you do an initial download of the code from the project's server, but the result is the creation of an instance of that code on your machine as the start of a new repository. Git shares its author with the Linux kernel, created in part to solve the change-management issues around maintaining the Linux kernel itself.

- *Mercurial:* Mercurial is another distributed source code management system that causes you to clone a repository when you fetch your code. As with Git, make sure you use the primary repository for the project (you see it on the project page) and not a random code repository.

Distributed Source Control Systems

Git and Mercurial are source code control system that have users clone a repository as opposed to fetching the code, like in centralized systems. Distributed source code control systems intend to match the distributed nature of open source development, instead of imposing a centralized source control system on a decentralized development process.

A distributed system makes it easier for you to make changes to your local repository while still getting updates from another repository, because the cloning process effectively creates another branch of the project. You can make revisions without contacting another server, making these systems ideal for when you're coding on your laptop some place with dicey Wi-Fi connectivity.

Using CVS

The process for getting code from CVS is to log in and perform a checkout of a module. To log in, you need to know the URL for the CVS project, the module name, and a user name. All this information is called a *connection string.* Open source projects that expect users to get the source provide an anonymous login. An example CVS login string looks like the following:

`:pserver:anonymous@the.project.url.org:/path/to/repository`

Table 13-1 breaks down this connection string and explains each part.

Table 13-1. *Explaining CVS Connection String parts*

Parameter	Meaning
pserver	The authentication method, which in this case uses the CVS pserver method. Other support types are kserver for Kerberos and gserver for GSSAPI, but these are much less common.

anonymous	The user name for login. If not provided, you're asked for this when authenticating.
the.project.url.org	The URL of the server containing the CVS repository.
/path/to/repository	The path of the repository on the host.

You can pass this connection string to CVS each time you contact CVS, or you can set the CVSROOT environment variable with this value. The following example works by setting the environment variable, logging in to a server, and checking out a module:

```
$ export CVSROOT=:pserver:anonymous@project.org:/what/directory
$ mkdir ~/project.org
$ cvs login
$ cvs co module-name
```

In this example, a directory project.org is created to hold the contents of the project. This is strictly a housekeeping operation, because the project can have several modules, and each module occupies its own directory named after the module. After this operation, you have the following directory structure:

```
~/
        project.org/
                        module-name/
                                <files and directories>
```

The project may instruct you to check out a certain *tag* or group of files that have been labeled. Do this with the -r argument:

```
$ cvs co -r tag-name module-name
```

Getting the changes to the code because the checkout was performed is called *updating.* You do this by logging in, changing directories to where the module was checked out, and then issuing the cvs update command.

Using Subversion

Subversion works much like CVS in that you get a copy of the source tree from a repository. Unlike CVS, there is no need for a login for anonymous access: modules can just be checked out, if the server has been properly configured. The overwhelming majority of open source projects using Subversion are configured in this manner. Because of this, you can check out a module with fewer commands. For example:

```
$ mkdir ~/project.org
$ svn co svn://project.org/path/to/module-name
```

Subversion also maintains the concept of tags, where a set of files is labeled so they can be downloaded all at once. After this operation, the directory structure looks like this:

```
~/
        project.org/
                module-name/
                        <files and directories>
```

To fetch files from a module with a certain tag, the syntax is the following:

```
$ svn co svn://project.org/path/to/module/tags/tag-name
```

where *tag-name* is the tag to use for the fetch. You may also be asked to check out a branch of code; you do so using syntax like the following:

```
$ svn co svn://project.org/path/to/module/branches/branch-name
```

To update your code to the latest version, use the `update` command in the top level directory of the module:

```
$ cd ~/project.org/module-name
$ svn up
```

That gets the latest version of the code for the entire module.

Using Git

The Git[2] code repository system is very different from CVS and Subversion in that it's a distributed system that doesn't have a single central server. Instead, each user has a *clone* of some code base (if you're imagining a tree structure of clones with one root, this is the wrong mental model) and has complete control over that clone. Because of the Git's distributed nature, getting the code takes a bit longer the first time around. Subsequent operations are much faster.

To create a clone of a Git tree, use this command (which is for the glibc sources):

```
$ git clone git://sourceware.org/git/glibc.git
```

When the command prompt returns, you have the latest revision of the tree. To refresh the tree with the latest versions of the file, use the `pull` command from the top level of the repository:

```
$ git pull
```

Using Mercurial

With Mercurial, like Git, you don't just retrieve a version of the source code. You create a branch of the project that has all the source code control goodies like branching, tagging, and change management

---

[2] *Git* is a mildly derogatory term akin to the original usage of the U.S. word *dude*, with the additional slant that the person was conceived outside the bonds of Holy Matrimony.

that you get when you run a source code control system—because you are! Use the following command to set up a source tree (in this case, I'm using the great `crosstool-ng` project as an example):

```
$ hg clone http://ymorin.is-a-geek.org/hg/crosstool-ng
destination directory: crosstool-ng

requesting all changes
adding changesets
adding manifests
adding file changes
added 1582 changesets with 5331 changes to 2509 files (+6 heads)
updating working directory
1025 files updated, 0 files merged, 0 files removed, 0 files unresolved
```

This process takes some time, because the system is fetching not only the code but the source code history for the project. On my system, this project took about 5 minutes to clone; your times will vary depending on your ISP's speed, network conditions, and phase of the moon.

When a repository is cloned, the system keeps track of the source. You can get changes by doing the following:

```
$ hg pull
pulling from http://ymorin.is-a-geek.org/hg/crosstool-ng
searching for changes
no changes found
```

Cross-Compiling

Cross-compiling a project means invoking the compilation tools for the target board instead of using the tools on the host. Open source code is designed to be compiled on many different systems, and therefore most packages include software to determine the state of the system and whether it has the right set of tools for cross-compilation. The software used to interrogate the system is called the *autotools* suite, and the primary interface for embedded engineers is the `configure` script created by the tools.

The `configure` script runs a variety of tests and writes the output into an include file used by the rest of the project. It runs a tool called `automake` to create the make files used to build the project. The interrogation process involves looking to see if files are present on the host system or compiling and running programs to test system capabilities. The last item, running programs, is problematic for embedded engineers in that the cross-compiler used to compile the test program produces code that runs on a host very different from the one used for compilation. When the configure script finds that it can't run a program to get a result, it stops processing the script and produces an error message.

There are two ways around this problem: fix the script so that it can supply what it needs to know without running a program; or add a value into a cache file to short-circuit the test, because when the value is cached, the offending program isn't run.

Using configure

There are two usage patterns for `configure`: one is running the `configure` script from within the source directory, and the other is creating an empty directory and running `configure` there. The main advantage of running `configure` in an empty directory is that the files created by the configure system aren't intermixed with the source files; so, if you're creating a patch, there's no chance of it including random files created by the configure process. Some projects refuse to let `configure` be run in the source directory, leaving you no choice in the matter. Likewise, some `configure` scripts don't run properly in an empty directory.

When you're cross-compiling, the best practice is to put all your commands in a script file. Doing so captures all the environment settings in one place and makes the build process repeatable; this is important because it makes the build process easier when the code being built is patched or a new revision is released. The rest of this section walks through building the script used to compile the package.

The script is parameterized enough that the package being built shouldn't be that important.

Creating the Script

This first part of the script overrides the environment variables that tell the `configure` script what programs to run in order to build a program. When not cross-compiling, the system uses default values that are the same as the environment variable, but lowercase. When you set these environment variables, the system instead invokes the cross-tools to compile. This script has a shortcut: the prefix for the cross-tools is reused, which is more a matter of style than anything else.

The very minimum of tools that must be overridden are `CC` and `LD`, for the C compiler and linker respectively. The next set of tools is less frequently used, and the last set is nearly never used:

```
#!/bin/sh

export PATH=$PATH:/home/gene/x-tools/powerpc-405-linux-gnu/bin

prefix=powerpc-405-linux-gnu

# this is the bare minimum
export CC=${prefix}-gcc
export LD=${prefix}-ld

# these are frequently used
export AS=${prefix}-as
export AR=${prefix}-ar
export OBJCOPY=${prefix}-objcopy
export CXX=${prefix}-g++

# these are rarely used
export CPP=${prefix}-cpp
export NM=${prefix}-nm
export STRINGS=${prefix}-strip
export OBJDUMP=${prefix}-objdump
```

For each of the tools, the system looks for am environment variable with the suffix `_FLAGS`. For example, for the C compiler, the environment variable is `CC_FLAGS`. You can now add this to your script in order to run the configuration process:

```
./configure -host=powerpc-linux-gnu
```

If you run the script from the project directory, these are the first few lines of output:

```
configure: WARNING: If you wanted to set the --build type, don't use --host.

    If a cross compiler is detected then cross compile mode will be used.
checking build system type... i686-pc-linux-gnu
checking host system type... powerpc-unknown-linux-gnu
checking target system type... powerpc-unknown-linux-gnu
checking for a BSD-compatible install... /usr/bin/install -c
checking whether build environment is sane... yes
```

The interesting thing to note is that the `configure` script picks suitable values for the build and target systems. Their names are somewhat confusing; here's what each means:

- *Build system:* The computer where the build is running. The `configure` script guesses this accurately; you don't need to specify the build system unless the documentation tells you it's necessary.

- *Host system:* The system where the code will be run. In this case, you're targeting a PowerPC Linux system. *Host* may sound like the computer you're working on, but that's the build system.

- *Target system:* The system used for building cross-compilers. It isn't used when compiling packages. The tools running on the host system should generate code suitable for the target system. The default value is the host system.

The values for the build, host, and target systems are called *triplets* and can contain up to four parts. The general format is

```
<cpu>-<manufacturer>-<os>-<kernel>
```

In the example case, the value

```
powerpc-linux-gnu
```

is missing the manufacturer field. However, for an ARM processor, which could be made by any of a number of companies, this field would be populated with the company that fabricated the chip—or more frequently with unknown to indicate no specific manufacturer. There's no listing of all the acceptable values, and as a result you may be uncertain about the correct value. If you're unsure, use the same string as the prefix to your cross-compiler for this value.

On the topic, you may wonder how the triplets and the environment variables for the tools relate. Why is it necessary to set the host system when the cross-compiler frequently has the same prefix? Why is it necessary to set CC, LD, and the others when you're telling `configure` via the –`target` parameter what system the code will be running? The answer is that the `configure` script uses the –`target` parameter to decide what tests to run and how to execute the configure process, but not how to build the code itself. Plus, not coupling the environment variables to the –target string makes it possible to use tools that don't follow the naming conventions.

You may get output like this, which says that the `configure` script can't find the compiler—but that isn't the real problem. In this case, I've added an extra character to cause the process to fail; if the path isn't correct or there's a misspelling, this error is produced, leading you to believe that the compiler was invoked but didn't produce suitable output:

```
checking for powerpc-linux-gnu-gcc... powerpc-405-linux-gnu--gcc
checking for C compiler default output file name... configure: error: \
C compiler cannot create executables
```

Gaming the Cache

One common problem that's encountered when building a project is a configure script that wants to run code on the host machine in hopes of finding out something about the target machine. When these configure scripts aren't cross-compiling, the host and target machines are the same, and this strategy makes sense; however, when cross-compiling, the code refuses to run, and the configure script generates an error.

The most direct way around this problem is to create an entry in the configure script's cache; in the interests of efficiently, the script doesn't attempt to run the program if it has a value from a prior run. Creating cache entries is just a matter of putting a key-value pair in a file and telling configure the location of the cache file. The real question is what those keys and values should be. When configure fails to run, the system produces an error listing in the config.log file that looks something like this:

```
configure:2307: error: 'somethingcritical' undeclared (first use in this function)
configure:2307: error: (Each undeclared identifier is reported only once
configure:2307: error: for each function it appears in.)
```

This shows that the error occurred on line 2307 of the configure script, which contains code that looks something like this:

```
if test "${ac_cv_somethingcritical+set}" = set; then
  echo $ECHO_N "(cached) $ECHO_C" >&6
else
  ac_cv_somethingcritical=no
ac_save_CC=$CC
        #more code follows
```

Looking at this script file, it's clear that putting ac_cv_somethingcritical into the cache file will result in the offending code not running. Putting this value into the cache is the matter of creating the file config.cache and adding this line:

```
ac_cv_somethingcritical=yes
```

Knowing what the value should be is a matter of understanding the target system and reading the code the configure script is trying to run. When a small C program is executed, copy that source code into a file, cross-compile, and run it on the target to get the result. To keep all the information about building a file in one place, a good practice is to use a *here file* to create the config.cache file in the build script itself—for example, adding these lines creates the config.cache file each time the script runs:

```
cat << EOF
ac_cv_somethingcritical=yes
```

```
EOF > config.cache
```

Specifying the -C parameter with `configure` results in the `configure` file reading the cache, which sets the variables; then the offending code doesn't run. Putting all these commands together looks like this in the script file:

```
cat << EOF
ac_cv_somethingcritical=yes
EOF > config.cache
./configure -C –host=powerpc-linux-gnu
```

Installation

The installation directory is known as the *prefix*, which is a name that seems to have nothing to do with where things are installed, at least at first. For an embedded system, the installation directories are appended to the prefix to form the complete installation directory. When you're constructing an embedded device, the practice is to make the root file system a directory somewhere on the development host, populate that directory with files, and then use a program to convert that directory's contents into a binary image that is placed on the device for production.

In this case, *prefix* makes perfect sense, because the prefix is the directory on the development host system containing the root file system for the board. For example, a root file system being assembled in the /opt/board/rfs directory has that directory as the prefix, so when the files are installed in the /bin directory, the complete installation directory is /opt/board/rfs/bin.

Using the example, the command line for the configure process is

```
./configure -C –host=powerpc-linux-gnu \
      --prefix=/opt/board/rfs
```

The important thing to note is that the installation doesn't happen at this step; rather, the `configure` process creates the scripts and files necessary to install the program after it has been built. The value of a prefix can also be used by the program at runtime to look for certain files, like configuration files or libraries; in this case, use the directory where the files will be installed as the target, and install the files into the root file system directory by hand (or with another script if you're automating your root file system build). Of course, how do you know how the program uses a prefix? This is a matter of reading the program's documentation; most don't operate in this fashion, and the exceptional programs make note of this usage pattern.

Setting Other Configure Options

There's more to the `configure` script than just setting the build tools. Using –help shows all the options you can set. For the example program, this is the output (a little has been clipped):

```
Optional Features:

  --disable-FEATURE            do not include FEATURE (same as --enable-
FEATURE=no)
  --enable-FEATURE[=ARG]       include FEATURE [ARG=yes]
  --disable-dependency-tracking Speeds up one-time builds
  --enable-dependency-tracking  Do not reject slow dependency extractors
```

```
  --disable-rpath            do not hardcode runtime library paths
  --disable-nls              do not use Native Language Support
  --enable-debug             enable debugging (requires GNU compiler, default:
no)
  --enable-compat            enable all old compatibility switches (default: no)
  --enable-oldhexdump        use the old style hexdump format (default: no)
  --enable-oldtelnet         use old telnet codes parsing policy (default: no)

Optional Packages:

  --with-PACKAGE[=ARG]       use PACKAGE [ARG=yes]
  --without-PACKAGE          do not use PACKAGE (same as --with-PACKAGE=no)
  --with-gnu-ld              assume the C compiler uses GNU ld default=no
  --with-libiconv-prefix=DIR search for libiconv in DIR/include and DIR/lib
  --without-libiconv-prefix  don't search for libiconv in includedir and libdir
  --with-libintl-prefix=DIR  search for libintl in DIR/include and DIR/lib
  --without-libintl-prefix   don't search for libintl in includedir and libdir
  --with-included-getopt     use the internal getopt library (default: auto)
```

The switch name indicates the default value of the option. When the option says without-PACKAGE, that means the package has already been selected; when the option is with-PACKAGE, the package isn't selected. The same is true with enable/disable showing the opposite state of the option. The difference between an option and a package is that the package typically links to another software package, whereas an option changes the compiler flags.

Configuration Process for Non-Automake Projects

Infrequently, you find a project that doesn't use configure to create a build environment. In this case, take time to read the documentation to understand what is necessary to cross-build the project. Even if the project doesn't use configure, it has a make file (very few don't), and that make file uses the environment variables CC, LD, AR, AS, and so on to compile the project. If the documentation isn't clear about what to do, open the make file and see if there are any provisions for cross-compiling. Many make files have lines like this:

```
CC=$(CROSS_COMPILE)-gcc
LD=$(CROSS_COMPILE)-ld
```

You only need to do the following when running make, given the test environment:

```
export CROSS_COMPILE=powerpc-linux
```

However, if the make file doesn't override any of the environment variables, assigning them in the same way as configure results in make invoking the correct tools for the compilation. To get a view of what the make file will do, use the -recon parameter:

```
$ make--recon
```

When you use -recon, none of the commands are executed; make prints what it *would* execute. This is an approximation of what make will do when it runs; for more complex projects, commands run earlier in the make process will affect how later files are built.

It's important to read the documentation and mailing lists first and then the build script's source code to understand the steps necessary to cross-build the project. Projects that have their own build processes include documentation about how to cross-build the software, even if it's located in the make file itself as comments.

Building and Installing

After the environment has been configured, running make is a matter of doing the following:

```
make
```

That's it! The automake tools handle any build issues and create a make file so that building just means issuing this command. If you're not using automake, make uses the environment variables that set the compiler and tools to build the project. Problems during the build process require you to look at the error, read the code, and understand what to change in the configuration process to sidestep the error; or fix the code. When the project finishes building, you're returned to a command prompt.

The build process creates many object files, but only a subset of those are copied over to the embedded system. The make file includes an install target that copies the files to their ultimate destinations:

```
make install
```

After the installation runs, the software is in the root file system for the target device, as specified by the --prefix parameter during the configure process. The next thing to do is to get the board running and test that your program works as expected. If the package uses --prefix to control runtime behavior, you need to skip this step and copy the executables and libraries by hand.

Commonly Used Projects

This section lists the more frequently used open source projects for embedded Linux projects. This is by no means an exhaustive catalog, but if you wonder what's available to you as a Linux engineer, it serves as an excellent starting point. One project not listed is BusyBox, because it merits a chapter unto itself (Chapter 14).

DirectFB

DirectFB is a graphics library that runs directly on top of the framebuffer device and provides functionality similar to X windows. DirectFB doesn't have the device management, extensibility, or hardware support as X windows.

Dropbear

This project offers a complete SSH 2 server and client in as little as a few hundred kilobytes. The project was created for small systems and has maintained a very small footprint over the years. Despite its small amount of memory, Dropbear has some extra features like X11 forwarding; you can even configure the program to use public keys for easy login. Even if the device isn't on a public network, having ssh running makes diagnostics easier, because you have an easy way to access the device.

Dropbear's maintainers have accepted patches so that the program cross-compiles nicely with small C libraries like uClibc and dietlibc.

QT/Qtopia

QT is a product that offers a graphics environment for embedded devices. The QT environment provides much more than just graphics: hidden within the QT library, you can find an impressive collection of general-purpose tools like XML parsers and, with the new version, a small browser. QT was designed from the start to be a toolkit for embedded developers: the project gives you plenty of flexibility when building the project to minimize the size, and cross-compilation works like a charm. Unlike many of the projects here, QT doesn't use the standard GNU configuration and build scripts; the project instead uses its own code to prep the code for compilation.

QT includes everything necessary to run a GUI. Applications just need to link against the QT libraries. One item in the minus column is that QT uses C++, which isn't always available for a target board. Also, some embedded engineers scoff at the idea of using C++ for their projects.

The licensing for QT is a bit vexing and boils down to the following: buy a license for QT, and you needn't concern yourself with complying with an open source license. For many companies, not having the perceived risk of an open source license (along with the support) justifies the expense.

JamVM

JamVM is a Java virtual machine. Although it isn't targeted specifically at embedded devices, it cross-compiles against a wide range of platforms, and it's described at compact. JamVM contains nearly all of the features found in Sun's Java, such as JIT code compilation, mark-and-sweep garbage collection, and a complete JNI interface for when a native language is necessary.

One advantage of JamVM is that it's written in C and assembler, so if you have a toolchain good enough to compile the kernel, you can compile JamVM.

Rzsz

This library contains the x-modem and z-modem serial communication protocols popular from the bulletin board days of yore. These protocols allow for the dependable transfer of data over a serial connection with very low system overhead in terms of processing power or memory. Even though many embedded devices contain Ethernet networking, the serial port is still the lowest resource way to transfer data. The protocols in this package basically do what TCP does for an Ethernet network: convert a stream of data into packages, transmit the packets, and ensure that they're received in the order sent with perfect fidelity. If there's an error, the protocol requests a retransmit of the data and retries several times before giving up.

Netcat

This amazingly useful utility can be used to stream data over a socket the same way that cat streams data over a pipe. Netcat can be used for both sending and receiving data. And because it's an executable that can be run from a shell script, very little programming is necessary to create a simple yet robust way to communicate over the network.

TinyXML

This is a library that is designed to parse and XML file and do so with the minimum amount of resources. XML is a commonly used way for disparate systems to communicate, and many networked devices need to understand XML because it's the format used by the programs issuing commands to the device. Although you could write a simple parser, having a complete parser makes for much less work and testing.

The XML language is simple, but it uses some rather complex constructs like schemas and document type definitions (DTDs) to describe the contents of the file and render data like XSL for layout. The TinyXML parser doesn't do much more than get the entities and properties stored in the file, but it does this very well and requires only about 60KB of program space.

Micro_httpd

This is one of the many tools available at Acme Software's site and deserves special mention. It's a simple HTTP server written in C and is just a few hundred lines. This is the perfect project for when your device needs to serve web pages that do some processing. Instead of writing a CGI script, modify the HTTP server and link your code directly into the server. Then, all you need to do is watch for when the user passes in the URL that should run your code.

The server runs as an inetd service, so it expects to receive its input from stdin; data is sent by writing it to stdout. If you're unfamiliar with inetd, it's a program that listens for incoming connections; when a host initiates attempts to open a socket on a port, inetd fulfills the request and then maps the socket to the standard in and out of a process. This makes testing easy as well, because you can write a script that pipes data into the server and captures the output.

Stupid-FTPd

Some devices need FTP for file transfer. The Stupid-TFPd3 server isn't fast, configurable, or secure like the VSFTPs and PROFTPs of the world, but it's small and simple to configure. By setting a few options in a file, you're off and running. Even without a configuration file, the software still runs with reasonable parameters.

Quagga

This software is the ancestor of the Zebra routing software suite of tools. If the target device is one that will be offering network services like Routing Information Protocol (RIP) or Open Shortest Path First (OSPF), Quagga offers an open source solution. These tools don't change the features that already exist in the Linux kernel for managing software routes; they offer a layer on top of kernel to make managing routes easer and to let routers talk to each other so that routing information doesn't need to be configured manually.

Tslib

The tslib system is designed to provide a common interface for touch screens and is used in conjunction with QT or X Window.

fgetty

Linux has many programs that acquire a `tty` and run the login process, but fgetty is the smallest of the bunch. This program is great for systems that need getty functionality but aren't using BusyBox, which supplies a larger program that does the same job.

---

[3] I used this in a project, and the customers asked that I rename the project to something else because their boss might be put off by the name. I decided on Simple FTP.

CHAPTER 14

■ ■ ■

BusyBox

BusyBox is an open source project that is a key part of many embedded systems. It supplies limited-functionality implementations of most of the command-line executables found on a desktop Linux system; BusyBox calls these *applets*. What the applets lack in functionality is more than compensated for in their size: a complete, full-featured BusyBox system weighs in at 1.5MB and can be much smaller when unused applets are dropped. In addition to being small, BusyBox is also clever about how it's deployed on an embedded target: it's just one file. Symbolic links named after the applications they replace point to the BusyBox executable. This makes BusyBox easy to deploy and manage.

The infrastructure for creating applets is very organized. Creating new applets for features you add is good idea, because they can take advantage of the existing code, resulting in a smaller code base. If a system is based on BusyBox, you can save considerable space by creating applets instead of independent executables. Because this is open source software, you're encouraged to contribute your applets back to the BusyBox project if they're general-purpose tools; applets specific to your project may still be welcome, but they may be of little use to the open source community at large.

BusyBox's project maintainers are always pleased to hear about products using their code. Visit www.busybox.net/products.html to see who is currently using the project, and don't be shy about telling the maintainers that you're using the project as well; with your permission, they'll add your company/application to the product page. Because this is open source, you're participating in the project, so feel free to contribute any bugs, bug fixes, changes, or enhancements. You can find information about how to participate at www.busybox.net/developer.html. If you read through the mailing list, you'll find that BusyBox's developer community is much like any other in the open source world: friendly and welcoming.

How a BusyBox-Based System Is Structured

The BusyBox build process creates one executable that is a collection of applets. Each applet is an independent unit of code that can be included in the BusyBox executable and that corresponds directly to a utility executed from the command line. Many users learning about this software are genuinely puzzled about how BusyBox runs applets, especially in the case of using symlinks to execute applets. In summary, BusyBox figures out what applet to run in one of two ways:

- *Looking at the first parameter:* If the program being run is called busybox, the software uses the first parameter as the name of the applet to run. For example:

      /bin/busybox ls

  Most users don't use BusyBox in this way; instead, they using symlinks, as described next.

- *Looking at the name of the executable:* Most BusyBox systems have root file systems composed of either hard or symbolic links to the busybox executable. When that link is executed, BusyBox looks at the executable name to run the correct applet. This is a little disorienting. Here's an example:

  ls -> /bin/busybox

  In this case, ls is a symbolic link to the program /bin/busybox; a *symbolic link* is an entity in the file system that points to another file. When the symlink refers to an executable, running the symlink is the same as executing the file to which it refers, with one important difference: the name of the file being run is that of the symlink. You can figure out the name of the program being run by inspecting argv[0] (at least, this is what a C programmer does; your favorite programming language may be different), and this is exactly how /bin/busybox solves this problem as well.

  BusyBox can also be instructed to create hard links to files. The principal advantage of hard links is that they refer directly to the file and don't need to go through the extra step of resolving the soft link's reference to a file into the BusyBox executable. Recall that hard links refer directly to the i-node for a file, whereas symlinks contain the name of a file that the operating system uses to find the i-node. For this reason, hard links are slightly smaller as well.

  Using this method is by far the more popular approach. By using links, the BusyBox applets appear to be just like their larger counterparts; and existing scripts can be used as is, minus changes necessary because of features not supported by the applet.

Like any program, BusyBox can be linked statically or use shared libraries. If you're using shared libraries, these must also be present on the system; otherwise the operating system can't load and run the program.

Building a BusyBox-Based System

Creating a system with BusyBox isn't that much different than building any other open source project; in fact, the project uses some of the same build infrastructure and practices as the Linux kernel project. Like the kernel, BusyBox has a menu-based configuration step where you can control how the application is built, followed by a build step that creates the binary. BusyBox also has an installation step that creates a minimal root file system containing all the symlinks for applications built into the BusyBox executable. The basic outline for building BusyBox is as follows:

1. Download the software. You can fetch BusyBox in a tar file, or you can access the Git repository. The Git repository always contains the most recent version of the code, and the tar files contain development snapshots. In general, as with any embedded project, the tar files are more stable than the code fresh from the developers.

2. Configure. This step allows you to specify the configuration parameters for the build and what applets are included in the BusyBox binary file. The configuration tool is the same as the tool used for the Linux kernel, so the interface and workings should be familiar.

3. Build. This step is uninteresting because the configuration work already been done. Here, you just need to tell the make file what cross-compiler to use and wait for the process to finish.

4. Install. This step creates a directory with the applets and the BusyBox executable. There's some additional work to do in order to get a complete system so you can test whether the build boots on the board.

Download the Software

The BusyBox project resides at www.busybox.net, and the www.busybox.net/download.html page contains a history of releases and any follow-on patches. As an example, you'll use the 1.14.1 release on this page, but understand that the release will be different by the time this book makes it to press:

```
$ wget http://busybox.net/downloads/busybox-1.14.1.tar.bz2
$ tar xjf busybox-1.14.1.tar.bz2
```

At this point, the busybox-1.14.1 directory has the sources for BusyBox ready for compilation. The source is also available using Git, by doing the following:

```
$ git clone git://busybox.net/busybox.git busybox
```

This creates a clone of the Git repository in the directory ./busybox. The Git clone process takes a few minutes, even with a fast Internet connection. If you want to follow a certain branch of BusyBox, use this command to fetch the changes for the branch

```
$ git checkout remotes/origin/1_<branch>_stable
```

where <branch> is the version of BusyBox. In this example, using 14 for the branch fetches the changes for the 1.14.x line of development:

```
$ git branch -a
* (no branch)
  master
  origin/0_60_stable
  origin/1_00_stable
  origin/1_00_stable_10817
  origin/1_10_stable
  origin/1_11_stable
  origin/1_12_stable
  origin/1_13_stable
  origin/1_14_stable
(more output clipped)
```

You should run these commands from the directory containing the Git repository; in this example, it's ./busybox. Following a branch makes sense when you want to get just the minor changes for a release and not larger-scale changes that may affect your project.

Configure

BusyBox must be configured before being built. In the configuration process, you specify what applets to compile and how to build the project. The system used is the same as the Linux kernel, so when you do the following

```
$ make menuconfig
```

you see a very familiar interface (see Figure 14-1).

```
BusyBox 1.14.1 Configuration
```

```
────────────────────────── Busybox Configuration ──────────────────────────
  Arrow keys navigate the menu.  <Enter> selects submenus --->.  Highlighted
  letters are hotkeys.  Pressing <Y> includes, <N> excludes, <M> modularizes
  features.  Press <Esc><Esc> to exit, <?> for Help, </> for Search.  Legend:
  [*] built-in  [ ] excluded  <M> module  < > module capable
  ┌──────────────────────────────────────────────────────────────────────┐
  │        Busybox Settings  --->                                         │
  │    --- Applets                                                        │
  │        Archival Utilities  --->                                       │
  │        Coreutils  --->                                                │
  │        Console Utilities  --->                                        │
  │        Debian Utilities  --->                                         │
  │        Editors  --->                                                  │
  │        Finding Utilities  --->                                        │
  │        Init Utilities  --->                                           │
  │        Login/Password Management Utilities  --->                      │
  │        Linux Ext2 FS Progs  --->                                      │
  │        Linux Module Utilities  --->                                   │
  │        Linux System Utilities  --->                                   │
  │        Miscellaneous Utilities  --->                                  │
  │        Networking Utilities  --->                                     │
  │        Print Utilities  --->                                          │
  │        Mail Utilities  --->                                           │
  │        Process Utilities  --->                                        │
  │        Runit Utilities  --->                                          │
  │        Shells  --->                                                   │
  └─v(+)─────────────────────────────────────────────────────────────────┘

              <Select>     < Exit >     < Help >
```

Figure 14-1. *The Busybox Configuration GUI.*

When you're running the configuration for the first time, no applets have been selected, meaning the root file system doesn't have anything to run. This is probably not you want. Selecting a minimal set of applets requires much tedious clicking, even after you know what constitutes a minimum set of applets. In order to get a set of applets approximating what would be on a desktop system, do the following:

```
$ make defconfig
```

The configuration process shows how it's configured by producing the following output:

```
(output clipped)
POSIX math support (SH_MATH_SUPPORT) [Y/n/?] y
  Extend POSIX math support to 64 bit (SH_MATH_SUPPORT_64) [Y/n/?] y
Hide message on interactive shell startup (FEATURE_SH_EXTRA_QUIET) [Y/n/?] y
cttyhack (CTTYHACK) [Y/n/?] y
*
* System Logging Utilities
*
syslogd (SYSLOGD) [Y/n/?] y
  Rotate message files (FEATURE_ROTATE_LOGFILE) [Y/n/?] y
  Remote Log support (FEATURE_REMOTE_LOG) [Y/n/?] y
  Support -D (drop dups) option (FEATURE_SYSLOGD_DUP) [Y/n/?] y
  Circular Buffer support (FEATURE_IPC_SYSLOG) [Y/n/?] y
    Circular buffer size in Kbytes (minimum 4KB) (FEATURE_IPC_SYSLOG_BUFFER_SIZE) \
[16] 16 logread (LOGREAD) [Y/n/?] y
      Double buffering (FEATURE_LOGREAD_REDUCED_LOCKING) [Y/n/?] y
klogd (KLOGD) [Y/n/?] y
logger (LOGGER) [Y/n/?] y
```

The default configuration isn't the smallest configuration. It contains nearly all of the applets, but it's the fastest and easiest way to get started. When you need to economize on space, you can reduce the number of applets to what your system needs, but that's a matter of economization.

Build

BusyBox is now ready to be built. Building the project is much like building any other project that relies on standard make files:

```
$ make CROSS_COMPILE=arm-linux-uclibc-
```

BusyBox is targeted for embedded developers, so cross-compiling has been baked into the project from the start. Just set the CROSS_COMPILE symbol to the prefix of the toolchain, and don't forget the trailing dash. The build process takes a few minutes, after which the following appears:

```
Trying libraries: crypt m
 Library crypt is not needed, excluding it
 Library m is needed, can't exclude it (yet)
Final link with: m
  DOC     busybox.pod
  DOC     BusyBox.txt

  DOC     BusyBox.1
  DOC     BusyBox.html
```

Static or Shared?

Under the BusyBox Settings/Build Options menu is the option "Build BusyBox as a static binary." This is false by default, resulting in the BusyBox file being linked with shared libraries. Thus the final BusyBox binary is much smaller because a large chunk of the code resides in another file: the C standard library used when compiling the software that must also be present on the final root file system. When you're using a shared library, the operating system performs the final link at runtime by loading both the executable and shared library and fixing the references in the program to run code in the shared library.

When statically linked, all the code the program uses resides in the file. The code is loaded into memory and executed. This is a much faster operation than loading a file with shared libraries, in exchange for a larger memory footprint, because a fresh copy of the code is loaded for each instance of BusyBox executed.

If the BusyBox executable contains just a few executables, the rule of thumb is about a 200KB program size. Static linking then makes sense because of the increased performance and savings from not needing the shared libraries. On the other hand, if the other programs on the system require shared libraries, using them for BusyBox as well makes perfect sense.

Install

After the build process runs, use the installation target to create a directory containing the BusyBox binaries and symlinks to the applications. For the purpose of illustrating how BusyBox works, this example uses the standard installation settings. The default installation directory is _install. It contains the start of a root file system, which follows the pattern of building the root file system for the target board in a directory and later using a tool that creates a file suitable for the flash, or other mass storage, device on the board:

```
$ make install
-------------------------------------------------
You will probably need to make your busybox binary
setuid root to ensure all configured applets will
work properly.
-------------------------------------------------
```

The installation step points out one of the things you need to do in order to have a working BusyBox root file system. There are a few more steps, as outlined here at a high level so you can understand the basic process:

1. Copy libraries. If the BusyBox project was built with shared libraries, those need to be located and copied into the root file system. You also need the dynamic library loader.

2. Update init scripts. If they aren't present, BusyBox uses a minimal initialization script when the system starts. The script allows a system to boot with reasonable defaults.

3. Update permissions. The BusyBox build and installation runs as a regular user (if you're usually logged in as root, shame on you!), and you must set the ownership of the files to root.

4. Create additional folders. Some standard folders need to be created. These are used to mount file systems like proc and temp.

5. Create required device nodes. Every Linux system requires two device nodes: /dev/null and /dev/console.

The following sections cover these steps in detail. After making these additional changes, your system will be ready to boot and start.

Copy Libraries

, If BusyBox was built with shared libraries, you need to copy them into the root file system and place them into the /lib directory. These files can be copied from the sysroot directory of the toolchain. BusyBox links against the m and c libraries, but you can prove this for yourself by doing the following from the directory where BusyBox was built, assuming installation in the default directory:

```
$ strings _install/bin/busybox | grep ^lib
libm.so.6
libc.so.6
```

This command says, "Get all the strings from the file, and only show the lines that begin with *lib*." The program ldd can't be used, because the program has been cross-compiled and won't run on the development host.

These files should be fetched from the sysroot directory of the toolchain. Most modern toolchains have been configured with a sysroot, which is a directory that contains the files from the toolchain likely to appear on a root file system of a system targeted by the toolchain. To check if your toolchain has sysroot support, try the following:

```
$ arm-linux-gcc -print-sysroot
<install dir>/arm-unknown-linux-gnueabi/bin/arm-linux-gcc
```

If this is a valid path, this is where the files should be copied from. If no path is displayed, use find to locate a sysroot directory in <*install dir*>, or use find to look for libc.so:

```
$ find . -name libc.so
```

After you've located libc and libm, create the _install/lib directory and copy them there. The files are likely symlinks to other files, so be sure to gather them all. The next file to get is the dynamic loader, normally called ld-linux-<*version*>, which also resides in the lib directory along with libc.so.*. Copy that to the _install/lib directory. Your system now has all the shared libraries and the loader, so BusyBox can run.

Default Init Scripts

If you skipped over the startup section of the book, I'll summarize: when Linux boots, it looks for an initial program to run if you don't give it explicit instructions to run something else. Under most circumstances, the program run at system start-up is init. This program reads a file, /etc/inittab, and then starts some number of tasks, as designated by this file. The default inittab for BusyBox is

```
::sysinit:/etc/init.d/rcS
::askfirst:/bin/sh
::ctrlaltdel:/sbin/reboot
::shutdown:/sbin/swapoff -a
::shutdown:/bin/umount -a -r
::restart:/sbin/init
```

Translated into English, this file says, "Run /etc/init.d/rcS when the system starts, and then ask you to press any key before starting a shell; if you presses Ctrl+Alt+Del, reboot the system; when the system shuts down, turn off swapping and unmount the file systems." Most users want more control over the inittab on their system and write their own. However, true to BusyBox, the init applet supports a subset of the features that appear in the desktop init; it also offers some additional features just for embedded systems.

The inittab file is a series of records, one per line, with : being the field delimiter. BusyBox's inittab records are very similar to the standard init:

```
tty:runlevels:action:command
```

Each of the fields is explained in Table 14-1. Because BusyBox implements a simpler version of this utility, the meaning of the fields is slightly different.

Table 14-1. *Busybox Fields as Available in inittab*

Field	Meaning
tty	Optional. When this field is populated, this is the tty used for the process. For an embedded device with several ttys, this allows you to start a process like rxtx or log in on one of the serial ports. The value that appears here needs to have a device node entry in the /dev file system.
runlevels	The contents of this field are ignored. BusyBox's init applet doesn't have runlevels; all processes are in runlevel 0.
action	This indicates when init should perform the action. The following actions are supported: sysinit, wait, askfirst, once, respawn, restart, ctraltdel, and shutdown. The items are executed in the order they appear in the file.
command	This specifies what to execute. It can be anything that can be run from the command line.

The actions work a little differently as well. Table 14-2 explains the actions; the order in which they appear in the table is the order in which they're run by BusyBox. Actions are executed in the order of appearance in the file.

Table 14-2. *Busybox Actions*

Action (in order of execution)	Effect
Sysinit	This is the first thing the system runs during startup.
Wait	A wait action follows sysinit and runs the command and waits until it completes. When the file contains several wait commands, BusyBox executes them, one after another, in the order of appearance.

once	Once actions follow wait, and the init program makes no attempt to ensure that any of these tasks complete before moving to the next step. These programs are run once during bootup but aren't serialized like wait actions, meaning that several can be run at the same time. Don't list several once actions with the expectation that they will run in order.
askfirst	This action results in a message that requests you to press Enter before running the command.
respawn	Respawn actions run the command and run the same command again if it stops. Your system should have at least one of these so that the system keeps running. The most common respawn action is to run a getty program that waits for a login.
restart	This is the command executed when you restart the init command. This is different than sysinit, which runs just once after the system boots; restart can be run as many times as init restarts. Use this to include code that alters the system-wide state, like the routing table.
ctrlaltdel	If your computer supports rebooting with Ctrl+Alt+Del, this is the script that is called.
shutdown	When you request a reboot or shutdown, this is the last script executed.

Update Permissions

When the files are created in the installation directory, the owner and group equal that of you running the command. When running on a target system, the owner of some of these files should be root or some other privileged user rather than the random user account used for installation. Some file systems allow you to force all the files to be owned by root, and others use the permissions and ownership of the files as they are on the file system.

Most embedded systems have a root user as well as the individual owner and the group owner of the files. You can do this with the following command:

```
$ sudo chown -R root:root _install/
```

Create Additional Folders

The system needs directories that serve as mount points for file systems required by the kernel or your application. Most systems need /dev, /proc, and /tmp directories. Creating these is a matter of using the mkdir command:

```
$ sudo mkdir _install/tmp
$ sudo mkdir _install/proc
$ sudo mkdir _install/dev
```

The tmp directory is necessary to mount a file system where temporary files are stored. This file system is usually a small RAM disk. The /dev file system contains the device nodes for the system.

Device nodes are a way to communicate with the kernel; these device nodes can be stored in any location on the file system, but a large amount of existing software expects these files to reside in /dev. Last is the /proc file system. It contains a view into the kernel's data structures; some commands read the contents of this file system, such as the mount command.

Create Device Nodes

Linux requires just two device nodes: console and null. Your system may require more nodes, say for flash file devices or serial ports:

```
$ sudo mknod _install/dev/console c 5 1
$ sudo mknod _install/dev/null c 1 3
```

Like changing the file owners, some file systems allow you to create the device nodes when creating the file system image. Which approach you take depends on your ability to become a privileged user, because the file system tools that create device nodes can't be run by a regular user.

Some devices use udev to create device nodes when the system starts, based on the devices present in the system. Systems that have external USB ports are candidates for udev, because it can populate the /dev file system with the appropriate nodes as you plugs-in new devices.

What Makes BusyBox Small?

One of the first questions about BusyBox is, "If it's smaller, what's missing?" BusyBox's tools are smaller than their full-sized cousins for the following reasons:

- *Less functionality:* BusyBox applets contain less functionality. Consider the difference between grep on BusyBox and the GNU grep found on a desktop system: absent is support for Perl regular expressions, special handling for line formatted data, and binary files. This isn't a criticism of the applet, because the GNU grep tool has been growing in functionality for decades without much consideration of the size of the application—on a desktop system, functionality trumps size.

- *No backward compatibility:* The tools that run on a desktop system need to work in a uniform manner, because an upgrade can't break scripts that expect the program to work in a certain way, even if that behavior is a bug. BusyBox doesn't concern itself with backward compatibility.

- *Less help:* Although you can remove the command-line help (if a user will never see the help, it's a waste of space), even the help present is more terse than that found on a desktop-oriented utility. Online help consumes space and doesn't contribute to the functionality of the applet; in that way, it can be viewed as deadweight.

- *Engineered to be small:* The size matters to BusyBox developers. There's a focus on making sure that a minimum amount of code is added to implement a feature and that you have control over what goes into the final executable. Not only do you have control over what applets get built, but you also control what features are in those applets, to squeeze every byte from the binary.

The most important difference is that the engineering is concentrated on making the code as small as possible. Even as the features have increased for BusyBox, the focus on making the code small has resulted in a very favorable code-to-functionality ratio. In addition, BusyBox is highly configurable, allowing you to create a build containing just the required applets and leaving you in control of the size and resource consumption.

The missing functionality means that some shell scripts that use the full sized tools won't work when you use BusyBox applets, because they require options that aren't supported. There isn't a tool to find these problems; it's a matter of testing the scripts to verify that they work properly.

Creating Your Own Applet

BusyBox contains just about every application that's on your desktop machine, but if it's missing something, you're free to add it and submit a patch with your work. In addition, the application you're building may need an additional program or two, and using BusyBox as the infrastructure is a great way to get something done quickly. The following is an overview of the process. Each step is explained in detail:

1. Create your applet code. Each applet resides in a file with an entry point similar to that of a regular C file. A more complex applet may have several source files, but the example has one.

   This step puts a line in the build file so the applet is built if the user chooses it in the configuration step. The make files for BusyBox handle the details of building. You just need to tell it the name of your applet and the configuration parameter that needs to be set in order to include it in the binary file.

2. Add the applet to the configuration file. BusyBox uses the same configuration system as the kernel. Adding a few lines to the configuration input file in the directory where the applet code is located is all that's necessary. After you add this code, you can use the configuration program to control if the applet is built just like any other BusyBox applet.

3. Register the applet with BusyBox. In this step, you tell the main BusyBox program the name of your applet; the program uses that name to create the call to the entry point. This little bit of code also tells BusyBox where the symlink for your application should reside in the installation directory.

4. Add help text. The help text for all applets is stored in the same directory. When you call your program with –help, this text is output.

There's also a bonus step of using the tools BusyBox offers to see how much additional code your changes added to the BusyBox binary. Because BusyBox focuses on the size of the program, this is a good habit to adopt while you're working on this project; it's even more important if you're contributing applets or other patches.

Create the Applet Code

This example creates a small "Hello World" application. Start by putting the application in the misc directory. Create a file called hellotest, put the following in the hello.c file, and store it in the miscutils directory in the BusyBox source tree:

```
#include "libbb.h"
int hello_main(int argc, char **argv) MAIN_EXTERNALLY_VISIBLE;
int hello_main(int argc UNUSED_PARAM, char **argv UNUSED_PARAM)
{
```

```
    printf("Hello World\n");
    return 0;
}
```

Notice the UNUSED_PARAM macros following argc and argv. Remember, in BusyBox, size matters; unused parameters waste stack space as well as adding a trivial amount of time necessary to set up the function call. However, sometimes unused parameters occur, as when you're implementing a general-purpose function (in the example, main()) and don't have a use for all the parameters. Sometimes, you're working on code and haven't yet implemented the code that will use the parameters. In order to suppress the warnings generated by the build, put the macro UNUSED_PARAM after the unused parameter. But remember, you should use this sparingly, because unused parameters add bytes to the code without adding functionality.

Add the Applet to the Make File

Next, you need to tell BusyBox to build the applet. You do so by creating an entry in the Kbuild file of the directory of the applet source: in this case, miscutils/Kbuild. This file lists entries in alphabetical order. If you're submitting your applet to the BusyBox project, you need to follow this convention. If the applet will be used just for your project, putting it at the end makes merging changes from open source easier. In this example, you break the rules and add this file to the end of the file:

```
lib-$(CONFIG_HELLO)        += hello.o
```

The next step is to create an entry in the miscutils/Config.in file that lets you control whether this file is included in the binary. This file follows the same syntax as the Linux kernel configuration tool. Like the Kbuild file, the entries here are in alphabetical order, and you should adhere to the convention if you want your applet to be accepted into the BusyBox project. For this example, add your entry to the bottom of the list:

```
config HELLO
      bool "Hello World"
      default n
      help
        This is a simple program that says Hello, World
```

The first line specifies the name of the configuration variable that will be set for this applet, in this case HELLO; this is stored in the configuration file as CONFIG_HELLO. The next line specifies the type (boolean) and the text that will appear in your interface for this menu item. The default n line tells the configuration tool not to select this by default. The help section is always last and continues until the next empty line or config statement.

Register Applet with BusyBox

In this step, you add the program to the registry that BusyBox uses to figure out how to run your applet. All applets have an entry in the include/applets.h file, which BusyBox uses to build an array that is searched with a binary lookup to find the entry point for the applet. As such, this file has applets in alphabetical order; your application must be added in the correct alphabetical location, or your changes will break BusyBox's application lookup code (which expects these entries to be ordered). In other parts of the BusyBox project, keeping things in alphabetical order is a convention—in this case, it's a requirement.

The entry for the hello applet looks like the following:

```
USE_HELLO(APPLET(hello, _BB_DIR_USR_BIN, _BB_SUID_NEVER))
```

So that you can understand what's happening, the APPLET macro is used to invoke the correct *<applet>* main function and tells BusyBox where the symlinks should be located when the applet is installed—in this case, the usr/bin directory.

Add Help Text

Finally, this program needs an entry in the online help. You do this by adding an entry to the include/usage.h file that looks like this:

```
#define hello_trivial_usage \
       "No options"
#define hello_full_usage "\n\n" \
       "This just says hello"
```

These options are also in alphabetical order, but for the purpose of creating an example program, you can add the entry to the end of the file. All the usage options are located in one file because that makes it easy for BusyBox to centralize how help is output. This saves space and makes it easy for the build process to exclude all help from the executable file if you request.

Build and Verify

You're ready to run configure to add your applet to the build. Before doing that, you build as the system is configured and create a baseline for sizing purposes. Recall that a goal of BusyBox is to be efficient with resources; creating a baseline enables you to later check out much code your utility added to the size of the BusyBox binary. Follow these steps to create the baseline:

```
$ make
$ make baseline
```

Now, test that everything builds by running the configuration tool and selecting your application:

```
$ make menuconfig
```

Select Miscellaneous Utilities from the first menu, and then scroll to the bottom. If you followed the directions verbatim, the following appears:

```
[ ] Hello World (NEW)
```

Press the spacebar to select and exit the configuration program. You're asked to save the current configuration; make sure you affirm. After changing the configuration, build by doing the following:

```
$make
$make install
```

Notice that this code isn't cross-compiled. At this point, you need to build some code that runs on your local machine so you can test that you performed all the steps necessary for the applet to compile and run. This is much easier to validate on your development host. When you're satisfied that the applet compiles, it can be cross-compiled for the target.

In the installation directory, the default is `./_install`. The scripts should have created a `/usr/bin/hello` symlink to BusyBox:

```
$./_install/usr/bin hello
hello
```

Running this file produces the "Hello, World" text you put in the `printf`:

```
$./_install/usr/bin hello
Hello, World
```

You can also check that the help works as expected:

```
$ ./_install/usr/bin/hello --help

BusyBox v1.14.1 (2009-08-12 22:08:06 EDT) multi-call binary


Usage: hello No options

This just says hello
```

This is what you placed in the `include/usage.h` file. If your help was different from the text, your output will be similarly different here.

That's it! You've added an applet and gotten it installed and running. Writing a more complex applet means writing more code. The mechanics of having BusyBox include it in the build and installation have been handled.

Earlier in the process, you created a baseline to see how much more memory your applet added to BusyBox. After verifying that the applet is installed properly and works, check how much code it added by doing the following:

```
$ make bloatcheck
function                    old     new     delta
packed_usage                25817   25839   +22
hello_main                  -       14      +14
applet_names                2029    2035    +6
applet_main                 1212    1216    +4
applet_nameofs              606     608     +2
------------------------------------------------------------------------

(add/remove: 1/0 grow/shrink: 4/0 up/down: 48/0)
                                                       Total: 48 bytes

    text      data      bss      dec      hex  filename
```

```
1511678   2452   19574   1533704   176708   busybox_old

1511738   2452   19574   1533764   176744   busybox_unstripped
```

As you can see, your new code is responsible for adding 48 bytes to the size of the executable. Most of that (22 bytes) is in the help function, called `packed_usage`; your increase in code size is a mere 14 bytes.

Getting Help

Similar to the other projects mentioned in this book so far, the BusyBox project offers support through a mailing list and keeps a history of the conversations. Searching the mailing list archives is an excellent way to get an answer to your question quickly, but don't be shy about asking a question or responding to a query you can answer. As is the case in any other open source project, the people on the list tend to help those who do their best helping themselves, so if you have question or don't understand something, put some effort into finding the resolution yourself. You may find the answer; and if you don't, your questions will be much more focused and easer for those monitoring the list to respond to.

Anybody interested in the project can join the BusyBox mailing list. You can find information on this page: `www.busybox.net/lists.html`. Notice that there's a mailing list for active developers. Please don't post support questions to this list in hopes that it's being monitored by people who know more than those on the general mailing list.

What's Next

The next chapter concentrates on system configuration: how to pick a root file system, and what's necessary to get everything in order to boot the system. This has been covered in bits and pieces throughout the book, because it's necessary to assemble a working system in order to verify that the code created thus far works. However, this chapter is more systematic and covers more of the "why" rather than just the "how."

■ ■ ■

## CHAPTER 15

System Design

Up until now, the goal has been to get a system up and running well enough for testing, but not for production. In this chapter, you go through the process of systematically creating a root file system that is proper for deployment on a production device. This process involves thinking about how the device is produced and how the user is using the device. This process shouldn't be haphazard, which means understanding and selecting the right tools for the job and taking the time to study and understand the alternatives offered by the environment around Linux.

The Big Picture

Getting a system ready for production means gathering the files to be deployed and preparing them so they can be placed on the device prior to shipping. Along with the root file system contents, the design and deployment entails selecting the right root file system and boot-up method for the device. The kernel must be prepared as a step in the process, along with any additional files needed to support the application running on the device. Going one level back, the boot loader is also a necessary component; some work is involved in getting it configured so the boot loader passes the right parameters to the kernel at boot time, if necessary. When you've completed all these steps, you have what's necessary to deploy Linux on the target.

For many embedded systems, the manufacturing (or production) takes place at a contract manufacturing company that performs the actual deployment of Linux. The company doing the fabrication of the device just knows that file X should be placed in the flash on the target device; it doesn't know or care about the contents of the file, just that it has the file, can verify its integrity, and understands where to put in on the device. Depending on the relationship with the manufacturer and the requirements of the project, a company may ask for a way to test that the software has been loaded on the device and that it's functioning correctly. Such a test is usually more detailed than "it boots" and likely includes a small smoke test[1] to ensure that the peripherals, such as the touch screen and any external buttons or lights, are working as expected.

This chapter covers the following steps:

---

[1] The phrase *smoke test* comes from hardware engineers who powered equipment and waited for the smoke to rise from miswired or failing components. This is the first test performed on equipment, with the goal of determining whether the device works at all under any conditions. After passing the smoke test, the equipment is deemed worthy of additional, more extensive testing. In software, you're deprived of actual smoke and an oddly enjoyable smell when the software fails when it first runs, but the general concept is the same.

- *Configuring the boot loader and kernel:* The boot loader and the kernel are intertwined at this point. How the kernel is built largely depends on the needs of the boot loader.

- *Selecting the root file system:* Many developers work on a file system that's been mounted over a network or are using what happens to work with the board. Now, you need to select the root file system type for the production builds. This affects the kernel, because the driver necessary to access the file system must be built into the kernel.

- *Deploying your application:* This is the process of getting your application in the root file system along with any dependencies. Because you built your application, you should be aware of the dependencies; nevertheless, this section has some simple checks to validate your assumptions.

- *Configuring the system:* An embedded Linux system is like a desktop system in that is has some system requirements that need to be met in order for it to work correctly. Plus, depending on the application, you may want to use some of the security features found on bigger Linux systems.

Configuring the Boot Loader and Kernel

As we already know, the first part of an embedded Linux system to run is the boot loader. The boot loader is responsible for getting the system in such a state that the kernel can run; the kernel in turn runs your application. The kernel boot process used in development, where the kernel is copied from flash into RAM, may be tweaked a little during deployment, because the image may be loaded to a different location or even be executed directly out of flash memory.

During development of the kernel, you probably skipped the step of writing the kernel into flash, because this process is time consuming in a relative sense—the extra 30 seconds feels much longer than the clock on the wall says. Extra time aside, putting the kernel into flash and then booting doesn't change how the kernel operates after it's booted, so this step can be factored out to reduce the amount of time in the development process. Now that you've completed the kernel work, the goal is to build a kernel file that can be booted on the device using the desired boot loader.

Because code size is a constant theme in embedded development, this section covers how to remove unnecessary code from the U-Boot boot loader. U-Boot is used for the example project to illustrate the concepts of size reduction; your boot loader may be different, but the concepts for making it smaller will be the same.

U-Boot

When you're doing development, U-Boot is built with features like flash management, documentation, a command line available through a serial port with editing facilities similar to that of a shell, and networking. During deployment, you can remove most of these features if they aren't used in the target device; they consume resources and make it easier for the device to become compromised—for example if a user is able to access the serial port and interrupt the booting process. Continuing the example, the online help included in the project is a complete waste of space for a commercial device where the user will never have access to the boot loader.

When you compiled U-Boot in Chapter 14, you used the default configuration parameters, which are excellent for development but contain features that would be unused in deployment. Here you rebuild U-Boot and remove some of the features, but you need to study your target board's usage patterns and determine what else can be removed.

When you build U-Boot boot code with parameters different from the default, you need to modify the configuration file for the board. You start by configuring U-Boot to build for a certain board and then update the default configuration files. For example, if you use the configuration for an Atmel 9100 board, you do this to configure the board:

```
make at91rm9200rk_config
```

This uses the C-style header file to configure the build process:
`include/configs/at91rm9200rk.h`

You edit this file to customize U-Boot for deployment. Table 15-1 describes the common settings for a production system. These settings reside in an include file that is used when building the U-Boot binary, so you must follow C syntax.

Table 15-1. Common U-Boot settings

Parameter	Meaning
CONFIG_ETHADDR	The MAC address for the Ethernet device. Some boards don't set this automatically.
CONFIG_IDENT_STRING	Vendor information that is appended to the U-Boot boot-up message.
CONFIG_ENV_OVERWRITE	When built with this flag, the user can't overwrite the MAC address built into U-Boot.
CONFIG_SYS_CONSOLE_INFO_QUIET	Turns off the console output when booting. Although it creates only a small amount of output, it sends some unnecessary chatter to the screen and increases boot time.
CONFIG_EXTRA_ENV_SETTINGS	A list of environment variable settings to include in the build. This list is a string with the format `envvar1=value\0envvar3=value\0`
CONFIG_BOOTCMD	The command string used to boot the kernel. This command is executed automatically after U-Boot is up and running. An example is `nboot kernel ; bootm` This loads the kernel from flash and then runs it from memory. To test this string, type it directly at the U-Boot prompt.
CONFIG_BOOTDELAY	The number of seconds to wait before executing CONFIG_BOOTCMD. For production boards, this value should be 0 unless there's a reason to delay the booting process.

Here's an example of the changes to the file:

```
#define CONFIG_BOOTDELAY 0
#define CONFIG_BOOTCMD "nboot.e kernel ; bootm"
#define CONFIG_ENV_OVERWRITE
```

U-Boot also has a tool for adding metadata to the Linux kernel: `mkimage` puts information in the kernel file, such as where it should be loaded into memory, the starting address, and version information. U-Boot has its own format for Linux kernels that it boots, and `mkimage` takes a kernel image and transforms it into something that U-Boot knows how to handle by adding this metadata. When you're building a Linux uImage target, which is the U-Boot–specific binary that has been processed by `mkimage`, the kernel make file sets the metadata to reasonable default values. The default values are adequate for development, but for a production kernel, you can set them to something specific to your application.

You set the metadata using the `mkimage` command, which is invoked with reasonable defaults when you build the kernel. To see the parameters for the command, build the kernel with the `V=1` option:

```
make uImage CROSS_COMPILE=<cross-compiler> ARCH=<arch> V=1
```

Close to the end of the build, you see a command line similar to this one, but with different values for your board:

```
mkuboot.sh -A arm -O linux -T kernel \
        -C none -a 0x30008000 -e 0x30008000 \
            -n 'Linux-2.6.31-rc4' \
            -d arch/arm/boot/zImage arch/arm/boot/uImage
```

Note that the command being run in `mkuboot.sh` is a small script in the kernel's script directory tree that calls `mkimage`; it fails with an informative error message if `mkimage` can't be found on the system.

The parameter you're likely to change is `-n`, which is the version string assigned to the kernel. This string can contain any value, because it's only informational; you can add information such as your company name, build date, or build number. For example:

```
$ mkimage -A arm -O linux -T kernel \
                -C none -a 0x30008000 -e 0x30008000 \
                -n 'MySpecialKernel' \
            -d arch/arm/boot/zImage arch/arm/boot/uImage
```

This command is run from the top of the kernel build tree for a kernel built for an ARM processor located at `arch/arm/boot/zImage`. Although this is the most common usage pattern for `mkimage`, you can run it from outside the kernel source tree on an arbitrary kernel image file; the output file can be changed as well. That makes it possible to name the kernel something different without a complete kernel rebuild. For instance, you may produce a kernel named Test Build; but when it passes QA, it's renamed Production Build *some version* to provide visual feedback about the contents of the file.

The other parameters of note are `-a` and `-e` along with their arguments. The first parameter adds to the file the address in RAM where the file should be placed when it's copied from storage. The second parameter is the address in RAM that should be executed after the copy process completes.

Other Boot loaders

The uImage is specific to U-Boot. Other boot loaders accept formats like a zImage or an srecImage. Unlike U-Boot, these file formats don't have any additional metadata regarding where to store the image or the ability to add a text version string. If your board uses a boot loader like this, there isn't much to do other than ensure that the kernel from the build process boots correctly. This file can then go to production as is. Most organizations change the name of the file to indicate the version number.

Execute in Place

Using execute in place (XIP) technology, the kernel code is run directly from flash, meaning the code isn't loaded into RAM before being run. In order to use the kernel like this, you need to build with the Kernel Execute-In-Place from ROM flag set; and you need to know where in the flash the kernel will reside, so it can link the files with the correct offsets.

This technology doesn't mean the kernel doesn't consume any RAM memory. The kernel still uses RAM memory for the stack and heap (the Linux memory model was discussed in Chapter 1), but because the code is running from the flash memory space, the kernel consumes that much less memory. The kernel isn't compressed when stored in flash, so less flash memory is available for storing the root file system. A smaller amount of flash may not be a consideration if RAM is a scarcer resource than flash. On the other hand, flash memory is more expensive than RAM; if the parts cost for the device is critical, using more flash than RAM memory may increase the per-unit cost of the device. This isn't much of a consideration if you're using a stock board where the RAM and flash are fixed and can't be changed, but it's an issue when you're creating a custom board.

Using U-Boot as an example, creating an image ready for XIP involves sending an additional -x parameter to mkimage:

```
mkimage -x -A arm -O linux -T kernel \
        -C none -a 0x30008000 -e 0x30008000 \
        -n 'MySpecialKernel' \
          -d arch/arm/boot/zImage arch/arm/boot/uImage-xip
```

This step ensures that the image is ready for XIP booting by U-Boot. If you're using a different boot loader, check the documentation to see what steps are appropriate.

Selecting a Root File System

The root file system plays a key role in an embedded device. Linux, following its Unix roots, defines a *file system* as a collection of files and directories, where directories may contain zero or more files and directories. The *root* file system is the file system that starts at the root (/) directory. Like everything in Linux, the sheer number of choices means you must dedicate time and effort to picking the file system most appropriate for the application. In addition to your application's requirements, the hardware also determines what root file system types you can use. The primary groupings for file systems fall into these categories:

- *Block-based file systems:* These are the file systems found on the hard drive of a desktop or laptop, working with a device that can read and write units of data called *blocks* in any sequence. An embedded device like a kiosk[2] is likely to have this type of storage because economizing on power consumption, size, and operating noise aren't the usual requirements.

- *MTD file systems:* A memory technology device (MTD) file system uses what is commonly called flash memory for storage. Flash memory has a duty cycle that is much lower than a block device, and the file system must be smart enough to distribute the updates around the device so that one area isn't used much more than another. Also, in order to write data to a flash device, you must take special steps to prepare the media.

- *RAM buffer–based file systems:* This type of file system resides in RAM, because the file system cache is never written to any storage medium. This file system type appeared in the 2.6 kernel and is most commonly known through the initramfs file system. This is different than a RAM disk: a RAM disk reserves some portion of RAM and uses a driver to make that portion appear as though it's a block-based device. Prior to the 2.6 kernel, there was the concept of RAM disks that were similar in nature to the RAM initramfs systems; the functionality still exists in the kernel, but it's use isn't recommended because these older RAM disks are much less efficient.

All of these file systems can be read-only. Several file systems are intrinsically read-only, which means they don't have the capacity to accept writes. This concept can be unsettling, but it makes sense when you understand that the storage requirements for an embedded device are frequently very small and that the user has little control over what programs are run. In that context, a read-only root file system isn't as constricting as you may immediately assume.

No matter what file system you use, it appears to be the same from the system's perspective. Although an MTD file system may be doing very different work from a block-based file system, it's not apparent from the application's perspective: opening a file residing in a RAM disk works the same as opening a file on a flash drive. This uniform access to system resources is why Linux is a leading choice for embedded development.[3]

Block-Based File Systems

A block-based file system is by far the most commonly used type of file system on desktop systems; it also is a frequent choice for embedded systems. An important note is that any block-based file system can be used on an MTD device, as long as it's mounted read-only. For example, an ext2 file system can be placed on the flash media and will work fine as long as it isn't used for writing; this can be enforced by

---

[2] This is a device like a touch screen or other input device (such as a scanner or credit-card reader) that takes the place of a person who used to perform a task like checking in your baggage at the airport or paying your parking bill. An ATM machine is a special sort of kiosk that ejects money after you swipe your bank card, supply your password, and wander through the menu system looking for the "give me cash, pretty please" entry.

[3] I'm working on a project with hardware engineers who are amazed that I can experiment with several different file systems with no change in my code.

mounting the file system as read-only. This section describes each of the file systems so you understand when one is more appropriate than another for your project.

One of the niceties of using a block-based file system is that tools readily exist to both create and inspect the file system. File systems like ext2 and ext3 include the necessary tools with nearly every Linux distribution.

■ **Caution** When you're experimenting with the low-level block devices on your development computer, proceed with care. If you access these devices directly, nothing is stopping you from making a mistake that can result in losing all the data on your hard drive. Use a virtual machine to protect your real hardware, or be confident in your backups.

A block-based file system can also be *loopback* mounted, a technique that allows you to create the file system in a file and then mount the file as though it was a block device. This approach is necessary to create an image of the file system that can be placed on the device directly. Delivery of the file system to the manufacturer is generally in this form.

Before getting into the mechanics of creating a loopback, it helps to understand what you're doing and why. Consider your desktop machine: it has the root file system mounted to /dev/sda<*number*> or something similar. For example:

```
$ mount | grep " / "
/dev/sda1 on / type ext3 (rw,relatime,errors=remount-ro,commit=600)
```

Looking at the /dev/sda device shows that this is a block device. This means writing to the /dev/sda1 device begins writing sequentially to the device, starting at the first block. Writing *directly* means you're accessing the device at the lowest level possible available through Linux's device model. When you create a file system on a loopback device, the data stored in the file is exactly what would be stored on the production device. During the production of the device, having this file makes it possible for the data to be placed on the device without Linux, because the manufacturer has a hardware-level tool that quickly deposits the data on the device.

This example shows how to loopback mount an ext2 file system. This technique works for any block-based file system in this section:

```
$ dd if=/dev/zero of=~/myrfs bs=1k count=1000
$ sudo losetup -f ~/myrfs
```

Depending on your configuration, when running dd, you may be asked to continue even though ~/myrfs isn't a block device; respond with Yes. The first line creates a 1MB file containing just zeros. The next command associates a loopback device with the file, picking the first unused /dev/loop device. To see what device was selected, use `losetup` again with the `-a` parameter; the output is similar to this:

```
sudo losetup -l
/dev/loop0: [0801]:8266313 (<your home directory>/myrfs)
```

This means the loopback device /dev/loop0 is the device you want to use to create your file system. To create an ext2 file system, use the `mkfs.ext2` command with the defaults:

```
$ sudo mkfs.ext2 /dev/loop0
Filesystem label=
OS type: Linux
Block size=1024 (log=0)
Fragment size=1024 (log=0)
128 inodes, 1000 blocks
50 blocks (5.00%) reserved for the super user
First data block=1
Maximum filesystem blocks=1048576
1 block group
8192 blocks per group, 8192 fragments per group
128 inodes per group
```

Now that you've created the file system, you can mount the loopback device like any other device:

```
mkdir ~/mountpoint
sudo mount -t ext2 /dev/loop0 ~/mountpoint
```

You can copy files into ~/mountpoint, and that data is deposited into the ~/myrfs file. After unmounting the device, this file can be copied to the device's block device that is mounted as a root file system. After a file has been created for loopback mounting, you can mount it again with a shortcut in the mount command:

```
mount -t ext2 -o loop ~/myrfs ~/mountpoint
```

This approach to creating a root file system makes it possible to use common tools like `cp` and `mknod` for configuration and population of the root file system. All block file systems can be mounted this way; however, if the file system is read-only, using a loopback mount doesn't add read/write capabilities.

Ext2

This is the file system that was included in Linux's first release. Ext2 includes the full complement of permissions, owner information, timestamps, and file types. It's an extensively tested and deployed file system that serves as the reference for testing changes that are made to the underlying virtual file system infrastructure of the kernel. This is a common file system for read-only flash devices, because of its simplicity and complete implementation. It has the ability to store extended attributes and therefore can be used on a system running SELinux, described later in this chapter.

The tools for creating ext2 file systems are included by default with every Linux distribution, so creating file systems is very easy.

Ext3

The ext3 file system is the successor to ext2 and includes features such as journaling and larger file systems, with a maximum size of 8 terabytes. Although this amount of memory seems very large for an embedded system, the maximum size is important if the embedded system will be used as a backup device, a multiuser file server, or a ready-to-use device that indexes data for search and retrieval at a medium-sized organization. This file system is widely deployed and is the default file system for most Linux distributions. A journaling file system writes changes to the file system in a temporary area before committing the changes to the file system. There is a performance penalty in that changes must be written twice: first to the temporary journal and then to the file system itself. With the high performance of disk drives, this overhead generally isn't noticeable.

Other improvements to the file system include increased capacity, both in volume size and the number of files that can be stored on the file system. Although the typical embedded system doesn't need a very large file system, for those that do, ext3 is an excellent choice.

Because journaling relates to changes to the file system, note that ext3 isn't an appropriate choice for a read-only file system, because journaling only occurs when writing. This means the kernel has a large chunk of code (over 100KB) that is never used. If you need the size of ext3 but in read-only, consider SquashFS.

SquashFS

This is a read-only file system that was designed for embedded systems but has found use as the file system used for most Live CD Linux distributions. Unlike ext2 or ext3, SquashFS works with compressed data; when the file system is created, all the data is compressed, making for a much smaller file system.

SquashFS is unique in this category because it can be used to create file systems that have an endianness different from that of the target platform. For most platforms, the host and target endianness are the same, so this isn't a differentiating feature; but if you're targeting a big-endian processor, this feature is very important.

SquashFS doesn't have the extended attributes necessary for SELinux.

CramFS

CramFS is a read-only file system that compresses data but stores the metadata for the files uncompressed. CramFS has been written to be as small as possible, and the file system kernel code is among the smallest in the group. This file system does have a much lower limit for the size (about 270MB) than others, but for many embedded systems, that size is large.

Romfs

The romfs file system is the simplest of the group. This file system has no compression and, true to its name, is read only. This is the absolutely smallest of the group, with a code size of around 4KB. Romfs is small because it does very little: it doesn't maintain file ownership or groups (everything belongs to uid/gid 0), file creation, extended attributes, or access times. For devices where space is at a premium, this is the best choice for a file system.

MINIX

This file system is used more frequently than you may expect in embedded Linux applications. It's a good choice considering that it supports reading/writing and all the permissions and ownership information necessary, matching the features in ext2. The limitation of MINIX is that it only supports smaller volumes—less that 36MB—but this isn't an issue for many embedded devices.

If you want to learn about how Linux handles file systems or want to create your own (maybe you need some features that don't exist in Linux), MINIX is a great system to use as a starting point. The simplicity of the implementation makes it easy to see the big picture of how Linux interacts with a file system.

MTD File Systems

The general name for flash storage is MTD. Flash hardware can't be read from and written to like a regular block-base device and therefore require special file systems. For starters, these file systems store data on a medium with a much lower duty cycle than a disk drive and must have special code built in so that the data is spread over the media—a process called *wear leveling*. Without wear leveling, certain parts of the media would be used too frequently, wear out, and become unusable. Although the duty cycle is low, it's not so low that you should fret over using the device in an application or worry about damaging a flash drive during development when there's much more writing than during regular use.

The USB stick used to store data has a microcontroller that handles this wear leveling, so no special file system is necessary for that device. This bit of software in the microcontroller is called a Flash Translation Layer (FTL). Similarly, there are flash drives that have IDE, SCSI, or Serial IO interfaces that also have an FTL, which means you don't have to worry about having an FTL in software. The Linux kernel also provides FTL services through the `mtdblock` devices that appear in the `/dev` file system for each MTD device.

■ **Note** The Linux operating system lets you create an ext2 file system on an MTD block device, and you can read and write to the device with apparently no problem—but sooner or later, you'll damage the device. Why? Because the Linux driver doesn't perform the wear-leveling required by this type·of device.

MTD devices come in two flavors: NAND and NOR flash. Each design is named after the arrangement of the individual logic gates that store the data on the chip. NAND is becoming a more popular design because the density can be higher: NAND gates require less circuitry than NOR gates. From a performance standpoint, NAND can perform read operations faster than NOR, but NOR is a faster technology for writing. Both flash file systems discussed next support both NOR and NAND flash. When you use a file system that runs on top of these devices, there is one difference: the file system driver in the Linux kernel (in this case, specifically, JFFS2 or YAFFS2) handles the details for you.

The next two sections cover two production file systems for MTD devices. JFFS2 is the leader, but it's playing catch-up to YAFFS2 from a technical perspective.

JFFS2

This is the most commonly used file system for MTD devices and has been part of the kernel since 2.4. It compresses the file data and meta-data, so it makes very good use of limited flash memory; however, accessing compressed data has a performance penalty. JFFS works by running a background thread in the kernel that garbage-collects space on the media, compacting data and performing other bookkeeping operations so that new information can be written across the media without any one part of the media being used more than another. JFFS2 attempts to write data in such a way that the least-used area is selected first when a write operation needs to be performed.

JFFS2's primary drawback is poor performance when mounting a root file system, because the driver performs a scan of the media at that time to locate bad blocks and build up its internal data structures. As media sizes increase, the delay related to scanning is becoming prohibitive. Newer versions of the JFFS driver contain features that reduce the amount of time necessary to mount the file system, as discussed later in the chapter

YAFFS2

This file system was created for NAND devices, initially, and has been updated to handle NOR flash technology. YAFFS2's primary advantage is the greatly reduced time necessary to mount the file system. The key difference is that YAFFS2 doesn't compress data, so both reading and writing subtract one step; on a slower machine, compression represent a considerable overhead. Mount times for YAFFS2 are sub-second and don't change much depending on the size of the file system.

Because YAFFS2 was designed for NAND memory from the start, it's optimized for the page-oriented access model of this memory type. NAND also stores less data in memory than JFFS2.

RAM Buffer–Based File Systems

These file systems reside in RAM memory. As soon as the device is reset, all changes to the file system disappear. This type of file system is perfect for storing temporary data, such as what appears in the /tmp file system. Because RAM file systems are very fast, they're also reasonable caches, where data is stored before another process moves it to a slower device for longer-term storage.

Rafms

The ramfs file system is a clever hack where data is written into the data cache for Linux and remains there. When writing to any file system, the kernel stores data to a cache to increase performance; in a RAM file system, that data goes into the cache but is never written to a physical device.

This is a very fast file system that has a small amount of overhead (just a few KB), but it continues growing until all the memory on the device is consumed. When the file system is mounted as read-only, this problem doesn't arise, making this a safer choice for a production system.

Tmpfs

The tmpfs file system is just like the ramfs file system with the additional feature of limiting the amount of memory the file system can consume. This is very important, because a defect that results in writing a large amount of data to a file, or systems that continue running for a long time and build up large /var/log/messages files, can't crash the system by consuming all the memory. tmpfs, unlike ramfs, uses swap memory for storing data; but on an embedded system, swap memory is typically disabled.

Initramfs

The initramfs file system is a special case of ramfs. The data in this file system is stored in a cpio format and then written into RAM during the computer's boot process. After this priming from cpio data, this file system behaves exactly like a ramfs file system. The intent behind initramfs was to have it serve as a temporary root file system before another root file system could be mounted and the boot process continued. Embedded developers have begun to use initramfs as the only file system by not mounting another file system at root.

File System Pairings

Considering that some of these file systems are read-only and the Linux system requires a few writable directories, such as /tmp and /home, the common approach is to use a RAM-based file system for several directories in the root file system. Even when you're using an MTD-based file system, it's advisable to use a RAM-based file system to store temporary files, because the wear-leveling code occasionally imposes large latencies as the file system finds a suitable location on the device for the data.

Assembling a Root File System

The process of assembling a root file system is less complicated than you may think: it mainly involves gathering the right bits and pieces and putting them in one place so the tools used to create the file system itself can create the binary image that is then placed into the embedded device's storage area. Here are the coarse-grained steps involved:

1. Create the staging area. The *staging area* is where the files reside to create the file system. Although this sounds complex, the process isn't much more than creating a directory.

2. Create a directory skeleton. A Linux system has some requirements as to the directories that must exist on a root file system. Some of these directories serve as mount points for virtual file systems.

3. Gather libraries and required files. This step involves getting together the files for your application, along with any libraries that are necessary. At this point, you also want to add files for logging into the host, if that's how it will be used.

4. Create initialization scripts. When the system starts, you need to run any background processes, perform any configuration steps, and get the application running.

5. Set permissions. The files in the staging area may be owned by root or some other user. The permissions, such as files being readable or writable, may also need to be changed.

A section is dedicated to each step. When there are several different approaches, the tradeoffs for each are explained. To a certain degree, the process of creating a root file system should be scripted so that the process can be repeated. Repeatability is important because you should create this critical part of the project in a controlled manner, if for no other reason than to avoid human error (which seems to inflict damage at the most inopportune times).

Create the Staging Area

The staging area is a directory where the files are assembled into the root file system. This directory is the virtual root directory when it's deployed on the target device.

There is nothing special about this directory, and there's no need to set any special permissions. If you're constructing a script to create your root file system, a best practice is assign the root file system directory to an environment variable, so that when it changes, minimal rework to your script is required:

```
$ ROOTFS=~/rfs
$ mkdir  $ROOTFS
```

The rest of this section refers to the root file system by its symbolic name, $ROOTFS.

Create a Directory Skeleton

The file system needs some top-level directories that are used to store files or serve as mount points for other file systems. A *mount point* is a directory where a file system is mounted; in the case of Linux, several virtual file systems should be mounted in order for other programs that expect their presence to function. The most commonly required file system is mounted at /proc. It represents a view into the kernel's state, showing what processes are running and the state of other system resources.

This command creates the basic directories necessary for a minimal file system:

```
cd $ROOTFS
mkdir -p tmp proc sys bin sbin lib etc
```

That's it. Later in the chapter, you populate these directories with files or use them as mount points for virtual file systems. Some of these directories are candidates for RAM-based file systems if the primary file system is read-only or MTD based.

Gather Libraries and Required Files

Many systems use shared libraries (sometimes called *shared objects*). These binary files contain code that is linked into the executable at runtime. Shared libraries help conserve space because multiple programs aren't loading the same code into memory several times; this comes at the expense of a slightly slower program load, because the system must perform the dynamic linking operation.

Some libraries are linked explicitly, whereas other are used and linked by ld automatically—the C library, for example. For libraries linked explicitly or those created during the build process, you can verify what libraries are in use by using a few simple techniques. Although you can find this data by inspection, the engineers working on the project (maybe that's you) should keep a list of the shared libraries used in the project. If nothing else, you can reconcile this list against what you found through inspection.

To see what libraries an executable loads, run the program on the target, use the LD_TRACE_LOADED_OBJECTS environment variable. A utility on your host machine, ldd, shows what shared objects are loaded with a file. This is a shell script, and digging through the file shows that this program sets the environment variable LD_TRACE_LOADED_OBJECTS=1 and then runs the executable. You can get the same output as ldd on the target by doing the following when running a program:

```
$ LD_TRACE_LOADED_OBJECTS=1 some-program
        libz.so.1 => /lib/libz.so.1 (0xb7dcc000)
        libc.so.6 => /lib/libc.so.6 (0xb7c68000)
        /lib/ld-linux.so.2 (0xb7ee5000)
```

This shows that this program loads the libraries libz.so.1 and lib.so.6, which are both mapped to the files /lib/libz.so.1 and /lib/libc.so.6 on the file system. The last entry, /lib/ld-linux.so.2, is the loader that performs the dynamic link process. These files must exist on the target system in order for the program to load and function. Use this script to find all the executable files and print a unique listing of the libraries required:

```
$find / -perm /111 -print | while read f; do \
    LD_TRACE_LOADED_OBJECTS=1 $f \
done | cut -f 1 -d' ' | sort | uniq
```

This uses `find` to get all the files that can be executed and runs them with the `LD_TRACE_LOADED_OBJECTS` flag set. The program isn't actually executed; instead, the loader outputs the libraries (as in the prior example) and `cut` selects the first column of the output; the column is sorted, and duplicates are removed.

In this strategy, you don't need to have a target to run the commands; instead, you find the information by inspection. Your toolchain includes a utility, `strings`, which can be used to extract the text strings from an executable file; however, you can use `strings` for your host machine as long as it has the same endianness (or byte order) as the target. This command scans a directory for strings in executable files that start with `lib`:

```
$ find <rfs dir> -perm 111 | while read f ; do \
strings $f \
done | sort | uniq
```

Now that you have this list of files, open it in an editor, and inspect it to find out whether it has any stray entries. Adjust the `grep` pattern so that those entries aren't included in the file. You can then use that file to fetch the libraries and place them in the root file system to validate that the root file system in the staging area has the necessary libraries installed.

Required Files

In order for you to log in to the device, the file system must have at least `group` and `passwd` files. You can easily create these files created with the following scripts. This creates the `passwd` file, with one entry for the root user:

```
$ echo "root:x:0:0:root:/root:/bin/bash" > $ROOTFS/passwd
```

The real password is stored in the /etc/shadow file. There isn't a good way to populate the /etc/shadow file in another root directory other than the one where the `passwd` command is run. To create your accounts, use the `passwd` program to change password for a user, and copy that line into the script for your shadow password. Shadow passwords are required for BusyBox systems configured with shadow-password support; if you don't need them, you can skip creating this file.

The next step is to create the /etc/group file. *Groups* in Linux are ways to assign file access rights to sets of users instead of individuals. This command creates a group file with the expected groups for a Linux system:

```
cat > $ROOTFS/etc/group << "EOF"
root:x:0:
bin:x:1:
sys:x:2:
kmem:x:3:
tty:x:4:
daemon:x:5:
```

```
disk:x:6:
lp:x:7:
dialout:x:8:
audio:x:9:
adm:x;10
EOF
```

Depending on the software installed on the target, you may have various configuration files in your root file system. This requires reading the documentation for the packages used in the project, copying those to the root file system, and populating them with the correct values. One such file is $ROOTFS/etc/inittab, as discussed in Chapter 16.

In order to get a scripted build of the root file system, you need a list of these files along with their expected content. If the files are fairly static, you can put them in tar archive that starts at / and unarchive them into the $ROOTFS directory, or you can create a script with a series of here files to produce the output.

Create Initialization Scripts

The Linux kernel can run any file as init, as long as that process continues running. As soon as that process stops, the kernel panics and stops running. Embedded systems use a program aptly called init that is designed to run certain processes at startup and restart processes that stop running. Although you can write your own init, the program included with BusyBox is small and packs enough power to be well suited to an embedded system.

Initialization scripts have a few jobs to perform on a Linux system:

1. Mount any file systems necessary for the system to operate. Find a selection of the most common filesystems in Table 15-2. As noted earlier in the chapter, the root directory skeleton contains several empty directories that are then used for virtual file systems.

2. Create any necessary files and perform other housekeeping chores. Any daemon process tasks should be run at this time. For example, if the device is connected to a network and expects the address to come from a DHCP server, the dhcpd daemon needs to be run at this time. If files need to be created in order for the application to run, this is the right place for that activity.

3. Get the main application running, and keep it running. Remember, when the main program stops, the kernel stops. The initialization needs to get that program running and make sure it keeps running. The init program should also be simple enough that it continues to run as well—if it crashes, the system will panic.

This section talks about using the init program, both using a script and using a regular program to start the system.

Table 15-2. Common File Systems Found on Embedded Systems

Mount Point (required, optional, recommended)	File System/Purpose
/proc (required)	The proc file system gives a view into the kernel of what is running and the current state of the system. This file system is used by many different programs, mount being one of them, and the proc file system should be mounted at this location for all systems.
/sysfs (recommended)	The sys file system contains driver and hardware information. This file system is recommended because it's the preferred way for the kernel to communicate information about the hardware configuration of the system to userland. In this way, sysfs file systems supports the udev device-management system.
/tmp (required)	This file system stores temporary data. Data stored here can be deleted at any time; there's no guarantee that data stored in this file system will survive a reboot. This directory isn't required as a mount point, but most embedded systems mount a small RAM file system at this directory, because writing temporary data to flash is time-expensive or impossible if the root file system is mounted as read-only.
/dev (required)	This file system contains the device nodes, so you can access system resources. Although theoretically optional, it makes sense to have a file system on the device. If the device has a read-only file system but is using udev or supporting a dynamic set of devices, a RAM-based file system is mounted here as well.

Using Init and Inittab

When you use init, the /etc/inittab file can be used to hold both the system initialization code and the application program for the device. Consider the following /etc/inittab file:

```
::sysinit:/bin/mount -t proc none /proc
::sysinit:/bin/mount -t sysfs none /sys
::sysinit:/bin/mkdir /dev/pts
::sysinit:/bin/mount -t devpts devpts /dev/pts
::sysinit:/sbin/ifconfig lo 127.0.0.1 up
::sysinit:/sbin/route add -net 127.0.0.0 netmask 255.0.0.0 lo
# now run any rc scripts
null::respawn:/usr/bin/appRunner
```

This file contains what would normally be in a script file as sysinit lines in the /etc/inittab; it ends with a respawn of /usr/bin/appRunner, which is the script that executes the application for the target board. The sysinit entries run in the sequence in which they appear in the file, and the init program waits until the current command ends before running the next. The respawn command ensures that the program appRunner is restarted if it stops running, thus avoiding a system panic.

Some users don't like the style of having multiple `sysinit` lines serve as a startup script or need to use looping structures that are more complex than can be placed on one line. In this case, the `/etc/sysinit` file looks like the following:

```
::sysinit:configureDevice
::respawn:/usr/bin/appRunner
```

Then, the script file `configureDevice` contains the series of `sysinit` lines. During startup, `init` runs the file `configureDevice`; it serves the same function as the lines in the `/etc/sysinit` that it replaces.

Using a Script

If you want something simpler, there's always the script file that has an infinite loop at the end to run the program. This method has advantages in that you have much more control over system startup; and the script is likely smaller than the `init` in BusyBox, although by a small amount. By using a script, you can create the code necessary to start the system in high language that's very easy to change. Because the initialization happens just once, and briefly, using a shell script doesn't introduce a noticeable performance penalty.

Given the examples, the script to start the file looks similar to this using:

```
#!/bin/sh
/bin/mount -t proc none /proc
/bin/mount -t sysfs none /sys

/bin/mkdir /dev/pts
/bin/mount -t devpts devpts /dev/pts
/sbin/ifconfig lo 127.0.0.1 up
/sbin/route add -net 127.0.0.0 netmask 255.0.0.0 lo

# run your program forever..
while true ; do appRunner ; logFailure ; done
```

If you save this file on the file system as `/etc/app`, the following kernel parameter results in this program being run at startup: `init=/etc/app`.

When you're thinking about how to get the system started, understand that Linux grants you a great degree of freedom. Using something like a simple shell script with an infinite loop is a perfectly acceptable way to get the system ready and to keep your program running. The `logFailure` script is added in this example to show that the shell script can be more complex than just mindlessly restarting the task.

Using a Program

Initialization code can be part of the application program or part of a very small program that initializes the system and keeps the application running. Although using a shell script is easier, having this code as part of the application saves space and gives you the most control over how the system starts. The C standard library includes a handy function, `system()` that runs a command and waits until it finishes before advancing to the next line. Enclosing this system() call in a loop ensures that the program restarts when it fails. The C code to do this looks like the following:

```
int main(int argc, char **argv) {
  while (1)
    system("theapplication");
  return 0;
}
```

Under the covers, the system() call does a fork, then an exec() call, and finally waits on the newly created process. This code is an endless loop that attempts to rerun the program if it fails. In a real system, you would likely put in some additional code to print an error message on failure and possibly wait for several seconds if the program failed to execute more than a certain number of times in a certain number of seconds. This is left as an exercise for you.

Using this approach has some additional overhead that you can remove by calling the fork() and exec() functions manually. For instance, the system() call runs the program in a new shell, which may create unnecessary overhead. The previous solution also requires at least two programs on the system: the application and the program that runs the application in a loop. The next bit of code shows a system that uses fork() and exec() to run the same instance of a program, with one instance responsible for restarting the forked instance in the case of failure:

```
int main(int argc, char **argv) {
    pid_t pid;
    int waitCode;

    configureDevice();  /* mounts file systems */
    while (1) {
        switch(pid=fork()) {
            case -1:
        /* error condition, system panic */
                exit(1);
            case 0:
        /* run the application */
                appEntryPoint(argc, argv);
            default:
        /* parent process waits for child to die */
                wait(&waitCode);
        }
    }
    return 0;
}
```

When the program ends, in the form of appEntryPoint finishing, the application restarts. This approach is very simple and doesn't require much in terms of resources; but it requires the most engineering, because the code in C necessary to mount file systems and otherwise configure the system is much more verbose than what can be written in a shell script. On the other hand, the resulting code is the smallest and runs the fastest; depending on the needs of the project, this may be a worthwhile tradeoff.

You may notice that this code results in two instances of this code being in memory at the same time: as long as the application acquires the resources it needs to run in the `appEntryPoint()` function, the memory footprint of the parent process is small. Depending on the size of the application, the memory footprint of this is usually smaller than the prior example that uses a small program to run a second program. There is no rule of thumb; you must measure the image sizes and memory consumption for your application to decide what is best.

Set Ownership and Permissions

When you create a root file system, many files are copied into the `$ROOTFS` directory; and when they're copied there, they're created with the permissions of the user doing the `copy` command. In a production system, this isn't desirable. The ownership and group should be set to some well-known value or root. You can set the owner and groups for the files in the root file system en masse as follows:

```
$sudo chown -R root:root $ROOTFS
```

Some file systems don't store ownership information; instead, all files are owned by root by default. If your system requires more complex ownership information, you need to construct a script that that changes the permissions as necessary.

Setting permissions is a more complex operation; because this typically can't be done simultaneously like setting ownership, you must set permissions with a greater degree of control. For example, some files need to have the execute permission set for just the owner, whereas other files can be executed by any user on the system. The process of setting permissions on a group of files involves two steps:

First, get the files in the root file system with their current permissions. You can use the Linux `find` command to fetch this information. Try the following command (recall that `ROOTFS` is the directory containing the root file system for the target board):

```
$ find $ROOTFS -printf "%#m %p\n" > /tmp/fscontents
```

The contents of this file look like the following:

```
0777 ./project_build_arm/device/root/bin/pwd
0777 ./project_build_arm/device/root/bin/umount
0777 ./project_build_arm/device/root/bin/linux32
0777 ./project_build_arm/device/root/bin/cp
0777 ./project_build_arm/device/root/bin/tar
```

The first number on the line is the permissions mask written in octal, and the second is the name of the file. You can then edit this file to change the permissions to the acceptable value for the target.

Most users rely on the symbolic settings for permissions, but octal isn't that difficult to use when you get the hang of it. Each of the digits represents a three-bit number, where the lowest bit is execute (1 when set), the next is write (2 when set), and the highest is read (4 when set). Sum the set bits to calculate the value for that field.

The three digits from left to right represent the permissions of the owner, group, and other (that is, a user who is neither the owner nor a member of the group), respectively. If you want to set the file to read, write, and execute for the owner, read and write for the group, and only read for the other users, the permission mask is

```
(4+2+1)(4+2)(4) = 0764
```

The first sum (4+2+1) is the owner's permissions, with all the permission bits set. (4+2) is the group permissions, with the read and write bits are set (4 and 2, respectively). And the last is for other users, who can only read the file, so only the highest bit is set (2).

Next, you use the inventory you just created to customize the permission settings. When you're satisfied with the permissions, you can feed the file to chmod to set permissions in the following manner:

```
while readline p ; do
    chmod -v %p
done < /tmp/fscontents
```

The file can contain wildcards like this to make the script less brittle as new files are added or removed:

```
0777 ./project_build_arm/device/root/bin/*
```

The -v argument results in verbose output for the script, making debugging easier, in case you have an incorrect octal value or stray characters in the filename. The verbose flag also results in the script producing a record of how the permission were configured when the software was shipped; this information can be stored with the engineering documentation for the project and used for QA or technical support. Without the -v switch, the system produces no output on success, and there is only a record of what fails and not what succeeds.

Security

Linux has a wide range of choices for security, starting with the ones you're most familiar: user name and password required for login to the system, and permissions set on files that control what can be done based on your identity. For lack of a better term, call this the *default* security model. The default security model has flaws in that what can be controlled thereafter is fairly sparse: you can control what files can be executed, read, and written, but not what system functionality can be accessed. This means that a user who gains the rights to execute files on the system has free reign over what that executable can do; for example, it could open network ports and begin sending data, or install kernel modules that could crash the system. In order to have fine-grained access control, you need to use SELinux or PAM to control the system; these systems allow the administrator to control what resources can be accessed and which files can be read and written to.

The need for security is to some extent dictated by the device and the configuration of the kernel. A device, for example, without an Ethernet port or networking built into the kernel isn't susceptible to attacks across the network; therefore, spending effort to ensure that this isn't possible is wasteful. Before deciding on a security technology, understand the susceptibilities of the system and how it is used so you can formulate requirements in order to judge what security works best for the device.

All security mechanisms just described rely on the Linux Security Model (LSM) infrastructure, which is a generalized framework for handling security enforcement. The LSM doesn't make decisions about what to do but checks with software providing security policy information to see if the requested action is permissible.

Built-In Security

This is the standard Linux security, which is much like the standard Unix security from decades past: you're challenged for your password at login, and if you present the right one, you're allowed access to the system. Users can belong to a number of groups, with one group having the same name as the user.

Based on your group and user, you have the ability to read, write, create, or execute files. Files and directories are owned by a certain user; being owner gives you the ability modify the permissions for a file.

True to its name, the built-in security system is a part of Linux. There's nothing you have to do to get what's offered. Because it's built into Linux as the default security system, is doesn't add anything to the size of the system—and for those who are counting every byte, this matters. Using this system is as easy as creating additional entries in the /etc/groups and /etc/passwd files, assigning files to groups and owners using chown, and then setting permissions using chmod.

Just as with a desktop system, the regular user for running applications shouldn't be root; rather, you should create a user for running the application and make an entry in /etc/passwd for that user.

SELinux

SELinux is a project undertaken by the National Security Agency (NSA) to harden the Linux kernel; the changes were accepted into the Linux kernel early in the 2.6 release cycle. The patches, now incorporated as part of the Linux kernel project, involve controlling access to kernel resources like memory, the file system, networking, and external buses like PCMCIA and USB. By configuring access rights to these resources, the system administrator can grant specific rights to specific users to not only execute programs but also control what in the operating system those programs can do while running.

■ **Note** SELinux can only be used with a file system that supports extended attributes. Currently, these are JFFS2, YAFFS2, and ext2/3/4.

SELinux is a good security model for an embedded system that is offering services over a network or a system that is running a set of programs that may not be known when the device ships. Consider a device like a network switch or a cell phone: these devices leave the factory with a set of programs, and third parties can then write additional software that the user loads on the device. In this case, it's important to guard the system from programs that either accidentally or purposely compromise the system by accessing resources that belong to another process.

In order to get SELinux running on your board, you need to enable it in the kernel and have some user-space programs help with creating security profiles. To enable SELinux in the kernel, visit the Security page which you can see in Figure 15-1 inside the kernel configuration, and select the following options:

```
Enable different security models
NSA SELinux Support
```

.config - Linux Kernel v2.6.30.1 Configuration

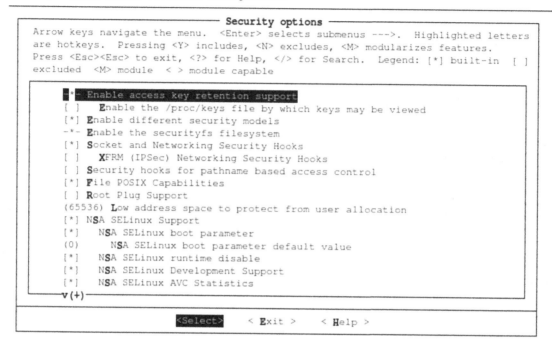

Figure 15-1. Configuring the kernel to use SELinux

When you configure SELinux, you have the opportunity to enable the ability to disable SELinux when booting the kernel. Production kernels don't have this feature (as you can obviously see the gaping security hole this opens); but during development, it's useful to have this feature available so you can disable SELinux without compiling the kernel. Do this by configuring these kernel options:

```
NSA SELinux boot parameter
NSA SELinux boot parameter default value, set to 0 to disable, 1 to enable
NSA SELinux runtime disable
```

The kernel now has the infrastructure to process SELinux security checks. You need to define access rules to allow a user or process access to kernel resources; this is called a *policy*, and creating your own is time consuming and error prone. There are two basic approaches to getting policy information:

- Use reference policies.

- Use the SEEdit tool to create policies.

Each is explained in the following sections. Both approaches have merits and drawbacks.

Reference Policies

You can obtain reference policies from the Tresys Reference Policy project at
http://oss.tresys.com/projects/refpolicy. Policy information is stored in files that you later
compile. To get the policy source files, download this Git tree:

```
$ git clone http://oss.tresys.com/git/refpolicy.git
```

This company is the maintainer of the policy information that is used in Linux distributions. In the
policy/modules folder, you find directories for each of the major policy areas of SELinux. These can be
edited to meet the needs of the target system and the programs being run on that system. For example, if
the target doesn't have a physical network device and the kernel doesn't include a TCP/IP stack, the
security policies for networking aren't useful. You can then copy the security policy information to the
/etc/selinux directory on the target machine. Using this command updates the initial file attributes:

```
(target) # load_policy
```

Using SEEdit

SEEdit is a group of tools and starting-point security policies created for embedded Linux targets by
Hitachi, LTD. The goal of this project is to have a simple set of policies that are both small in size and
appropriate for embedded systems and that can be installed with ease. The tool also includes a GUI-
based policy editor that insulates you from some of the complexities of editing SELinux policies. As part
of this project, a set of SELinux commands have been added to BusyBox: load_policy, setfiles,
restorecon, and is_selinux_enabled. This means you don't have to cross-compile the larger SELinux
commands for the target. When you're configuring BusyBox on a system that is using SELinux, you need
to enable Support NSA Security Enhanced Linux under the General Configuration menu in the BusyBox
configuration menu. After you do so, SELinux Utilities appears on the top-level menu, and you can select
the BusyBox builds of these commands.

■ **Note** For more information regarding the Simplified Policy Description Language (SPDL) used by the SEEdit
project, visit http://seedit.sourceforge.net/doc/2.1/spdl_spec. SPDL is simpler because it reduces
access control specifiers to just a filename and allowed ports.

The project is hosted at http://seedit.sourceforge.net/. Follow this link to get the newest
version of the software. In order to compile the code, you need to have SELinux installed on your host
computer. This is necessary because the make files for the project reference some headers on the host
machine to create the GUI tool. This tool is located in the GUI directory, where you can also find the
source tarball. Install it by typing

```
$ sudo make install
$ ./seedit-gui
```

The GUI presents you with entry points for editing policy information, which you can then compile into policy data for the target computer. To do this, unpack the SEEdit tools and do the following from the project's root directory:

```
$ cd core
$ make
 ;  make cross-install DESTDIR=/your-project/selinux
$ cd ..
/policy
$ make cross-install DESTDIR=/your-project/selinux
```

This creates the basic skeleton of SELinux files at /your-project/selinux. From this directory, use the ./seedit-load command to compile the files into something usable for the target:

```
$ seedit-load -cd
```

This command prepares the policy files and produces the output in the policy_root directory. You can place these files in the /etc/selinux/seedit directory of the target machine. At this point, you need to switch to the target machine and do the following so SELinux can use the policy and context information on the root file system of the target:

```
(target) # load_policy ; restorecon -R
```

It takes a few minutes to initialize the additional file attributes on the root file system. These extended attributes must be modified on the target; there isn't a way to set extended attributes when you're creating a root file system.

PAM

Pluggable Authentication Modules (PAM) is an access-control system that provides an authentication system. This means PAM provides the tools to verify the identity of the user making the request for resources; it then lets the program decide what powers to grant the user based on that information. This is very different from SELinux, even though SELinux performs the job of authentication like PAM. SELinux also contains the rules for what resources the user can access, which is unlike the way PAM modules do their job.

The *Pluggable* part of PAM come from the configuration files that PAM uses to decide what code to use in order to satisfy an authentication request. This data can be stored in a /etc/pam.conf file, with the following format:

```
service type    control      module          arguments
```

Here's an example line:

```
sftp    auth    required      pam_module.so
```

The following explains each of the columns in this file:

- *Service:* This is the name of the program that is requesting the authentication services. If you wrote a special application that required PAM services, the value for service would be `special-app`. The service name `other` is reserved to mean the default method to be used if no other service matches. A system can have a set of PAM rules for only the `other` service, which means those rules are the default for all services.

- *Type:* This is the type of PAM service for the module. Valid values for this field are as follows:

    `auth`: What action to perform for authentication. Usually, this provides a username and then a password.

    `account`: Checks to see if the user's account is valid and whether they have access to the service after they're authenticated.

    `password`: The mechanism to update the password for the account.

    `session`: Actions to perform after the user has been authenticated. Actions may include logging operations or making resources available to the user so the service can operate properly.

- *Control:* This specifies how PAM searches for a module that can provide authentication information. A service can have several different modules offering authentication services; it also tells PAM how to search those modules for information and when to stop searching. Valid values for this field are as follows:

    `required`: This module must agree that the credentials are valid; other modules can still be used to further validate the user information.

    `sufficient`: This module checks the credentials, and PAM authenticates the user, even if some other sufficient control rejected the user information. Use this if there are several possible services and only one needs to be available for authentication to be successful.

    `requisite`: This module must agree with the user's credentials. Failure means no further checks occur.

- *Module:* This is the name of the module that performs the validation. This is a shared object file that is available in the system's `/lib` directory.

- *Arguments:* These are arguments passed to the module. The valid values for this field are module specific.

On a desktop system, the directory `pam.d` contains a file for each of the PAM modules. This is an acceptable configuration for an embedded system, but it requires a little more space. Putting all the PAM information for an embedded system in one file isn't as flexible but does save a little space. Most embedded systems aren't as complex as a desktop system, so the additional administrative overhead of managing more than one file isn't worth the marginal gain in flexibility.

The configuration files specify some number of PAM modules, so those modules must be cross-compiled for your target machine. To get sources for these modules, download the PAM sources, stored at `ftp://ftp.kernel.org/pub/linux/libs/pam/library/`. In this directory is a file named `LATEST_IS_<filename>` with the name of the file in the directory to download. For this example, download this file:

```
$ wget ftp://ftp.kernel.org/pub/linux/libs/pam/library/Linux-PAM-1.0.4.tar.gz
```

```
$ tar xzf Linux-PAM-1.1.0.tar.gz
```

This project uses a standard configuration script to cross-compile the code, so do the following:

```
$ CC=arm-linux-gcc ./configure --host=arm-linux \
        --prefix=$ROOTFS
$ make ; make install
```

The process puts a complete installation of PAM in your root file system, which may be more than is necessary for the embedded device. You need to remove the modules not used in your PAM configuration file; for example, unused PAM modules in the /lib/security directory can be removed, and the remainder can be stripped to further reduce space requirements. In addition to the extra library files, a standard PAM installation includes a group of files installed under etc/security that you can remove if you aren't using PAM's access-control features.

One thing that may sneak past you as you're configuring this program is that it attempts to compile the program even if it can't find a symbol it needs: yywrap, which is part of the flex tokenizer package. PAM uses Flex to parse the configuration files that it uses. You need to cross-compile Flex for your toolchain if the compilation fails with a message that yywrap can't be found. You can download and build Flex by doing the following:

```
$ wget http://prdownloads.sourceforge.net/flex/flex-2.5.35.tar.gz?download
$ tar xzf  flex-2.5.35.tar.gz
$ CC=arm-linux-gcc ./configure -host=arm-linux -prefix=/path/to/sysroot
```

/path/to/sysroot is the sysroot path of your toolchain. These files can be installed in any directory on your development machine, as long as the linker is able to find them. You shouldn't install these files in the root file system of the target device, because they're only used to build the PAM libraries and helpers.

After it's built and installed, the software on the target device can begin using PAM for authentication. For example, if the device is running Samba, then Samba needs entries in the pam.conf file if you want to use something different than the "other" configuration. Samba also needs to be configured with the right settings so it knows to use PAM for authentication. When you're working on the project, you need to ensure that each of the services you expect to use PAM is properly configured, because this is a package-specific setting.

What's Next

The next chapter digs into system tuning, meaning all things necessary to make a system smaller and boot faster. For an embedded device, RAM and storage are fixed; for some projects, there is great pressure to reduce the amount of both used in a project. Tuning also means making a system boot faster, or at least appear to boot faster, by reducing the things that happen during boot and producing output so the user feels like the system is booting faster. This is one of the most fun, addictive parts of embedded systems work, because shaving a few bytes from the system size and making the system boot just a little faster produces its own positive feedback loop that is difficult to escape.

■■■

## CHAPTER 16

System Tuning

Small is a relative term. Embedded systems seem to divide into three groups: those with just a few megabytes of storage, those with around 16–32MB, and those with a hard drive with gigabytes of storage. This chapter is aimed squarely at the first two groups, because as soon as your system contains a storage medium over a few hundred megabytes, there is no real need to economize on the size of the system— on such a this system, a desktop Linux distribution fits comfortably. However, you may be interested in decreasing the amount of time required to get the system up and running, so don't flip past this chapter quite yet.

There three possible things that you can reduce in a Linux system with respect to size: the kernel, the root file system, and the application itself. Although the application is technically part of the root file system (well, mostly, unless drivers are involved), it's a separate part of the system from a logical standpoint. As the developer of the application, you have much more control over the code than you would have over an open source project. Not that you cann't make any changes necessary in an open source project—it's just that learning a different code base to be able to reduce the size may not be feasible in the time budgeted for the application.

The size of the system as it resides in storage is a different matter from the size of the application while running. Code that is small in terms of number of instructions may be larger when running. Writing code that is efficient with respect to the amount of memory it uses during runtime is a classic software engineering size-versus-speed tradeoff, because the increased size represents information that is cached in memory rather than being calculated when necessary.

This chapter looks at ways you can reduce the size and runtime memory requirements of your application. You also examine some tools you can use to see where in the system you should be focusing your efforts. Although every system has resource constraints, in the embedded world those constraints are more a part of everyday programming than in other software engineering fields. Before getting started, it helps to understand roughly where you fit into the spectrum of being resource constrained, because that colors your entire system-tuning approach.

Three or Fewer Megabytes

Systems that fit into this category have application requirements just above a microcontroller. This device may attach to a network but uses something low-powered like ZigBee and a partial IP networking stack. Another characteristic of these devices is that they're generally battery powered, and therefore contain a processor with a low clock rate.

■ **Note** A *microcontroller* is a simple microprocessor with some peripherals like timers, serial connections, GPIO lines, and maybe a few analog-to-digital converters. The microprocessor operates in the tens of kilohertz range, and the available memory is just a few thousand kilobytes. Microcontrollers are designed to consume very little power when operating and can be put into sleep modes where the power draw is less than a milliwatt.

The user interface for this device is probably a few LEDS or a small LCD readout. In terms of input, the user interface may consist of a few buttons in addition to an on/off switch. Because of the low-resource nature of these systems, creating a small distribution is easier than you may think: eliminate all file systems, networking, and input devices, and the kernel shrinks dramatically. The resource constraints of this device demand that any and all non-essential code be removed.

The same applies for the root file system in this situation. The simplicity of this device means the application running on the board isn't complex either. Most likely the board has one and only one program that it runs on boot and should relaunch if it fails.

Because the device forces simplicity and economy on you, you don't have the temptation to do much more than the minimum—and that rescues you from attempting anything other than getting the application running.

16–32 Megabytes

This is a dangerous amount of memory. It's enough that the device does more sophisticated tasks like running a small, full-color LCD, equipped with a touch screen, and there is probably some networking or voice processing. The device may also have a keyboard (like the mini keyboards kids have on their phones today) and a mouse-like device. Many consumer devices fall into this range, resulting in pressure to both reduce per-unit costs and offer more features for the end user. Making the problem a little more complex, the devices are frequently battery powered, so the processor must operate at a low clock rate to conserve battery resources. Because the expectations are so high, cramming all the required functionality onto the device while leaving enough memory for the application is a difficult challenge.

Another set of devices that fit into this category are DVRs and inexpensive routers/gateways for residential use. DVRs have a very nice user interface through a remote control and television screen, whereas your home router may be *headless* (that is, it has no monitor) and use a small web server for the user interface along with some LEDs and a switch or two.

When you're optimizing these sorts of devices, the goal is to make the application as small as possible and get the device ready to use quickly after power-on. The key is making sure the kernel has only what it needs, reordering startup to get the application running faster, and measuring to identify trouble spots.

It's worth mentioning that the bottom range for this amount of memory is 16MB because that's a commonly available memory part and less memory is frequently more expensive than a single 16MB part. During the design of your system, you may be surprised that due to ingenuous economical and electrical engineering, you have more resources than you anticipate.

More than a Gigabyte

This type of device has a hard drive: it's either a traditional device with platters and a spindle or a solid-state drive with some hardware (likely a microcontroller) serving as a flash translation layer, so the device appears like a traditional drive. No matter the hardware configuration, there is so much storage on the device that effort spent on reducing the size of the operating system won't result in an appreciable increase in the proportion of free storage space.

If you have this sort of device, you may be unconcerned about memory used by the operating system and application, but you may have a great deal of interest in decreasing the device's boot time. For example, if the device is a vending machine plugged into a wall, the size of the hard drive doesn't concern you; however, the time in which that machine can start and begin selling products is very important. The same concept applies to a retail kiosk or self-service retail POS system.

Just like the 16–32MB devices, many embedded devices in this category have the amount of resources they do because it's cheaper to get the larger memory parts or source a complete board with this amount of memory. This is another case where the electrical engineering may result in more resources than you expect.

Reducing the Size of the Root File System

This is the best place to start optimization because it has the greatest potential for wasted space. Starting from zero also forces you to think through the addition of each new component and understand why you're adding it to the system. In the starting-from-zero approach, you also see that what was once done as a shell script becomes part of the application, to avoid the overhead of the shell executable and script.

Start from Zero

This book includes references to several different distribution building tools like OpenEmbedded and Buildroot. These are great tools for creating a Linux distribution, but they don't create a *minimal* Linux distribution. The best way to make a small distribution is to start with nothing and work upward from zero rather than try to whittle down an existing root file system and hope nothing breaks. You can create the minimal contents for a root file system by doing the following:

```
$ mkdir ~/minimal-rfs; cd minimal-rfs
$ mkdir ./proc ./tmp ./dev
$ sudo mknod ./dev/console c 5 1
$ sudo mknod ./dev/null c 1 3
```

The application resides in the root of the file system and must continue running or the system will halt, because at least one process must kept running in a Linux system. This root file system can be built as an initramFS and therefore assembled with the kernel and included in the kernel image file deployed on the device.

The application is placed in the root directory of the target machine and is statically linked, so it doesn't require any additional files. This root file system adds about 3KB on top of the application, meaning the flash drive of a few megabytes looks like a huge amount of space by comparison. Applications operating at this level are usually quite simple; they may read a value from a measurement or wait for the user to scan a bar code and perform a query. Whatever the application, it's small enough that is can easily fit into the remaining few MB of space in flash.

When you use this approach, the kernel's init= parameter must be set to the application or the application must be named linuxrc so that it's run when the system starts; remember, the init program can be anything the kernel can execute This system is so small, in fact, that as a side effect it also boots very quickly, assuming the application code is reasonably efficient. As a rule, systems that have been built up from zero boot quickly because the drive to be small reduces the system to the essentials, jettisoning even a shell for scripting.

This minimal file system usually prompts people to say things like, "I thought I needed...." Table 16-1 clears up many of those questions and explains why a certain component is missing.

Table 16-1. Minimum Requirements for a Root Filesystem

I Thought I Needed...	Why You Don't
Some way to log in.	A login isn't necessary. When Linux runs init, it executes as user id 0, group id 0, which is conveniently the root user who has all system privileges. You only need a login for development or as a back door for maintenance.
/etc/passwd and /etc/groups.	There's never a login, so the user name and group are empty strings.
A shell, like sh or bash.	There's no shell scripting, so there's no need for a shell.
A special program like init to boot the system. Same with the /etc/init.d directory.	The init program can be anything that is an executable. In the case of a small system, the initialization program is the only program that ever runs, so it becomes init.
Something in /lib.	As long as the application is statically linked, no libraries need to be copied onto the target.
Scripts to initialize the network.	The network can be configured during the kernel boot with a static address or can request one from a BOOTP/DHCP server. Configuration can also be done in the application and not through a shell script.
Kernel modules.	On the smallest of computers, the kernel has all modules compiled directly into itself, meaning there's no need for the modules or the scripts that load them.
The contents of /dev.	Most of the devices in this directory are created as a result of running udev, which scans the /sys file system to create device nodes as needed. All device nodes for this system are created manually.
/var/log/messages.	This file is created by a kernel logger program that reads an area of shared memory and deposits the data in this file. Without this logging function running, the logging data remains in shared memory, and the oldest data is overwritten when the area is filled.

Mounting Small File Systems

There's one additional twist to account for when you're mounting such a small file system stored on a flash drive: The device doesn't have the additional file nodes for the MTD block device. In fact, creating that file wastes a few bytes of memory, and you're doing your best to conserve. When you mounted a root file system in the past, you used the symbolic name for the device:

```
root=/dev/mtdblock3
```

However, because you don't want a byte to go to waste, the device can be mounted using its major and minor number. These are the numeric identifiers that the kernel uses to decide what driver to use for the device. In this case, the identifier for the device looks like the following

```
root=6703
```

where the first two integers are the major and minor device numbers for /dev/mtdblock3 in hex. The easiest way to discover these values is to use ls -l on the board to print them out:

```
$ ls -l /dev/mtdblock3
crw------- 1 root    root        90,  3 2009-10-02 07:41 console
```

For this device, the identifier is 5A03, because 5A is the hex value of 90 and 03 is the hex value for 3; a zero pads the field so the value can be parsed correctly. Putting it all together, you have the following as the root device on your kernel command-line:

```
root=5A03
```

If your target board includes a dev directory full of data, these items are being created by a helper program that's part of the udev project and that has code to scan your system and then create corresponding entries in the /dev directory. In a simple production system, dynamic device-node creation is pure overhead because the result is always the same—there is no way to change the hardware. Symbolic names are also overhead, because the device is always mounted by the kernel at startup; the lack of a shell means you can't readily log in.

Shared Libraries

More complex applications use shared libraries, which means they must be collected from the toolchain and then placed in the target machine's root file system. Shared libraries require a loader in order to work, as discussed in prior chapters; the loader performs a dynamic linking step for a program before it's run. Shared library loaders are small, are statically linked, and must reside at the location specified in the executable. Finding out the name of the loader is as simple as using strings on the program:

```
$ strings <your program> | grep ld
```

You're looking for a file called /lib/ld-linux.so.X or /lib/ld-uClibc.so.X, where X is a version number. This file must be located on the target file system at the same path contained in the executable file—there's no way to relocate this file.

You can also get the shared libraries used by an executable through brute force with strings. In this example, <your program> is fc-list, a font-management program. The program you use will produce different results based on the libraries it uses:

```
$ strings <your program> | grep "lib*"
/lib/ld-uClibc.so.0
libfontconfig.so.1
libiconv.so.2
libfreetype.so.6
libz.so.1
libexpat.so.1
```

But for these files, the readelf program packaged with your toolchain can do this more elegantly. Searching for random strings in the file can produce false positives. Here's what readelf reports for the same file as the prior example:

```
$ arm-linux-readelf -d <your program>  | grep NEEDED
 0x00000001 (NEEDED)                      Shared library: [libfontconfig.so.1]
 0x00000001 (NEEDED)                      Shared library: [libiconv.so.2]
 0x00000001 (NEEDED)                      Shared library: [libfreetype.so.6]
 0x00000001 (NEEDED)                      Shared library: [libz.so.1]
 0x00000001 (NEEDED)                      Shared library: [libexpat.so.1]
 0x00000001 (NEEDED)                      Shared library: [libc.so.0]
```

This command parses the elf header of the program; the -d parameter tells the program to only print the dynamic information, and the grep command shows the entries for shared libraries in this section. Performing this action for all of the executables will get you a list of the files you need to include in the target root file system.

When you have this list and you're gathering the files from the toolchain, notice that each shared library has one file and several symlinks that point to that file. This exists so that the system can accommodate several different versions of the same shared library. For example:

```
$ ls -l $ROOTFS/lib/libc*
-rw-r--r-- 1 gene gene 13043 2009-06-30 20:57 libcrypt-0.9.30.1.so
lrwxrwxrwx 1 gene gene    20 2009-06-30 23:57 libcrypt.so.0 -> libcrypt-0.9.30.1.so
lrwxrwxrwx 1 gene gene    21 2009-06-30 23:57 libc.so.0 -> libuClibc-0.9.30.1.so
```

Notice that the shared library libc.so.0 is a symlink to libuClibc-0.9.30.1.so. Although it's just a few bytes on the file system, that symlink is wasted space because on many systems, the root file system won't change. Nor do you need to worry about versioning something as critical as the C library. If the change is that far reaching, the entire root file system is replaced; and it's likely that would happen on a new device, leaving the devices in the field running the older software .With that in mind, you can copy the library to the root file system and rename it libc.so.0 as a way to economize on space. The savings may appear small; but most embedded systems have more than a few libraries, so the savings sum to something substantial.

Compiling to Save Space

GCC has a few tricks to reduce the amount of object code produced for a given amount of source code. The most common and frequently most successful approach uses the -Os switch, which compiles code to produce the smallest image size. Other approaches remove sections of comments, debugging, or other data stored in the binary that isn't necessary for program execution.

All these approaches should be used in conjunction with carefully coding your application so it does what's necessary and nothing more. If you routinely work in embedded systems, this is a reflexive action; but if you're new to the craft, keeping in mind how much memory will be consumed by taking one approach over another is something new and often forgotten. Stepping off the soapbox, let's look at the most successful ways you can reduce the size of your code when you're reasonably sure it's not bloated due to non-embedded coding habits.[1]

GCCs -Os

Compiling programs with the -Os parameter in GCC results in the compiler generating the smallest code possible. Using this option is as easy as doing the following:

```
$ arm-linux-gcc -Os <program>
```

Smaller code doesn't always mean faster code, so this switch may not be the right choice for all programs on the system. The exact optimizations that occur depend on the target architecture; but as a general rule, -Os is the same as -O2 without these optimizations, because they increase the code size:

```
-falign-functions
-falign-jumps
-falign-loops
-falign-labels
-freorder-blocks
-freorder-blocks-and-partition
-fprefetch-loop-arrays
-ftree-vect-loop-version
```

All the flags that start with falign move code so that it starts on a new page, which makes the addresses faster to fetch from memory. The freorder functions shifts generated code around to reduce the number of branches the CPU performs. The last two options optimize loops by caching data before the loop executes to reduce the time spent waiting for instructions or data to be fetched from memory.

■ **Note** The GCC size optimizations decrease the code size, but not by a substantial amount. Don't count on this to magically reduce the size of your program.

Static Linking

Static linking as a way to reduce code works by including all the code in the application's binary image during the linking process. A program that is statically linked is larger than a program that uses shared libraries; however, the smaller program needs the much larger shared library (and the shared library

---

[1] True story: while working on a project that needed to fit on a very small device, I found that the project contained a library with wrapper functions for fprintf(stderr,...) to control error reporting and logging, on a device with no networking, serial, or other way of ever reading this data. All told, these functions and calls to them consumed well over 100KB, or about a fifth of the program's size. With some #define hackery, they were removed for production builds, thus reclaiming sorely needed memory.

loader) to be present on the system as well. Creating a statically linked application is as easy as adding the -static flag during the linking process:

```
$ arm-linux-ld -static -l corefunctions file1.o file2.o -o app
```

If you're linking GCJ-generated object files, you need to add -static-libgcj as well:

```
$ arm-linux-ld -static -static-libgcj -main=Class1 Class1.o Class2.o -o app
```

During the linking process for the first example, the functions used by file1 and file2 are gathered from corefunctions and the C library (which is linked by default) and copied into app. However, the final size of the program has much to do with the structure of the object files used in the linking. Consider the library corefunctions, which is stored on the file system as libcorefunctions.a. The library file libcorefunctions.a is created by grouping a collection of .o files using the ar command, and the .o file is the smallest unit that the linker knows how to handle.

For instance, suppose libcorefunctions contains the following:

```
core1.o
        functiona()
        functionb()
core2.o
        functionx()
        functiony()
        functionz()
```

If file1.o calls functiona() and file2.o calls functionz(), all of core1.o and core2.o is included in the final image, resulting in the program containing a large amount of dead code: that is, functionx, functiony, and functionb. The result is that the statically linked program has the same footprint on the root file system as if libcorefunctions was a shared library; minus the shared library loader, which consumes some additional space as well. To avoid this problem, put each function inside of its own .o file; that way, the linker can create the smallest executable file possible. To get a view of how a library is structured, use the ar command included with your toolchain. This output is from the BusyBox static library:

```
$ arm-linux-ar t ./busybox-1.14.2/libbb/libxfuncs.o
(clipped)
xreadlink.o
xrealloc_vector.o
xregcomp.o
```

■ **Note** The .o file is the smallest unit for linking in C/C++. If any symbol is required in the .o file, the entire contents of the file are included in the executable. So, if the .o file contains functions that are unused, the target system has dead code that will never be executed but still consumes memory. If you're using static linking to conserve memory, be sure to structure your code so that each .o file contains one function, giving the linker the greatest opportunity to create the smallest program.

This has been wisely structured so that just about every function is in its own .o file, giving the linker the best opportunity to produce a small executable. Some of the functions in the library may call each other; but because each function is contained in its own .o file, the linker includes the minimum amount of code. Because the output is large enough to scroll away, use the wc command to get a count of the object files in the archive:

```
$ arm-linux-ar t ./busybox-1.14.2/libbb/libxfuncs.o | wc -l
115
```

If you find that your project looks more like the libcorefunctions example, dividing the code into smaller pieces is a fairly mechanical process, unless variables are shared by several functions in a single file. Although this isn't in the best form, it's a common practice that makes separating functions into their own files more work. If this is the case, create a file that contains the shared variable with a get and set function, and then replace the direct references with calls to the function.

Stripping

ELF formatted binaries include metadata primarily used for debugging. When deployed on a target system, this data is of no use and therefore is a waste of space that could be used for other purposes. To remove this data, use the strip utility included with your toolchain. Running strip replaces the current file with one that doesn't have debugging information:

```
$ arm-linux-strip <file>
```

This replaces <file> with a file that is smaller due to the removed sections. strip works with a wildcard as an argument if you want to update many files at once. You can use strip in conjunction with find to check all files in a root file system:

```
$ find <rfs root> -type f -exec arm-linux-strip {};\
```

This command starts at <rfs root> and runs the strip command for all the files it locates. The strip command checks whether the file is an ELF-formatted executable before attempting to change the file, so there's no need to structure the find command to locate files of the appropriate type.

Reducing the Size of the Kernel

The kernel isn't that much different from a regular executable file. The first step to reducing its size is finding code that will never be executed and remove it. However, unlike regular programs, the kernel comes equipped with a great tool for picking and choosing code that goes into the build: the configuration editor. The kernel's configuration editor lets you remove large chunks of code by quickly and easily disabling features or removing support for hardware that isn't in the project. This work is divided into two basic parts: removing drivers that aren't used, and removing kernel features. Let's look at drivers first, because that's where you can get the greatest reduction very quickly.

Removing Unneeded Features and Drivers

There isn't a magic way for you to know what to remove in terms of drivers; it's a matter of removing from the kernel drivers that support hardware that isn't on your target board. The best approach is to make a list of the hardware on the device and then remove support for peripherals that aren't present. Because most embedded devices have a fixed inventory of devices, you can safely remove the drivers for components that aren't on the board or will never be used, because that code will never be run.

The question is: what can be removed? The kernel has no "make this smaller" utility; instead, you must understand what your system needs in terms of drivers and functionality and then remove what's unneeded. The configuration files for the kernel keep track of what components rely on the one selected, so if the component you want to remove is required by something else, you can't remove it until its dependencies are removed.

Here are some general guidelines to help you figure out what to remove from the kernel:

- *File systems:* Your system will only use a few file systems, but the kernel build you have probably includes several unused file system drivers. For example, a device that uses a flash file system likely doesn't need the ext2 or ext3 file system (it may if the device has a USB interface or some other interface for external storage; the point is that you need to understand your application before removing things from the kernel), and these are often included in the kernel by default. Any file system that's not being used now or in the future can be removed. The NFS file system is a particularly large item, taking several hundred KB of memory and about twice that during runtime. A convenience while debugging, the NFS file system on a device not connected to the network is a waste of resources.

- *Hardware drivers:* Hardware that won't be used shouldn't have a corresponding driver built into the kernel. Many systems-on-chip (SOCs) have Wi-Fi drivers, video, serial, and other hardware interfaces that will never be used and therefore have no need for a driver. In fact, drivers for unused hardware leave a security risk open on the device.

- *Input and output:* Although this seems like the hardware drivers already mentioned, it's a little different in that the kernel has special drivers for using the mouse and VGA console. On devices that contain a serial port or use a graphics driver on the frame buffer, a console on the same device as the UI wastes memory and resources. Likewise, keyboard support for a device with only a touchscreen is also wasted memory.

- *Debugging and profiling:* Under the Kernel Hacking entry on the main menu are many options designed for those doing kernel debugging. In a production system, all options under this menu entry can be disabled.

- *Networking:* A device without networking hardware that doesn't also use networking for interprocess communication, so you can remove the networking stack. The networking stack contributes about 200KB to the Linux kernel. Before removing this feature, check that the programs aren't using TCP connections to localhost or 127.0.0.1 as a way to communicate between processes. Using TCP as a way to transport data between processes is common, even if the device doesn't have a physical network adapter, because the localhost device is a logical network adapter that doesn't have a physical termination point.

■ **Note** The kernel doesn't necessarily need a physical networking adapter in order to use networking. The TCP/IP stack included with the Linux kernel can be, and frequently is, used without a physical network device; in this case, the loopback device (address 127.0.0.1) is used as a tool for interprocess communication.

Recommendations for Embedded Systems

The kernel configuration program now has a menu that aggregates the most common items embedded engineers change when configuring the kernel. Go to the General Setup menu , and look for "Configure standard kernel features (for small systems)." Enabling this option results in the following items becoming visible under this menu:

- *Enable 16-bit UID system calls:* This is for compatibility with older programs that used system calls where the UID was a single byte. Generally, these programs were created when the 2.4 kernel was current; it used an older glibc version. Because you control what is running on the OS and you're likely using newer software, this compatibility option can be disabled, saving a marginal amount of memory.

- *Sysctl syscall support:* When the sys file system was first introduced, early in the 2.6 release cycle, some of the paths used numbers and not strings to represent their corresponding kernel object. The string method of accessing data in the sys file system is now the default; unless you know you're using the older style, this can be dropped to save a few kilobytes.

- *Load all symbols for debugging/ksymoops:* When the kernel dies due to panic, the output contains the names of the functions in the call stack before the crash. Unselecting this item removes the symbolic information from the crash dumps. If your embedded system doesn't have a good way to view crash-dump information, the extra data this produces is wasted. Unselecting this option yields a substantial drop in size—over 200KB—because this information is the text for all of the kernel's function call names.

- *Support for hot-pluggable devices:* This code supports the dynamic assignment of USB device nodes when a new hardware device appears on the USB wire. If your device doesn't have USB, this code isn't necessary; if your device does have USB and you're supporting a known subset of items, and therefore have created the /dev entries for the devices, you can also disable this feature.

- *Enable support for printk:* Printk is the kernel equivalent of printf. Many drivers and kernel modules use it as a way of reporting the state, errors, and other information. This is the data that eventually makes its way into /var/log/messages. Disabling this results in printk turning into a macro that basically does nothing. This is a great way to reduce the size of the kernel, but at the expense of losing valuable diagnostic data that makes diagnosing problems much easier. However, if your device has no user interface but an LED or two and no way to store printk data, removing printk is a perfectly sensible thing to do. If you're working with a device that has some storage and a way to access it, consider disabling this only for the final production build.

- *BUG() support:* The BUG() macro is the kernel equivalent to assert. For most embedded systems, this can be removed, because the opportunity to act on this information is limited.

- *Enable ELF core dumps:* When a process dies, it can produce a dump of its memory state, or what's called a *core dump*. If your system doesn't have the room to store this file or you can't easily get it from the device, disabling this item saves a few kilobytes.

- *Enable full-sized data structures for core:* Unselecting this item reduces memory usage at runtime by reducing in the kernel various data structures and buffers, including the number of lines kept in the console rollback buffer and the maximum process ID (PID). These reductions help control the amount of RAM Linux needs while running.

- *Enable futex support:* Removing this option drops support for Fast User Space Mutexes. These are the building blocks for much of the POSIX interthread communication. Although this saves a few KB, most applications depend on this code being present, so removing it isn't recommended.

- *Enable eventpoll support:* The event-poll set of functions provide a superset of poll() functions. Most programs don't use this functionality, and it can be dropped from the kernel.

- *Enable signalfd() system call:* This system call allows you to create a file descriptor that receives signals sent to the program, instead of registering a signal handler. You should leave this enabled unless you know it isn't used on your system, because this new feature is quickly becoming a common way for a program to handle signals.

- *Enable timerfd() system call:* Like the signalfd, this is functionality that wraps timer events in file-based semantics. It doesn't require much space and should be left enabled.

- *Enable eventfd() system call:* An eventfd is a low-resource notification system that works something like a semaphore. It's an IPC call that notifies another process that an event has occurred; it can be used to replace a pipe that passes one character (or other token) to notify the listening process of a state change. This is a very low resource feature that you should leave enabled unless you know for certain it isn't being used.

- *Use full shmem filesystem:* Disabling this code replaces the internal file system used to manage memory resources with a much less complex RAM-based solution. If you have an embedded systems without swap memory, unselect this item and enjoy the extra few kilobytes of memory.

- *Enable AIO support:* Asynchronous I/O (AIO) means input/output requests are scheduled by the kernel, and the caller doesn't wait for an I/O operation to complete before it gets control back. Having control over I/O is helpful for embedded systems, because the kernel has fewer places where the system can become blocked waiting for an IO device; otherwise, it can be disabled.

Measuring

For each directory in the kernel build, each file is compiled into a .o file that is then linked together with the other .o files in the directory into a built-in.o file. The subdirectories' built-in.o files are gathered together into a smaller number of built-in.o files that the kernel build process then links into the final kernel image, along with some other supporting code to get the kernel booting and the contents of the initramfs (remember, even if you never include an initramfs, the kernel still creates a small empty one that consumes a few bytes). This makes getting a measurement of what components are taking the most code space a matter of scanning the kernel directory and looking at the size of the built-in.o files. Here's a simple one-line command that accomplishes that task on a directory that contains a kernel that has been compiled:

```
$ cd <kernel source directory>
$ find . -name built-in.o -type f | xargs arm-linux-size
```

This produces output that looks similar to this (your system will have different numbers because it was built with a different compiler with different options; a match is unlikely):

```
text    data    bss     dec     hex     filename
512     0       0       512     200     ./usr/built-in.o
6862    1796    1184    71603   117b3   ./block/built-in.o
13223   7028    368     20619   508b    ./kernel/irq/built-in.o
241851  16196   86472   344519  541c7   ./kernel/built-in.o
3260    72      24      3356    d1c     ./kernel/power/built-in.o
(many lines clipped)
```

The command looks for all the built-in.o files and then uses the size utility to print out the sizes of the different sections. You may notice that the sum of all built-in.o files is far greater than the size of the final kernel image. This is a result of the built-on.o files of parent directories containing built-in.o files of their subdirectories. To find out the size of the final kernel image, use the following command from the top of the kernel directory after building:

```
$ arm-linux-size vmlinux
text       data       bss        dec        hex        filename
5255980    224768     177412     5658160    565630     vmlinux
```

■ **Note** The whole is the sum of its parts. Knowing the size of each built-in.o file is important because that makes it clear when you need to economize as you're reducing the size of the kernel. When all the built-in.o files are combined into the kernel image, finding the low-hanging fruit with respect to reducing the memory footprint of the kernel is much more difficult.

Because the output from the size command is a little cryptic, the following explains what each column means:

- text: This section is the code of your program or object file. No string constants are stored in this section, despite a name that leads you to believe the contrary.

- data: This section contains variables that are initialized to a constant value.

- bss: This section contains global variables that are initially set to zero. BSS means Block Started by Symbol and refers to file layout from the days of yore.

- dec / hex: These two columns have the sum of text, data, and bss, displayed in decimal and hex formats.

The following code snippet shows all these parts in context so you can get a better understanding of what goes where:

```
// this string would be in the data section
char g_text[] = "message: %s -> %s";

// space for this variable would be in the bss section
static long g_lastsize;

// this code would appear in the text section
void print_message(char* str, char* str2) {
        g_lastsize = strlen(str);
        printf(g_text, str, str2);
}
```

A few items in the list are the core of the operating system; they serve as the infrastructure for the rest of the kernel. The size of these elements can't be changed much by twiddling with the kernel build parameters:

- arch/<your arch>/<directory>/built-in.o: These directories are specific to your board and processor and contain the enabling code the rest of the kernel needs to do things like handle interrupts and manage memory. Most of this code is in assembler and is very low level, even for an operating system.

- drivers/base/built-in.o: This file contains the infrastructure code used by the rest of the drivers handled by the kernel. Even if you have a few drivers loaded, this code is required.

- init/built-in.o: This is the initialization code for the kernel, or the equivalent of the main() function in a C program. Much of the code here concerns itself with gathering the parameters from the user at boot time and initializing the system.

- kernel/built-in.o: This is the core of the operating system. The scheduler, interrupt handling, process, and thread handling all happen here. You can do some things to reduce this part of the kernel, such as removing debugging and kernel-hacking features.

- mm/built-in.o: The code in this directory handles memory management. If your system doesn't have paged, virtual memory, removing that feature reduces the size of this component appreciably.

Using the Bloat-O-Meter

Linux includes a tool that allows you to view the size of the kernel and compare it against prior builds, showing the size different between the two. This utility gives the most detail about the size of the kernel by showing you the amount of memory consumed by each item. This is the best way to see how a far-reaching change like removing printk affects the size of the kernel binary. To use this tool, do the following:

1. Make a copy of the vmlinux file in the top directory of the kernel source tree.

2. Use the kernel configuration tool to make your changes.

3. Rebuild the kernel.org.

4. Use the bloat-o-meter to check the size difference.

As an example, the second kernel has no debugging or an NFS file system:

```
$ cd <kernel source tree>
$ cp vmlinux vmlinux.old
$ make menuconfig ARCH=<your arch>
$ make ARCH=<your arch> CROSS_COMPILE=<your cross compiler>
$ ../scripts/bloat-o-meter vmlinux.old vmlinux
twofish_setkey                   -      7936    +7936
pktgen_if_write                  -      7728    +7728
rmd320_transform                 -      7460    +7460
rmd160_transform                 -      7392    +7392
ieee80211_invoke_rx_handlers     -      7140    +7140
sha512_transform                 -      6732    +6732
sha256_transform                 -      6348    +6348
static.__compound_literal       728     6768    +6040
pktgen_thread_worker             -      5928    +5928
sd_revalidate_disk               -      5864    +5864
rfcomm_run                       -      5044    +5044
camellia_encrypt                 -      4856    +4856
rmd128_transform                 -      4796    +4796
rmd256_transform                 -      4764    +4764
```

The output from this code is very granular. You can see how the size of each function has changed and what symbols have been removed as a result of kernel development or changing the kernel's configuration.

Minimizing Boot Time

Reducing boot time is a matter of doing one of the following: reducing what happens during boot or delaying activities so that the boot-up time is broken up and the system appears to start more quickly. This section looks at what to do from a kernel and root file system perspective.

Reducing Kernel Boot-Up Time

The kernel boots rather quickly, even with no attempts to make it go faster. In the example later in this chapter, an unmodified kernel for a 400Mhz arm board boots in about seven seconds from power-up, and three of those seconds are spent by the boot loader waiting for the user to interrupt the boot process (the measurement was done on a device still used for development). This means the device is ready to run user programs in about four seconds. This also means speeding up the kernel boot process is a series of changes that reduce the speed in the quarter- to half-second range; with effort, you can reduce the time to about two or three seconds, which is in the range of a digital camera.

Also notice that the choice of root file system is the largest predictor of boot time for the kernel. In the example, using a JFFS2 file system takes a breathtaking six seconds to mount for 50MB flash storage. When using a read-only file system, the mount time is in the subsecond range. If you need to have a large, solid-state drive, consider getting hardware that has flash memory that appears as though it's a standard block-based device, similar to a USB memory stick.

Uncompressed Kernel Image

Most boot loaders expect the kernel to be in a compressed format. The boot loader uncompresses the image during the boot process: this process takes time, and sometimes a kernel that is uncompressed starts booting faster. You have to measure on your target system to be sure, because the time to uncompress varies greatly and there's no rule of thumb about what performs faster.

If you have U-Boot as your boot loader, you need to create an uncompressed U-Boot image. Do so with the following command:

```
$ mkimage -A <your arch> -O linux \
-C none -T kernel \
-a 20008000 -e 20008000 -n linux-2.6 \
-d arch/<your arch>/boot/Image uImage
```

This command is very similar to the command used to create a compressed kernel image file. It uses the uncompressed object file (Image) instead of the compressed one (zImage). Of course, this file is larger. That's a classic engineering tradeoff: size for speed. Because creating an image like this is fairly easy, you should test what works best on the target system if flash space isn't at a premium.

No Console Output on Boot

No doubt you've watched the messages go by during the boot process. Producing these messages costs time, because the system must interact with a much slower I/O device to print out the data. If that slow device is a serial connection, the messages themselves can produce a delay of close to a second. On the target board, try the following commands:

```
$ dmesg | wc -c
```

Or copy the contents of the dmesg command to your development host, and use the wc command. wc -c counts the number of characters in the file. Divide this number by the baud rate of the serial port, and you can estimate in seconds the time to get this output written to the console. For example, if wc -c returns 18530 and the baud rate for the serial port is 115200, the kernel spends almost a fifth of a second waiting for output to be written to the serial port. When the output rate of the port is 9600 baud, the delay is nearly two seconds. The time differences are less for a VGA console, which is about twice as fast as a 115200 serial line, but this is still wasted time.

To remove these messages, add the parameter `quiet` to the kernel command line. Unlike when you disable `printk`, the messages are still generated, but they aren't displayed to the console during boot time. Using `quiet` instead of removing `printk` from the kernel means you can easily return to the more verbose output without recompiling the kernel; you just need to change the parameters passed to the kernel by the boot loader.

Deferred Initialization

Deferred initialization works by delaying the initialization code for kernel modules that have been compiled into the kernel. After the kernel boot, you write into the `/proc/deferred_initcalls`, and the remaining initialization code runs. This feature makes sense when there are peripherals that you won't be using immediately under most circumstances. For a device that periodically collects data and uses the network to report batches of data, you can delay initialization of the network device so the device can begin collecting data as soon as possible. It's important to note that the same time elapses, but some of the code is run later when time is less critical.

Using this feature requires you to apply a patch to your kernel. This patch has been tested with a kernel version that's always a few releases behind the mainline kernel. You can download the patch by doing the following:

```
$ wget http://elinux.org/images/1/18/Deferred_initcalls.patch
```

After you apply the patch, you need to modify the source files of the modules for which you want to delay initialization. Using the prior example, if the device's network card (SMC91x) can be initialized later, you modify the driver like so:

```
module_init(smc_init);
```

to

```
module_deferred_init(smc_init)
```

The function call `module_deferred_init` queues up initialization calls until you request that they be executed. This is done through a file like so:

```
echo 1 >/proc/deferred_initcalls
```

This then begins executing all f the initialization functions queued up through calls to `module_deferred_init`. This operation can occur only once; subsequent writes to `/proc/deferred_initcalls` will produce an error message indicating that the call was already performed. Recall that the proc file system doesn't exist on disk but is a view into the kernel's data structures. The `/proc/deferred_initcalls` file isn't really a file in the traditional sense; when a write occurs on `/proc/deferred_initcalls`, the result is the execution of the initialization calls instead of that data being stored some place.

Because the initialization of a driver requires poking at the hardware, this is a time-consuming process. Being able to bring up the essential devices for your target can produce a substantial time savings. The biggest drawback of this approach is that is requires modifications throughout the kernel and a knowledge of how the device is used so that you defer initialization of the correct set of drivers.

No Kernel Modules

A Linux *kernel module* is code that is linked into the kernel at runtime. The process of inserting a module depends on its size and the number of symbols the kernel must link; however, this time can be reduced to zero if the kernel eschews loading modules and instead has all the modules linked directly into the kernel. For embedded systems with fixed hardware configuration, this makes perfect sense; but for systems that may have changing hardware configurations, adding the drivers directly into the kernel also removes the need to load the correct module at boot or some other time, at the expense of having additional code present that may never be run.

The time required to load a module is only one part. Before loading the module, some code is executed to decide whether the module should be loaded in the first place. This logic commonly exists in a shell script. A shell script is very slow, both in terms of raw execution speed and because most shell scripts busily invoke many other programs in order to do their job. The clock is always ticking.

If your target must use modules, and boot time is an issue, consider using a C program to contain the logic necessary to figure out what modules need to be loaded. This approach doesn't reduce the amount of time necessary to load a module into the kernel, but it reduces the amount of time necessary to determine what modules should be loaded.

Measuring Kernel Boot-Up Times

This section describes three tools for determining how long the kernel takes to boot. Some of the tools also measure the time consumed after the kernel has handed control over to the init process. The first is the most simple method, but it doesn't provide much information about why the boot process is slow. The techniques presented give you a better picture of where time is being spent during boot-up so you can focus your attention on the biggest startup delays.

/proc/uptime

This is a deceptively easy yet effective way to see how fast the system boots: dump the results of /proc/uptime to the console. Making this the first line in your init scripts tells you how long the system has been running and therefore how much time was spent booting. For example:

```
$ cat /proc/uptime
1.20 0.00
```

The first column shows the number of seconds the machine has been running, and the second shows the amount of idle time, or the time the CPU was sleeping because it was waiting for I/O or some other external input. Because of the nature of process accounting during the kernel boot process, the second number is zero (or very nearly zero) if executed as the first program. When you print it out after executing initialization scripts, the second number accurately reports the time tasks spend in a sleeping state, waiting for hardware or other input.

Grabserial

This script prefixes output from the serial port with a timestamp so you can see how much time each action takes that has some output via printk. You can then correlate this to a driver and decide if you want to include the driver or delay the startup. Using this code requires that the device produce boot information on a serial port or a USB port acting like a serial port. This is a very easy program to use and makes it simple to find slow spots in the kernel boot process. To use this program, do the following:

> ■ **Note** Grabserial is also a great tool for measuring the amount of time used by the system initialization scripts.

```
$ wget http://elinux.org/images/b/b6/Pyserial-2.2.zip
$ wget http://elinux.org/images/b/bf/Grabserial
$ chmod +x ./Grabserial
```

This program is written in Python and requires the Python serial library. This library isn't usually present, so it must be installed first:

```
$ unzip Pyserial-2.2.zip
$ cd ~/pyserial-2.2
$ sudo python setup.py install
running install
running build
running build_py
running install_lib
(clipped)
```

When this is installed, you can run the Grabserial program. It works by pointing at a serial device and then starting the boot process:

```
./Grabserial -d /dev/ttyS0 -b 115200 -t -e 360
```

The program grabs data from the serial line and then begins printing it out with timestamp information:

```
[    0.003957]
[    0.004153] Loading from NAND 64MiB 3,3V 8-bit, offset 0x60000
[    0.011949]    Image Name:   Linux-2.6.31
[    0.013036]    Created:      2009-09-18  19:34:52 UTC
[    0.017110]    Image Type:   ARM Linux Kernel Image (uncompressed)
[    0.027601]    Data Size:    1951248 Bytes =  1.9 MB
[    0.034704]    Load Address: 30008000
[    0.039209]    Entry Point:  30008000
[    2.335971] ## Booting kernel from Legacy Image at 32000000 ...
[    2.341174]    Image Name:   Linux-2.6.31
[    2.344641]    Created:      2009-09-18  19:34:52 UTC
[    2.355510]    Image Type:   ARM Linux Kernel Image (uncompressed)
[    2.357363]    Data Size:    1951248 Bytes =  1.9 MB
[    2.358740]    Load Address: 30008000
[    2.361558]    Entry Point:  30008000
[    2.366123]    Verifying Checksum ... OK
[    3.092168]    Loading Kernel Image ... OK
[    3.712171] OK
[    3.715954]
[    3.716102] Starting kernel ...
```

```
[    3.716804]
[    3.727919] Uncompressing Linux.................. done, booting the kernel.
[    4.819974] Linux version 2.6.31 (superrpoject@shost-1)
[    4.829198] CPU: ARM920T [41129200] revision 0 (ARMv4T), cr=c0007177
[    4.835957] CPU: VIVT data cache, VIVT instruction cache
[    4.852953] Machine: MINI2440
(clipped)
[    7.976855] RPC: Registered udp transport module.
[    7.982516] RPC: Registered tcp transport module.
[    7.986593] s3c2410-rtc s3c2410-rtc: setting system clock to
[   15.191973] Empty flash at 0x033472ac ends at 0x03347400
```

A brief analysis of this output results in alarm at the last line, which is from the JFFS2 file system. As Grabserial scans a volume before startup, it shows a delay well over six seconds, or close to the time the kernel has spent booting thus far. This means you can cut the boot time almost in half by using a file system that mounts more quickly.

Because the Grabserial command needs the serial port and for some devices, it's the only way to communicate with the host: the typical usage pattern is to reboot the host, leave the serial communication program, and then start Grabserial and have it start logging output. Using the -m feature of Grabserial results in the program resetting its timer counter when it sees a line matching a certain pattern. For example, to start timing output when the line starting with U-Boot is received, use the following command:

```
./Grabserial -d /dev/ttyS0 -b 115200 -m "^U-Boot"
```

The -m command can accept any regular expression, so you can have it start counting when the kernel begins booting or after a driver has loaded. Table 16-2 describes the parameters to Grabserial.

Table 16-2. Grabserial Parameters

Parameter	Example	Meaning
-d --device	-d /dev/ttySAC0	What serial device to use as input for the program. The default is /dev/ttyS0.
-b --baudrate	-b 9600	What baud rate to use for the device. The default value is 115200.
-w --width	-b 7	The default bits per character. The default value is 8.
-p --parity	-p N	If the word contains a parity bit, the default value is N.
-s --stopbits	-s 1	The Number of stop bits. The default is 1.

-x -xonxoff	-x	Use xon/xoff flow control. The default is no flow control.
-r -rtscts	-r	Use rts/cts flow control. The default is no flow control.
-t --time	-t	Print the time for each line received. This isn't set by default, but it should be. Make sure you add this to your command line.
-m --match	-M "^Linux Version"	A pattern that resets the clock. Use this when you want to focus on how much time a subset of the boot process requires to run. This expression is empty by default, which results in no effect.
-v --verbose	-v	Verbose program operation. If you're having trouble getting the program to communicate with the target, use this setting for additional diagnostic information.

Initcall_debug

Initcall_debug is the opposite of quiet when it comes to boot time output. By adding initcall_debug to the kernel command line, you get output that looks like this:

```
initcall init_sunrpc+0x0/0x58 returned 0 after 8145 usecs
rootcalling  init_rpcsec_gss+0x0/0x4c @ 1
initcall init_rpcsec_gss+0x0/0x4c returned 0 after 237 usecs
calling  init_kerberos_module+0x0/0x28 @ 1
initcall init_kerberos_module+0x0/0x28 returned 0 after 226 usecs
calling  s3c24xx_dma_sysdev_register+0x0/0x70 @ 1
initcall s3c24xx_dma_sysdev_register+0x0/0x70 returned 0 after 9878 usecs
calling  init_oops_id+0x0/0x40 @ 1
initcall init_oops_id+0x0/0x40 returned 0 after 372 usecs
calling  disable_boot_consoles+0x0/0x48 @ 1
initcall disable_boot_consoles+0x0/0x48 returned 0 after 12 usecs
calling  pm_qos_power_init+0x0/0xac @ 1
initcall pm_qos_power_init+0x0/0xac returned 0 after 14959 usecs
calling  max_swapfiles_check+0x0/0x8 @ 1
initcall max_swapfiles_check+0x0/0x8 returned 0 after 4 usecs
calling  random32_reseed+0x0/0x68 @ 1
initcall random32_reseed+0x0/0x68 returned 0 after 166 usecs
calling  seqgen_init+0x0/0x1c @ 1
initcall seqgen_init+0x0/0x1c returned 0 after 162 usecs
calling  rtc_hctosys+0x0/0x13c @ 1
initcall rtc_hctosys+0x0/0x13c returned 0 after 7436 usecs
```

This shows every driver initialization call and the length of time necessary for it to complete. This kernel was compiled with the symbols present; so the symbolic name of the function was printed. If these are removed (as they are in many systems to conserve space), you need to use the `addr2line` program to resolve the symbol into something more understandable.

In this output, a few lines have initialization numbers large enough to merit examination:

```
initcall init_sunrpc+0x0/0x58 returned 0 after 8145 usecs
initcall pm_qos_power_init+0x0/0xac returned 0 after 14959 usecs
initcall rtc_hctosys+0x0/0x13c returned 0 after 7436 usecs
```

The last two items relate to configuring hardware devices (the power-management hardware and the real-time clock) and can't be changed, because they're essential and the amount of time is strictly related to the underlying hardware. The first, however, is a target for optimization, because it's for the code that is used for handling NFS connections. For this device, NFS is built into the kernel to aid development, but it's consuming a considerable amount of time during startup to configure itself.

Reducing Root File System Startup Times

Reducing the amount of time necessary to get Linux up and running after the kernel is done booting is much more direct. The kernel mounts a root file system and then runs a program that is responsible for starting all the other processes in the system. In the vast majority of standard Linux systems, like servers and desktop machines, that program is called `init`, and it runs several other programs to boot the system; this program is designed for flexibility, not expediency. In an embedded system, the primary concern is booting the system to the point that the user can begin using the device as soon as possible. In order to get the fastest booting speeds, the initialization routines skip the flexibility offered by the startup systems on a desktop or server system.

The following sections cover proven techniques that reduce the time necessary to get a system up and running as quickly as possible. Unlike the kernel boot process, where effort results in subsecond savings, putting effort into streamlining the boot process when the kernel hands control to the `init` program can result in a boot process that shrinks by tens of seconds.

Use a Read-Only File System

Many users pick the JFFS2 file system for devices that have flash storage; if you need to write to a flash device, this is a practical choice. JFFS2 has very long mount times, because it performs an inventory of the media's free blocks on mount so that it can perform its wear-leveling job. There have been updates to JFFS2 to reduce this time; however, it's still in the few-second range for media in the 1GB range. The way around this problem is to use a read-only file system like cramfs for the root file system and mount a JFFS2 file system after the user program is up and running. This is a small change that has a large impact on the speed at which the system gets going.

However, the system needs some read/write file systems, notably /tmp and /var. In a system with a read-only file system, these directories are created and used as mount points for the read/write file system—typically, a file system that exists in memory, like tmpfs. When the system starts, the initialization scripts mount over the read-only directory. The tradeoff is that some of the device's RAM memory is consumed for temporary files, meaning less is available for the application.

When you're creating a temporary file system, the key is to limit the size so it doesn't consume all the available memory in the system. The tmpfs file system is the recommended file system to use for RAM-based temporary drives, because you can limit the amount of space it consumes. As an example, this line in the /etc/fstab file mounts a tmpfs file system at /tmp and limits the size to 512KB:

```
tmpfs              /tmp           tmpfs    defaults,size=512k 0     0
```

For most embedded systems, the amount of space the user can use for writing data is small compared to the root file system, which is effectively read-only, because the user shouldn't be able to overwrite the code running the device. Because the mount time for JFFS2 is proportional to the size of the media, mounting a smaller area for read-write access also means a quicker mount time.

Because you may be accustomed to writing anywhere on a root file system, there is a bit of a learning curve; and you may need to do some testing to see where the program is writing in unexpected places. You can easily change a root file system to be read-only by doing the following as root:

```
# mount -n -o remount,ro /
```

Run the application to see what breaks.

■ **Note** Creating a read-only file system requires far more planning than a read-write file system, because you're habituated to being able to write just about anywhere. Furthermore, updating a read-only root file system requires rebuilding and reflashing the entire image, which is a time-consuming process that makes experimentation difficult.

In the boot-up code earlier in the chapter, the mount time for the root file system is close to six seconds. Using a read-only file system, the same volume mounts and is ready to use in less than half a second.

Replacing Initialization Scripts

The system doesn't need a script in order to initialize the system. For the quickest boot time, write a program that performs via fork()/exec() the commands necessary to start services instead of relying on scripts to perform this task. This is the fastest way to get the system configured and booting, but it requires the most engineering work.

If you feel you must use scripts, then combine all of the init scripts in the system into one large script and factor out redundant code. This coding trick keeps the shell from being loaded once each time a script is executed. By performing any checks at the start of the script, those checks won't happen once for every script that is loaded.

Consider the initialization script that is included with buildroot:

```
for i in /etc/init.d/S??* ;do
    # Ignore dangling symlinks (if any).
    [ ! -f "$i" ] && continue
    case "$i" in
        *.sh)
            # Source shell script for speed.
            (
                trap - INT QUIT TSTP
                set start
                . $i
            )
```

```
            ;;
    *)
            # No sh extension, so fork subprocess.
            $i start
            ;;
    esac
done
```

Here's the pseudo code for this script:

1. Find all the directory entries in /etc/init.d that start with *S* and at least two characters. The for statement gets the list of files to execute based on the mask S??. The shell returns the list of files in sorted order, so S01foo is processed before S02bar.

2. If the directory is a file that doesn't exist, skip processing to the next file. It's possible that the directory entry is a symlink that doesn't point to a file on the file system. The check [! -f "$i"] && continue ensures that the file exists; if not, the next file in the list is processed. Conceivably, on a production system, you can skip this step because when the file system was created, the engineer ensured that all the files in the /etc/init.d directory existed on the system.

3. If the file ends in sh, assume it's a script, and run it. Files that end in .sh are assumed to be shell scripts and are read into the current script using the . command (a shortcut for the keyword source) and executed. By reading the code into the current script, the system doesn't need to run another instance of the shell in order to run the script, saving time and memory.

4. Otherwise, execute the file with the parameter start. At this point, the script thinks the program in the directory is an executable and so runs it with the parameter start.

5. Move to the next file to process. Go to step 2. When the current program is finished running, the code returns to the top of the for loop and processes the next file in the list. This loop continues until there are no more files to process.

This is a very minimal startup script and is much more efficient than the standard initialization scripts found on a desktop system, but it's much less efficient than combining all scripts into one file and then executing them at once. On a system that will always have the same scripts to run, there's no need to scan a directory for a list of scripts, because that list is always the same. This exercise also forces you to examine the scripts one by one to eliminate waste.

Consider the script to start the Dropbear ssh server, which weighs in at 56 lines (not printed here!) and does the following:

1. Checks to ensure that the /etc/dropbear directory exists

2. Checks for the existence of the RSA and DSA keys, generating them if they aren't present

3. Echoes several status messages

4. Starts Dropbear

Steps 1 and 2 can be performed during the build process of the root file system that is placed on the device. Therefore this code doesn't ever have to perform the checks, because these files are present. Step 3 can be eliminated on an embedded device without a console, because the user won't see the device booting. This leaves a script containing just step 4, which is one line, resulting in a 56-to-1 reduction in the code size. Continue this process for all user initialization scripts to reduce boot time by a second or two.

Inittab Abuse

Many systems rely on SysV init (or its BusyBox cousin) to start the system. Recall that the init program reads the file /etc/inittab to figure what to run when. One of the things you can specify is that commands are to be executed once while the system is booting. There is no limit on the number of commands that can appear, and they're executed in order of appearance—that sounds a lot like a script. Exploiting this means you can use the inittab file instead of a separate script file to boot the system. Consider this /etc/inittab file and /etc/init.d/rc file:

/etc/inittab	/etc/init.d/rc

`::sysinit:/etc/init.d/rc`
`::respawn:/usr/bin/the-app`
	`#!/bin/sh`
	`/bin/mount -t proc none /proc`
	`/bin/mount -t tmpfs -o \`
	`    size=128k,mode=0755 none /dev`
	`/bin/mount -o remount,rw /`
	`/sbin/ifconfig lo 127.0.0.1 up`
	`/sbin/route add -net 127.0.0.0 \`
	`    netmask 255.0.0.0 lo`

In this example, the init process launches the /etc/init.d/rc file that then performs the necessary startup configuration work. In the following example, all the commands that were in the /etc/init.d/rc file have been moved into the /etc/inittab script. This change results in a savings of a dozen or so milliseconds, but every little bit helps:

/etc/inittab	/etc/init.d/rc

`::sysinit:/bin/mount -t proc none /proc`
`::sysinit:/bin/mount -t tmpfs -o \`
`    size=128k,mode=0755 none /dev`
`::sysinit:/bin/mount -o remount,rw /`
`::sysinit:/sbin/ifconfig lo 127.0.0.1 up`
`::sysinit:/sbin/route add -net 127.0.0.0 \`
`    netmask 255.0.0.0 lo`
`::respawn:/usr/bin/the-app`
	Empty!

Also note that the same amount of work happens in both cases—it's just that there's less overhead in running the commands from the inittab than from a separate script. This approach also results in a slightly smaller root file system, but that isn't the primary reason for taking this approach.

Link with GNU Hash Style

When you're compiling with shared libraries, there is a section containing hash values for the symbols that need to be resolved by the dynamic linker. To create look-up information for these systems, they're identified with a hash code. When more than one symbol produces an identical hash code, the linker searches sequentially through the symbols with the same hash code until a match is found. Using a different hashing system, such as one that has a high chance of producing a unique hash, means the linker doesn't have to perform a sequential search nearly as frequently, if at all.

The GNU hash style does just that, creating a hash key with a lower chance of name collision. This results in faster linking times because there's no need to perform sequential searches. Some compilers turn this on by default. To see for yourself, use the -### option of GCC, which shows you exactly what steps GCC does in order to build an executable. Using this option is as easy as adding the parameter -Wl,--hash-style=gnu to your compilation (or link) step:

```
$ arm-linux-gcc -Wl,--hash-style=gnu app.c -o app
```

You can verify whether a program is using GNU hashing by looking at the dynamic section of the file—for example, by using this command:

```
$ arm-linux-readelf -d app
Dynamic section at offset 0xf18 contains 24 entries:
  Tag        Type                         Name/Value
 0x00000001 (NEEDED)                     Shared library: [libc.so.6]
 0x0000000c (INIT)                               0x8350
 0x0000000d (FINI)                               0x85c0
 0x00000019 (INIT_ARRAY)                 0x10f0c
 0x0000001b (INIT_ARRAYSZ)              4 (bytes)
 0x0000001a (FINI_ARRAY)                 0x10f10
 0x0000001c (FINI_ARRAYSZ)              4 (bytes)
 0x6ffffef5 (GNU_HASH)                  0x81a8
 0x00000005 (STRTAB)                             0x8278
 0x00000006 (SYMTAB)                      0x81e8
 0x0000000a (STRSZ)                          92 (bytes)
```

This change only affects the program being compiled; there is no need to recompile the libraries or other programs in the system in order to take advantage of this feature. Speed improvements are proportional to the number of symbols used by the program. If your program uses a few functions from shared libraries, load times can be further decreased by linking statically.

■ **Caution** Not all target boards support GNU hashing. MIPS, for example, doesn't. Try compiling your application with this setting and then running it on the target board to ensure that the dynamic linker works as expected.

What's Next

The next chapter looks at handling common issues when the device is deployed: updating the kernel and programs on a running device and what techniques work best. As more and more devices come equipped with networking (wireless networking being more pervasive on embedded devices), the problem of getting the new software on the board isn't as complex as it used to be a few years back.

CHAPTER 17

▪▪▪

Deploying Applications

Embedded applications aren't installed like traditional applications. Nonetheless, code is installed on the target, and time needs to be allotted for the process of getting the program on the target in such a way that it's ready to run when the board starts. This is a nontrivial undertaking. During the design process, how the device will be built, where, and in what quantities affects what effort goes into automating the deployment process.

Deploying an application on an embedded device is very different from the task of deploying an application on a regular desktop system, because this process is additive in nature: the system is already running, so the task of deploying means putting the application in the appropriate place and updating any configuration files. On a desktop system, the program being deployed is one of several applications running on the device, and you may not know what else is running on the target machine along with your application. For an embedded system, however, deploying the software means creating everything that is necessary to execute the application and having that ready to be burned on the device during manufacturing. As an embedded engineer, you have a lot of control over what applications appear on the device and how they're initially configured; this relieves you from some of the problems that an engineer working on a traditional project needs to solve, but it introduces some new issues that you need to address.

After the device is in the field, the user may be able to add arbitrary applications—think of a cell phone with a marketplace of applications or a networking switch with applications for routing data that can be added after the device is deployed. The device may be customized after it leaves the factory, but the initial boot loader, kernel, and set of applications must be placed on the device so that when the consumer powers-on the device, it's ready to be used. Of course, if the device is designed to be customizable, one of the programs in the initial software load is the code necessary to download and install new applications.

The point of this chapter is to get you thinking about how the application will get onto the target device as soon as possible in the design process, which is why so much space has been dedicated to describing the general process for an embedded device. The design of the device and its manufacture greatly affect how the application is deployed, meaning that deployment must be designed into the product at the earliest stages of product development—indeed, beginning in industrial design. For that reason, this chapter starts by taking a step back and looking at the entire development process for an embedded device and how to think about deployment at each step.

Deployment for Embedded Devices

To understand the deployment issues that embedded devices engender, you need to see the development process for an embedded device from beginning to end. Embedded software must go through a manufacturing stage that regular software doesn't; that phase colors the deployment process and must be considered from the start of the project. It's a good idea to start with a high-level view of what happens during an embedded device's development cycle. Understanding this development process makes it clear why deploying on an embedded device is so much different than deploying standard applications. The following is an explanation of each step and how deployment fits in at that step. Figure 17-1 illustrates a waterfall design process; but in reality, representatives from all seven steps (except manufacturing, unless that is performed in-house) are present for most design meetings.

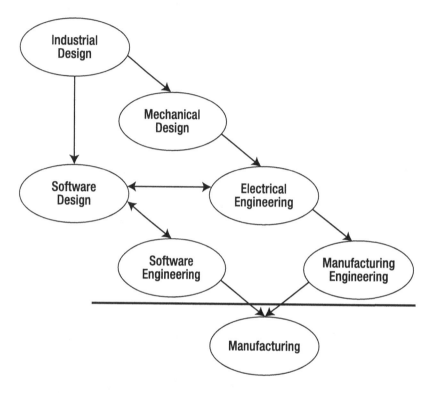

Figure 17-1. *Embedded development process*

Requirements

Embedded devices are made for a purpose, and that purpose is spelled out by requirements. Requirements say what the device should do, how much it costs, what it looks like, and how it's packaged. When the requirements are drafted, they take into consideration who is buying and/or using the device (as parents know, the buyer of a cell phone isn't always the user) and how it's used.

The requirements for the device govern all of the following steps: an inexpensive device won't have a aluminum case, a device that is sold to IT departments needs to fit in a 19-inch telco rack, and a music player should have a long battery life and lots of memory. The act of designing the device has an impact on the requirements as it's tested with potential users: the user of the music player may use the device while exercising, so a heart monitor, calorie counter, or stopwatch may be an essential or differentiating feature of the device.

As an engineer working on a project, it's key to understand the requirements so they be translated into the device's hardware and software design. Because engineering involves trade-offs, such as making the device bigger to accommodate batteries or external connectors, it's important to record when the device strays from the requirements due to engineering limitations. Keeping track of why changes are made and the fact that they're made deliberately is as important as the changes themselves.

Industrial Design

At this step, the look and feel of the device are created. *Look and feel* doesn't mean just the software UI; the case materials, weight, and shape of the device all contribute to its look and feel. Marketing knows about the anticipated target user and market, how the device should be perceived by the buyer, and the features necessary to differentiate the device in the market. During this stage, little attention is paid to the tech parts of the device unless there is an overwhelming marketing need, such as a requirement that the device be a certain size or weight. The output of this process is either a high-resolution drawing called a *rendering* or a hand-made model, usually created with a stereo lithography device, contact cement, and paint.

The industrial designer is responsible for leading this process. This person knows how people interact with objects, how users think a device should operate based on its physical properties, and the types of materials that are durable enough for the device's intended usage patterns. If you're in a meeting and somebody says "emotional response" or "iconic, yet playful shape," you're talking to an industrial designer (bonus hint: this person will also be wearing black and shop at Whole Foods).

Consumer devices spend a long time in this phase, because the device's appearance drives sales. Some products, like medical devices, also have a long industrial design phase because of their safety-critical nature: great care is taken to make sure the user doesn't push the wrong button and that the machine's output is clear and obvious. At some point, the model of the device is tested with potential users to ensure that the industrial design is correct.

Very little deployment thinking occurs now, other than making sure the device has input and output ports to cover the necessary mechanics of deploying the software. (Of course, the device may have other devices to get data from the user or interact with the outside world, which can be used for deployment as well.) Much of the mechanical part of the process is delayed until the next step; but if the designer wants a wafer-thin device that needs an 10-Base-T Ethernet port, it's time to speak up. Likewise, if the development schedule is tight, the device should have a physical configuration that allows connectors to be attached so something can be downloaded to the device.

The interesting parts of the process from a deployment perspective occur in the next steps and result in the alteration of the industrial design to meet the desired hardware requirements.

Mechanical Design

This is where a mechanical/electrical engineer figures out how to put the technology parts into the device case created by the industrial designers. If the device contains an LCD, the engineer working on the project looks at the possible components that can fit into the design case. The end result of this part of the project is a high-level drawing that shows the location of the electronics, batteries, connectors, and openings for external ports, as well as placement of speakers and microphones.

It's here that the nuts and bolts of the design process occur. The mechanical designer tries to find parts to meet the industrial design and specifies how the board is constructed. A processor is selected at this phase, along with the amount of RAM and storage memory. The engineer also looks to see if an off-the-shelf board is available that fits the requirements of the project and that can be adapted to the industrial design. How the processor will communicate with the peripherals is also determined at this stage. For instance, if the processor needs to control mechanical devices, the analog-to-digital and digital I/O devices are selected if the chosen CPU part needs more than it already includes.

During this step, you need to specify what ports you need on the device so that you can perform programming and testing. Some of these may be the same as the devices used for the user interface. For instance, this is the time to request a diagnostic serial port and JTAG leads on the board. The physical connector may not look like a serial port, but the leads let you connect or solder on a serial connection to some boards after they've been manufactured so you can perform programming and/or testing.

This is also the time to catalog all the devices on the board and understand what drivers and programs are necessary to make them operational. For example, if the board will have a speaker and play sounds, an audio software stack is required; likewise, if Wi-Fi is a requirement, the chip set selected by the electrical engineer should be supported by Linux. If there are codec licensing issues to understand—for example, to use a certain video driver—this should be recorded and understood. A video chipset with a closed source license can be replaced with a similar one that has a more open driver model.

At this point, a flurry of activity occurs in the software design. What happens affects the hardware design and vice versa. Tension also exists between the industrial and mechanical designers, because the technical bits and pieces frequently don't fit inside the industrial design. The nice thin design may not house enough batteries or doesn't dissipate enough heat and must be adjusted to work from an mechanical perspective. Likewise, if the external connectors for the device can't be accommodated by the industrial design, it must be updated.

Electrical Engineering

At a high level, this process consists of putting the electrical parts on the boards and wiring them up to each other. This is a complex process that involves getting components with different voltage and signaling requirements working together with a minimum amount of supporting circuitry. The electrical engineering process proves that the mechanical design can accommodate all the technology parts specified by the mechanical design and whether it fits inside the case created by the industrial designers. The electrical engineer frequently finds problems that result in changes to the mechanical or electrical design. The output of this step is a schematic used to create the device. At this point in the process, you should get a test fixture that has all the technical bits wired up and working. Not everything is installed in a case, but it's mounted on a board so you can get to the technical parts when necessary.

From a deployment perspective, enough of the device is created that you can test whether the deployment will work as expected. Even if you have a very rough Linux distribution created for the target device, this is the time to use the facilities on the board to copy the boot loader and operating system to the board and make sure they work correctly. Depending on the components selected in the prior step, you may need the engineering group to solder on the leads for the cabling used for diagnostics and programming or create a custom cable that splits the pins on one header on the board into standard JTAG, Ethernet, and serial connectors. Having one header that supplies a variety of interfaces is a common solution for embedded systems; when the board goes into production, the physical connector is left off, which makes the device less accessible to end users.

Diagnostics appear in this phase, because the electrical engineer needs to both make sure the board works correctly and test the electrical design to make sure it works as expected. The engineer will likely add areas of a board where a meter can be attached, to watch for board behavior. Then, questions about testing what appears on the board will arise. For instance, the electrical engineer can add a testing point to ensure that the serial port has a physical connection, but the software group must provide testing and validation code to prove that the connection can move data at a certain rate; this ensures that the quality of the connection falls within acceptable parameters.

The test fixture should be used to test your assumptions about how the device functions when first powered-on, so that it can be programmed with the right tools. If the order volume for the device is very large (in the 10,000+ range), the company that creates or resells the flash storage components will put the boot loader and operating system on the chips as part of a production run. In that case, the manufacturer will tell you the format of the files and hand-create a few chips for your test fixture to be sure they work correctly.

> ### Programming Tape and Reel Services
>
> For large-quantity orders, wholesale hardware resellers offer a programming service for flash memory parts. You supply the images that go on the device(s), and the reseller puts it on the chip for you. The programmed chip is then put on mylar tape and wound onto a reel that is used by the manufacturing robots to build the board.

Manufacturing Engineering

Here, an engineer figures out what steps are necessary to assemble the unit. The engineer takes the mechanical design and creates the tools[1] necessary to mold the plastic parts for the device and ensure that the parts fit as specified. This involves creating a manual that a contract manufacturer can follow to assemble the item and ensuring that all the parts specified by the electrical engineering step are available and specified. Manufacturing engineering usually contributes earlier in the design process to help the industrial and mechanical engineers create something easier to fabricate, but the bulk of the manufacturing engineering work happens at the end of the process.

The manufacturing engineer inspects all the parts necessary to assemble the device and makes the first few units by hand, creating a *first article* report that is essentially a bug list for the parts. If there is a fixture for programming and testing the board, the manufacturing and testing engineer tests those as well, ensuring that the software load and testing procedures work as expected.

The manufacturing engineer is primarily concerned with creating the design as presented with the greatest fidelity possible. The focus is on creating instructions that another group will follow and how to ensure that those instructions are performed as requested. The testing program is of great interest to this engineer because the goal is to get the code on the target quickly and then equally as fast be sure the device is working correctly. The initial software load on the device includes some testing code so that the device can be verified as working from a higher-level perspective. This means testing programs must be part of the root file system that is placed on the unit as part of the initial software load. If the device doesn't have enough resources for both the testing programs and the application, a special root file system and/or kernel must be created to contain the testing code. When the unit has passed testing, this software is replaced with the software for the end consumer.

Software Design

About the same time that the industrial design happens, the software team begins designing what will run on the device. This has a direct impact on the industrial and mechanical designs: for instance, will the device have a touchscreen, a keypad, or both? Or will the output be a few lines on an LED readout? What peripherals are necessary to meet the requirements, and what software is necessary to drive them? This is the point in the process where the decision to use Linux or some other operating system occurs.

The software design needs to consider what is stored on the device and how many and what applications the device is running. For instance, does the device need to be manufactured with all the applications on the root file system, or will the user customize the set of applications running on the

---

[1] A tool isn't used in the same manner as a wrench or screwdriver: *tools* are the plastic molds and stamping dies necessary to create the pieces that are assembled into the final part. Creating industrial tooling is an art.

board? How will these new programs get on the board? Can this system be used to install the first bits of the software?

If the software is placed on the unit after manufacturing, the device needs the additional services in order to install the software. For example, a networking device has a number of Ethernet ports that can be used as avenues for installing software. A consumer electronics device has a USB port that can be used as the data-transfer mechanism, but that means the device must have the necessary drivers and tools in place to take advantage of the hardware.

Software Engineering

The nuts and bolts of creating the software specified during the design happen during this stage. You're probably familiar with this phase and the software design steps. The output of this process is the bits that are placed on the device during manufacturing.

Most of what happens at this phase in terms of deployment involves ensuring that the design is implemented as specified and tested properly. As the industrial design processes, testing can be performed on more complete units and eventually on a unit that is a manufacturing sample, sometimes called a *first article*. The goal of this step is ensuring that the process for putting the software on the board is completely repeatable and can be accomplished with the peripherals and connectors on the board. The software engineering step sometimes exposes problems that must be resolved by changing the mechanical or electrical engineering, so the sooner you think about how the final software (and subsequent updates) will get on the board, the better.

The manufacturing engineer also helps in understanding the requirements of the manufacturing team in terms of the formats of the files used to write the data on the device. If the board is programmed through the boot loader on the serial port, you must create the scripts to interact with the boot loader to copy the data. Using the boot loader is becoming a more common method because NAND memory can have a fairly high number of bad blocks and the software writing the data must properly work around these problems. If the board has NOR flash memory, bad blocks are the exception, rather than the rule, so the memory can be programmed with the assumption that the NOR media will contain no errors.

The last bit of deployment work is creating software to ensure that the device is in working order. This file is included on the root file system and is run by the manufacturer on a sample of the units to ensure that they work as specified. Because this diagnostic code is on all units, the code is activated by pressing the right sequence of keys or sending a properly formed packet to the device. (Congratulations, you've created an Easter egg![2])

It's worth nothing that for very large production runs, a testing *jig* is created: it's supposed to take the place of the testing software performing tests on the electrical level. Some additional testing software may be required, but the testing jig does the majority of the testing work. However, for smaller production runs, the cost of creating a separate testing fixture can't be amortized over the production run without adding a substantial cost per unit. For this reason, low-production, cost-sensitive devices favor software-level testing over hardware-level testing.

---

[2] An *Easter egg* is a software feature that is undocumented and not intended for the end user. Easter eggs are different than defects (although it could be argued that defects are harder to write) in that the behavior isn't the result of a programming mistake.

Quantity Matters

Although embedded devices may have the same process, the number of units produced ultimately governs the amount of time spent managing deployment. A production run of 50 devices may not have a highly automated installation and testing process, because a person can perform the task more economically; but a device with a production run of 50,000 needs a completely automated deployment in order to be produced profitably.

That isn't to say a low quantity automatically means low automation. Devices produced in low quantity where deployment must be carefully done (as example, industrial control devices that may harm people if not properly configured) have highly automated procedures to reduce human error during the deployment step.

Manufacturing

The line above this process in Figure 17-1 emphasizes that it's detached from the rest of the development steps. The process of putting together the different components occurs at a contract manufacturer, probably in another country. If the unit is assembled in-house, you still need the same level of detail; but with reduced barriers in terms of distance and language, the process can tolerate a little more ambiguity.

The manufacturing step is performed by a company that knows how to run injection molders and screw things together but has very little domain knowledge about what they're assembling: today robot toys, tomorrow your device. That's why it's vital that the steps for deploying the software be as mechanized as possible (Table 17-1). The people and/or robots will take care to assemble the unit to the best of their ability, but they can't make technical decisions.

The output from this process is your finished device. The units are delivered to your site in bulk packaging or, if your volume is high enough, are put into a box and shipped out directly to the supply chain and eventually sold to end users.

Table 17-1. *What to Think About When Deploying the Application*

Development Step	Think about deployment...
Industrial design Goal: Make sure the design accommodates deployment.	How does the user know about what software is running on the device?
	Will the user be running arbitrary software on the device?
	Will the user have access to the technical elements? Will the user have an interest in the technical elements?

Mechanical design

Goal: Ensure that the device has the proper parts and hardware interfaces to put the software on the board and has enough resources to run the application.

What physical access ports will the device have? USB, Network, Wi-Fi?

How will those ports be configured? Will the device have standard or nonstandard connectors.

How fast does the device need to boot?

How much room is available for memory and memory expansion?

What processor can be used? What is the battery life?

How will the user communicate with the peripherals on the device?

Electrical engineering

Goal: Make sure the device has the right connectors, and get the pin-outs if custom cables are needed for development purposes. Add any necessary diagnostic test points or LEDs.

Does the board have all right parts for development?

If chip-specific features are required, are the pins wired so they can be accessed?

Can a connector for a serial port and JTAG be placed on the design?

What diagnostic indicators can be placed on the board?

Manufacturing engineering

Goal: Validate that what has been developed during mechanical and electrical engineering can be done in the desired production volumes. Create the plans so that a third party can easily test and validate the device.

How does the software get burned on the flash?

What testing software can be put on the board so manufacturing has an easy, unambiguous way to see that the electrical components are working?

Software design

Goal: Put the necessary software on the device to make deployment as mechanized as possible, given the production quantities. Identify areas where the end user needs to supply data to the device that can't be done at the factory, and ensure that there's a way to collect this information.

What needs to happen from a software perspective the first time the user powers-on the device?

What diagnostic features can be made available to the user?

What user-specific information must be collected before the device is functional? How does the device function before receiving this information?

What calibration steps must be performed? Where is the calibration information stored?

How does the user update the software on the device? What connections are supplied for communication?

Software engineering

Goal: Make the deployment process as easy to perform as possible, being very explicit about problems and defects so that devices aren't released from the factory unless the software and hardware are in working condition.

Manufacturing

Goal: Make the installation and test process easy to perform. If the device will have a large production run, test and validate the procedures. Ensure that deployment problems are easy to identify.

Does the board have enough resources to store user-specific information?

Will the board be running the right services for deployment?

If the software won't be ready by the release to manufacturing stage, can the file system and kernel be updated after the board is assembled?

How can the manufacturer quickly assess that a unit is ready to ship?

How can the manufacturing step be as error-free as possible?

How can the manufacturing company tell that an error has occurred while deploying the software or creating the device?

What remedies can be performed to fix problematic devices?

Deployment Strategies and Tactics

Now that you understand the process around deploying Linux, you need to be familiar with several different use cases that you may encounter. Like all embedded projects, these use cases are driven by the type of hardware used in the system. The following encompass the most common use cases:

- *Single-purpose device, resource constrained:* This is the simple "runs one application" device that has just enough memory and storage to run the designed application. These devices were once created with microcontrollers, but additional requirements, such as a working Wi-Fi stack and more sophisticated display, resulted in Linux being selected as the operating system.

- *Multipurpose device, fewer resource constraints:* This is a consumer electronics device like a cell phone, digital picture frame, IP telephone, test and measurement fixture, or other device. These devices don't have hard drives (unlike those in the next category) but do have storage in the multi-megabyte range. One of the key differentiators of this device is that the manufacturer may not know the programs that eventually run on the target. Resources are constrained on these devices in order to reduce BOM (Bill of Material, or manufacturing) costs and extend battery life, if the device is battery powered.

- *Multipurpose device, plenty of resources:* These are kiosk or network-management devices that don't have the penny-counting constraints[3] of a consumer electronics device. Essentially, no ceiling on the amount of storage and processing power means you can skip the care taken to minimize resources on the other types of devices. The unit includes a few different ways to communicate with the outside world: maybe several network ports, USB connectors, and a serial port or two.

These use cases are considered throughout the remainder of the chapter. If you're presently working on an embedded project, think of where it appears on this list and what sort of manufacturing will occur. Devices that are mass-produced (thousands per year) should be programmed with minimal human intervention: even a month of development effort can be cost-justified by saving 5 minutes of labor per device, if that makes the final software deployment less complex or error-prone.

Boot Loaders

The boot loader is the first code to run on the system. The job of the boot loader is to load the operating system, which eventually gets the application for the device running. But boot loaders have become more capable and can be a part of the deployment process. This section covers getting the boot loader on the board, configuring it for booting, and using it as a way to get the initial kernel and root file system installed.

Depending on the hardware design, the board may have the boot loader preinstalled; the hardware vendor may program it on for you, depending how many devices you order. However, you may be responsible for programming the boot loader on the target board; this is something you need to add to your development plans. No matter how the boot loader gets on the board, you must configure it so that it will boot your application.

In General

Boot loaders are much more sophisticated now and can serve as tools to do more than boot the board. Some boot loaders, like UBOOT and GRUB, have a set of features that rival the first general-purpose operating systems. All these features can be used to your advantage when you're deploying software. You also need to make some deployment-related configuration changes to the boot loader so that it does the right things when the device starts.

For example, during development, the boot loader was likely configured to pause during the reboot process so it can be interrupted to get to a command prompt—this is the type of feature you remove from the production version of the boot loader (unless you want this feature to be available to your users). Likewise, configuration parameters control what initial set of commands the boot loader has; when you were doing development, those were probably typed into the boot loader's command line and saved into flash memory. Those parameters are built into the boot loader as well.

This section covers a few use cases that you're likely to encounter for your embedded project. To provide concrete examples, UBOOT is used to illustrate how to solve these problems; many boot loaders

---

[3] I worked on a product for which a week of the schedule was dedicated to removing costs from the device. Cables were shortened, a less-expensive touchscreen part was selected, and nearly five cents was saved by eliminating a USB connector internal to the device.

are in use, so you may not be using UBOOT for your project; but the examples serve as a template when you use the boot loader on your board:

- *Configuring the boot loader to run the kernel:* When the boot loader initially starts, it need to know what to do in order to run the kernel. In a boot loader like GRUB, this information comes from a configuration file. Some boot loaders allow you to make this information part of the executable itself. This example shows how to modify the source to specify the command to run at startup.

- *Getting the initial boot loader on the board and performing initial configuration:* The boot loader needs to be copied on the board. Physical aspects aside, such as having the contacts on the board to support a serial, network, or JTAG connection, you may need to create code to automate this process or work with the manufacturer to deliver the right binary files so the production system can do the work.

- *Using the boot loader to program the root file system for the board:* For smaller production runs, you may be responsible for the deployment of the software. The boot loader can be very helpful with this task because it can work with the low-level hardware and can be scripted. The use cases show scripting done with expect, but you can use just about any serial scripting tool.

UBOOT: Configuring Initial Parameters

The boot loader deployed on the board must be configured so that it's as ready as possible to boot on the board. In order to make the process as error-proof as possible, the boot loader should be prebuilt with the settings for the board compiled-in by default. For example, suppose you use the following command on the text fixture to start the kernel using UBOOT:

```
UBOOT # load kernel ; bootm
```

This command should be set as the default bootup command for UBOOT, and the boot delay time should be set to 0 so the board begins the booting process as soon as possible. When UBOOT is configured for the board, it includes a block of predefined environment variables for the board; you needs to change this so the boot loader placed on the board has the right settings by default. To do so, set the CONFIG_BOOTARGS and CONFIG_BOOTCMD for the board to the proper values. For UBOOT, these settings reside in the include/configs/<*board name*>.h file. For example:

```
#define CONFIG_BOOTARGS  \
                "mem=56M console=ttyS0,115200n8 root=/dev/hda1 rw noinitrd ip=dhcp"

#define CONFIG_BOOTCOMMAND  \
"nboot kernel ; bootm"
#define CONFIG_BOOTDELAY  0
```

When the board boots, it has the right set of commands to load the kernel from flash and start booting. When you use a boot loader like UBOOT, the initial boot command can be more sophisticated, because several steps must be done to initialize UBOOT. The usual sequence of commands (which is different for each board—this serves as an example to illustrate the concept) is something like the following.

First, the dynamic area of flash must be set, because this is where the environment variables are stored. The first saveenv command writes the default environment variables into this location:

```
# dynenv set 40000
# saveenv
```

These commands initialize the flash memory, checking for bad blocks and storing the data in the aptly named *bad block table*. For devices that use NAND flash, this step is essential and must be performed before writing any data to the target device. These commands want the operator to press Enter, so you can use expect (as explained in the next section) to automate the keypress:

```
UBOOT # nand scrub
UBOOT # nand createbbt
```

In this section, you set the environment variables for communicating over an IP connection. The server IP address is used when downloading a file via TFTP:

```
UBOOT # setenv serverip 10.0.0.2
UBOOT # setenv ipaddr 10.0.0.1
```

This is the pointy end of the stick: these commands download the kernel into memory at address 0x32000000 and then write it into flash. The nand write.e command is used because it detects and works around back blocks in NAND memory:

```
UBOOT # tftp 32000000 zImage
UBOOT # nand write.e 32000000 kernel 23400
```

If the board contained a separate root file system, that would be downloaded and written to flash in the same manner. The last thing to do is change the bootup parameters so that when the board restarts, it loads the kernel that was burned into flash and runs it, which results in the application running:

```
UBOOT # setenv bootcmd 'nboot.e kernel; bootm'
UBOOT # setenv bootdelay 0
UBOOT # saveenv
UBOOT # reset
```

You can put all these commands into the CONFIG_BOOTCOMMAND variable so that the first power-on for the board can program the flash with the appropriate data when the board boots. But several of the commands require that you confirm your intentions by pressing Enter, meaning the process requires human intervention. In order to fully automate the process of putting Linux on the board, you must use an automation tool like expect.

Expect

If the boot loader for the board doesn't support scripting or you need to do more sophisticated work when initializing the board, the tool of choice is expect. With expect, you can program the system to wait for a certain string of characters; when they appear, the system responds with another string. Expect is an extension of the TCL language, so you're free to program an expect script that does nearly anything; but in practice, the scripts are simple.

This tool is for controlling the boot loader so that other binaries—such as another boot loader, the kernel, and/or the root file system—can be written to the board. Expect in this case is used in a testing and/or manufacturing fixture and isn't used on the production device. For small-volume devices, the manufacturing fixture may be as simple as a PC with a network, power, and a serial cable, with a place to secure the board while it's being programmed. Large-scale production runs include a budget for bespoke manufacturing and testing fixtures; in this case, you use expect to automate testing of the final code that is given to manufacturing to be burned on the board.

Installing Expect

Expect isn't part of a typical Linux distribution; nor is the tool it's based on, TCL. However, it's widely available as part of the set of packages for all major Linux distributions, so you can install it by doing the following on a dpkg-based system

```
$ apt-get install expect
```

or this if you're using RPM:

```
$ yum install expect
```

Because the package managers get all the dependencies necessary for these packages, you may see that TCL is being installed as well.

Expect on Windows

Running Microsoft Windows (it couldn't have happened to a nicer person) and need to automate scripting? Using a virtual machine for embedded development means you can also use that virtual machine to run expect, but sometimes that isn't possible. A native port of expect to Windows is available at http://downloads.activestate.com/ActiveTcl/Windows. This doesn't require that you have any other software installed on your machine to use TCL; this is a native implementation of expect that runs using the standard Microsoft Windows libraries.

Using Expect

Expect can be used with any boot loader that uses the serial port for communication, which is just about all boot loaders. After you master it, expect is the tool of choice for scripting boot loaders: it's flexible and can be used to build scripts containing robust error-handling that can't be quickly programmed with a boot loader's scripting capabilities.

For instance, imaging that the board in question uses RedBoot and is communicating over a serial port. In order to get the software on the board, you need to perform a number of steps to initialize the board the first time it boots, such as downloading the kernel and programming it into the segment of flash called kernel. The RedBoot commands to accomplish this are as follows:

```
RedBoot> load -r -b 0xd1000000 zImage.redboot
RedBoot> fis write -b 0xd1000000 -l 0x1000 -e 0xd1000000 kernel
* CAUTION * about to program FLASH
            at 0x00020000..0x0002ffff from 0x0606f000 - continue (y/n)? y
```

Automating this with expect is easy, because all expect needs to do is wait until it see the text RedBoot> to know that it can issue its next command. This makes it very easy to write a script to automate this process, as follows:

```
set port /dev/ttyS0

set baud 115200

set timeout 60

set spawned [spawn -open [open $port w+]]

stty $baud < $port
```

These commands configure port $port, open it for reading and writing by TCL, and essentially map the standard in and out to the current TCPL process. Setting the values of port and baud is for readability only, but setting the timeout variable controls how long expect waits for the data before considering it a timeout and moving to the next command in the file:

```
#!/usr/bin/expect -f
expect {

    "RedBoot> "    {

        send "load -r -b 0xd1000000 zImage.redboot\n"
        timeout exp_continue

}

expect {

    "RedBoot> "    {

        send "fis write -b 0xd1000000 -l 0x1000 -e 0xd1000000 kernel\n"
        expect { "continue (y/n)? " send "y" }
        timeout exp_continue
host
}
```

As you can see, the general format of an expect script is a series of expect commands where each one waits for some text before sending data in reply. The data that expect waits for can be a constant (as the example shows) or a regular expression. When expect gets text matching that expression, it moves inside the next block (delimited with {}) and begins executing the commands. The timeout exp_continue causes expect to continue to the next command instead of stopping the script completely if there are no matches in the timeout duration.

This is only an example of what is necessary for one command. An expect script can be as complex as necessary in order to program the board. Expect is a feature of TCL, so you can program just about anything. If you need to do additional processing for each board, such as assigning a MAC address to your Ethernet adapters, you'll appreciate the flexibility of TCL.

Using TCL and expect isn't limited to interacting with boot loaders. You can use the same approach to establish a shell session with the target and begin executing commands required to configure the device.

Beyond Expect

If you shun TCL, don't like the idea of learning yet another language, or need to so some complex programming work while programming your board, there are several alternatives to expect. Of note for Python programmers are pexpect (http://www.noah.org/wiki/Pexpect) and expectpy (http://sf.net/projects/expectpy), which are both adequate tools for expect-like automation.

If you prefer Perl for scripting tasks, you can use the expect module (available on CPAN) that provides the same basic features as the TCL-based expect tool.

Boot Loaders Are Just Programs

The boot loader that contains all the functionality necessary to flash the device and maintain the file system presents security risks that may not be acceptable for some devices. In addition, a boot loader that uses the serial port during boot is a security risk, because the device could be hacked during bootup and data stored on the device could be removed in an unauthorized manner. Devices that fall into this category are those used for medical purposes or other devices that may have a safety impact if hacked. How can you use the boot loader to program the system but avoid these security risks?

The answer is easy: build one boot loader with the functionality to flash the device and perform all the startup and programming tasks, and then use this boot loader to replace itself with a lower-functionality boot loader that boots the system for the customer. This process uses two boot loaders:

- *The full-featured boot loader:* This boot loader has the necessary features to communicate over a network or USB device to download the kernel and root file system and burn them into flash. This boot loader isn't deployed but is used only as a way to program the board. Because this boot loader has features such as programming flash and using the serial console that aren't used in a production device, it consumes resources on the board needlessly and presents a security risk.

- *The limited-functionality boot loader:* This boot loader is the production code for the board. It doesn't have the engineering conveniences of the full-featured boot loader: it's engineered to boot the device and take up as little time and memory as possible in the process. Because the user never interacts with this software, you can remove the user interface software, for example.

Consider this example of using a full-featured boot loader to load and program a lower-functionality boot loader into flash, along with the kernel and application. A boot loader can be loaded into memory in an arbitrary location and then executed; after all, the boot loader is code that the board can run without an operating system.

Using UBOOT as an example, you can easily experiment with this by doing the following from the UBOOT command line:

```
# setenv serverip 10.0.0.1
# tftp 3000000 uboot.bin
# go 30000000
```

These commands download the file uboot.bin from the TFTP server at 10.0.0.1 and place the data starting at memory location 30000000. The last command sets the instruction pointer, and the program starts running. Following this strategy, the steps will be as follows during the manufacturing of the unit:

1. Load the full-featured boot loader into memory via the JTAG port. When the board is designed, the electrical engineer brings out the JTAG lines someplace where they can be reached during manufacturing. Depending on the device, the JTAG connector may be points on the board, a post header, or some other connection. The electrical engineer works with the manufacturing engineer to make something appropriate for the expected manufacturing process.

2. Use full-featured boot loader to obtain the low-feature boot loader, root file system, and kernel. During manufacturing, the full-featured boot loader is loaded; its job is loading and writing to flash the Linux distribution with the application that is running on the board. If these programs are to be downloaded via a serial or Ethernet connection, the electrical engineer makes a header on the board with the pins for this interface.

3. Reset the parameters for production booting.

4. Change the parameters and the configuration so that the board is ready to boot the deployment system.

Devices that use this method of programming usually require a jumper to be connected in order for the ports to work on the electrical level, ensuring that reprogramming in the field is difficult. Other devices have contact points that the manufacturing system makes contact with for programming, making it difficult to attach leads in the field.

The programming fuse

Some boards (or the components used on the boards) have a very low-power fuse that is blown after programming. This means performing a write to the device is no longer be possible at an electrical level. Blowing the programming fuse is obviously done after the software has been written to the device.

Having such a feature isn't necessary, but it does add a layer of protection that software can't provide. In some flash parts, the programming fuse is integral to the chip: an adventurous user with a soldering iron can't route around it if the fuse is located on the board itself.

Deployment Root File Systems

The root file system contains the application for the device. Much has already been written to describe what should be on the file system, how to make it small, and how to make it boot quickly. This section is about getting that root file system ready for deployment on the device. When you're preparing to deploy the root file system, these are the factors to consider:

- *Default accounts and file ownership:* If the file system has the capacity to store file-permission information (recall that some low-memory file systems support file ownership only by root), those accounts must exist. and the files need to be assigned to those users. File systems like JFFS2, YAFFS2, and ext2/3 allow users to assign a default user id and group id for files within the file system or change the ownership information for all files to the root user.

- *First-boot requirements:* Some applications have programs that must be run just once, the first time the board is booted; then you never need them again. Devices with first-boot requirements must have the ability to detect that they've been booted once, implying some read/write capability.

- *Mount points that must be created:* The board's root file system contains at least the proc, sys, and tmp file systems. For a read-only file system, these directories must exist before you create the root file system image.

- *Putting the application in the root file system:* When the application is built, it must be copied into the root file system before using the tools to create the RFS. The application files and all the libraries necessary to get the application to work have to be copied to the RFS as well. If the application needs certain environment variables set or created, put that information into a script that runs the application. This seems like an obvious statement, but many times this step is forgotten.

Application Files and Libraries

There is a standard for the name and location of files and directories in the Linux system, called the File System Hierarchy (FSH) standard. It's maintained by the Linux Foundation and is located at www.pathname.com/fhs/. This document describes the names and expected contents of a standard set of directories that Linux systems should obey. The standard goes as far as describing what files should appear in what directory: for example, the specification says that the /etc directory contains the inittab, passwd, and group files.

When you follow the FSH standard, your application, along with any other nonsystem applications, should appear in the /opt directory, under a directory specific to your company (called *provider* in the FSH standard). If the software has variable data like a log file, it resides in /var/opt/<*provider*>; configuration data is stored in /etc/opt/<*provider*>. No other application files should appear outside of these directories, with the exception of device nodes, which should be stored in the /dev directories, and lock files for device nodes, which are in /var/lock.

If the embedded device is created assuming that users or partners can install arbitrary packages, following these rules closely is the best practice. This is the case with embedded systems that are essentially desktop computers wrapped in a different casing, such as kiosks and point-of-sale systems. For these systems, you require a packaging system to manage the root file system for the device (like RPM or dpkg). You also need to follow the FSH rules because doing so reduces deployment problems when you use packages from multiple sources.

Small Root File Systems

For very small systems, breaking the FSH standard in a minor sort of way is the standard and recommended course of action. What does *minor* mean? The FSH standard, for example, describes the top-level root file system, what is mounted at / and prohibits the addition of additional directories, but it gives more leeway for users' home directories and the files stored in /opt and /etc. Obeying the standard of no additional directories or files in root makes sense; but after that, when it comes to saving space, anything else is fair game. The approach you take depends on the nature of the small root file system. For file systems that are read-only, application files can be stored in the /opt directory and configuration files stored under this directory, which complies with the FSH standard.

For some systems, it makes sense to store all the executable, library, and configuration files under one file system. Even configuration files for peripheral programs, like the touchscreen interface, go into this directory. The thinking is that putting all these files in one directory makes it easier to create the distribution and consumes a little less space.

Given a hypothetical application called datasampler, the directory looks like this:

```
/home/app
        datasampler
        libsampler.so
        pointercal
        ts.conf
        datasampler.conf
```

In this example, the program uses a touchscreen and the Xfbdev X screen buffer server, which is stored in the root file system in the standard location. The script that starts this program looks like the following:

```
#!/bin/sh

# configure the pointer calibration
export TSLIB_TSDEVICE=/dev/input/event0
export TSLIB_TSEVENTTYPE=INPUT
export TSLIB_CONFFILE=/home/app/ts.conf
export TSLIB_CALIBFILE=/home/app/pointercal
# point the library loader to this directory for the shared library ↲
export LD_LIBRARY_PATH=/home/app

# start X
Xfbdev

# start your application
./datasampler
```

Following the standard, these files should be stored in different locations in the root file system. By storing all this data in one directory, you can configure the flash file system with one partition for the program files, meaning the deployment of the program is separate from the core Linux operating system. In addition, this approach saves a little space on the root file system by not creating any additional directories for these files.

This bit of indirection means that the final development push causes changes in only one small part of the file system. The remaining parts of the system can be frozen from a development perspective, thereby isolating changes.

If you take this approach, this partition can be mounted as a read-write file system without a large boot-time penalty. You're also assuming that the application and supporting files aren't in the tens-of-megabytes range, making it easy for the application to store configuration data. In this example, the device wants to include the tslib pointer calibration program, which can place results in this read/write directory.

First Field Update at the Factory

For devices that are updated in the field as part of their normal operation, configuring the system to perform its first field update at the factory is the best way to ensure that this process works as expected and puts the system in the proper state for the next update. Any problems that occur during the update process can be addressed at the factory, where it's less expensive than fixing the problem on site. Furthermore, when a customer has a problem on site, it can affect their business operations and gives them the opportunity to form a less-than-favorable impression of your product and company.

What's Next

The next chapter covers the process for performing field updates. Software is always subject to change and updates, and with the additional connectivity, storage, and processing power of embedded devices, getting new software on the device is a more reasonable proposition than ever before. Chapter 18 explores the tools and techniques that are available for performing field updates for all types of embedded systems.

CHAPTER 18

■ ■ ■

Handling Field Updates

Change is as ever-present as death and taxes. Companies sometimes ship embedded devices with a set of software that fulfills requirements, only to find out that what the software does and what the customer wants don't quite match. Software passes through code reviews and test suites with flying colors but fails in the field. The new industrial designer likes rounded corners and blue, not square corners and earth tones. A competitor has released a similar device, getting rave reviews for features your product managers said nobody would ever want. No matter what the reason, the software that goes on the device as it leaves the factory will need some sort of update. The question isn't about the need but rather how to fulfill that need.

One way to update devices is to have them returned to your customer service department, where a technician opens the device, connects a serial cable, and follows instructions to load a new kernel and root file system on the board. This is the least risky approach, but it's easily the most expensive and, as I'm sure you've heard from your management, not "scalable."

This chapter looks at the process of updating devices after they've been shipped to customers or creating highly-automated update systems that your in-house customer service group or partners can use. Field updates need not be complex; you can create a reasonable solution with a few straightforward shell scripts;—no major surgery is necessary. However, if the need arises for a more complex solution, the same tools used to update the packages on your Linux desktop can be used on devices with modest resources, granting you nearly endless flexibility.

Root File System Updates

Updating the root file system is the first topic, because you can use many of the concepts and practices to update the kernel as well. In many cases, the ability to update the root file system fulfills the requirements for field updates, and the kernel itself remains unchanged over the life of the product.

The root file system on an embedded device is frequently stored on a flash device. Even though that device can be written to, the actual file system is read-only, meaning the entire root file system must be replaced. The "Basic Strategies" section describes the different ways you can update a root file system; which strategy fits best for your application depends on the device's resources, the frequency of updates, and the complexity of the software deployed on the device. Some devices contain a root file system that's identical for each device shipped, whereas others have a mix of software installed depending on the configuration of the device. There is no "right" solution, just the one that best fits how the device is used by your customers and their expectations.

Basic Strategies

You can follow a few basic strategies to update the programs on a root file system. No matter what approach you take, because you're updating an embedded system that you control, the update strategy isn't as difficult as a desktop system; but it does present challenges in that the device is likely resource constrained and may not have the most complex user interface. For example, the user can't be prompted for information if the update process can't figure out what to do. Each of the strategies is listed here and then each described in detail later in the chapter.

All of the strategies require a good communication mechanism to fetch the new binaries and enough data to for temporary storage, if just to have a temporary root file system that can start in case the root file system update system fails:

- *Forklift upgrade:* This means the complete replacement of the old root file system with something new. On an embedded system, you replace the entire root file system with a new flash image. This is a hold-over from the days when the software in telco equipment could only be upgraded by replacing the existing equipment with new.

- *Parallel systems:* This approach works by having two kernels and two root file systems. One root file system and kernel pair is the production system, and the other is the staging system for upgrades. You first upgrade the staging system; when the staging system is considered ready, the boot loader is changed to point at the staging system, and the board is rebooted. Obviously, this works best where the device has sufficient resources to store a second root file system and kernel.

- *Build your own:* In this option, you distribute the software changes as a tar or cpio archive with a script or other software that then updates the system. For an embedded system with little to no variation of the software on the target, this is a very practical choice.

- *Package manager:* No doubt you're familiar with the concept of a package manager and have used one, like RPM and Debian packages. Both of these systems are geared toward desktop systems and have facilities not only to distribute software but also to build the software from source. Embedded systems also use a lighter-weight packing system, IPKG; like many embedded tools, it favors simplicity over features.

In all cases, you need a way to handle failures. If the update process fails, the device needs to know how to go back to some state where it can attempt the upgrade process again, or revert to the original state. When the device reverts, the user needs to know that a failure happened so that they can contact technical support or attempt the upgrade process again. Of course, knowing about a failure means that upgrade process needs some software that decides whether the update process worked in the first place, not just that it failed. The sections for each of the update types cover these areas with solutions appropriate to the approach.

Forklift Upgrade

Going this route means making a new image of the root file system that is burned on the flash storage. For a read-only file system, a forklift upgrade is a necessity because the file system drivers can't write data: that is one way they manage to economize on space. Most of the work involves figuring out how to get the new root file system to the device and where to store it before copying to the target. In order to forklift-upgrade a root file system, you need at least the following:

- *MTD utilities:* The flash device on the board can't be written to without first performing an erase process. In addition, boards with NAND memory need a special tool when writing, because the standard /dev/mtdblockX device driver doesn't handle bad blocks properly.

- *Extra storage space and communications link:* In order to get your shiny new root file system on the board, there must be some way of accessing an external storage device, or additional storage must be on the board to hold the root file system image before it's copied to the target. It isn't recommended that you copy the new root file system image from the network or by some other means and then directly overwrite the original root file system. There are too many opportunities for error, and recovering can become difficult if not impossible. However, this is an acceptable route if the environment is controlled enough; for example, if the upgrade process is performed by a technician rather than by a consumer, it works in the majority of cases. In the example, the device has enough memory to store a copy of the new RFS in RAM along with the existing root file system, which is copied into RAM as a backup in case the upgrade goes horribly wrong.

- *Tools on the OS:* You need some additional tools to perform the copy process and ensure that it worked. These tools are nothing special; in fact, they're what you find on a desktop system. You just need to make sure these tools are on the target system.

Designing for Forklift Upgrades

If this is the route you want to use to upgrade your device, you can make it easier by adjusting the software configuration of the device in order to make it simpler to upgrade in the first place. The most practical change is to store your application in a segment of flash that is separate from the core operating system so that you can upgrade the application independently from the OS. This process involves a little more work up front, but it makes the remaining process much easier and failsafe because a possible failure to upgrade the file system containing the application won't disturb the rest of the operating system. This approach also gives you the greatest ability to accommodate failures.

Note If you're planning on the forklift upgrade, the best practice is to create a separate flash partition for your application programs. This is the only partition that is modified during the upgrade process.

The tradeoff is that the rest of the operating system is off limits when you're performing an upgrade. You can mitigate this issue by having first in the path some directories in the application directory that can be used to store upgraded system utilities and also by using the LD_LIBRARY_PATH environment variable to control what shared libraries are used. There are also programs and tools that normally appear in the root file system under /bin or /sbin that are subject to frequent change. They're placed in the application file system and appear in the path first. There are no generic criteria for selecting applications for this process; you'll know which application to choose by understanding your application in detail.

MTD Utilities

This process requires some special utilities that probably aren't installed on the target system: MTD utilities. This set of programs is maintained by the developers who brought you the JFFS2 file system and can be used to work with flash memory, even if it isn't using JFFS2. In order to use these utilities, you need to fetch them using Git and cross-compile them:

```
$ git clone  git://git.infradead.org/mtd-utils.git
$ make CC=arm-linux-gcc \
        LDFLAGS="-static" \
        WITHOUT_XATTR=1
```

After these are compiled, they need to be available on the board, because they're used during the upgrade process. These utilities were built with static linking because they may be placed in a file system that doesn't have a C library available to use for dynamic linking. WITHOUT_XATTR disables extended attribute handling for supporting SELinux, but this has an effect only when you're building the mkfs.jffs utility.

Forklift-Upgrade Example

This is an example process for performing an upgrade of a read-only root file system. It has some components cooperating to ensure that the upgrade process worked and that the embedded system has a reasonable chance of booting. It works by mounting a small file system with the necessary tools as root, and then upgrading the flash file system with the new image. This example assumes the device has enough RAM memory to store the file system before it's copied into the flash partition:

```
#!/bin/sh
# create the files you need

FLASH_DEVICE=/dev/mtd2
FILELIST="image md5"
APP_NAME="your_app"
APP_MOUNT_POINT=/app
FIFO=/tmp/upgrade

mkdir /tmp/newrfs
mount -f tmpfs -o size=xxK nodev /tmp/newrfs
```

This is a simple example that gets a fixed list of files from an FTP server. Because you're replacing the entire file system, which contains a group of files, this is a reasonable approach. If you want a more flexible system, change this script to download a file that then contains a list of files to download. At that rate, why stop at a list of files to download? You can download a script and execute it on the machine, although that is advisable only for systems in a controlled setting, because that leaves the device open for all sorts of exploits. Coding either of these is simple and is left as an exercise for you:

```
# fetch from the target the necessary files
for f in $FILELIST; do
  if ! ftpget -u username -p secret \
     hostname /tmp/newrfs/$f /remote/path/$f ; then
        echo "failed to download file $f"
```

```
        exit 1
done
```

Here, you check that the downloaded files have the expected content:

```
# check that the file is what you wanted
if ! md5sum -c md5 > /dev/null  ; then
        echo "md5 sum did not match"
        exit 2
fi;
```

■ **Note** Recall that a FIFO (First In, First Out) is a special file that allows you to pass data between processes. In this case, the data is a side effect, because you're using the FIFO to control the execution flow of the processes.

The little trick here is that the system knows it's starting to upgrade. The target application is killed, and the init process should restart the application when it dies; however, you don't want to restart while upgrading, so you can use something simple like a FIFO to have the script or program that launches the application wait until the upgrade is over. With a FIFO, the program that does the read blocks until data appears in the input, so this is acting like a semaphore for your upgrade process:

```
mkfifo $FIFO
killall $APP_NAME
umount $APP_MOUNT_POINT
```

Now you have all the files necessary for the upgrade. You just need to switch out the root file system and restart the application by writing something into the FIFO:

```
mtderase $FLASH_DEVICE
if ! mtdcopy /tmp/newrfs $FLASH_DEVICE ; then
    echo "problem copying new rfs"
            ## notice, that you did not write to the fifo
    exit 3
fi
mount -t cramfs $FLASH_DEVICE /app
umount /tmp/newrfs
echo go > $FIFO
rm $FIFO
```

The script that runs the application needs to wait on the end of the FIFO, which can be done by attempting to read a line from the file:

```
if [ -f $FIFO ] ; then
        read l < $FIFO
        # the environment variable l will have "go" from the prior code
```

```
fi
```

The key to this script is that is only updates a small part of the system in such a way that the core operating system bits keep running. Because the application code is segmented from the rest of the operating system, the code used to start the application can perform additional checks to ensure that the flash partition containing the application is in a proper state and goes into diagnostic mode or attempt to restart the upgrade process in case it hasn't worked correctly on the first attempt.

Parallel Systems

Parallel systems work somewhat like forklift upgrades, the difference being that the changes happen to a file system other than the root file system currently in use. This has several advantages over the forklift upgrade:

- *Safer:* No matter how badly the upgrade process goes, all the changes are made to the staging system, which isn't the one being used by the system. If the reboot into the new system fails, you have a fallback, working root file system and kernel. The worst possible case is that the machine needs to download a complete root file system, which means the update will take longer.

- *Better diagnostics:* Because the system being upgraded is a matter of updating a second partition, the software performing the upgrade can easily keep track of the process because it still has a complete, working file system.

- *Less disruptive:* This is an oft-overlooked benefit: because the staging root file system isn't in use, the update process can be done a little at a time without causing disruptions. For the forklift upgrade, the system needs to be stopped while performing the upgrade; but in this case, the system can keep running while the update occurs.

However, this approach requires enough space to store three copies of the changes: the production root file system, the staging root file system, and the updates stored in the production file system before they're copied to the staging root file system. The production copy of the root file system doesn't need all the data for the update, because the changes to the staging root file system can happen in smaller chunks to conserve space.

Parallel System Example

In this example, you perform an update of the system by downloading a root file system and putting it into a flash partition. After the root file system has been written, the boot loader's environment variables are changed so that the next time the system boots, it uses the new root file system. The boot loader in the example is U-Boot, because it has tools that let you easily change the variables in flash from Linux. To do this, you configure the environment for the Atmel 9263 development board and build the environment update tools:

```
$ cd <u-boot sources>
$ make at91sam9263ek_config
$ make env
```

The last step built the tool ./tools/env/fw_printenv. You can use this tool to print the state of the environment and write to the environment when the filename is fw_setenv; to accomplish this, create a symlink to the file with the following command:

```
$ cd tools/env
$ ln -s ./fw_printenv fw_setenv
```

When fw_printenv is copied to the target machine, you need to also copy or re-create the symlink This program uses the flash layout stored with the configuration for the board to know what memory to change in flash. If you change the flash layout of the board, you need to recompile this program as well; otherwise, it will write to the wrong areas of flash.

Now you do the work on the target system. You fetch the root file system from the update server and store it in the current root file system:

```
$ wget http://yourdomain.com/path/to/new/rootfilesystem/newrfs.
```

The U-Boot boot loader allows environment variables to contain references to other environment variables that are expanded when the board boots. Because you may change the root file system used to boot the device, you create a kernel command line that looks like the following in your U-Boot environment:

```
UBOOT> setenv bootargs 'console=ttyS1 rootfstype=jffs2 root=${rootdev}'
```

The environment variable ${rootdev} is set to the production root file system in the boot loader's environment. To change the root file system after the new root file system has been written to the flash device, you run the fw_setenv command. For example, a script to accomplish this looks like the following:

```
FLASH_DEVICE=/dev/mtd4
mtderase $FLASH_DEVICE
if mtdcopy /tmp/newrfs $FLASH_DEVICE ; then
        fw_setenv rootdev $FLASH_DEVICE
fi
```

The next time the system reboots, it will use the new root file system.

Do It Yourself

There still is one more option on the table for handling updates: doing it yourself. The primary benefit of this approach is also its greatest source of reliability, because you have control over everything. However, by using the high-level tools on the system for bundling and compressing files as well as fetching data from a remote host, you're relieved of most low-level coding problems. This relief comes at the cost of a solution that has a larger footprint.

All these package-management tools are wrappers around lower-level archive tools. In the case of dpkg and ipkg, the underlying tools are tar and gzip, whereas RPM uses cpio and gzip. The point isn't to lessen the value of the tools, but to point out that if you really need just the bare minimum in package management, you can use tar and zip to create a reasonable solution that doesn't have all the bells and whistles but does enough that updates get to the target computer.

The most reasonable choice would be to use tar or cpio because BusyBox has tools for working with these file formats. Depending on the size of your application and the amount of memory on the board, compression is optional.

Do-It-Yourself Example

To make this an easy and simple example, create a directory on your development host to hold the files that is sent to the target device; call this the ‹*build dir*›:

```
<build dir>/
  lib/
    libapp.so.0
    libapp.so -> libapp.so.0
  bin/
    appfile
```

To create a tar file for this directory, do the following in a script file:

```
BUILDDIR=<build-dir>
OUTPUTFILE=<output-file>
tar -C $BUILDDIR tf $OUTPUTFILE *
```

The output file can now be sent to the target machine and uncompressed from the root directory in order to install its contents. The command looks much like the command to build the system. Using ftpget to fetch the tar file, the script looks like the following:

```
 if ftpget -u username -p secret \
     hostname /tmp/newfile.tar ; then
        tar -C / -xf /tmp/newfile.tar
done
```

After putting the new code on the system, you need to restart the application so the changes take effect.

Using Package Managers

As a user of a desktop system, you're familiar with package managers, because nearly every Linux distribution has its origins in some base set of packages that were compiled and turned into ISO images used to boot Linux on your desktop machine. Package-management systems have the ability to track what has been installed previously on a system. They also track information about individual packages such as the files in the package, some grouping information, and a list of other packages that must be installed in order for the software inside the package to function correctly. The information about package dependencies is paired with an online database where the package-management software can download not only a package but all the dependencies the package needs.

Using a package-management system means the device has a root file mounted as read/write, so devices using flash use JFFS2 or YAFFS2. If the device has a read-only file system, there is no way the package manager can perform the updates on the media. The entire root file system doesn't need to be read/write, only the parts where the package-management software is writing files and keeping the database.

There are several package-management systems: this section looks at two systems frequently used on desktop systems, RPM and dpkg, and another that was created just for embedded systems, ipkg. A nice thing about using a package-management system is that it generally includes the ability to create a store of packages on a remote site and have the software download new packages and any related packages in one transaction, as described earlier. For instance, if your software says it needs packages one, two, and three, and package three needs A and B, the package-management software can use the package-dependency information to download packages one, two, three, A, and B and install all of them before attempting to install your application.

RPM

RPM was created by Red Hat as a way to maintain the build and installation of the company's distribution. On an embedded system, RPM can be used to install packages on the system in the same way it does on your desktop system. Downloading packages from a remote system is done through a separate program called YUM that works with RPM packages. You can use RPM without YUM if desired.

Creating a binary RPM is a matter of making a spec file that tells RPM where to look for the files to add to the archive, the file types, and their permissions settings when installed. Many people think an RPM can only be created by compiling a source RPM, but this isn't the case. You can create an RPM by creating a simple specification file that looks for a list of files to copy to the target, regardless of how they're built. Having the ability to create a RPM binary without using RPM as your build system means you can still use RPM for package management, but you don't have to give up your current build system. Here, you see the contents of an example file that builds a binary RPM from packages that have been built elsewhere. Although RPM likes the idea of you building your application from source using RPM, that isn't always practical. This procedure creates an RPM file from a file system containing binaries built using outside of RPM:

```
Summary: Embedded Application
Name: embedded-app
Version: 1.1
Release: 001
Group: Applications/Misc
URL: http://your.url
Packager: Resource 1,
BuildRoot: %_buildsystem
License: GNU

%description
The application for the target system

%files
%defattr(-,root,root)
/usr/bin/appfile
/usr/lib/libapp.so.0
/usr/lib/libapp.so
```

In order to have this build correctly, you need to have the following ~/.rpmmacros file:

```
%_buildsystem %(echo $HOME)/<build dir>
%_targetcpu    arm
%_topdir       %(echo $HOME)/<output dir>
```

The RPM build process reads the files from <build dir>, which mirrors the root file system of the target device, and then creates an RPM that is placed in the <output dir> directory. These directories can be anyplace on the machine; the example uses the home directory for simplicity. After creating these files, you can use RPM build to read the spec file:

```
$ rpmbuild -v -bb --target arm app.specfile
Building target platforms: arm
Building for target arm
Processing files: embedded-app-1.1-001
Requires(rpmlib): rpmlib(CompressedFileNames) \
        <= 3.0.4-1 rpmlib(PartialHardlinkSets) \
        <= 4.0.4-1 rpmlib(PayloadFilesHavePrefix) <= 4.0-1
Checking for unpackaged file(s): \
        /usr/lib/rpm/check-files /home/gene/book-code/build
Wrote: /home/gene/book-code/output/RPMS/arm/embedded-app-1.1-001.arm.rpm
```

This produces an RPM file ready for installation on a target machine. You can take two paths to install this RPM file: copy it to the target and use RPM to install the file, or create a store and have YUM manage copying the file and its dependencies. Let's take a look at each.

Using RPM

By using RPM, you can either build the full RPM binaries for your system to use the RPM utilities included with BusyBox. The BusyBox rpm utility, fitting the BusyBox project's philosophy, is a minimal implementation and doesn't include dependency checking or a database to record what has been installed on the system: it copies the files out of the RPM and deposits them in the right spots in the file system. For most embedded systems, this is perfectly acceptable.

To install the file created in the example, you copy the RPM you intend to install to the target machine, using whatever utilities are the most convenient. For this example, the files are copied to the /tmp directory using ftpget (a BusyBox utility) and installed from there.

This is the list of files to copy from the remote machine and the name of the target application. You'll use these later in the script; the macros make the code easier to read:

```
FILELIST="file.list md5"
APP_NAME="your_app"
```

Here you fetch the files and put them in the /tmp file system. You copy all the files to the target machine so that if you have multiple files, you can ensure that all files are present on the host before attempting an upgrade. This script downloads a list of files and then attempts to download all the files in the list:

```
for f in $FILELIST; do
  if ! ftpget -u username -p secret \
     hostname /tmp/$f /remote/path/$f ; then
        echo "failed to download file $f"
        exit 1
done


if ! md4sum -c /tmp/md5 > /dev/null ; then
        echo "list of files not downloaded properly
```

```
fi;

while read f ; do
        if ! rpm -i $f ; then
            echo error installing $f
            exit 4
        fi
done < /tmp/file.list
```

Now that all the files have been copied, you can delete them to free up the resources they were consuming. You do so in a separate step to give the most freedom for handling errors:

```
for f in $FILELIST; do
        rm /tmp.$f
done
```

After you upgrade the system, you can restart the application. If you have the system configured to restart the main application if and when the program ends, the following line causes the application to restart:

```
killall $APP_NAME
```

Using YUM

The YUM system works with RPM files to create a way to download an RPM, along with any dependencies. After YUM has downloaded all dependencies, it then installs them on the target system.. YUM isn't a fit for all systems because it uses Python and some systems may not have the additional storage space for the files required by YUM. Using YUM means creating a repository that is placed on a machine reachable by the target board. To create the repository, you need the createrepo utility. Even if you have a Red Hat system and use YUM, this tool isn't always present. To download, build, and install, follow these steps:

```
$ wget http://createrepo.baseurl.org/download/createrepo-0.4.11.tar.gz
$ cd createrepo-0.4.11/
$ make
$ sudo make install
```

Creating a repository is straightforward. Consider the build of the PRM file earlier in the chapter; you can use that as your repository, located at $REPO_DIR, which is any directory where you have write access. To create the YUM repository for that directory, do the following:

```
$ createrepo $REPO_DIR
Saving Primary metadata
Saving file lists metadata
Saving other metadata
```

Now that the repository is ready for use, you need to put the contents of REPO_DIR in a location that is accessible by your HTTP server so remote devices can locate the data with an HTP URL. This example refers to this location as REPO_URL.

The next thing to do is to build and configure YUM so it can read this repository. When you're experimenting with YUM, you can use your development machine, so long as you don't try to install, because the mismatch between the RPM's architecture and your development host will likely result in the RPM refusing to install due to the differences in architecture. In order to use YUM on the target, you first need to download and build the tool, if it isn't installed on your system already:

■ **Note** YUM is Python-based. If you want to use YUM on your target board, Python must be present.

```
$ wget http://yum.baseurl.org/download/3.2/yum-3.2.24.tar.gz
$ tar xzf yum-3.2.24.tar.gz
$ cd yum-3.2.24.tar.gz
$ make
$ sudo make install DESTDIR=/path/to/board/rfs
```

This step ensures that the components necessary for YUM are available on the board. On the board, you need to create a configuration file so that YUM knows to use that URL when updating the system. Create this file in the /etc/yum/repos.d directory; you can give it any filename as long as it ends in .repo:

```
[embedded]
name = EmbeddedApp
baseurl = file:///tmp/output/repodata
```

Before you can use the YUM repository, you need to create a cache. This process must be done every time new packages are added to the cache. In this example, the repository is small, so the time to create the cache is very small:

```
$ sudo yum makecache
embedded                            100% |================|  951 B     00:00
Metadata Cache Created
```

The next step is to ensure that the cache contains what you expect. You can do this check on any machine that can reach the URL where the repository is stored. In this example, you use a file URL, so this test is run from the machine where the YUM repository was created:

```
$ yum repolist
repo id                  repo name                                          status
embedded                 EmbeddedApp                                        enabled:
1
repolist: 1
```

You're now ready to use this repository. You can adjust the base URL to be something under your HTTP document root or served by FTP for remote hosts. The board accessing the repository needs to know this in order to reach the YUM update service, which means the devices need an appropriately configured /etc/yum directory when building the root file system.

Dpkg

The Debian package system is the underlying package-management system for the Debian distribution and is used by Ubuntu, one of the more popular Debian-based distributions. The Debian package system works much like the RPM system: you create a file with the package metadata and then combine the metadata into a package that another program uses to install the software on another system. Debian has the notion of source and binary packages, and ideally you should build your binary package sources. However, not all projects can accommodate this, so packages can be built from binaries as well.

This packaging system also has the ability to build a repository of packages that can be accessed by remote clients who can request the latest version of a package along with its dependencies. The following sections look at how to create a simple package and repository.

Creating a dpkg

You build a dpkg using a control file, similar to the way RPM files are built using a spec file.. Referencing the example project from the RPM, here's a Debian package control file for the same binary project:

```
Package: embedded-app
Version: 1.1
Section: application
Priority: required
Architecture: arm
Essential: yes
Installed-Size: 1024
Maintainer: Resource 1 <resource1@company.url>
Description: The application for the target system,
             now with positive electrons,
             just like marketing asked!
```

This file contains the metadata to describe the package so that the device installing it can decide whether it's the right file, say by comparing the architecture or version of the package with that of the host. The example shown is the minimal set of information to create a package; thus, you can keep a focus on the higher-level process of creating a package and using it in a repository.

In the example package, the files are built into a directory, build/, that looks like the root file system on a device. For example:

```
build/
   lib/
   libapp.so.0
   libapp.so -> libapp.so.0
bin/
   appfile
```

In order to have dpkg build this directory (using default file locations, which is the easiest route by far), you name this control file DEBIAN/control, resulting in a directory structure that looks like the following:

```
build/
   lib/
```

```
    libapp.so.0
    libapp.so -> libapp.so.0
bin/
    appfile
DEBIAN/
    control
```

After the control file is in the correct location,[1] use the `dpkg build` command to build the package:

```
$ dpgk -b build embedded-app.deb
dpkg-deb: building package `embedded-app' in `embedded-app.deb'
```

The file is now built and ready for use. If you want to inspect the contents, use the `less` command to get a quick overview:

```
$ less embedded-app.deb
```

■ **Note** BusyBox is the Swiss army knife of embedded systems, and `less` is the Swiss army knife of your desktop system. Use 17.300 `less` to display nearly any type of file, and it does the right thing.

Remote Update with Debian

After `embedded-app.deb` is on the target system, BusyBox contains a set of applets for installing Debian packages. Getting these packages on your system and installing them works much the same way as the RPM example: instead of using RPM, you use dpkg, and the modified part of the earlier script looks like this:

```
while read f ; do
        if ! dpkg $f ; then
            echo error installing $f
            exit 4
        fi
done < /tmp/file.list
```

The rest of the script is exactly the same. In fact, you can make the command that performs the installation a macro so you can easily test both systems to see which one you prefer, although a resource-sensitive embedded engineer will never waste a few bytes that way.

---

[1] Unlike the spec file, which resides somewhere outside of the directory structure of the files going into the package, the dpkg file resides along with the files. As somebody who learned RPM first, I found this a little disquieting.

Using APT

You may not be keen on creating and maintaining a script that figures out what to download in order to update a system. It may be that the systems in the field have enough variations in their configuration that a simple script that downloads a list of packages and installs them isn't sufficient to update the system. The Debian analogue to YUM is apt-get (part of the Debian Advanced Packaging Tool [APT] collection of utilities), and you can use it to create a pool of packages with dependency information so the user can fetch a package and all of its dependents in one operation.

Creating an APT repository involves creating a set of directories to hold the packages and using a tool to create the supporting files for the APT tools to use to access the repositories. To get the necessary tools, fetch the package reprepro:

```
$ sudo apt-get install reprepro
```

Next, create the directories for the repository. In this example, you create them in the /tmp directory, but any directory where you have write privileges can be used:

```
mkdir -p /tmp/apt/conf
mkdir -p /tmp/apt/incomming
```

Next, the repository needs a configuration file so that when clients access the repository, they know what types of packages they can expect to find there. This is an example configuration file appropriate for the files you adding for the embedded device. This file needs to be stored as /tmp/apt/conf/distributions:

```
Origin: Embedded Company
Label: Embedded Device Software
Suite: stable
Codename: edasich
Version: 1.0
Architectures: arm
Components: main
Description: This is an embedded code repository for an embedded device
```

After this file has been created, you can add the embedded-app file to the repository with this command:

```
$ reprepro -b /tmp/apt includedeb edasich \
  <path to package>/embedded-app.deb
Exporting indices...
```

You can verify that the package is located inside the repository by doing the following:

```
$ reprepro -b /tmp/apt list edasich

edasich|main|arm: embedded-app 1.1
```

Now that the repository is ready, it's a matter of getting the tools ready to run on the target board. The apt tools are written in C++, so they don't need additional tools like Python on the target to work (that is, if you're not already using Python). In order to get the sources, use the `apt-get source` command:

```
$ apt-get source apt
dpkg-source: extracting apt in apt-0.7.20.2ubuntu6

dpkg-source: info: unpacking apt_0.7.20.2ubuntu6.tar.gz
```

The apt project uses the `autoconf` tools to build, so creating them for your target board should be a familiar process. For the compilation process to work correctly, you also need the curl library for your toolchain; if it isn't present, download it and build it first:

```
$ wget http://curl.netmirror.org/download/curl-7.17.0.tar.gz
$ CC=arm-linux-gcc ./configure \
        --host=arm-linux-gnu \
        --prefix=<toolchain sysroot> \
        --disable-ldap --disable-ldaps
$ make
$ make install
```

Curl is a tool that allows high-level processing of URLs. This configuration command drops support for the LDAP and LDAPS authentication schemes, because these aren't present in most toolchains and require additional steps to build. Unless you plan to use LDAP authentication, you can leave these out and save some space as well. After they're installed, you can build the apt library like so:

```
$ cd apt-0.7.20.2ubuntu6
$ CC=arm-linux-gcc CXX=arm-linux-g++ \
    CPPFLAGS="-I <path to your toolchain sysroot>"
        ./configure --host=arm-linux-gnu \
        -prefix=<path to your rfs>
$ make
$ make install
```

When it's installed on your target machine, you need to tell apt-get to use your repository when doing an update. You do so by putting an entry in the `/etc/apt/sources.list` file on the target machine. Using what you've created so far, the entry is

```
deb     file:///tmp/apt edasich
```

The board can now be read from the repository and download packages when requested. This line says to check the repository at `file:///tmp/apt`, which contains packages for the `edasich` distribution, which is the label you've assigned to the set of packages. This file can have several lines and can use HTTP and FTP URLs. The example uses a file URL to make it as simple as possible.

Ipkg

The Itsy Package Manager (ipkg) is part of the Open Handhelds project and is designed for low-resource machines. Originally, this project was a collection of shell scripts that unpacked a `tar` file. Not that this was a bad thing; rather, it was a great, low-resource way to manage updates. The code has since been rewritten in C with a mind toward doing the job as simply as possible while adding some of the features found in the other, bigger package-management tools. If you're short on resources (both RAM and flash), but you still require a more structured way of interacting with packages on the system, ipkg is a great solution.

Getting the Sources

The tools for ipkg aren't available in a standard Linux desktop distribution, so you need to download some sources and compile them for use on the development machine. These sources are compiled later for the target, but having them handy on the host machine is very helpful. The Open Handhelds site has an area where you can download snapshots or get the sources from CVS; this example gets the sources from a snapshot file:

```
$ wget http://www.handhelds.org/download/packages/ipkg/ipkg-0.99.163.tar.gz
$ tar zxf ipkg-0.99.163.tar.gz
$ ./configure
$ make
$ sudo make install
```

The snapshot I used didn't copy the library file used by ipkg to the /usr/lib directory, so the program wouldn't work after installation. To get around this problem, copy it yourself using these steps:

```
$ sudo cp ./.libs/libipkg.so /usr/lib
$ sudo ln /usr/lib/libipkg.so /usr/lib/libipkg.so.0
```

You also need the utilities for creating ipkg packages. These are stored on www.handhelds.org, but in this example they're downloaded from a mirror because the link on www.handhelds.org sometimes doesn't work.

```
$ wget ftp://ftp.cerias.purdue.edu/pub/os/gentoo/distfiles/ipkg-utils-1.7.tar.gz
```

These files are a combination of shell and Python scripts, so no compilation is necessary. To make accessing these files easier, you can copy them into /usr/bin or append to your search path the directory where there were unpacked. Because these files won't be on the target, you don't take the same level of care to make them small.

Creating an Ipkg

This process works much like the Debian process for creating a package: you create a special file in a well-known directory, in this case CONTROL/control. The CONTROL directory is a peer of other directories that is included in the build of the ipkg, similar to the way Debian creates packages. Going back to the example, an example CONTROL/control file looks like the following:

```
Package: embedded-app
Priority: required
Version: 1.1
Section: base
Architecture: arm
Source: none
```

```
Maintainer: Valued Resource 1<vresource1@yourdomain.here>
Description: Primary application.
 Comment remarking about the new electrons
added at the behest of marketing.
```

After the file is created, use the `ipkg-build` command to create a package file:

```
$ ipkg-build build-ipkg

*** Removing the following files: ./CONTROL/control~

Packaged contents of build-ipkg into \
        <parent dir>/embedded-app_1.1_arm.ipk
```

Creating a Feed

The ipkg system also supports fetching packages from a remote location, called a *feed*. Feeds are very easy to create: make a directory in a place accessible via FTP or HTTP, copy the ipkgs you want to make available, and use a tool to prepare the feed. This section goes through the process one step at a time:

1. You need to create directories in some place that can be reached by a web server (it can be any web server type; there's no requirement for Apache). In this example, the web server's document root is DOCROOT to make the directory's location clear. This directory can be any directory; the one chosen was named to make the example clear:

```
mkdir $DOCROOT/ipkg-feed
```

2. Copy in package files. Any ipkg files that need to be part of this feed must be copied into this directory. Using the example package:

```
cp <package dir>/ipkg-feed/embedded-app_1.1_arm.ipk \
        $DOCROOT/ipkg-feed
```

3. Run the indexer to create the index file that the ipkg file uses to see what's available on the target machine. This tool is designed to use Python 2.2. If it isn't present on your system, the script produces a "no such file or directory" error message. Because most systems use Python 2.4 or newer, you need to modify the first line of the script to use the Python on your system. The `ipkg-make-index` script contains this as the first line:

```
#!/usr/bin/python
```

However, on newer systems, you should use the Python interpreter on the path, so the first line of the file read

```
#!/usr/bin/env python
```

After the script has been changed to run on your system, invoke it by doing the following:

```
$ cd $DOCROOT/ipkg-feed
$ ipkg-make-index -v . > Packages
Reading in all the package info from .
```

```
Reading info for package ./embedded-app_1.1_arm.ipk
Generating Packages file
Writing info for package None
MD5Sum: 19c92f2ebc4a942b4e5c47d3c528c44f
Size: 824
Filename: embedded-app_1.1_arm.ipk
```

The system is now ready for a client to connect and download files. To test your work, you can also use the ipkg tools created for the host to query the repository. The next step is getting ipkg running on the target computer; to do this, you need to cross-compile the ipkg tools and put them on the root file system. Using the sources unpacked earlier in this section, you can do the following from the directory where the ipkg files were unpacked:

```
$ make clean
$ CC=arm-linux-gcc ./configure \
        --host=arm-linux-gnu \
        --prefix=<target board rfs>
$ make ; make install
```

The board needs a configuration file so it knows where to look for ipkg files. This file is called /etc/ipkg.conf, and for this example it contains the following:

```
src edasich http://<some host>/ipkg-feed
dest root /
```

This configuration file says that files belong to the edasich group can be found in the http://<some host>/ipkg feed directory and that these files should be installed in the root directory. A file can have multiple feeds; the field after the src command is the label used by ipkg to keep track of what feeds belong to what section.

Initramfs Root File Systems

Some users opt for a root file system that uses the initramfs file system. For review, this file system is stored alongside the kernel as a cpio archive that is uncompressed into the file system cache so it works like a RAM disk. This file system is read/write, but all changes are lost when the system reboots. If you have initramfs as your root file system, you need to replace the entire kernel as a way of making updates.

Kernel Updates

The kernel is the other part of the system that you can update in the field. Updating the kernel is often approached with trepidation, because the problems are often viewed as catastrophic. In fact, a failure updating the kernel leads to nearly the same level of nonfunctionality as a botched update to the root file system and results in a kernel panic because the main application won't run.

Even though kernel updates are no more risky or problematic than updating the root file system, the need to update the kernel is much less frequent. On a desktop system, a user may update the kernel to take advantage of new peripherals or get performance updates or patches that affect security. For an embedded system, with fixed hardware and very controlled communication, these needs typically don't arise due to the nature of the device. However, with more consumer electronic devices that are more open, the need for security updates is more prevalent.

Basic Strategies

The strategies for updating the kernel are much like those for the root file system. The strategy you eventually take depends on factors around the application, which are discussed with each of the strategies. These choices aren't mutually exclusive; after reading them, you may pick both options. Whatever option you select, you need to be careful with your implementation because if the kernel doesn't update properly, you can cripple your system:

Update Kernel Modules

Using kernel modules lends a great amount of flexibility to the kernel. Kernel modules are essentially files containing relocatable object code linked into the kernel at runtime, much as a program uses a shared object. During development of the kernel, if it becomes apparent that some modules are subject to changes after the product is shipped, these should be put on the root file system as modules.

How does a module make itself apparent? Here are some factors to weigh when deciding if you should create a kernel module:

- *Problematic during development:* Modules that caused grief when developed will likely continue being troublesome when released.

- *Works with new hardware:* Code that enables new hardware is another good candidate, because the documentation for the hardware isn't always clear or doesn't fully describe how the deice works. Another indicator is hardware that is changed close to the shipping date, because you don't have as much time to test it as desired.

- *Frequently changing hardware:* In this case, the supported hardware on the device is sourced from several different and subject to change over the production run. LCD displays are a good example, because this component is subject to price fluctuations and the buyer is constantly looking for a good deal.

- *Expected upgrades:* Any kernel functionality that is likely to be upgraded while the kernel remains running is a candidate, because these modules can be unloaded and updated and then new versions can be loaded.

If you can afford the time and space necessary to load kernel modules during the boot process, then use kernel modules, because they make updating the kernel a much easier process.

Forklift Upgrade

This is like the update for the root file system where the contents of the flash partition containing the kernel are erased and updated with a new kernel image. The methodology for this approach is nearly the same as replacing the root file system. For resource-constrained devices, this is the most practical approach. Even if the system uses kernel modules, you still may need to replace the core kernel, necessitating a forklift update approach.

The following sections look at examples for implementing a field update for the kernel.

Modules

The easiest way to conceptualize this approach is to think of kernel modules as being no different than updating any other sort of file that can be updated on a root file system. This means a package manager can be used to replace the kernel modules on the root file system. The system reboots to take advantage of the change; or, if the device needs to stay operational, the module can be unloaded and then the new version loaded.

There is no requirement that kernels use the modprobe utility to load and manage modules, but it certainly makes life easier; and for systems that use modules, this utility pays for its overhead through added flexibility. However, not using modprobe gives you additional control over how modules are loaded. This section looks at both approaches, because each has its advantages and liabilities.

No matter what approach you take, it's worth mentioning that a writable file system is required in order to store the updated modules and possibly update some configuration files in the root file system. The entire root file system doesn't need to be writable, just the mount point containing the kernel modules subject to update.

Using Modprobe

Modprobe exists to make managing modules easier, by using a configuration file to contain information about the module and formalizing where the modules are stored on the system. For the purposes of this section, you stick to the subset of capabilities offered by the BusyBox implementation of modprobe.

The modprobe utility use a file /etc/modprobe.conf to hold the modules that can be loaded on the system. A typical modprobe.conf file looks like the following:

```
alias network eepro1000
alias gpio-input gpio-keys-2
options eepro1000 irq=4
```

Each line that starts with alias allows a module stored on the disk to be loaded through its alias's name, as in the example:

```
modprobe network
```

This results in modprobe attempting to load the module eepro1000.

The options line lets you define default options that are passed into the kernel module when it loads. Modprobe expects modules to be located in the directory /lib/modules/`uname -r`, where uname -r is the kernel release string; when surrounded by backtick ` characters, it tells the shell to execute the command between the backticks and substitutes the result. The backtick syntax only works from a command shell prompt. On a typical system, this expression evaluates to /lib/modules/2.6.28-11-generic, but with the kernel version matching what is running on the system.

The indirection that modprobe allows through the configuration file lets you download kernel modules with a revision number associated with the name, but still have consistent module names in other scripts in the system. For example, on the file system, before an update, these files exist in the root file system:

```
/lib/modules/2.6.11-yourkernel/
        somemodule-rev1.ko=
```

After an update, the following are in the file system:

```
/lib/modules/2.6.11-yourkernel/
        somemodule-rev1.ko
        somemodule-rev2.ko
```

Before performing an update, the modprobe conf file contains the following:

```
alias somemodule somemodule-rev1.ko
```

Post update, the modprobe.conf file contains the following:

```
alias somemodule somemodule-rev2.ko
```

The script performing the update is responsible for ensuring that the module somemodule-rev2.ko is the correct file before making the change. By keeping the old module file in the system, if the somemodule-rev2.ko file doesn't load properly, the prior revision is still available. A simple way to quickly test if a module is present and conforms to the format of a module, and is thus likely to load, is to use the modinfo utility. For example, if you have a list of modules to check, the could looks something like this:

```
MODULE_LIST="module1 module2"
ERRORS=0
for   m in $MODULE_LIST ; do
        if ! modinfo $m > /dev/null ; then
            let "ERRORS = $ERRORS + 1"
        fi
done
if $ERRORS == 0 ; then
        update_modules_conf
fi;
```

Notice that this section doesn't include information regarding how to get the modules on the target system. Because the modules are no different from any other file on the file system, they can be put into a Debian, ipkg, or RPM for delivery to the target machine. Using a package manager also allows you to package the script for maintaining the modprobe configuration file as part of the package itself; encapsulating that information with the modules removes a step from the deployment process and makes the update process easier to test and validate.

Roll Your Own

If you have complex module-loading requirements, such as loading some modules conditionally or from nonstandard locations, the modprobe utility may not be sufficient for your application. Module loading without modprobe means using the insmod utility; insmod is much lower level than modprobe—it just loads the requested module into the kernel, passing along any parameters.

Systems that use insmod also need to keep track of module load order. That can be done with a simple script that loads the modules in the right order instead of using the module dependency information modprobe uses to do the same job. For example, a common approach is to put the modules to be loaded in a directory with a small shell script that loads then with the right parameters in the right order. For example:

```
/var/modules-rev1
    somemodule.ko
    anothermodule.ko
    loadmodules
/var/modules-rev2
    somemodule.ko
    anothermodule.ko
        athirdmodule.ko
    loadmodules
/var/modules-current -> /var/modules-rev2
```

In this example, the `loadmodules` script (for the first directory) contains a few lines of code to load the modules in the directory:[2]

```
insmod somemodule
insmod anothermodule
```

In this example, when a new set of modules is added to the system, they go into a separate directory so they don't overwrite the existing set of modules, in case the modules were in a package that was corrupted.

Notice in the example that the directory tree contains a symlink to the current set of modules to load. This symlink makes it so the script that loads the modules can be the same no matter what set is being loaded. When the new modules have been checked and are considered in a good state, the script changes the symlink to point to the correct directory.

Forklift

The forklift upgrade for the kernel is also very similar to the forklift upgrade of the root file system, but with one important difference: once the kernel is loaded into memory, it doesn't have a dependency on the partition like a file system. No dependencies mean that the upgrade routine doesn't need to do anything to make sure that the data in the partition will remain untouched during the update process. Much of the code for updating the root file system forklift-style was ensuring that the update had exclusive accesses to the partition.

Here's an example script that performs an update for the kernel:

```
KERNEL_FILE=uimage.new
FLASH_DEVICE=/dev/mtd1
```

---

[2] This script could be much more complex: using a numerical prefix to the filename to control load order, for example. However, because this script becomes more complex, it really reimplements `modprobe`; chances are, if you're an engineer taking this approach, the desire is to make things as simple as possible.

```
mtderase $FLASH_DEVICE
if [ -f $KERNEL_FILE && -f $FLASH_DEVICE ] ; then
        mtdcopy $KERNEL_FILE $FLASH_DEVICE
fi
```

The next logical step in this system is to use a package-management tool to contain a package with this new kernel and the script that was run after the files were installed on the target. The mechanics for this step are slightly different for each package manager, but all support the concept of a post-installation script. The advantage of using a package manager is that it ensures that the package downloads and unpacks successfully before attempting to run any installation scripts.

After the copy process finishes, the system can be reset, or you can wait for the user to reset the system so the new kernel loads.

Field Update Failures

Just as change is ever-present as death and taxes, there is another omnipresent, universal constant: screw-ups. The sections in this chapter include a fair amount of code and practice to make sure that when the update occurs, the data written to the device is good in a formal sense; that is, it may not perform to specifications, but it won't crash the device. Thus, the chances of a failure are greatly reduced; but no matter what happens, there's the possibility that the upgrade process will fail.

What do you do in such a case? You can take several approaches.

Report Failure, Stop

This seems like a non-solution, but telling the user that the device is in a compromised mode and requires service is much better than nothing at all. For a very minimal machine, a LED that can be turned on by the boot loader and then off by the kernel during the boot process gives the user some idea that the device isn't functioning normally. A device with a screen offers much more bandwidth for communicating failure and how the user should get help.

Failsafe Root File System

This is a great use for the initramfs file system. The initial file system has the primary job of ensuring that the last boot or system update did not end in failure. Failure can be detected by the file system not mounting or a file being present on the device indicating that the boot process didn't complete. The job of the failsafe root file system is to determine what steps are necessary to get the device back in working order, typically by downloading and installing on the board a failsafe root file system that can then run through the process again.

The nice feature about a failsafe root file system is that you have a great degree of control over how the failure should be handled. In some cases, the device can retry the update process; in others, the device can present a message telling the user the nature of the problem and direct them to technical support.

Failsafe Kernel

In this case, the board contains a kernel (with a small root file system) that is never changed. This failsafe kernel is the first thing to boot and is responsible for checking that the system booted properly the last power cycle. This communication is accomplished by writing data to an agreed-upon register or memory location, after the fail-safe kernel has determined that the system has booted improperly.

The GRUB boot loader has fail-over support as a feature. Consider the following GRUB configuration file:

```
fallback 1

title "Primary Kernel"
root (hd0,0)
kernel /primary.kernel

title "Fallback Kernel"
root (hd1,0)
kernel /fallback.kernel
```

The fallback kernel is Fallback Kernel, as indicated by the `fallback 1` statement; that kernel is booted if the first kernel fails to boot or panics. Recall that GRUB numbers boot entries starting at zero, from the top of the file to that bottom.

In order to have a system that's as survivable as possible, the fallback kernel has its own root file system located at (hd1,0), The root file system used by the fallback kernel should never be updated in the field so that it can't be corrupted and therefore is unavailable to boot the system. As an extra measure of safety, the fallback kernel should also include a small initramfs so it can perform minimal tasks in case the fallback root file system can't be mounted.

After the primary kernel boots, another command needs to be issued. Thus, the boot loader knows to use the primary kernel for the next boot cycle. This command must be run each time the primary kernel boots successfully:

```
$ grub-set-default
```

If you don't issue this command, GRUB doesn't know if the boot was successful; and the next time the system restarts, GRUB will try to use the fallback kernel.

In Summary

Keeping the software on the device doesn't get the attention it deserves because for many workers in the embedded field, the devices lacked the ability to update themselves—the software that was put on the device as part of the production software load was the software that ran on the device. Linux, with its excellent communication capabilities paired with the tools to perform an update, gives you the ability to update nearly any device. Linux offers choices for updating systems that span the complete resource spectrum, so you have a great deal of freedom to pick the update system that works best for your device and users. Some of the update approaches work best on a system with a high-bandwidth connection whereas others are perfectly suited for low-resource devices that communicate over a serial line.

All the update choices mean you also need to think about software updates sooner in the development process. That way, you can put the right tools on the board and test the update features before they leave the factory, ensuring that your users will have trouble-free updates.

Index

C

■ D

■M

S